'The Republic won an empire, and destroyed itself in doing so. Tom Holland tells the story of how this came about, and does so with splendid verve . . . His writing is as pellucid as Macauley's'
Allan Massie, *Spectator*

'Engrossing . . . a lively narrative style . . . A thoroughly worthwhile and timely project – an account of a formative period of Western history that manages to be accessible and not over-simplified'
Harry Eyres, *Daily Telegraph*

'A master of the telling detail . . . *Rubicon* is unrivalled in revealing the humbug behind the cant and stripping Julius Caesar and company of their moral finery'
Frederic Raphael, *Sunday Times*

'Tom Holland's excellent new study of the fall of the Republic . . . re-evaluating Rome for a new generation'
Robert Harris, *Sunday Times*

'For the student of contemporary politics as well as the classicist, Tom Holland's account of the last century or so of the Roman Republic is timely. It enables the reader to re-live the slow, bloodstained collapse of a system, not only as a fascinating drama in its own right, but as a morality tale . . . This gripping narrative resurrects some of the half-forgotten personalities and events that shaped who we are. In the light of the parallels between the two great imperial republics, it can be recommended as an instructive beach-read for senior politicians on both sides of the Atlantic'
Anthony Everitt, *Independent*

'Fresh and vivid . . . Holland's strength is as a narrative historian and there is no better and clearer guide to the tangled political events of 100–44 BC . . . if a new readership is to be won for ancient history, it is books like this that will pave the way'
Frank McLynn, *New Statesman*

'*Rubicon* . . . is no dry history: it is immensely readable, a perfect combination of authoritative scholarship and racy narrative . . . all Holland's people are real and alive. Sometimes they even talk'
David Wishart, *The Scotsman*

'Holland paints a vivid social portrait of the Roman world . . . Ideal bedside reading for George W. Bush'
Max Hastings, *Sunday Telegraph*

'Explosive stuff . . . a seriously intelligent history of the late republic that approximates as closely to the condition of the novel as should be allowed. Concentrating on the characters, plotting their interactions, rise and fall with considerable narrative skill, writing with élan and gusto . . . It is a history for our times . . . One can see classicists like Paul Wolfowitz in the White House eagerly seizing this book to find out how to deal with those tricky middle-easterners . . . a wickedly enjoyable book and a very sharp "reading" of the late Roman republic'
Peter Jones, *BBC History Magazine*

'Holland brings to vivid life the names found in thousands of schoolbooks . . . and gives them both personality and relevance. . . . With authoritative prose, this comes as recommended reading for those interested in the ancient world'
Good Book Guide

'Always readable and often beautiful . . . essential reading for anyone interested in ancient history. However, it also says more about our modern civilisation than many books that more overtly address the contemporary political and social issues . . . [Holland] blows the dust off an ancient civilisation, and shows that we still have plenty to learn from the past'
Sunday Business Post

Tom Holland has adapted Herodotus, Homer, Thucydides and Virgil for BBC Radio. He lives in London with his wife and two children.

'Holland brings a diverse cast of characters to life and in his descriptions of the skullduggery, luxury and squalor of ancient Rome he's marvellously entertaining'
Evening Herald

'Stunning . . . *Rubicon* is unusually well informed by any standard and impressive for its large but not overwhelming cast of characters. The roster goes well beyond the expected Marius and Sulla, Pompey and Crassus, Caesar and Cicero. Look out for prototypical metrosexuals, high-class oyster purveyors, overprivileged aristo table-dancers, back-alley prostitutes and a small army of political bit players – mercifully, not all identified by name. Holland keeps his narrative moving at chariot-race speed'
Corey Brennan, *Newsday*

RUBICON

The Triumph and Tragedy
of the Roman Republic

Tom Holland

ABACUS

An *Abacus* Book

First published in Great Britain by Little, Brown in 2003
This edition first published by Abacus in 2004

A CIP catalogue record for this book
is available from the British Library.

ISBN 0 349 11563 X

The publisher wishes to acknowledge that the maps in this book are
after maps that appear in the *Barrington Atlas of the Greek and Roman World*
(Princeton University Press, 2000), *The Cambridge Ancient History* Volume IX
(second edition) (Cambridge University Press, 1999), and *The Times Atlas
of World History* (Times Books Limited, 1979).

Typeset in Spectrum by M Rules
Printed and bound in Great Britain by Clays Ltd, St Ives plc

Abacus
An imprint of
Time Warner Book Group UK
Brettenham House
Lancaster Place
London WC2E 7EN
www.twbg.co.uk

For Eliza.
Welcome to the world.

Contents

Acknowledgements

I owe a debt of gratitude to many people for their help with the writing of this book. To my editors, Richard Beswick and Stephen Guise in London, and Bill Thomas and Gerry Howard in New York. To that best of agents and dearest of friends, Patrick Walsh. To Jamie Muir, for being the first to read the manuscript, and for all his unstinting friendship, encouragement and advice. To Caroline Muir, for being such a help whenever my failure to be a stern *pater familias* threatened to overwhelm me. To Mary Beard, for saving me from more errors than I can bear to count. To Catharine Edwards, for doing the same. To Lizzie Speller, for being as obsessed by Pompey's quiff as I was, and for all her conversation and support. To everyone at the British School in Rome, and to Hilary Bell, for not complaining (too much) as I dragged her round yet another coin collection. To the staff of the London Library, and the library of the Society for the Promotion of Roman Studies. To Arthur Jarvis and Michael Symonds, for first introducing me to the late Republic. And above all, of course, to my beloved wife and daughter, Sadie and Katy, for keeping me sane when it seemed that I would never have time for anything except for the Romans: '*ita sum ab omnibus destitutus ut tantum requietis habeam quantum cum uxore et filiola consumitur.*'

List of Maps

Note on Proper Names

Where familiar use has served to anglicise proper names, I have chosen to employ the modern rather than the classical usage: Pompey rather than Pompeius, for instance; Naples rather than Neapolis.

Preface

January 10th, the seven-hundred-and-fifth year since the foundation of Rome, the forty-ninth before the birth of Christ. The sun had long set behind the Apennine mountains. Lined up in full marching order, soldiers from the 13th Legion stood massed in the dark. Bitter the night may have been, but they were well used to extremes. For eight years they had been following the governor of Gaul on campaign after bloody campaign, through snow, through summer heat, to the margins of the world. Now, returned from the barbarous wilds of the north, they found themselves poised on a very different frontier. Ahead of them flowed a narrow stream. On the legionaries' side was the province of Gaul; on the far side Italy, and the road that led to Rome. Take that road, however, and the soldiers of the 13th Legion would be committing a deadly offence, breaking not only the limits of their province, but also the sternest laws of the Roman people. They would, in effect, be declaring civil war. Yet this was a catastrophe for which the legionaries, by marching to the border, had shown themselves fully steeled. As they stamped their feet against the cold, they waited for the trumpeters to summon them to action. To shoulder arms, to advance – to cross the Rubicon.

But when would the summons come? Faint in the night, its waters swollen by mountain snows, the stream could be heard, but

---

* Usually quoted in Latin – '*alea iacta est*' – but in fact lifted from the Athenian playwright Menander, and spoken by Caesar in Greek. See Plutarch, *Pompey*, 60 and *Caesar*, 32.

still no blast of trumpets. The soldiers of the 13th strained their ears. They were not used to being kept waiting. Normally, when battle threatened, they would move and strike like lightning. Their general, the governor of Gaul, was a man celebrated for his qualities of dash, surprise and speed. Not only that, but he had issued them with the order to cross the Rubicon that very afternoon. So why, now they had finally arrived at the border, had they been brought to a sudden halt? Few could see their general in the darkness, but to his staff officers, gathered around him, he appeared in a torment of irresolution. Rather than gesture his men onwards, Gaius Julius Caesar instead gazed into the turbid waters of the Rubicon, and said nothing. And his mind moved upon silence.

The Romans had a word for such a moment. '*Discrimen*', they called it – an instant of perilous and excruciating tension, when the achievements of an entire lifetime might hang in the balance. The career of Caesar, like that of any Roman who aspired to greatness, had been a succession of such crisis points. Time and again he had hazarded his future – and time and again he had emerged triumphant. This, to the Romans, was the very mark of a man. Yet the dilemma which confronted Caesar on the banks of the Rubicon was uniquely agonising – and all the more so for being the consequence of his previous successes. In less than a decade he had forced the surrender of 800 cities, 300 tribes and the whole of Gaul – and yet excessive achievement, to the Romans, might be a cause for alarm as well as celebration. They were the citizens of a republic, after all, and no one man could be permitted to put his fellows forever in the shade. Caesar's enemies, envious and fearful, had long been manoeuvring to deprive him of his command. Now, at last, in the winter of 49, they had succeeded in backing him into a corner. For Caesar, the moment of truth had finally arrived. Either he could submit to the law, surrender his command, and face the ruin of his career – or he could cross the Rubicon.

'The die is cast.'* Only as a gambler, in a gambler's fit of passion, was Caesar finally able to bring himself to order his legionaries to advance. The stakes had proved too high for rational calculation. Too imponderable as well. Sweeping into Italy, Caesar knew that he was risking world war, for he had confessed as much to his companions, and shuddered at the prospect. Clear-sighted as he was, however, not even Caesar could anticipate the full consequences of his decision. In addition to 'crisis point', '*discrimen*' had a further meaning: 'dividing line'. This was, in every sense, what the Rubicon would prove to be. By crossing it, Caesar did indeed engulf the world in war, but he also helped to bring about the ruin of Rome's ancient freedoms, and the establishment, upon their wreckage, of a monarchy – events of primal significance for the history of the West. Long after the Roman Empire itself had collapsed, the opposites delineated by the Rubicon – liberty and despotism, anarchy and order, republic and autocracy – would continue to haunt the imaginings of Rome's successors. Narrow and obscure the stream may have been, so insignificant that its very location was ultimately forgotten, yet its name is remembered still. No wonder. So fateful was Caesar's crossing of the Rubicon that it has come to stand for every fateful step taken since.

With it, an era of history passed away. Once, there had been free cities dotted throughout the Mediterranean. In the Greek world, and in Italy too, these cities had been inhabited by men who identified themselves not as the subjects of a pharaoh or a king of kings, but as citizens, and who proudly boasted of the values that distinguished them from slaves – free speech, private property, rights before the law. Gradually, however, with the rise of new empires, first those of Alexander the Great and his successors, and then of Rome, the independence of such citizens everywhere had been stifled. By the first century BC, there was only one free city left, and that was Rome herself. And then Caesar crossed the Rubicon, the Republic imploded, and none was left at all.

As a result, a thousand years of civic self-government were brought to an end, and not for another thousand, and more, would it become a living reality again. Since the Renaissance there have been many attempts to ford back across the Rubicon, to return to its far bank, to leave autocracy behind. The English, American and French revolutions were all consciously inspired by the example of the Roman Republic. 'As to rebellion in particular against monarchy,' Thomas Hobbes complained, 'one of the most frequent causes of it is the reading of the books of policy, and histories of the ancient Greeks, and Romans.'[1] Not, of course, that the desirability of a free republic was the only lesson to be drawn from the dramas of Roman history. It was no less a figure than Napoleon, after all, who went from consul to emperor, and throughout the nineteenth century the word most commonly applied to Bonapartist regimes was 'Caesarist'. By the 1920s and 1930s, when republics everywhere appeared to be collapsing, those crowing over their ruin were quick to point out the parallels with the death-throes of their ancient predecessor. In 1922 Mussolini deliberately propagated the myth of a heroic, Caesar-like march on Rome. Nor was he the only man to believe that a new Rubicon had been crossed. 'The brown shirt would probably not have existed without the black shirt,' Hitler later acknowledged. 'The march on Rome was one of the turning points of history.'[2]

With fascism, a long tradition in Western politics reached a hideous climax, and then expired. Mussolini was the last world leader to be inspired by the example of ancient Rome. The fascists, of course, had thrilled to its cruelty, its swagger, its steel, but nowadays even its noblest ideals, the ideals of active citizenship that once so moved Thomas Jefferson, have passed out of fashion. Too stern, too humourless, too redolent of cold showers. Nothing, in our aggressively postmodern age, could be more of a turn-off than the classical. Hero-worshipping the Romans is just *so* nineteenth century. We have been liberated, as John Updike once put it, 'from all those oppressive old Roman values'.[3] No longer, as they were for centuries, are they regarded as a mainspring of our modern civic rights. Few pause to wonder why, in a continent unimagined by the ancients, a second Senate should sit upon a second Capitol Hill. The Parthenon may still gleam effulgent in our imaginings, but the Forum glimmers barely at all.

And yet – we flatter ourselves, in the democracies of the West, if we trace our roots back to Athens alone. We are also, for good as well as ill, the heirs of the Roman Republic. Had the title not already been taken, I would have called this book *Citizens* – for they are its protagonists, and the tragedy of the Republic's collapse is theirs. The Roman people too, in the end, grew tired of antique virtues, preferring the comforts of easy slavery and peace. Rather bread and circuses than endless internecine wars. As the Romans themselves recognised, their freedom had contained the seeds of its own ruin, a reflection sufficient to inspire much gloomy moralising under the rule of a Nero or a Domitian. Nor, in the centuries since, has it ever lost its power to unsettle.

Of course, to insist that Roman liberty had once been something more than a high-sounding sham is not to claim that the Republic was ever a paradise of social democracy. It was not. Freedom and egalitarianism, to the Romans, were very different things. Only slaves on the chain gang were truly equal. For a citizen, the essence of life was competition; wealth and votes the accepted measures of success. On top of that, of course, the Republic was a superpower, with a reach and preponderance quite new in Western history. Yet none of this – even once it has been admitted – necessarily diminishes the relevance of the Republic to our own times. Just the opposite, it might be thought.

Indeed, since I started writing this book, the comparison of Rome to the modern-day United States has become something of a cliché. For the historian, the experience of being overtaken by current

affairs is more common than might be thought. It is often the case
that periods which have appeared foreign and remote can come
suddenly, disconcertingly, into focus. The classical world in particular, so similar to ours, so utterly strange, has always had this
kaleidoscopic quality. A few decades ago, in the late 1930s, the great
Oxford classicist Ronald Syme saw in the rise to power of the
Caesars a 'Roman revolution', a prefiguring of the age of the fascist
and communist dictators. So Rome has always been interpreted,
and reinterpreted, in the light of the world's convulsions. Syme
was heir to a long and honourable tradition, one stretching all the
way back to Machiavelli, who drew from the history of the Republic
lessons both for his own native city of Florence, and for that namesake of the Republic's destroyer, Cesare Borgia. 'Prudent men are
wont to say – and this not rashly or without good ground – that he
who would foresee what has to be should reflect on what has been,
for everything that happens in the world at any time has a genuine
resemblance to what happened in ancient times.'[4] If there are periods when this claim can seem outlandish, then there are periods
when it does not – and the present, surely, is one of them. Rome
was the first and – until recently – the only republic ever to rise to
a position of world power, and it is indeed hard to think of an
episode of history that holds up a more intriguing mirror to our
own. Nor is it only the broad contours of geopolitics, of globalisa-
tion and the *pax Americana*, that can be glimpsed, albeit faint and
distorted, in the glass. Our fads and obsessions too, from koi carp to
Mockney to celebrity chefs, cannot help but inspire, in the historian
of the Roman Republic, a certain sense of *déjà vu*.

Yet parallels can be deceptive. The Romans, it goes without
saying, existed under circumstances – physical, emotional, intellectual – profoundly different from our own. What strikes us as
recognisable about aspects of their civilisation may be so – but not
always. Often, in fact, the Romans can be strangest when they

appear most familiar. A poet mourning the cruelty of his mistress, or a father his dead daughter, these may seem to speak to us directly of something permanent in human nature, and yet how alien, how utterly alien a Roman's assumptions about sexual relations, or family life, would appear to us. So too the values that gave breath to the Republic itself, the desires of its citizens, the rituals and codes of their behaviour. Understand these and much that strikes us as abhorrent about the Romans, actions which to our way of thinking are self-evidently crimes, can be, if not forgiven, then at least better understood. The spilling of blood in an arena, the obliteration of a great city, the conquest of the world – these, to the Roman way of thinking, might be regarded as glorious accomplishments. Only by seeing why can we hope to fathom the Republic itself.

Naturally, it is a hazardous and quixotic enterprise to attempt to enter the mindset of a long-vanished age. As it happens, the last twenty years of the Republic are the best documented in Roman history, with what is, for the classicist, a wealth of evidence – speeches, memoirs, even private correspondence. Yet even these only gleam as riches for being set against such darkness. One day perhaps, when the records of the twentieth century AD have grown as fragmentary as those of ancient Rome, a history of the Second World War will be written which relies solely upon the broadcasts of Hitler and the memoirs of Churchill. It will be one cut off from whole dimensions of experience: no letters from the front, no combatants' diaries. The silence will be one with which the ancient historian is all too familiar, for, to twist the words of Shakespeare's Fluellen, 'there is no tiddle taddle nor pibble pabble in Pompey's camp'. Nor in the peasant's hut, nor in the slum dweller's shanty, nor in the field slave's barrack. Women, it is true, can sometimes be overheard, but only the very noblest, and even those invariably when quoted – or misquoted – by men. In Roman history to search for details of anyone outside the ruling class is to pan for gold.

Even the narrative of great events and exceptional men, however magnificent it may appear, is in truth a mutilated ruin, like an aqueduct on the Campagna, arches striding, and then, abruptly, fields. The Romans themselves had always dreaded that this might be their destiny. As Sallust, their first great historian, put it, 'there can be no doubting that Fortune is the mistress of all she surveys, the creature of her own caprices, choosing to broadcast the fame of one man while leaving that of another in darkness, without any regard for the scale of what they might both have achieved'.[5] Ironically, the fate of his own writings was to illustrate this bitter reflection. A follower of Caesar, Sallust composed a history of the years immediately preceding his patron's rise to power, a work unanimously praised by its readers as definitive. Had it only survived, then we would have had a contemporary's account of a decade, from 78 to 67 BC, rich in decisive and dramatic events. As it is, of Sallust's masterwork, only scattered fragments remain. From these, and from other scraps of information, a narrative may still be reconstructed – but what is gone can never be repaired.

No wonder that classicists tend to be nervous of sounding overly dogmatic. Write so much as a sentence about the ancient world and the temptation is immediately to qualify it. Even when the sources are at their most plentiful, uncertainties and discrepancies crop up everywhere. Take, for example, the celebrated event after which this book is titled. That the crossing happened as I described it is probable but by no means certain. One source tells us that the Rubicon was forded after sunrise. Others imply that the advance guard had already passed into Italy by the time that Caesar himself arrived on the river's bank. Even the date can only be deduced from extraneous events. A scholarly consensus has formed around 10 January, but any date between then and the 14th has been argued for – and besides, thanks to the vagaries of the pre-Julian calendar, what the Romans called January was in fact our November.

In short, the reader should take it as a rule of thumb that many statements of fact in this book could plausibly be contradicted by an opposite interpretation. This is not, I hasten to add, a counsel of despair. Rather, it is a necessary preface to a narrative that has been pieced together from broken shards, but in such a way as to conceal some of the more obvious joins and gaps. That it is possible to do this, that a coherent story may indeed be made out of the events of the Republic's fall, has always been, to the ancient historian, one of the great appeals of the period. I certainly see no reason to apologise for it. Following a lengthy spell in the dog-house, narrative history is now squarely back in fashion – and even if, as many have argued, it can only function by imposing upon the random events of the past an artificial pattern, then that in itself need be no drawback. Indeed, it may help to bring us closer to the mindset of the Romans themselves. Rare, after all, was the citizen who did not fancy himself the hero of his own history. This was an attitude that did much to bring Rome to disaster, but it also gave to the epic of the Republic's fall its peculiarly lurid and heroic hue. Barely a generation after it had occurred, men were already shaking their heads in wonderment, astonished that such a time, and such giants, could have been. A half-century later and the panegyrist of the Emperor Tiberius, Velleius Paterculus, could exclaim that 'It seems an almost superfluous task, to draw attention to an age when men of such extraordinary character lived'[6] – and then promptly write it up. He knew, as all Romans knew, that it was in action, in great deeds and remarkable accomplishments, that the genius of his people had been most gloriously displayed. Accordingly, it was through narrative that this genius could best be understood.

More than two millennia after the Republic's collapse, the 'extraordinary character' of the men – and women – who starred in its drama still astonishes. But so too – less well known perhaps than a Caesar, or a Cicero, or a Cleopatra, but more remarkable than any of them – does the Roman Republic itself. If there is much about it we can never know, then still there is much that can be brought back to life, its citizens half emerging from antique marble, their faces illumined by a background of gold and fire, the glare of an alien yet sometimes eerily familiar world.

Human nature is universally imbued with a desire
for liberty, and a hatred for servitude.

Caesar, *Gallic Wars*

Only a few prefer liberty – the majority seek
nothing more than fair masters.

Sallust, *Histories*

GAUL

ILLYRICUM

Marseille

CORSICA

Rome **ITALY**

Naples

SPAIN

SARDINIA

SICILY

Carthage

AFRICA

The Roman World in 140 BC

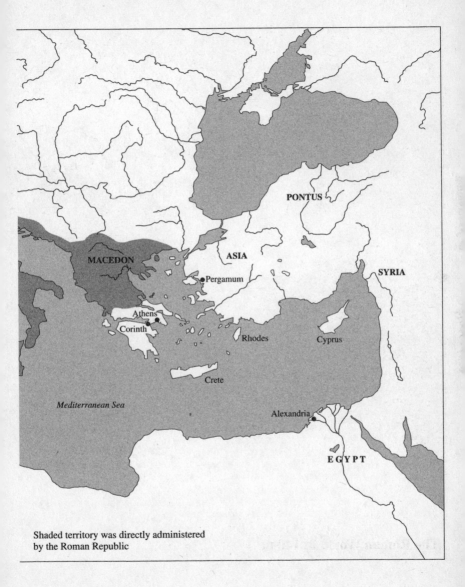

PONTUS

MACEDON

ASIA

SYRIA

●Pergamum

Athens

●Corinth

Rhodes

Cyprus

Crete

Mediterranean Sea

Alexandria●

EGYPT

Shaded territory was directly administered
by the Roman Republic

1

THE PARADOXICAL REPUBLIC

Ancestral Voices

In the beginning, before the Republic, Rome was ruled by kings. About one of these, a haughty tyrant by the name of Tarquin, an eerie tale was told. Once, in his palace, an old woman came calling on him. In her arms she carried nine books. When she offered these to Tarquin he laughed in her face, so fabulous was the price she was demanding. The old woman, making no attempt to bargain, turned and left without a word. She burned three of the books and then, reappearing before the King, offered him the remaining volumes, still at the same price as before. A second time, although with less self-assurance now, the King refused, and a second time the old woman left. By now Tarquin had grown nervous of what he might be turning down, and so when the mysterious crone reappeared, this time holding only three books, he hurriedly bought them, even though he had to pay the price originally demanded for all nine. Taking her money, the old woman then vanished, never to be seen again.

Who had she been? Her books proved to contain prophecies of such potency that the Romans soon realised that only one woman could possibly have been their author – the Sibyl. Yet this was an identification that only begged further questions, for the legends told of the Sibyl were strange and puzzling. On the presumption that she had foretold the Trojan War, men debated whether she was a compound of ten prophetesses, or immortal, or destined to live a thousand years. Some – the more sophisticated – even wondered whether she existed at all. In fact, only two things could be asserted with any real confidence – that her books, inscribed with spidery and antique Greek, certainly existed, and that within them could be read the pattern of events that were to come. The Romans, thanks to Tarquin's belated eye for a bargain, found themselves with a window on to the future of the world.

Not that this helped Tarquin much. In 509 BC he succumbed to a palace coup. Kings had been ruling in Rome for more than two hundred years, ever since the city's foundation, but Tarquin, the seventh in line, would also be the last.* With his expulsion, the monarchy itself was overthrown, and, in its place, a free republic proclaimed. From then on, the title of 'king' would be regarded by the Roman people with an almost pathological hatred, to be shrunk from and shuddered at whenever mentioned. Liberty had been the watchword of the coup against Tarquin, and liberty, the liberty of a city that had no master, was now consecrated as the birthright and measure of every citizen. To preserve it from the ambitions of future would-be tyrants, the founders of the Republic settled upon a remarkable formula. Carefully, they divided the powers of the exiled Tarquin between two magistrates, both elected, neither permitted to serve for longer than a year. These were the consuls,† and their presence at the head of their fellow citizens,

---

* Although, according to Varro, the great polymath of the late Republic, the Tarquin visited by the Sibyl was Tarquinius Priscus, the *fifth* king of Rome.
† Consuls were in fact originally called praetors. The murk of early Roman history is dense with such confusions.

the one guarding against the ambitions of the other, was a stirring expression of the Republic's guiding principle – that never again should one man be permitted to rule supreme in Rome. Yet, startling though the innovation of the consulship appeared, it was not so radical as to separate the Romans entirely from their past. The monarchy might have been abolished, but very little else. The roots of the new Republic reached far back in time – often very far back indeed. The consuls themselves, as a privilege of their office, bordered their togas with the purple of kings. When they consulted the auspices they did so according to rites that pre-dated the very foundation of Rome. And then, of course, most fabulous of all, there were the books left behind by the exiled Tarquin, the three mysterious rolls of prophecy, the writings of the ancient and quite possibly timeless Sibyl.

So sensitive was the information provided by these that access to them was strictly regulated as a secret of the state. Citizens found copying them would be sewn into a sack and dropped into the sea. Only in the most perilous of circumstances, when fearsome prodigies warned the Republic of looming catastrophe, was it permitted to consult the books at all. Then, once every alternative had been exhausted, specially appointed magistrates would be mandated to climb to the temple of Jupiter, where the books were kept in conditions of the tightest security. The scrolls would be spread out. Fingers would trace the faded lines of Greek. Prophecies would be deciphered, and advice taken on how best to appease the angered heavens.

And advice was always found. The Romans, being a people as practical as they were devout, had no patience with fatalism. They were interested in knowing the future only because they believed that it could then better be kept at bay. Showers of blood, chasms spitting fire, mice eating gold: terrifying prodigies such as these were regarded as the equivalent of bailiffs' duns, warnings to the

Roman people that they stood in arrears with the gods. To get back in credit might require the introduction of a foreign cult to the city, the worship of a divinity who had hitherto been unknown. More typically, it would inspire retrenchment, as the magistrates desperately sought to identify the traditions that might have been neglected. Restore the past, the way that things had always been, and the safety of the Republic would be assured.

This was a presumption buried deep in the soul of every Roman. In the century that followed its establishment, the Republic was repeatedly racked by further social convulsions, by demands from the mass of citizens for expanded civic rights, and by continued constitutional reforms – and yet throughout this turbulent period of upheaval, the Roman people never ceased to affect a stern distaste for change. Novelty, to the citizens of the Republic, had sinister connotations. Pragmatic as they were, they might accept innovation if it were dressed up as the will of the gods or an ancient custom, but never for its own sake. Conservative and flexible in equal measure, the Romans kept what worked, adapted what had failed, and preserved as sacred lumber what had become redundant. The Republic was both a building site and a junk yard. Rome's future was constructed amid the jumble of her past.

The Romans themselves, far from seeing this as a paradox, took it for granted. How else were they to invest in their city save by holding true to the customs of their ancestors? Foreign analysts, who tended to regard the Romans' piety as 'superstition',[1] and interpreted it as a subterfuge played on the masses by a cynical ruling class, misread its essence. The Republic was not like other states. While the cities of the Greeks were regularly shattered by civil wars and revolutions, Rome proved herself impervious to such disasters. Not once, despite all the social upheavals of the Republic's first century of existence, had the blood of her own citizens been spilled on her streets. How typical of the Greeks to reduce the ideal of shared citizenship to sophistry! To a Roman, nothing was more sacred or cherished. After all, it was what defined him. Public business – *res publica* – was what 'republic' meant. Only by seeing himself reflected in the gaze of his fellows could a Roman truly know himself a man.

And by hearing his name on every tongue. The good citizen, in the Republic, was the citizen acknowledged to be good. The Romans recognised no difference between moral excellence and reputation, having the same word, *honestas*, for both. The approval of the entire city was the ultimate, the only, test of worth. This was why, whenever resentful citizens took to the streets, it would be to demand access to yet more honours and glory. Civil unrest would invariably inspire the establishment of a new magistracy: the aedileship and tribunate in 494, the quaestorship in 447, the praetorship in 367. The more posts there were, the greater the range of responsibilities; the greater the range of responsibilities, the broader the opportunities for achievement and approbation. Praise was what every citizen most desired – just as public shame was his ultimate dread. Not laws but the consciousness of always being watched was what prevented a Roman's sense of competition from degenerating into selfish ambition. Gruelling and implacable though the contest to excel invariably was, there could be no place in it for ill-disciplined vainglory. To place personal honour above the interests of the entire community was the behaviour of a barbarian – or worse yet, a king.

In their relations with their fellows, then, the citizens of the Republic were schooled to temper their competitive instincts for the common good. In their relations with other states, however, no such inhibitions cramped them. 'More than any other nation, the Romans have sought out glory and been greedy for praise.'[2] The consequences for their neighbours of this hunger for honour were invariably devastating. The legions' combination of efficiency and ruthlessness was something for which few opponents found themselves prepared. When the Romans were compelled by defiance to take a city by storm, it was their practice to slaughter every living creature they found. Rubble left behind by the legionaries could always be distinguished by the way in which severed dogs' heads or the dismembered limbs of cattle would lie strewn among the human corpses.[3] The Romans killed to inspire terror, not in a savage frenzy but as the disciplined components of a fighting machine. The courage they brought to service in the legions, steeled by pride in their city and faith in her destiny, was an emotion that every citizen was brought up to share. Something uniquely lethal – and, to the Romans, glorious – marked their way of war.

Even so, it took time for the other states of Italy to wake up to the nature of the predator in their midst. For the first century of the Republic's existence the Romans found it a struggle to establish their supremacy over cities barely ten miles from their own gates. Yet even the deadliest carnivore must have its infancy, and the Romans, as they raided cattle and skirmished with petty hill tribes, were developing the instincts required to dominate and kill. By the 360s BC they had established their city as the mistress of central Italy. In the following decades they marched north and south, crushing opposition wherever they met it. By the 260s, with startling speed, they had mastered the entire peninsula. Honour, of course, had demanded nothing less. To states that humbly acknowledged their superiority, the Romans would grant such favours as a patron condescends to grant his clients, but to those who defied them, only ceaseless combat. No Roman could tolerate the prospect of his city losing face. Rather than endure it, he would put up with any amount of suffering, go to any lengths.

The time soon came when the Republic had to demonstrate this in a literal struggle to the death. The wars with Carthage were the most terrible it ever fought. A city of Semitic settlers on the North African coast, dominating the trade routes of the western Mediterranean, Carthage possessed resources at least as great as Rome's. Although predominantly a maritime power, she had indulged herself for centuries with bouts of warfare against the Greek cities of Sicily. Now, poised beyond the Straits of Messina, the Romans represented an ominous but intriguing new factor in Sicily's military equation. Predictably, the Greeks on the island could not resist embroiling the Republic in their perennial squabbles with Carthage. Equally predictably, once invited in, the Republic refused to play by the rules. In 264 Rome transformed what had been a minor dispute over treaty rights into a total war. Despite a lack of any naval tradition, and the loss of fleet after fleet to enemy action or storms, the Romans endured over two decades of appalling casualties to bring Carthage, at last, to defeat. By the terms of the peace treaty forced on them, the Carthaginians undertook a complete withdrawal from Sicily. Without ever having intended it, Rome found herself with the nucleus of an overseas empire. In 227 Sicily was constituted as the first Roman province.

The theatre of the Republic's campaigning was soon to grow even wider. Carthage had been defeated, but not smashed. With Sicily lost, she next turned her imperial attentions to Spain. Braving the murderous tribes who swarmed everywhere in the mountains, the Carthaginians began to prospect for precious metals. The flood of wealth from their mines soon enabled them to contemplate resuming hostilities. Carthage's best generals were no longer under any illusions as to the nature of the enemy they faced in the Republic. Total war would have to be met in kind, and victory would be impossible unless Roman power were utterly destroyed.

It was to achieve this that Hannibal, in 218, led a Carthaginian army from Spain, through southern Gaul and over the Alps.

Displaying a mastery of strategy and tactics far beyond that of his opponents, he brought three Roman armies to sensational defeat. In the third of his victories, at Cannae, Hannibal wiped out eight legions, the worst military disaster in the Republic's history. By every convention and expectation of contemporary warfare, Rome should have followed it by acknowledging Hannibal's triumph, and attempting to sue for peace. But in the face of catastrophe, she showed only continued defiance. Naturally, at such a moment, the Romans turned for guidance to the prophecies of the Sibyl. These prescribed that two Gauls and two Greeks be buried alive in the city's marketplace. The magistrates duly followed the Sibyl's advice. With this shocking act of barbarism, the Roman people demonstrated that there was nothing they would not countenance to preserve their city's freedom. The only alternative to liberty — as it had always been — was death.

And grimly, year by year, the Republic hauled itself back from the brink. More armies were raised; Sicily was held; the legions conquered Carthage's empire in Spain. A decade and a half after Cannae Hannibal faced another Roman army, but this time on African soil. He was defeated. Carthage no longer had the manpower to continue the struggle, and when her conqueror's terms were delivered, Hannibal advised his compatriots to accept them. Unlike the Republic after Cannae, he preferred not to risk his city's obliteration. Despite this, the Romans never forgot that in Hannibal, in the scale of his exertions, in the scope of his ambition, they had met the enemy who was most like themselves. Centuries later statues of him were still to be found standing in Rome. And even after they had reduced Carthage to an impotent rump, confiscating her provinces, her fleet, her celebrated war-elephants, the Romans continued to dread a Carthaginian recovery. Such hatred was the greatest compliment they could pay a foreign state. Carthage could not be trusted in her submission. The Romans looked into their own souls and attributed the implacability they found there to their greatest foe.

Never again would they tolerate the existence of a power capable of threatening their own survival. Rather than risk that, they felt themselves perfectly justified in launching a pre-emptive strike against any opponent who appeared to be growing too uppity. Such opponents were easy – all too easy – to find. Already, even before the war with Hannibal, the Republic had fallen into the habit of dispatching the occasional expedition to the Balkans, where its magistrates could indulge themselves by bullying princelings and redrawing boundaries. As the Italians would have confirmed, the Romans had an inveterate fondness for this kind of weight-throwing, reflecting as it did the familiar determination of the Republic never to brook disrespect. For the treacherous and compulsively quarrelsome states of Greece, however, it was a lesson which took some grasping. Their confusion was understandable – in the early years of their encounters with Rome, the Republic did not behave at all in the manner of a conventional imperial power. Like lightning from a clear sky, the legions would strike with devastating impact, and then, just as abruptly, be gone. For all the fury of these irregular interventions, they would be punctuated by lengthy periods when Rome appeared to have lost interest in Greek affairs altogether. Even when she did intervene, her incursions across the Adriatic continued to be represented as peace-keeping ventures. These still had as their object not the annexation of territory but the clear establishment of the Republic's prestige, and the slapping down of any overweening local power.

In the early years of Roman engagement in the Balkans, this had effectively meant Macedon. A kingdom to the north of Greece, Macedon had dominated the peninsula for two hundred years. As heir to the throne of Alexander the Great, the country's king had always taken it for granted that he could be quite as overweening as he pleased. Despite repeated punishing encounters with the armies of the Republic, such an assumption never entirely died, and in 168 BC Roman patience finally snapped. Abolishing the monarchy altogether, Rome first of all carved Macedon into four puppet republics, and then in 148, completing the transformation from peace-keeper to occupying power, established direct rule. As in Italy, where roads criss-crossed the landscape like the filaments of a net, engineering prowess set the final seal on what military conquest had begun. The via Egnatia, a mighty gash of stone and gravel, was driven through the wilds of the Balkans. Running from the Adriatic to the Aegean Sea, this highway became the vital link in the coffle joining Greece to Rome. It also provided ready access to horizons even more exotic, those beyond the blue of the Aegean Sea, where cities glittering with gold and marble, rich with works of art and decadent cooking practices, seemed positively to invite the Republic's stern attentions. Already, in 190, a Roman army had swept into Asia, pulverised the war-machine of the local despot and humiliated him before the gaze of the entire Near East. Both Syria and Egypt, the two local superpowers, hurriedly swallowed their pride, learned to tolerate the meddling of Roman ambassadors, and grovellingly acknowledged the Republic's hegemony. Rome's formal empire was still limited, being largely confined to Macedon, Sicily and parts of Spain, but her reach by the 140s BC extended to strange lands of which few back in Rome had even heard. The scale and speed of her rise to power was something so startling that no one, least of all the Romans themselves, could quite believe that it had happened.

And if they thrilled to their country's achievements, then so too did many citizens feel unease. Moralists, doing what Roman moralists had always done, and comparing the present unfavourably with the past, did not have to look far for evidence of the pernicious effects of empire. Ancient standards appeared corrupted by the influx of gold. With plunder came foreign practices and philoso-phies. The unloading of Eastern treasures into Rome's public places or the babbling of strange tongues on her streets provoked alarm as well as pride. Never did the hardy peasant values that had won the Romans their empire seem more admirable than when they were being most flagrantly ignored. 'The Republic is founded on its ancient customs and its manpower'[4] – so it had been triumphantly asserted in the afterglow of the war against Hannibal. But what if these building blocks began to crumble? Surely the Republic would totter and fall? The dizzying transformation of their city, from back-water to superpower, disoriented the Romans and left them nervous of the jealousy of the gods. By an uncomfortable paradox, their engagement with the world came to seem the measure of both their success and their decline.

For great as Rome had become, portents were not lacking of her possible doom. Monstrous abortions, ominous flights of birds: wonders such as these continued to unsettle the Roman people and require, if the prodigies appeared particularly menacing, con-sultation of the Sibyl's prophetic books. As ever, prescriptions were duly discovered, remedies applied. The Romans' time-sanctioned ways, the customs of their ancestors, were resurrected or reaf-firmed. Catastrophe was staved off. The Republic was preserved.

But still the world quickened and mutated, and the Republic with it. Some marks of crisis defied all powers of ancient ritual to heal them. Changes such as the Roman people had set in motion were not easily slowed down – not even by the recommendations of the Sibyl.

It required no portents to illustrate this, only a walk through the world's new capital.

All was not well in the seething streets of Rome.

The Capital of the World

A city — a free city — was where a man could be most fully a man. The Romans took this for granted. To have *civitas* — citizenship — was to be civilised, an assumption still embedded in English to this day. Life was worthless without those frameworks that only an independent city could provide. A citizen defined himself by the fellowship of others, in shared joys and sorrows, ambitions and fears, festivals, elections, and disciplines of war. Like a shrine alive with the presence of a god, the fabric of a city was rendered sacred by the communal life that it sheltered. A cityscape, to its citizens, was therefore a hallowed thing. It bore witness to the heritage that had made its people what they were. It enabled the spirit of a state to be known.

Foreign powers, when they first came into contact with Rome, would often find themselves reassured by this thought. Compared to the beautiful cities of the Greek world, Rome appeared a backward and ramshackle place. Courtiers in Macedon would snigger in a superior manner every time they heard the city described.[5] Much good it did them. Yet, even as the world learned to kowtow to the Republic, there remained a whiff of the provincial about Rome. Spasmodic attempts were made to spruce her up, but to little effect. Even some Romans themselves, as they grew familiar with the harmonious, well-planned cities of the Greeks, might occasionally feel a touch of embarrassment. 'When the Capuans compare Rome, with her hills and deep valleys, her attics teetering over the streets, her hopeless roads, her cramped back-alleys, against their own city of Capua, neatly laid out on a suitable flat site, they will jeer at us and look down their noses,'[6] they worried. Yet still, when all was said and done, Rome was a free city, and Capua was not.

Naturally, no Roman ever really forgot this. He might sometimes moan about his city, but he never ceased to glory in her name. It appeared self-evident to him that Rome, mistress of the world, had been blessed by the gods, and preordained to rule. Scholars learnedly pointed out that the location of the city avoided extremes of heat, which sapped the spirit, and cold, which chilled the brain; it was therefore a simple fact of geography that 'the best place of all to live, occupying as it does the happy medium, and perfectly placed in the centre of the world, is where the Roman people have their city'.[7] Not that a temperate climate was the only advantage that the gods had thoughtfully provided the Roman people. There were hills that could be easily defended; a river to provide access to the sea; springs and fresh breezes to keep the valleys healthy. Reading Roman authors praise their city,[8] one would never guess that to have built across seven hills was a contravention of the Romans' own principles of town-planning, that the Tiber was prone to violent flooding, and that the valleys of Rome were rife with malaria.[9] The love which Romans felt for their city was of the kind that can see only virtues in a beloved's glaring faults.

This idealised vision of Rome was the constant shadow of the squalid reality. It helped to generate a baffling compound of paradoxes and magnitudes, in which nothing was ever quite as it seemed. For all the 'smoke and wealth and din'[10] of their city, the Romans never ceased to fantasise about the primitive idyll that they liked to imagine had once existed on the banks of the Tiber. As Rome heaved and buckled with the strains of her expansion, the bare bones of an ancient city state, sometimes blurred, sometimes pronounced, might be glimpsed protruding through the cramped modern metropolis. In Rome memories were guarded closely. The present was engaged in a perpetual compromise with the past, restless motion with a reverence for tradition, hard-headedness with a devotion to myth. The more crowded and corrupted their city grew, the more the Romans longed for reassurance that Rome remained Rome still.

So it was that smoke from sacrifices to the gods continued to rise above the seven hills, just as it had done back in far-off times, when trees 'of every kind' had completely covered one of the hills, the Aventine.[11] Forests had long since vanished from Rome, and if the city's altars still sent smoke wreathing into the sky, then so too did a countless multitude of hearth-fires, furnaces and workshops. Long before the city itself could be seen, a distant haze of brown would forewarn the traveller that he was nearing the great city. Nor was smog the only sign. Nearby towns with celebrated names, rivals of the Republic back in the archaic past, now stood deserted, shrunk to a few scattered inns, emptied by Rome's gravitational pull.

As the traveller continued onwards, however, he would find the roadside lined with more recent settlements. Unable to accommodate a burgeoning population, Rome was starting to burst at the seams. Shanty-towns stretched along all the great trunk-roads. The dead were sheltered here as well, and the necropolises that stretched towards the coast and the south, along the great Appian Way, were notorious for muggers and cut-rate whores. All the same, not every tomb had been left to crumble. As the traveller approached Rome's gates he might occasionally find the stench from the city ameliorated by myrrh or cassia, the perfumes of death, borne to him on the breeze from a cypress-shaded tomb. Such a moment, the sense of a communion with the past, was a common one in Rome. Yet just as the stillness of a cemetery sheltered violence and prostitution, so not even the most hallowed and timeless of spots were immune to defacement. Admonitory notices were always being posted on tombs, prohibiting electioneering slogans, but still the graffiti would appear. In Rome, seat of the Republic, politics was a contagion. Only in conquered cities were elections an irrelevance. Rome, having neutered political life in other societies, was now supreme as the world's theatre of ambitions and dreams.

Not even the graffiti-ravaged tombs, however, could prepare a traveller for the bedlam beyond the city gates. The streets of Rome had never had any kind of planning imposed upon them. That would have taken a design-minded despot, and Roman magistrates rarely had more than a single year in office at a time. As a result, the city had grown chaotically, at the whim of unmanageable impulses and needs. Stray off one of Rome's two grand thoroughfares, the via Sacra and the via Nova, and a visitor would soon be adding to the hopeless congestion. 'A contractor hurries by, all hot and sweaty, with his mules and porters, stone and timber twists on the rope of a giant crane, funeral mourners compete for space with well-built carts, there scurries a mad dog, here a sow who's been wallowing in mud.'[12] Caught up on this swirl, a traveller was almost bound to end up lost.

Even citizens found their city confusing. The only way to nego-tiate it was to memorise notable landmarks: a fig-tree, perhaps, or a market's colonnade, or, best of all, a temple large enough to loom above the maze of narrow streets. Fortunately, Rome was a devout city, and temples abounded. The Romans' reverence for the past meant that ancient structures were hardly ever demolished, not even when the open spaces in which they might once have stood had long since vanished under brick. Temples loomed over slums or meat markets, they sheltered veiled statues whose very identities might have been forgotten, and yet no one ever thought to demol-ish them. These fragments of an archaic past preserved in stone, fossils from the earliest days of the city, provided the Romans with a desperately needed sense of bearing. Eternal, like the gods whose spirits pervaded them, they stood like anchors dropped in a storm.

Meanwhile, on all sides, amid a din of hammering, rumbling wagon wheels and crashing rubble, the city was endlessly being rebuilt, torn down and rebuilt again. Developers were always look-ing for ways to squeeze in extra space, and squeeze out extra profit.

Shanties sprouted like weeds from the rubble left by fires. Despite the best efforts of responsible magistrates to keep streets clear, they were always filling with market stalls or squatters' shacks. Most profitably of all, in a city long constricted by her ancient walls, developers had begun to aim for the sky. Apartment blocks were springing up everywhere. Throughout the second and first centuries BC landlords would compete with one another to raise them ever higher, a development frowned on by the law, since tenements were notoriously jerry-built and rickety. In general, however, safety regulations were too weakly imposed to inhibit the splendid opportunities for profiteering that a high-rise slum presented. Over six storeys or more, tenants could be crammed into tiny, thin-walled rooms, until invariably the building would collapse, only to be flung up again even higher than before.

In Latin these apartment blocks were known as *insulae*, or 'islands' – a suggestive word, reflecting the way in which they stood apart from the sea of life down on the streets. Here was where alienation bred by the vastness of the city was most distressingly felt. To those dossing in the *insulae*, rootlessness was more than just a metaphor. Even on the ground floors the *insulae* usually lacked drains or fresh water. Yet sewers and aqueducts were precisely what the Romans would boast about when they wanted to laud their city, comparing the practical value of their public works with the useless extravagances of the Greeks. The Cloaca Maxima, Rome's monstrous central drain, had provided the city with its gut since before the foundation of the Republic itself. The aqueducts, built with plunder from the East, were an equally spectacular demonstration of the Romans' commitment to communal living. Stretching for up to thirty-five miles, they brought cool mountain water into the heart of the city. Even Greeks might on occasion admit to being impressed. 'The aqueducts convey such volumes that the water flows like rivers,' wrote one geographer. 'There is barely a house in Rome which doesn't have a cistern, a service-pipe or a gushing fountain.'[13] Evidently, the slums had not been on his tour.

In truth, nothing better illustrated the ambiguities of Rome than the fact that she was at once both the cleanest and the filthiest of cities. Ordure as well as water flowed through her streets. If the noblest and most enduring virtues of the Republic found their expression in the murmuring of a public fountain, then its horrors were exemplified by filth. Citizens who dropped out of the obstacle race that was every Roman's life risked having shit — literally — dumped on their heads. *Plebs sordida*, they were called — 'the great unwashed'. Periodically, waste from the *insulae* would be wheeled out in barrows to fertilise gardens beyond the city walls, but there was always too much of it, urine sloshing over the rims of fullers' jars, mounds of excrement submerging the streets. In death, the poor themselves would be subsumed into waste. Not for them the dignity of a tomb beside the Appian Way. Instead their carcasses would be tossed with all the other refuse into giant pits beyond the easternmost city gate, the Esquiline. Travellers approaching Rome by this route would see bones littering the sides of the road. It was a cursed and dreadful spot, the haunt of witches, who were said to strip flesh from the corpses and summon the naked spectres of the dead from their mass graves. In Rome the indignities of failure could outlive life itself.

Degradation on such a scale was something new in the world. The suffering of the urban poor was all the more terrible because, by depriving them of the solaces of community, it denied them everything that made a Roman what he was. The loneliness of life on the top floor of an apartment block represented the antithesis of all that a citizen most prized. To be cut off from the rituals and rhythms of society was to sink to the level of a barbarian. To its own citizens, as to its enemies, the Republic was unyielding. It gave up on those who gave up on it. And after abandoning them, in the end, it had them swept out with the trash.

It was no wonder that life in Rome should have been a desperate struggle to avoid such a fate. Community was cherished wherever it was found. The potential anonymity of big-city life was not all-conquering. Vast and formless though the metropolis appeared, there were patterns of order defying its chaos. Temples were not the only repositories of the divine. Crossroads, too, were believed to be charged with spiritual energy. Shadowy gods, the Lares, watched over the intersection of all the city's high streets. These streets, the *vici*, were so significant as a focus for community life that the Romans used the same word to describe an entire urban quarter. Every January, at the festival of the Compitalia, inhabitants of a *vicus* would hold a great public feast. Woollen dolls would be hung beside the shrine of the Lares, one for every free man and woman in the quarter, and a ball for every slave. This relative egalitarianism was reflected in the trade associations that were also centred on the *vicus*, and were open to everyone: citizen, freedman and slave alike. It was in these associations, the *collegia*, rather than on the broader stage of the city, that most citizens sought to win that universal goal of a Roman – prestige. In a *vicus* a citizen could know his fellows, sit down to supper with them, join in festivities throughout the year, and live confident that mourners would attend his funeral. In a patchwork of communities across the metropolis, the intimacies of traditional small-town life still endured.

None of which calmed the suspicions of outsiders. Walk down a main street, and the snarl of narrow back alleys twisting off it might appear dark with menace, the air heavy with the stench of unwashed bodies, and trade. To refined nostrils, both were equally noxious. Fears that the *collegia* served as covers for organised crime combined readily with the upper classes' instinctive contempt for anyone obliged to earn his keep. The very idea of paid work inspired paroxysms of snobbery. It affronted all the homespun peasant values in which wealthy moralists, lounging comfortably in their villas, affected to believe. Their scorn for 'the mob' was unvarying. It embraced not only the wretches starving on the streets or crammed into *insulae*, but also traders, shopkeepers and craftsmen. 'Necessity', it was assumed, 'made every poor man dishonest.'[14] Such contempt – unsurprisingly – was much resented by those who were its object.* *Plebs* was a word never spoken by a nobleman without a curling of the lip, but the *plebs* themselves took a certain pride in it. A description once spat as an insult had become a badge of identity, and in Rome such badges were always highly prized.

Like other fundamentals of Roman life, divisions of class and status were deep rooted in the myths of the city's very origin. On the far side of Rome's southernmost valley stretched the Aventine Hill. This was where immigrants would invariably end up, the port of disembarkation possessed by all great cities, an area where new arrivals congregate by instinct, drawn to one another's company and shared confusion. Facing the Aventine rose a second hill. There were no shanty-towns to be found on the Palatine. Hills in Rome tended to be exclusive. Above the valleys the air was fresher, less pestilential – and therefore cost more to breathe. Of all Rome's seven hills, however, the Palatine was the most exclusive by far. Here the city's elite chose to cluster. Only the very, very rich could afford the prices. Yet, incongruously, there on the world's most expensive real estate stood a shepherd's hut made of reeds. The reeds might dry and fall away, but they would always be replaced, so that the hut never seemed to alter. It was the ultimate triumph of Roman conservationism – the childhood home of Romulus, Rome's first king, and Remus, his twin.

---

* Judging from funerary inscriptions – the only written evidence that has survived.

According to the legend, both brothers had decided to found a
city, but they could not agree where, nor what name it should
have. Romulus had stood on the Palatine, Remus on the Aventine,
both of them waiting for a sign from the gods. Remus had seen six
vultures flying overhead, but Romulus had seen twelve. Taking
this as incontrovertible proof of divine backing, Romulus had
promptly fortified the Palatine and named the new city after himself. Remus, in a fury of jealousy and resentment, had ended up
murdered by his brother in a brawl. This had irrevocably fixed the
two hills' destinies. From that moment on, the Palatine would be
for winners, the Aventine for losers. Success and failure, prestige
and shame – there, expressed in the very geography of the city,
were the twin poles around which Roman life revolved.

For just as a valley stretched wide between the hills of Romulus
and Remus, so too did the social chasm between the senator in his
villa and the cobbler in his shack. There were no subtle gradations
of wealth in Rome, nothing that could approximate to a modern
middle class. In that sense the Palatine and the Aventine were
indeed true *insulae*, islands apart. Yet the valley that separated the
two hills also joined them, by virtue of a symbolism almost as
ancient as Romulus himself. Chariots had been racing round the
Circus Maximus since the time of the kings. Stretching the entire
length of the valley, the Circus was easily Rome's largest public
space. Framed on one side by ragged shacks, on the other by grace-
ful villas, this was where the city came together in festival. Up to
two hundred thousand citizens might gather there. It was this
capacity, still unrivalled by any other sports arena to this day, which
made its gaze both so feared and so desired. There was no truer
mirror held up to greatness than that provided by the audience at
the Circus. Here was where a citizen could be most publicly defined,
whether by cheers of acclamation or by jeering and boos. Every
senator who looked down at the Circus from his villa was reminded

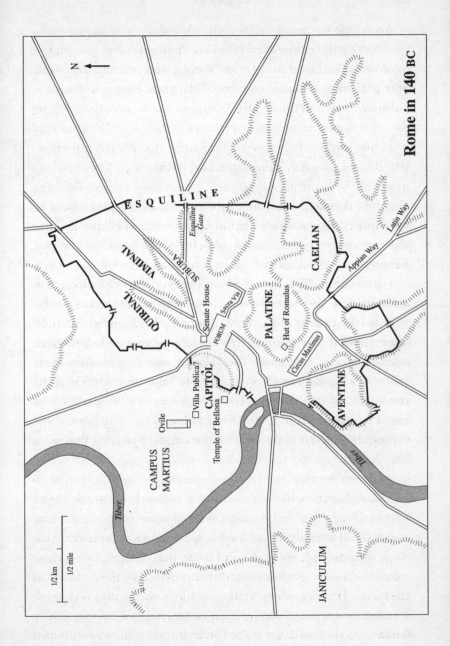

Rome in 140 BC

of this. So too was every cobbler who looked down from his shack. For all the gulf that yawned between them, the ideal of a shared community still held firm for millionaire and pauper alike. Both were citizens of the same republic. Neither Palatine nor Aventine was entirely an island after all.

Blood in the Labyrinth

The central paradox of Roman society – that savage divisions of class could coexist with an almost religious sense of community – had evolved through the course of its history. A revolution against the exactions of authority had, of course, inspired the Republic's very foundation. Even so, following the expulsion of Tarquin and the monarchy, the plebeians had found themselves quite as tyrannised by the ancient aristocracy of Rome, the patricians, as they had ever been by the kings. There were no snobs like patrician snobs. They had the right to wear fancy shoes. They claimed to hobnob with gods. Some even claimed to be descended from gods. The Julian clan, for instance, traced its lineage all the way back to Aeneas, a prince of the Trojan royal house, who in turn had been the grandson of Venus herself. This was a class of pedigree bound to give one airs.

Indeed, in the early years of the Republic's history, Roman society had come perilously close to ossifying altogether. The plebeians, however, refusing to accept they belonged to an inferior caste, had fought back in the only way they could – by going on strike. The site of their protests, inevitably, had been the Aventine.* Here they

---

* Piso and Livy disagreed over the destination of the plebeians' first walk-out, Piso claiming that it had been on the Aventine, Livy at the nearby Sacred Mount.

would periodically threaten to fulfil Remus' original ambitions by founding an entirely new city. The patricians, left to stew in their own hauteur across the valley, would gracelessly grant a few concessions. Gradually, over the years, the class system had become ever more permeable. The old rigid polarisation between patrician and plebeian had begun to crack. 'What sort of justice is it to preclude a native-born Roman from all hope of the consulship simply because he is of humble birth?'[15] the plebeians had demanded. No justice at all, it had finally been agreed. In 367 BC a law had been passed that permitted any citizen to stand for election to the great offices of the state – previously a prerogative of the patricians alone. In acknowledgement of their traditional intimacy with the gods a few minor priesthoods had remained the patricians' exclusive preserve. To the pure-bred families who had found themselves swamped by plebeian competition, this must have seemed small consolation indeed.

Over the centuries, many clans had faded away almost completely. The Julians, for instance, had found that descent from Venus did little to help them in reaching the consulship: only twice in two hundred years did they win the ultimate prize. Nor was it only their political stock that had gone down in the world. Far from the rarefied heights of the Palatine, stuck in one of the valleys where the poor seethed and stank, they had seen their neighbourhood gradually decline into a slum. What was once the small village of Subura had become the most notorious district in Rome. Like a stately ship taking in water, the lineaments of the Julian mansion had been submerged behind brothels, taverns and even – most shocking of all – a synagogue.

Privileges of birth, then, guaranteed nothing in Rome. The fact that the descendants of a goddess might find themselves living in a red-light district ensured that it was not only the very poor who dreaded the consequences of failure. At every social level the life of a citizen was a gruelling struggle to emulate – and, if possible, surpass – the achievements of his ancestors. In practice as well as principle the Republic was savagely meritocratic. Indeed, this, to the Romans, was what liberty meant. It appeared self-evident to them that the entire course of their history had been an evolution away from slavery, towards a freedom based on the dynamics of perpetual competition. The proof of the superiority of this model of society lay in its trouncing of every conceivable alternative. The Romans knew that had they remained the slaves of a monarch, or of a self-perpetuating clique of aristocrats, they would never have succeeded in conquering the world. 'It is almost beyond belief how great the Republic's achievements were once the people had gained their liberty, such was the longing for glory which it lit in every man's heart.'[16] Even the crustiest patrician had to acknowledge this. The upper classes may have sniffed at the *plebs* as an unwashed rabble, but it was still possible for them to idealise an abstract – and therefore safely odourless – Roman people.

Hypocrisy of this kind virtually defined the Republic – not a byproduct of the constitution but its very essence. The Romans judged their political system by asking not whether it made sense but whether it worked. Only if an aspect of their government had proven to be inefficient, or unjust, would they abolish it. Otherwise, they would no more have contemplated streamlining their constitution than they would have been prepared to flatten Rome and build her again from scratch. As a result, the Republic was as full of discrepancies and contradictions as the fabric of the city, a muddle of accretions patched together over many centuries. Just as the Roman streets formed a labyrinth, so the byways that a citizen had to negotiate throughout his public life were confusing, occluded and full of dead ends. Yet they had to be followed. For all the ruthlessness of competition in the Republic, it was structured by rules as complex and fluid as they were inviolable. To master them was a lifetime's work. As well as talent and application, this required contacts, money and free time. The consequence was yet further paradox: meritocracy, real and relentless as it was, nevertheless served to perpetuate a society in which only the rich could afford to devote themselves to a political career. Individuals might rise to greatness, ancient families might decline, yet through it all the faith in hierarchy endured unchanging.

For those at the bottom of the heap, this resulted in painful ambivalences. Legally, the powers of the Roman people were almost limitless: through a variety of institutions they could vote for magistrates, promulgate laws, and commit Rome to war. Yet the constitution was a hall of mirrors. Alter the angle of inspection, and popular sovereignty might easily take on the appearance of something very different. Foreigners were not alone in being puzzled by this shape-shifting quality of the Republic: 'the Romans themselves', a Greek analyst observed, 'find it impossible to state for sure whether the system is an aristocracy, a democracy, or a monarchy'.[17]

It was not that the people's powers were illusory: even the grandest candidates for magistracies made efforts to court the voters and felt not the slightest embarrassment in doing so. Competitive elections were crucial to the self-image as well as the functioning of the Republic.

It is the privilege of a free people, and particularly of this great free people of Rome, whose conquests have established a world-wide empire, that it can give or withhold its vote for anyone, standing for any office. Those of us who are storm-tossed on the waves of popular opinion must devote ourselves to the will of the people, massage it, nurture it, try to keep it happy when it seems to turn against us. If we don't care for the honours which the people have at their disposal, then obviously there is no need to put ourselves at the service of

their interests – but if political rewards are indeed our goal,
then we should never tire of courting the voters.[18]

The people mattered – and, what is more, they knew that they
mattered. Just like any electorate, they delighted in making candidates for their favours sweat. In the Republic 'there was nothing
more fickle than the masses, nothing more impenetrable than the
people's wishes, nothing more likely to baffle expectation than the
entire system of voting'.[19] Yet if there was much that was unpredictable about Roman politics, there was more about it that was
eminently predictable. Yes, the people had their votes, but only the
rich had any hope of winning office,* and not even wealth on its
own was necessarily sufficient to obtain success for a candidate. The
Roman character had a strong streak of snobbery: effectively, citizens preferred to vote for families with strong brand recognition,
electing son after father after grandfather to the great magistracies
of state, indulging the nobility's dynastic pretensions with a numb-
ing regularity. Certainly, a Roman did not have to be a member of
the ruling classes to share their prejudices. The aim of even the
most poverty-stricken citizens was not to change society, but to
do better out of it. Inequality was the price that citizens of the
Republic willingly paid for their sense of community. The class-
based agitation that had brought the plebeians their equality with
the patricians was a thing of the long-vanished past – not merely
impossible, but almost impossible to conceive.

That this was the case reflected an irony typical of the Republic.
In the very hour of their triumph the plebeians had destroyed
themselves as a revolutionary movement. In 367 BC, with the abolition of legal restrictions on their advancement, wealthy plebeians

---

* Almost certainly – although explicit proof is lacking – there was a property
qualification for public office.

had lost all incentive to side with the poor. High-achieving plebeian families had instead devoted themselves to more profitable
activities, such as monopolising the consulship and buying up the
Palatine. After two and a half centuries of power they had ended up
like the pigs in *Animal Farm*, indistinguishable from their former
oppressors. Indeed, in certain respects, they had come to hold the
whiphand. Magistracies originally wrung from the patricians as
fruits of the class war now served to boost the careers of ambitious
plebeian noblemen. One office in particular, that of the tribunate,
presented immense opportunities for grandstanding. Not only did
tribunes have the celebrated 'veto' over bills they disliked, but they
could convene public assemblies to pass bills of their own.
Patricians, forbidden from running for plebeian offices, could only
watch on in mingled resentment and distaste.

It could, of course, be dangerous for a tribune to overplay his
hand. Like most magistracies in the Republic, his office presented
him with pitfalls as well as opportunities. Even by the standards of
Roman political life, however, the unwritten rules that helped to
determine a tribune's behaviour were strikingly paradoxical. An
office that provided almost limitless opportunities for playing dirty
was also hedged about by the sacred. As it had been since ancient
times, the person of a tribune was inviolable, and anyone who
ignored that sanction was considered to have laid his hands upon
the gods themselves. In return for his sacrosanct status a tribune
was obliged during his year of office never to leave Rome, and
always to keep an open house. He had to pay close attention to the
people's hardships and complaints, to listen to them whenever they
stopped him in the street, and to read the graffiti which they might
scrawl on public monuments, encouraging him to pass or obstruct
new measures. No matter how overweening his personal ambition,
the aristocrat who chose to stand for election as a tribune could not
afford to appear haughty. Sometimes he might even go so far as to

affect the accent of a plebeian from the slums. '*Populares*', the Romans called such men: politicians who relied on the common touch.

Yet at the same time as he upheld the interests of the people, a *popularis* also had to respect the sensibilities of his own class. It was a balancing act that required enormous skill. If the tribunate was always regarded with suspicion by the more conservative elements in the nobility, then that was in large part because of the unique temptations that it offered to its holders. There was always a risk that a tribune might end up going too far, succumbing to the lure of easy popularity with the mob, bribing them with radical, un-Roman reforms. And, of course, the more that the slums swelled to bursting point, and the more wretched the living conditions for the poor became, the greater that risk grew.

It was two brothers of impeccable breeding, Tiberius and Gaius Gracchus, who finally made the fateful attempt. First Tiberius, in 133 BC, and then Gaius, ten years later, used their tribunates to push for reforms in favour of the poor. They proposed that publicly held land be divided into allotments and handed out to the masses; that corn be sold to them below the market rate; even, shockingly, that the Republic should provide its poorest soldiers with clothes. Radical measures indeed, and the aristocracy, unsurprisingly, was appalled. To most noblemen, there appeared something implacable and sinister about the devotion of the Gracchi to the people. True, Tiberius was not the first of his class to have concerned himself with land reform, but his paternalism, so far as his peers were concerned, went altogether too far and too fast. Gaius, even more alarmingly, had a consciously revolutionary vision, of a republic imbued with the values of Greek democracy, in which the balance of power between the classes would be utterly transformed, and the people, not the aristocracy, would serve as the arbiters of Rome. How, his peers wondered, could any nobleman argue for this, unless he aimed to establish himself as a tyrant? What struck them as particularly ominous was the fact that Tiberius, having finished his year of office, had immediately sought re-election, and that Gaius, in 122 BC, had actually succeeded in obtaining a second successive tribunate. Where might illegalities such as these not end? Sacred as the person of a tribune might be, it was not so sacred as the preservation of the Republic itself. Twice the cry went up to defend the constitution and twice it was answered. Twelve years after Tiberius was clubbed to death with a stool-leg in a violent brawl Gaius, in 121, was also killed by agents of the aristocracy. His corpse was decapitated, and lead poured into his skull. In the wake of his murder three thousand of his followers were executed without trial.

These eruptions of civil violence were the first to spill blood in the streets of Rome since the expulsion of the kings. Their grotesque quality vividly reflected the scale of aristocratic paranoia. Tyranny was not the only spectre that the Gracchi had raised from Rome's ancient past. It was no coincidence, for instance, that Gaius died on the spot most sacred to the plebeian cause, the Aventine. By taking refuge there, he and his supporters had deliberately sought to identify their cause with that of the ancient strikers. Despite the fact that the poor failed to rise in his support, Gaius' attempt to stir long-dormant class struggles struck most members of the nobility as a terrifying act of irresponsibility. Yet the reprisals too filled them with unease. Head-hunting was hardly the practice of a civilised people. In the lead-weighted skull of Gaius Gracchus an ominous glimpse could be caught of what might happen were the conventions of the Republic to be breached, and its foundations swept away. It was a warning that temperament more than fitted the Romans to heed. What was the Republic, after all, if not a community bound together by its shared assumptions, precedents and past? To jettison this inheritance was to stare into the abyss. Tyranny or barbarism – these would be the alternatives were the Republic to fall.

Here, then, was one final paradox. A system that encouraged a gnawing hunger for prestige in its citizens, that seethed with their vaunting rivalries, that generated a dynamism so aggressive that it had overwhelmed all who came against it, also bred paralysis. This was the true tragedy of the Gracchi. Yes, they had been concerned with their own glory – they were Roman, after all – but they had also been genuinely passionate in their desire to improve the lot of their fellow citizens. The careers of both brothers had been bold attempts to grapple with Rome's manifold and glaring problems. To that extent, the Gracchi had died as martyrs to their ideals. Yet there were few of their fellow noblemen who would have found that a reassuring thought. In the Republic there was no distinguishing between political goals and personal ambitions. Influence came through power, power through influence. The fate of the Gracchi had conclusively proved that any attempt to impose root and branch reforms on the Republic would be interpreted as tyranny. Programmes of radical change, no matter how idealistic their inspiration, would inevitably disintegrate into internecine rivalries. By demonstrating this to the point of destruction, the Gracchi had ultimately stymied the very reforms for which they had died. The tribunes who followed them would be more careful in the causes they adopted. Social revolution would remain on permanent hold.

Like the city itself, the Republic always appeared on the point of bursting with the fissile tensions contained within it. Yet just as Rome not only endured but continued to swell, so the constitution appeared to emerge stronger from every crisis to which it was subjected. And why, after all, should the Romans not cling to an order that had brought them such success? Frustrating, multi-form and complex it may have been, yet these were precisely the qualities that enabled it to absorb shocks and digest upheavals, to renew itself after every disaster. The Romans, who had turned the world upside down, could be comforted by knowing that the form of their republic still endured unchanged. The same intimacies of community bonded its citizens, the same cycles of competition gave focus to its years, the same clutter of institutions structured its affairs.

And even blood spilled in the streets might easily be scrubbed clean.

2

THE SIBYL'S CURSE

Sacker of Cities

Long before the murder of the Gracchi and their followers the Sibyl had foreseen it all. Roman would turn against Roman. Nor, according to the Sibyl's grim prognostications, would the violence be confined to mere scuffles in the capital. Her vision of the future was far bleaker, far more dystopian: 'Not foreign invaders, Italy, but your own sons will rape you, a brutal, interminable gang-rape, punishing you, famous country, for all your many depravities, leaving you prostrated, stretched out among the burning ashes. Self-slaughterer! No longer the mother of upstanding men, but rather the nurse of savage, ravening beasts!'[1]

Hardly the kind of forecast to delight the portent-haunted Romans. Fortunately for their peace of mind, however, these particular verses had not been copied from their own prophetic books, which remained locked up where they had always been, secure against any leaks, in the temple of Jupiter. Instead, the blood-curdling prediction had first begun to circulate far away from Rome, in the kingdoms of the eastern Mediterranean. The Romans, it appeared, were not the only people to have been visited by the

Sibyl. In Rome her prophecies may have been kept a closely guarded secret, but those she had given to the Greeks and Jews were widely broadcast. Many of these clearly referred to the Republic: 'An empire will rise from beyond the western sea, white and many-headed, and its sway will be measureless, bringing ruin and terror to kings, looting gold and silver from city after city.'[2] Nervous of prodigies the Romans may have been, but in the eyes of the world they were a prodigy themselves. The deadliest one of all – or so the Sibyl warned.

For her vision of the Republic's rise to greatness was dark indeed. Ancient cities, great monarchies, famous empires, all would be swept away. Mankind would acknowledge a single order. One superpower would rule supreme. But this would bring no dawning of a universal peace. Far from it. Instead, it would be the Romans' fate to surfeit on their own greatness. 'They will sink into a swamp of decadence: men will sleep with men, and boys will be pimped in brothels; civil tumults will engulf them, and everything will fall into confusion and disorder. The world will be filled with evils.'[3]

Scholars have dated these verses to around 140 BC. Rome's supremacy was so well established by then that its description would hardly have required the powers of an authentic Sibyl. Unlike their counterparts held by the Republic, the prophetic books circulating in the Greek East never suggested that the future could be altered. Before their vision of a series of great empires succeeding each other throughout history, with Rome's the greatest and most baneful of all, mere mortals were represented as impotent. No wonder that the poets hiding behind the pseudonym of the Sibyl, when they claimed to peer into the future, should have offered a vision of the Republic as a mother of 'ravening beasts', torn to shreds by her own children. It was a prophecy bred equally of wishful thinking and desperation, of an inability to imagine how else the Roman juggernaut might ever be stopped. 'They will bring despair to humanity – and then, once they have succumbed to their savagery and pride, the fall of these men will be terrible indeed.'[4]

There could have been no doubt, in the 140s, as to what the Sibyl was referring when she spoke of the Romans' savagery and pride. This was the decade when the brute fact of their power was demonstrated to the world beyond all possible doubt. Devastation shadowed the Mediterranean. First, the Republic decided to conclude unfinished business and bring the ghostly half-life of Carthage to an end. Even in Rome herself there were those who disapproved. Many argued that the Republic needed a rival who was worthy of the name. Without rivalry, they demanded, how would Rome's greatness ever be maintained? Such a question, of course, could have been asked only in a state where ruthless competition was regarded as the basis of all civic virtue. Unsurprisingly, however, a majority of citizens refused to stomach its implications. For more than a century they had been demonising the Carthaginians' cruelty and faithlessness. Why, most citizens wondered, should the standards of Roman life be applied to the protection of such a foe? This question was duly answered by a vote to push Carthage into war. By aiming at her complete annihilation, the Republic revealed what the logical consequence of its ideals of success might be. In such brutality, unmediated by any nexus of fellowship or duty, lay the extremes of the Roman desire to be the best.

In 149 the hapless Carthaginians were given the vindictive order to abandon their city. Rather than surrender to such a demand, they prepared to defend their homes and sacred places to the death. This, of course, was precisely what the hawks back in Rome had been hoping they would do. The legions moved in for the kill. For three years the Carthaginians held out against overwhelming odds and in the final stages of the siege the generalship of Rome's best soldier, Scipio Aemilianus. At last, in 146, the city was stormed, gutted of its treasures and set ablaze. The inferno raged for seventeen days. On the cleared and smoking ruin, the Romans then placed a deadly interdiction, forbidding anyone ever to build upon its site again. Seven hundred years of history were wiped clean.*

Meanwhile, just in case anyone was missing the lesson, a Roman army spent the same spring of 146 rubbing it into the noses of the Greeks. That winter a ragbag of cities in southern Greece had presumed to disturb the balance of power that Rome had established in the area. Such lese-majesty could not be allowed to pass unpunished. In a war that was over almost before it had begun, a Greek army was swatted like a bothersome wasp, and the ancient city of Corinth reduced to a heap of smoking rubble. Since Corinth had long been celebrated for two things in particular – the quality of her prostitutes and the splendour of her art – the opportunities for plunder were enthusiastically embraced. The women of the slaughtered citizens were enslaved, while on the harbour quays soldiers rolled dice on priceless paintings. Jumbles of statuary stood piled all around them, ready to be auctioned off in job lots or crated back to Rome.

The obliteration of not one but two of the greatest cities of the Mediterranean was a stunning outrage. No wonder, in the face of it, that the Sibyl imagined a curse laid against Rome, one borne upon the smoke from the twin scenes of annihilation. Even the Romans themselves felt a little queasy. No longer could it be pretended that they were conquering the world in self-defence. Memories of the looting of Corinth would always be recalled by the Romans with embarrassment. Guilt over Carthage, however, provoked in them

---

* The oft-repeated story that the Romans drove a plough over the foundations of Carthage and sowed them with salt appears to be just that – a story. Certainly, no ancient source refers to it.

something far more. It was said that even as Scipio watched the
flames lap at the crumbling walls of the great city, he had wept. In
the destruction of Rome's deadliest enemy he could see, like the
Sibyl, the baneful power of the workings of Fate. At the moment
when the Republic's supremacy had been so overwhelmingly
affirmed, when there was not an enemy who could hope to stand
against it, when the plunder of the whole world seemed its for the
taking, Scipio imagined its doom. Lines from Homer came to him.

> *'The day of the destruction of sacred Troy will arrive,*
> *And the slaughter of Priam and his people.'*[5]

But what he imagined might bring slaughter and destruction to the
Republic, Scipio, unlike the Sibyl, did not say.

Choking on Gold

Prior to the cataclysms of 146 there had been some confusion
among the Greeks as to the precise definition of 'freedom'. When
the Romans claimed to be guaranteeing it, what did this mean?
One could never be sure with barbarians, of course: their grasp of
semantics was so woefully inadequate. All the same, it did not
require a philosopher to point out that words might be slippery
and dangerously dependent on perspective. And so it had proved.
Roman and Greek interpretations of the word had indeed diverged.
To the Romans, who tended to regard the Greeks as fractious children in need of the firm hand of a *pater familias*, 'freedom' had meant
an opportunity for the city states to follow rules laid down by
Roman commissioners. To the Greeks, it had meant the chance to
fight each other. It was this incompatibility of viewpoints that had
led directly to the tragedy of Corinth's destruction.

After 146 there could be no more quibbling over diplomatic language. The treaties of friendship that governed relations between the Republic and her allies now stood brutally defined. They granted the Republic freedom of action, and her allies none at all. If the Greek cities were still permitted a nominal autonomy, then this was only because Rome wanted the benefits of empire without the bother of administering it. Cowed and obsequious, states far beyond the shores of Greece also redoubled their efforts to second-guess the Republic's will. Throughout the monarchies of the East, assorted royal poodles would jump whenever the Romans snapped their fingers, perfectly aware that even a hint of independence might result in the hamstringing of their war elephants, or the sudden promotion of rivals to their thrones. It was the last monarch of Pergamum, a Greek city controlling most of what is now western Turkey, who took the resulting spirit of collaboration to its logical extreme. In 133 he left his entire kingdom to the Republic in his will.

This was the most spectacular bequest in history. Fabled for the gargantuan splendour of her monuments and the wealth of her subject cities, Pergamum offered the prospect of riches beyond even the Romans' plunder-sated dreams. But what was to be done with the legacy? Responsibility for that decision lay with the Senate, an assembly of some three hundred of Rome's great and good, generally acknowledged – even by those not in it – to be both the conscience and the guiding intelligence of the Republic. Membership of this elite was determined not automatically by birth but by achievement and reputation – as long as he had not blotted his copy-book too outrageously, any citizen who had held high office could expect to be enrolled in it as a matter of course. This gave to the Senate's deliberations immense moral weight, and even though its decrees never had the technical force of law, it was a brave – or foolhardy – magistrate who chose to ignore them. What

was the Republic, after all, if not a partnership between Senate and
people – '*Senatus Populusque Romanus*', as the formula put it? Stamped
on the smallest coins, inscribed on the pediments of the vastest
temples, the abbreviation of this phrase could be seen everywhere,
splendid shorthand for the majesty of the Roman constitution –
'SPQR'.

Even so, as in any partnership, there was nothing like a dispute
over money to breed tension. News of the windfall from Pergamum
arrived just in time for that doughty champion of the people,
Tiberius Gracchus, to propose that it be spent on funding his ambitious reforms. The people themselves, naturally enough, agreed.
Most of Tiberius' fellow senators, however, did not, and dug in
their heels. In part, of course, this reflected distaste for Tiberius'
demagoguery, and indignation that he should dare to trample on
the Senate's august toes. But there was more to the opposition
than a simple fit of pique. The prospect of inheriting an entire kingdom did indeed affront long-held Roman principles. Pre-eminent
among these were an identification of gold with moral corruption
and a hearty suspicion of Asiatics. Senators, of course, could afford
to stand up for such traditional values, but there was also a more
practical reason why they should have regarded the bequest of
Pergamum as an embarrassment. Provinces, it was assumed, were
burdensome to run. There were subtler ways of fleecing foreigners
than by imposing direct rule on them. The Senate's preferred
policy, practised throughout the East, had always been to maintain
a delicate balance between exploitation and disengagement. Now, it
seemed, that balance was in danger of being upset.

So, initially, the Senate – aside from colluding in Tiberius'
murder – did nothing. Only when the kingdom's collapse into
anarchy threatened the stability of the entire region was an army
finally dispatched to Pergamum, and even then it took several years
of desultory campaigning before the Republic's new subjects were

brought to heel. Still the Senate refrained from establishing Rome's first province in Asia. Instead, the commissioners sent to regulate the kingdom were carefully instructed to uphold the regulations of the kings they were replacing. As was invariably the Roman way, the emphasis lay on pretending that nothing much had changed.

So it was that a governing class that had been responsible for guiding its city to a position of unparalleled world power, bringing the entire Mediterranean under its effective control, and annihilating anyone who dared to oppose it, still clung to its instinctive isolationism. As far as Roman magistrates were concerned, abroad remained what it had always been: a field for the winning of glory. While plunder was never to be sniffed at, honour remained the truest measure of both a city and a man. By holding to this ideal, the members of the Roman aristocracy could reassure themselves that they remained true to the traditions of their rugged forefathers, even as they revelled in the sway of their command. As long as the effete monarchs of Asia sent their embassies crawling to learn the every whim of the Senate, as long as the desert nomads of Africa reined in their savagery at the merest frown of a legionary commander, as long as the wild barbarians of Gaul dreaded to challenge the unconquerable might of the Republic, then Rome was content. Respect was all the tribute she demanded and required.

But if the senatorial elite, confident already in their own wealth and status, could afford to believe this, then businessmen and financiers, to say nothing of the vast mass of the poor, had very different ideas. The Romans had always associated the East with gold. Now, with the settlement of Pergamum, came the opportunity to start looting it systematically. Ironically, it was the Senate's insistence that the traditional governance of Pergamum be respected that pointed the way. Governance, to the Pergamene kings, had meant taxing their subjects for all they could get. It was an example from which the Romans had much to learn. While it had been a constant principle of the Republic that war should turn a profit, profit, to the Romans, had tended to mean plunder. In the barbarian West, it was true, conquest had generally been followed by taxation, but only because otherwise there would have been no administration at all. In the East administration had existed long before Rome. For this reason it had always seemed cheaper, and far less bother, to pillage with abandon, and then to top up funds with an indemnity or two.

Pergamum, however, illustrated that taxation could indeed be made to pay – that it was a glittering opportunity, in fact, and not at all a chore. Soon enough the officials who had been sent to administer the kingdom were wallowing in peculation. Extravagant rumours of their activities began to filter back to Rome. There was outrage: Pergamum was the property of the Roman people, and if there were pickings to be had, then the Roman people wanted their proper share. Mouthpiece for this resentment was none other than Gaius Gracchus, tribune in succession to his murdered brother, and just as keen to lay his hands on the Pergamene bonanza as Tiberius had been. He, too, was proposing ambitious social reforms; he, too, needed quick funds. So it was that in 123, after a decade of agitation, Gaius Gracchus finally succeeded in pushing through a fateful law. By its terms, Pergamum was at last subjected to organised taxation. The lid of the honeypot was now well and truly off.[6]

Pragmatic and cynical in equal measure, the new tax regime worked by actively fostering greed. Lacking the huge bureaucracies that the monarchs of the East relied upon to squeeze their subjects, the Republic turned instead to the private sector to provide the necessary expertise. Tax-farming contracts were publicly auctioned, with those who bought them advancing in full the tribute owed to the state. Since the sums demanded were astronomical, only the very wealthiest could afford to pay them, and even then not as individual contractors. Instead, resources would be pooled, and the resulting companies administered, as befitted huge financial concerns, with elaborate care. Shares might be offered, general meetings held, directors elected to the service of the board. In the province itself a consortium's employees would include soldiers, sailors and postmen, quite apart from the tax-collecting staff. The name given to the businessmen who ran these cartels, *publicani*, harked back to their function as agents of the state, but there was nothing public spirited about the services they provided. Profit was all, and the more obscene the better. The aim was not only to collect the official tribute owed to the state, but also to strongarm the provincials into paying extra for the privilege of being fleeced. If necessary, commercial know-how would complement the thuggery. A debtor might be offered loans at ruinous rates and then, once he had been leeched of everything he owned, enslaved. Far distant in Rome, what did the shareholders of the great corporations care for the suffering they imposed? Cities were no longer sacked, they were bled to death instead.

Ostensibly, Rome's subjects did have some recourse against the depredations of their tormentors. The taxation system may have been privatised, but the province's administration remained in the hands of the senatorial elite – the class still most imbued with the ideals of the Republic. These ideals obliged governors to provide their subjects with the benefits of peace and justice. In reality, so lucrative were the bribes on offer that even the sternest principles had the habit of eroding into dust. Roman probity fast became a sick joke. To the wretched provincials, there appeared little difference between *publicani* and the senators sent to govern them. Both had their snouts in the same loot-filled trough.

As a spectacle of greed, the rape of Pergamum was certainly blatant. The vast sway of the Republic's power, won in the cause of the honour of Rome, stood nakedly revealed as a licence to make money. The resulting goldrush was soon a stampede. Highways originally built as instruments of war now served to bring the taxman faster to his victim; pack-animals straining beneath the weight of tribute clopped along the roads behind the legionaries. Across the Mediterranean, increasingly a Roman lake, shipping sailed for Italy, crammed with the fruits of colonial extortion. The arteries of empire were hardening with gold, and the more they hardened, so the more gold Rome squeezed out.

As her grip tightened, so the very appearance of her provinces began to alter, as though giant fingers were gouging deep into the landscape. In the East great cities were ransacked for treasure – but in the West it was the earth. The result was mining on a scale not to be witnessed again until the Industrial Revolution. Nowhere was the devastation more spectacular than in Spain. Observer after observer bore stunned witness to what they saw. Even in far off Judaea, people 'had heard what the Romans had done in the country of Spain, for the winning of the silver and the gold which is there'.[7]

The mines that Rome had annexed from Carthage more than a century previously had been handed over to the *publicani*, who had proceeded to exploit them with their customary gusto. A single network of tunnels might spread for more than a hundred square miles, and provide upwards of forty thousand slaves with a living death. Over the pockmarked landscape there would invariably hang a pall of smog, belched out from the smelting furnaces through giant chimneys, and so heavy with chemicals that it burned the naked skin and turned it white. Birds would die if they flew through the fumes. As Roman power spread the gas-clouds were never far behind.

Initially, large areas of Spain had been regarded as too remote and dangerous to exploit, the haunt of tribesmen so irredeemably savage that they believed banditry to be an honourable profession, and used urine to brush their teeth.* By the last years of the second century BC, however, all except the north of the peninsula had been opened up for business.† Huge new mines were sunk across central and south-western Spain. Measurements of lead in the ice of Greenland's glaciers, which show a staggering increase in concentration during this period, bear witness to the volumes of poisonous smoke they belched out.[8] The ore being smelted was silver: it has been estimated that for every ton of silver extracted over ten thousand tons of rock had to be quarried. It has also been estimated that by the early first century BC, the Roman mint was using fifty tons of silver each year.[9]

As in Asia, so in Spain, the huge scale of such operations could not have been achieved without collusion between the public and private sectors. Increasingly, in return for providing investors back in Rome with docile natives, decent harbours and good roads, the Roman authorities in the provinces began to look for backhanders. The corruption that resulted from this was all the more insidious because it could never be acknowledged. Even as they raked in the cash, senators still affected a snooty disdain towards finance. The contempt for profit was even enshrined in law: no *publicanus* was allowed to join the Senate, just as no senator was permitted to engage in anything so vulgar as overseas trade. Behind the scenes, however, such legislation did little to fulfil its aims. If anything, by prescribing how governor and entrepreneur could best collaborate, it only served to bring them closer together: the one needed the other if they were both to end up rich. The result was that

---

* According to the poet Catullus, anyway (37 and 39). It was probably a joke, but one that must have played on Roman prejudices about Spanish standards of personal hygiene.

† The Iberian peninsula was not brought entirely under Roman control until 23 BC.

Roman government increasingly began to mutate into what can perhaps best be described as a military-fiscal complex. In the years following the Pergamene bequest motives of profit and prestige grew ever more confused. The traditional policy of isolationism came increasingly under threat. And all the while the provincials were exploited ever more.

Not that every ideal of the Republic was dead. There were some administrators so appalled by what was happening that they attempted to take a stand against it. This was a dangerous policy – for if the business cartels ever found their interests seriously threatened, they were quick to muscle in. Their most notorious victim was Rutilius Rufus, a provincial administrator celebrated for his rectitude who had sought to defend his subjects against the tax-collectors, and who in 92 BC was brought to trial before a jury stuffed with supporters of the *publicani*. Big business had successfully oiled the workings of the court: the charge – selected with deliberate effrontery – was extortion. After he had been convicted Rufus, with matching effrontery, chose as the place of his exile the very province he was supposed to have looted. There he was loudly welcomed with honours and scattered flowers.

The province was Asia: formerly the kingdom of Pergamum and still, forty years after it had been given to them, the Romans' favourite milch-cow. To the provincials, the conviction of Rufus must have seemed the final straw: proof, if proof were still needed, that Roman greed would never restrain itself. Yet what could be done? No one dared fight back. The charred rubble of Corinth testified eloquently to the perils of doing that. Despair as well as taxes crushed the Greeks of Asia. How could they ever hope to throw the Republic, its rapacious financiers and invincible legions off their backs?

Then, at last, three years after the conviction of Rufus, the provincial authorities pushed their money-grubbing too far.

Looking to widen their activities, Roman business interests began casting greedy eyes on Pontus, a kingdom on the Black Sea coast in the north of what is now Turkey. In the summer of 89 the Roman commissioner in Asia, Manius Aquillius, trumped up an excuse for an invasion. Rather than risk his own troops' lives, he preferred to order a client-king to do the fighting for him – having assumed, with fatal complacency, that any fallout from such a provocation would be easily containable. But the King of Pontus, Mithridates, was no ordinary opponent. His biography, carefully honed by a genius for florid propaganda, read like a fairy tale. Persecuted by his wicked mother as a child, the young prince had been forced to take refuge in a forest. Here he had lived for seven years, outrunning deer and outfighting lions. Nervous that his mother might still try to have him murdered, Mithridates had also developed an obsessive interest in toxicology, taking repeated antidotes until he was immune to poison. Not the kind of boy, in short, to let family stand in the way of a throne. Duly returning to his capital at the head of a conquering army, Mithridates had ordered his mother killed, and then, just for good measure, his brother and sister too. More than twenty years later he remained as power hungry and ruthless as ever – far too much so, certainly, for a reluctant Roman poodle. The invasion was contemptuously repelled.

Next, however, came a more fateful step. Mithridates had to decide whether to take the attack to Rome herself. Superpowers were not taken on lightly, but war with the Republic was a challenge for which Mithridates had been preparing all his reign. Like any ambitious despot, he had worked hard to beef up his offensive capabilities, and his army was shiny new – literally so, since its weapons were embossed with gold and its armour with bright jewels. But if Mithridates liked to make a splash, he also enjoyed playing at cloak and dagger: travelling undercover through Asia, he

had seen enough to convince him of the provincials' hatred of
Rome. This, more than anything, was what persuaded him to take
the plunge. Crossing into the province of Asia, he found the garrisons protecting it scanty and ill-prepared, and the Greek cities
eager to hail him as a saviour. In a matter of weeks Roman power in
the province had totally collapsed, and Mithridates found himself
standing on the shore of the Aegean Sea.

As a matricidal barbarian he was hardly the kind of champion
the Greeks would normally have taken to their hearts. But better
a matricidal barbarian than the *publicani* – the longing for freedom
was so desperate, and the loathing of Rome so visceral, that the
provincials were willing to go to any lengths to dispose of their
oppressors. In the summer of 88, when Rome's chains had already
been thrown off, they were to demonstrate this in a horrific explosion of violence. Aiming to bind the Greek cities to him
irrevocably, Mithridates wrote to them, ordering the massacre of
every Roman and Italian left in Asia. The Greeks followed his
instructions with savage relish. The atrocity was all the more terrible for the secrecy with which it had been prepared and the
perfect co-ordination of the attacks. Victims were rounded up and
slaughtered by hired assassins, hacked to pieces as they clung to
sacred statues, or shot as they attempted to escape into the sea.
Their bodies were left to rot unburied outside city walls. Eighty
thousand men, women and children were said to have been killed
on that single, deadly night.[10]

As a blow to the Roman economy, this was calculated and devastating; but as a blow to Roman prestige it was far worse.
Mithridates had already shown himself a master of propaganda,
resurrecting the Sibyl's prophecies and throwing in some new
ones of his own in order to make them appear more relevant to
himself. The common theme was the appearance of a great king
from the East, an instrument of divine retribution sent to humble

the arrogant and grasping superpower. The mass slaughter of businessmen was only one way in which Mithridates chose to dramatise this. Even more calculated for effect was the execution of Manius Aquillius, the Roman commissioner who had provoked Mithridates into war in the first place. Falling ill at just the wrong moment, the unfortunate Aquillius was captured and dragged back to Pergamum, shackled all the way to a seven-foot barbarian. After tying him to an ass and parading him through jeering crowds, Mithridates next ordered some treasure melted down. When all had been prepared, Aquillius' head was jerked back, his mouth forced open, and the molten metal poured down his throat. 'War-mongers against every nation, people and king under the sun, the Romans have only one abiding motive – greed, deep-seated, for empire and riches.'[11] This had been the verdict of Mithridates on the Republic and now, in the person of her legate in Asia, he exacted symbolic justice. Manius Aquillius choked to death on gold.

A Trumpet in the Sky

When a ship loaded with the pickings of empire sailed for Italy, it would most likely aim for the bare cone of Vesuvius. Sailors would scan the horizon, searching for the familiar, flat-topped silhouette of the volcano, and when they made it out raise a prayer of thanks to the gods for having brought them safely through the perils of their voyage. Ahead of them was journey's end. Across the glittering azure of the bay the sailors would see towns dotted along the coastline, picturesque touches of Greece on the Italian shore, planted there by colonists centuries earlier – for business, in the Bay of Naples, had always been international. Not that these old ports received much shipping now. Naples herself, for instance, basking in

the sun, made a living from a very different trade. Only two days'
ride from Rome, her ancient streets had recently begun to fill with
tourists, all of them keen to taste the Greek lifestyle – whether by
debating philosophy, complaining to doctors, or falling in love with
a witty, well-read whore. Meanwhile, out to sea, the giant freight
ships loomed and passed on by.

Nowadays, their port of call was a few miles up the coast. At
Puteoli, Roman businessmen had long since flattened all traces of
Greek heritage. Huge, concrete moles harboured shipping from all
over the Mediterranean, loaded with grain to feed Rome's monstrous appetite and slaves to fuel her enterprises, but also rarities
garnered from her far-off domains: sculptures and spices, paintings and strange plants. Only the wealthiest could afford such
luxuries, of course, but there was a growing market for them in the
villas that now dotted the coastline either side of Puteoli, and were
themselves the ultimate in consumer trophies. Like the super-rich
anywhere, the Roman aristocracy wanted to keep their favourite
holiday destination exclusive, and to this end had begun to buy it
up.

The property boom in the region had been fuelled throughout
the nineties by resourceful entrepreneurs – and in particular by an
oyster-breeder named Sergius Orata. Looking to capitalise on the
insatiable Roman appetite for shellfish, Orata had developed the
local oyster beds on a hitherto undreamed-of scale. He had built
channels and dams to regulate the flow of the sea, and lofty
canopies over the mouth of the neighbouring Lucrine Lake, which
he then promoted as home to the tastiest oysters in the world.
Contemporaries were so impressed by Orata's wizardry that they
claimed he could have bred shellfish on his roof had he tried. But it
was a further piece of technical innovation that really made Orata's
name: having cornered the market in oysters, he then invented
the heated swimming pool.

Such at least seems the likeliest meaning of a cryptic Latin phrase, *balneae pensiles* – literally, hanging baths.* We are told that this invention required the suspension of seas of warm water and was marvellously relaxing, properties which helped Orata to market it as successfully as oysters. Soon enough, no property could be called complete unless it had first had a 'hanging bath' installed. Of course, it was Orata himself who did the installing – buying up villas, building the swimming pools, then selling the properties on.

It did not take long for his speculations to make the Bay of Naples synonymous with wealth and chic. Nor was the boom confined solely to the coast. Inland too, in ancient cities such as Capua, where the scent of perfume hung thick in the streets, or Nola, a favoured ally of Rome for more than two centuries, marks of peace and softness were all around. Beyond their walls, fields of apple-trees and vines, olive groves and wild flowers stretched away, back towards Vesuvius and the sea. This was Campania, the jewel of Italy, playground of the rich, fertile, prosperous and luxuriant.

But not everywhere was booming. Beyond Nola, valleys wound from the lowlands into a very different world. In Samnium all was mountainous and austere. Just as the jagged contours of the landscape provided a brutal contrast with the plain below, so too did the character of the people who had to scratch a living from the stony, scrub-clad soil. There were no oysters in Samnium, no heated swimming pools, only lumbering peasants with comical, rustic accents. They practised witchcraft, wore ugly rings of iron round their necks,

---

* The exact nature of Orata's 'hanging baths' has provoked much speculation. Some have argued that they constituted a hot shower, others that Orata had invented the *hypocaust*, the under-floor central heating system built in to luxury villas. But if a shower, why describe it as a bath? And if a *hypocaust*, why invent a new phrase? For the best analysis of the various alternatives, see Fagan, 'Sergius Orata'.

and – scandalously – permitted barbers to shave their pubic hair in public. The Romans, needless to say, regarded them with scorn.

All the same, they could never quite forget that these savages had been the last Italian people to contest the mastery of the peninsula with them. Barely ten miles from Nola, at a mountain pass known as the Caudine Forks, the Samnites had inflicted one of the most humiliating defeats in Roman history. In 321 BC an entire army had been trapped in the defile and forced to surrender. Rather than slaughter their captives, the Samnites had elected to strip them to their tunics and drive them beneath a yoke formed of spears, while the victors, in their splendid armour, had stood and watched in triumph. By humiliating them in this manner, however, the Samnites had betrayed a fatal misunderstanding of their enemies. Peace was intolerable to the Romans unless they dictated it themselves. Despite the terms agreed and sworn to, they had soon found a way of breaking the treaty, and returned to the attack. Samnium had been duly conquered. Colonies were built on remote hilltops, roads driven over the valleys, the very ruggedness of the landscape tamed. To anyone lolling beside one of Orata's swimming pools, the age when the Samnites would sally forth from the mountains to devastate Campania must have seemed very ancient history indeed.

But then suddenly, late in 91 BC, the unbelievable happened. Long-held grudges, never entirely extinguished, flared back into flames. Warfare returned to the Samnite hills. The mountain-men armed themselves as though the long years of occupation had melted away. Pouring from their fastnesses, they did as their ancestors had always done, and swept into the plains. The Romans, unmindful of the storm about to break, had stationed only the barest military presence in Campania and were caught perilously short. All along the Bay of Naples, lately the scene of such indolence and peace, cities fell to the rebels like ripe fruit from a tree:

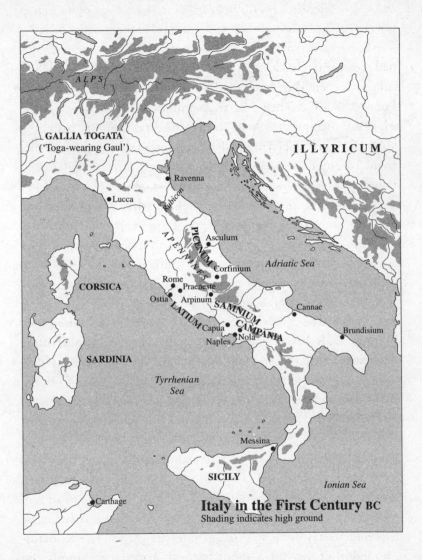

Italy in the First Century BC
Shading indicates high ground

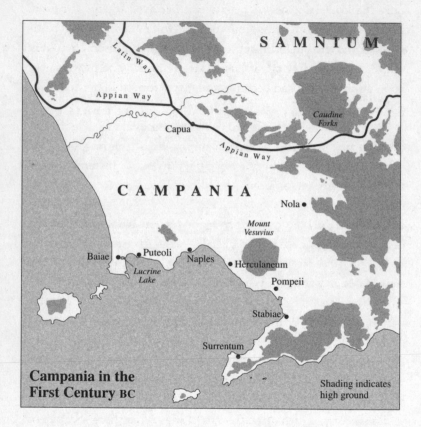

S A M N I U M

Latin Way

Appian Way

Caudine Forks

Capua

Appian Way

C A M P A N I A

Nola

Mount Vesuvius

Baiae

Puteoli

Lucrine Lake

Naples

Herculaneum

Pompeii

Stabiae

Surrentum

**Campania in the
First Century** BC

Shading indicates
high ground

Surrentum, Stabiae and Herculaneum. But the biggest prize of all –
by virtue of its strategic situation – lay further inland: Nola. After
only the briefest of sieges the city was betrayed to the Samnites.
The garrison was invited to join the rebel forces, but when its commander and the senior officers contemptuously refused, they were
starved to death. The city itself was strengthened and provisioned.
Soon enough Nola had become a mighty stronghold of the rebels'
cause.

That cause was not confined to the Samnites alone. The treachery that had delivered Nola into the hands of the rebels was far
from an isolated incident: the town of Pompeii, for instance, only a
few miles from Naples along the slope of Vesuvius, had been party
to the rebellion from the very start. Elsewhere in Italy, tribes and
cities whose previous campaigns against Rome belonged to an age
of barely remembered legend had also taken up arms. The particular focus of the rebellion, however, lay along the line of the
Apennines, in territory mountainous and backward like Samnium,
where the peasants had long been brutalised by poverty. It was this
which gave their eruption into the urbanised lowlands such a
savage quality. When the rebels captured Asculum, the first city to
fall to them, they slaughtered every Roman they could find. The
wives of those who refused to join them had then been tortured
and scalped.

The record of such atrocities might suggest nothing more than
a vengeful and primitive barbarism. Yet the hatreds of the peasantry would have counted for nothing without the oligarchies who
ruled the various Italian states having their own reasons for
unleashing them. It had always been Roman practice to flatter and
bribe the ruling classes of their allies – indeed, it was the success of
this policy that had done more than anything else to ensure the
Italians' loyalty in the past. Increasingly, however, those with the
crucial power to influence their communities – the wealthy, the

landed, the literate – had begun to find themselves alienated from Rome. Their resentments were many. The burden of military service in Rome's wars fell disproportionately on their shoulders. They held an inferior status in Roman law. Perhaps most unsettlingly of all, however, their eyes had been opened to a world of opportunity and power undreamed of by their ancestors. The Italians had not only helped Rome to conquer her empire, but had contributed enthusiastically to exploiting it. Wherever Roman arms had led, there Italian businessmen had been sure to follow. In the provinces the Italian allies were guaranteed privileges virtually indistinguishable from those of full Roman citizens, and the wretched provincials certainly found it hard to tell the two classes apart, loathing them equally as 'Romaioi'. Far from mollifying the Italians, however, the experience of living abroad as a master race seems only to have encouraged them in their determination to share in a similar status back in their native land. In an era when Roman power had grown so universal, it is hardly surprising that the limited privileges of self-determination that Rome had always granted Italian politicians should have come to seem very small beer. What was the right to determine a local boundary dispute or two compared to the mastery of the world?

Just as the teeming wharves of Puteoli or the sophistication of the nearby pleasure-villas spoke of a shrinking world, then so too, in its own way, did the Italians' revolt. The mass of their armies may have been fighting in defence of vaguely felt local loyalties, but their leaders certainly had no wish to return to the parochialisms of life before Rome. Far from trying to free their communities from the grip of a centralising super-state, they could think of no recourse other than to invent a new one of their own. At the start of the war, the rebel leaders had chosen Corfinium, in the heart of Italy, to be their new capital, 'a city which all the Italians could share in as a replacement for Rome'.[12] Just so that no one would miss the symbolism of this measure, both Corfinium and the new state itself had then been given the name of 'Italia'. Coins had been duly issued and an embryonic government set up. Not until the nineteenth century, and Garibaldi, would there be another such attempt to form an independent Italian state.

But if imitation is the sincerest form of flattery, then the establishment of Italia suggests that for the vast majority of the Italian leaders, at least, rebellion against Rome had been a gesture less of defiance than of frustrated admiration. From the constitution to the coinage, everything was copied from the Romans. All along, the rickety new state had never been anything more than second best to the Italians' real ambition – enrolment as citizens of Rome. Even among the common soldiers, to whom Roman citizenship would have brought few benefits, there are signs that resentment of the Republic was sometimes balanced by a mood of fellow feeling. Early in the war, following the defeat of Rome's main army in central Italy, the survivors found themselves engaged in a desperate holding action, against men at least as well trained and armed as themselves. All through the summer of 90 BC they fought a painstaking trench warfare, gradually rolling back the rebels' front until, as harvest-time drew near, and with it the end of the campaigning season, they prepared to engage the enemy one final time. But as the two armies lined up opposite each other soldiers on both sides began to recognise friends, calling out to one another, and then laying down their arms. 'The threatening atmosphere was dissolved and instead became like that of a festival.' As their troops fraternised the Roman commander and his opposite number also met, to discuss 'peace and the Italian longing for citizenship'.[13]

The talks failed – naturally. How could a Roman ever grant concessions to an enemy in the field? All the same, the very fact that a parley had been possible suggested that there were regrets on both sides. Of particular significance was the identity of the Roman general. Gaius Marius was the Republic's most celebrated soldier. Even though by now he was in his sixties, and not as light in the saddle as he had once been, he still had star quality. The rebels knew and admired him, many having been commanded by him in battle. Marius' imperious habit of awarding citizenship to entire cohorts of Italian allies as a reward for exceptional valour was gratefully remembered. So too was the fact that Marius was not even a native of the city of Rome: he had grown up in Arpinum, a small hill town a three-day journey from the capital, famous for its poverty and remoteness, and not much else. In primordial times it had been the stronghold of tribesmen who had themselves fought against the Romans, but defeat had been followed by assimilation, and – ultimately – by enfranchisement. This last step, however, had occurred less than a century before the other Italian allies had launched their own desperate bid for the citizenship, so that the career of a man such as Marius, who had risen from such unpromising beginnings to such extraordinary heights, could not help but serve the rebels as an inspiration.

And not only the rebels. There were plenty of Romans who sympathised with the Italians' demands. After all, what had Rome been founded as if not a city of immigrants? The first Roman women had been the abducted Sabines, back in the time of Romulus, who had flung themselves between their fathers and their new husbands, begging them not to fight but to live in peace as the citizens of a single state. The appeal had succeeded, and Romans and Sabines had settled down together on the seven hills. The legend reflected the reality that there had never been a city so generous with her citizenship as Rome. Men of diverse backgrounds and origins had always been permitted to become Roman, and to share in Roman values and beliefs. In turn, of course, it was an irony, if not quite a paradox, that chief among these was an attitude towards non-Romans of invincible contempt.

Tragically, however, in the years leading up to the Italian revolt, the arguments for openness and exclusivism had begun to grow dangerously polarised. To many, there had seemed a world of difference between granting citizenship to the occasional individual or community and enfranchising the whole of Italy. Roman politicians had not needed to be motivated entirely by chauvinism or arrogance – although plenty were, to be sure – to fear that their city was in danger of being swamped. How were Rome's ancient institutions to cope with the sudden enrolment of millions of new citizens, dotted throughout the length and breadth of Italy? To conservatives, the threat appeared so desperate that their efforts to combat it had grown desperate in turn. Bills had been passed expelling all non-citizens from Rome. More ominously, there had been increasing resort to violence against opponents bringing forward bills of their own. In 91 BC a proposal to enfranchise the Italians had been abandoned amid rioting and violent demonstrations, and its proposer, retiring in dudgeon to his home, had been stabbed to death in the twilight gloom of his portico. The murderer was never found, but the Italian leaders had certainly known who to blame. Within days of the assassination they had begun massing their hillsmen for war.

As news had reached Rome of the massacres and scalpings at Asculum the rival factions whose squabblings had precipitated the crisis were shocked into a dazed unity. Even those most identified with the Italians' cause had girded themselves for the fight. The grim doggedness of Marius' campaigning had been matched wherever the legions met their erstwhile allies, in a long, bloody slog to reverse the disastrous series of defeats that had marked the start of Rome's war. By the time Marius sat down to negotiate terms with his Italian adversary, the Roman cause had been stabilised throughout northern Italy; a few weeks later and the rebel cause began to crumble. The massacre at Asculum had heralded the revolt, and it

was news from Asculum again that enabled the Romans to celebrate their first decisive victory of the war. The triumphant general
had been Gnaeus Pompeius 'Strabo', possibly the most loathed man
in Rome, as notorious for the shadiness of his character as for the
squint that had given him his nickname. Strabo owned vast swaths
of territory in Picenum, on the eastern seaboard of Italy, and had
been blockaded there since the start of the war. With the onset of
autumn, however, and clearly unwilling to go hungry through the
winter, Strabo had launched two sorties that successfully caught
the enemy in a pincer attack. The remnants of the rebel army had
fled to Asculum, which Strabo, completing the reversal of fortune,
had settled down to starve into submission.

With victory now looking increasingly assured, the Senate
launched a pincer movement of its own. One wing of the attack was
continued military action beyond the campaigning season, harrying
the insurgents throughout central Italy, forcing their increasingly
bedraggled armies to retreat into the mountains where the winter
snows lay thickest. The second wing of the pincer was led by those
politicians who had always favoured granting citizenship to the
Italians. Confident that military success now enabled Rome to be
generous, they succeeded in persuading even the most die-hard
conservatives that there was no alternative, in the long term, to
enfranchising the allies. Accordingly, in October 90 BC a bill was
proposed and passed. By its provisions all the Italian communities
that had stayed loyal were granted Roman citizenship immediately, and the rebels were promised it in due course if they would
only lay down their arms. To many, the offer proved irresistible. By
the summer of 89 most of northern and central Italy was back at
peace.

In Samnium, however, where the struggle was rooted in ancient
loathing, a resolution was not so easily obtained. And it was at this
very moment, with the Republic exhausted and still preoccupied

with war in its back yard, that alarming news began to filter through from Asia. A chasm of difference might have seemed to separate the peak-hugging hamlets of the Samnites and the great cities of the Greek East, cosmopolitan as they were, adorned with monuments of marble and gold, but Roman rule had bridged it. There had certainly been no lack of Samnites among the hordes of Italian businessmen and tax-farmers who had battened on to Asia. There they had merrily contributed to the very resentment of Rome that back in Samnium had pushed their compatriots into revolt. Despite the war raging in Italy, the Romans and Italians of Asia had been far too busy screwing money out of the provincials to worry about fighting each other – or, indeed, anyone else.

Then came Mithridates. When, in 89, Roman rule in Asia collapsed, the shockwaves spread fast throughout the Mediterranean economy. Italy was plunged into a disastrous slump. Ironically, the rebel leaders had exploited their compatriots' business ties in the East to beg Mithridates to join them in their revolt, but now that Mithridates had finally taken up their invitation they found that it was Italian businessmen who were the hardest hit. In Rome, by contrast, in senatorial circles the prospect of a war with Mithridates was greeted with open relish. Everyone knew that Orientals were soft and fought like women. Even more invitingly, everyone knew that the reason for this was because Orientals were obscenely rich. No wonder that there was an almost audible sound of aristocratic lips being smacked.

One man in particular regarded the command as his by right. Marius had long had his eye on a war with Mithridates. Ten years previously he had travelled to Asia and confronted the King face to face, telling him with the bluntness of a man spoiling for a fight either to be stronger than Rome or to obey her commands. On that occasion Mithridates had managed to swallow his pride and back down from war. All the same, it may have been no coincidence that when at last he did rise to the bait the man who provoked him into doing so was a close ally of Marius. Manius Aquillius, the commissioner who incited Rome's puppet king to invade Pontus, had previously served as Marius' military deputy and consular colleague, and Marius in turn had helped secure Aquillius' acquittal on a charge of extortion. The events and sources are murky, but it is possible that there is an explanation here for Aquillius' otherwise seemingly cavalier attitude towards Rome's security in the East, at a time when, back in Italy, she was fighting for her life. He had been aiming to provide his patron with a glorious Asian war.[14]

But the plot – if such indeed it were – was to have fatal consequences: for Aquillius himself, for Marius, and for the Republic as a whole. To the contagion of faction-fighting that had infected Rome for decades, racking first her own streets and then the whole of Italy, a new and deadly strain was about to be added. An Eastern command was a prize so rich that no one, not even Marius, could take it for granted. There were others, hungry and ambitious, who wanted it too. Just how badly would soon become clear.

That autumn of 89 BC, looking to the future, the Roman people found themselves in the grip of a collective paranoia. A terrible war was drawing to a close, but despite the victory there was only a sense of foreboding. Once again, it seemed, the gods were speaking through strange signs of the Republic's doom. Most ominous of all was a trumpet, heard ringing out from a clear, cloudless sky. So dismal was its note that all those who heard it were driven half mad with fear. The augurs nervously consulted their books. When they did so they found, to their horror, that the meaning of such a wonder left little room for doubt: a great convulsion in the order of things was approaching. One age would pass away, another would dawn, in a revolution fated to consume the world.

3

LUCK BE A LADY

The Rivals

During the nineties Marius had gone shopping for real estate on the coast along from Naples. So had most of Rome's super-rich, of course, but Marius' investment in an area notorious for its indolence and effeminacy had raised particular eyebrows. Location, location, location: the great general had chosen a spot just south of the Lucrine Lake, where his villa would be conveniently situated not only for Orata's oyster-beds, but also for the sulphur baths of the nearby spa town of Baiae. The perfect retirement home, in other words – and, as such, a public-relations disaster. Shellfish and health resorts were not what the Romans cared to associate with their war heroes. The satirists had a field day. The man of steel, they jeered, had grown soft and obese.

But this mockery was misdirected. Marius' weight problems were only common gossip in the first place because, far from lounging by the side of his pool, the old general had chosen to remain in the public eye. Rome was the only conceivable theatre for a man of his fame, and Marius had never had the slightest intention of retiring. Ironically, this could be read in the architecture of the notorious villa itself. Built on a natural promontory, it mimicked the layout as well as the situation of a legionary camp, and displayed an enthusiasm for entrenchment that had always been the hallmark of Marius' generalship. In its blending of the military virtues with imposing splendour, it was in fact the perfect expression of how the great general liked to see himself.

One of his former officers, inspecting the villa, could only exclaim in rueful approbation that, compared to his old commander, everyone else was blind. In the summer of 89 BC that officer had good reason to appreciate the qualities that made for an exemplary encampment. Down the coast from Marius' villa, smoke billowed out over the orchards and vineyards of Campania as Lucius Cornelius Sulla, in command of a vast army of thirteen legions, blockaded the rebel-held cities of the plain, forcing their surrender one by one. No more apprenticeships for Sulla. Instead, a career marked by the struggle to emerge from Marius' shadow had finally brought him a reputation as perhaps the ablest officer in the war. Yet even though the rivalry between the two men, veteran general and ambitious protégé, had long since grown poisonous, Sulla never made the mistake of underestimating his old commander. Where others saw marks of flabby degeneracy in Marius' villa, Sulla found inspiration.

It was not only that its siting served as an object lesson in the science of entrenchment. On a coastline thronged with the resorts of the ruling classes the magnificence of Marius' estate stood out. Traditional Roman morality may have frowned upon conspicuous consumption, but it also fostered competition as the essence of life. It was his clients' scrabbling after status symbols that had enabled Orata to make such a killing. No Roman could afford to lose face, not even when it came to having a swimming pool installed. To the nobility, a villa was less important as a holiday home than as a public display of its owner's splendour and high birth.

And yet Marius was a provincial. His breeding lacked pedigree, his manners polish. He had won his prestige on raw ability alone. If his villa loomed above those of the aristocracy, then it served as all the more vivid a symbol of the status that an outsider could hope to win in the Roman Republic. And Marius' status was indisputable. Not only had he won election to just about every magistracy going – often several times over – but he had even married a bona fide Julian, patrician and still proud of it, despite her family's decline. So it was that a nobody from Arpinum could claim that he slept with a descendant of the goddess of love. Naturally, none of this did anything to boost the great man's popularity with the establishment. Even so, Marius' example was one that Sulla, though himself a patrician, would have been eager – and indeed anxious – to absorb.

For the younger man's career too had been a struggle against the circumstances of his upbringing. Despite his noble birth, his father had died leaving him virtually penniless, and throughout his youth Sulla's means had been humiliatingly disproportionate to his pretensions. He had gradually sunk into a world of seedy lodgings and even seedier companions – comics, prostitutes and drag-queens – to whom, however, he would display a touching loyalty all his life, to the immense scandal of his peers. Sulla had relished the *demi-monde* even as he struggled to escape from it; nor was he ever to lose his taste for slumming. Hard drinking and wisecracking, he combined the aptitudes of a bar-fly with the natural talents of a gigolo, being as physically striking as he was charming, with piercing blue eyes and hair so golden that it was almost red. Ultimately, indeed, it had been sex appeal that had redeemed him from the ranks of the déclassé, for one of Rome's best-paid courtesans had grown so obsessed with him that in her will she had left him everything she owned. At around the same time Sulla's stepmother had also died, having similarly appointed him her sole heir. Only at thirty, an age when most nobles had already spent years climbing the slippery

pole of advancement, had Sulla at last found himself with the funds
to launch his political career.

From that point on he had sought and gained prestige with a
rare brilliance. His talents may have been exceptional, but not his
ambition, for in Rome a man was reckoned to be nothing without
the fame that accrued from glorious deeds. Whether won in warfare or political office, the reward such fame brought was the
opportunity to try for ever greater achievements and ever greater
renown. And at the summit of this relentless uphill race, a summit
to which Sulla was now drawing close, the supreme prize beckoned. This, of course, was the consulship — still, more than four
centuries after its inauguration, a magistracy of literally regal scope.
If Sulla could only win election to this office, then his authority
would be sanctioned by the trappings, as well as the powers, of the
ancient kings. Not only would he inherit the toga bordered with
royal purple and a special chair of state; he would also be accompanied by lictors, a bodyguard of twelve men, each bearing on his
shoulder the *fasces*, a bundle of scourging rods, most dreaded of all
the attributes of monarchy. An escort, in short, sufficient to reassure anyone that he had indeed reached the very top.

Not that he would ever stay there for long. A consul was no
tyrant. His *fasces* served as symbols not of oppression but of an
authority freely bestowed by the people. Subject to the whims of
the voters, limited to a single year in power, and accompanied in
office by colleagues their precise equal, magistrates of the Republic
had little choice but to behave in office with scrupulous propriety.
No matter how tempestuous a citizen's ambitions, they rarely broke
the bounds of the Romans' respect for tradition. What the Republic
fostered it also served to trammel.

And so it had always been. Rare was a high achiever who had not
been oppressed by the resulting sense of tension. The ideals of the
Republic served to deny the very hunger they provoked. As a result,

1. The bronze head of an early Republican hero – traditionally identified as Brutus, leader of the coup against Tarquin, Rome's last king. Dating either from the third or first century BC, it powerfully illustrates how the Romans liked to imagine their ancestors: as paragons of dignity and manly virtue. *(Museo Capitolino, Rome/Fratelli Alinari)*

2. Elephants, the weapon of choice among Rome's more sophisticated enemies – most famously Hannibal, but also the Greek kings of the East. War elephants were invariably banned by the Republic whenever peace treaties were imposed. Those kept in contravention of the Republic's terms might be hamstrung by visiting weapons inspectors.
(Villa Giulia, Rome/AKG London/Erich Lessing)

3. As the Republic's empire expanded, so the gap between rich and poor widened. The idea of paid work filled the Roman aristocracy with snobbish horror; the *plebs* could not afford to be so sniffy. This is the shop-sign of a greengrocer who doubled as a butcher: the heads of rabbits can be seen sticking out from hutches under the counter. From the second century AD, but very similar in style to reliefs from the late Republic. *(Museo Ostiense, Ostia/Scala, Florence)*

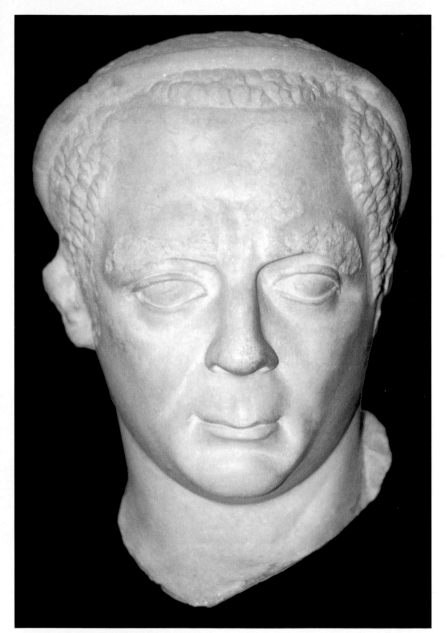

4. A diademed king of Pergamum, possibly Attalus III. In 133 BC, Attalus' bequest of his kingdom to the Republic opened up a honey pot which was soon crawling with Roman flies. The Senate's traditional aversion to imposing direct rule was fatally weakened, and the foundation stone of the Roman empire in the East laid.

(Ny Carlsberg Glyptotek, Copenhagen)

5. By the early first century BC, the Bay of Naples had become both a pleasure ground for Rome's super-rich, and the entry point for the flood of wealth from overseas into Italy. As this dreamy scene of a port suggests, artists preferred to emphasise the beauties of the Bay over any hint of its commercial energies. *(Museo Nazionale, Naples/Scala, Florence)*

6. The statue of a general, from Tivoli, early first century BC. Even though the expression, hard-faced and unsentimentalised, is all Roman, the pose is derived from images of Greek rulers. The wealth and sophistication of the Greek world made an eastern command the dream of every ambitious general. In this, as in much else, republican militarism was exemplified by Marius. *(Museo Nazionale Romano, Rome)*

7. Mithridates, the lion of Pontus. Eager to maximise his support among the Greeks – and no doubt as a result of vanity as well – he sedulously aped the portraits of Alexander the Great. His invasion of the Roman province of Asia in 89 BC – and even more his massacre of Italian businessmen the following year – established him as the Republic's most inveterate foe. A silver tetradrachm, 75 BC. *(British Museum, London/AKG London)*

8. The hairstyle of a playboy, the stare of a man on the make: a Roman portrait bust traditionally identified as Sulla. *(Fratelli Alinari)*

9. A stretch of the Republican city wall on the Aventine. No citizen bearing arms was normally permitted to pass inside the city gates. Sulla was the first general to lead a Roman army against his own city in four hundred and twenty-one years of the Republic's history. *(Scala, Florence)*

10. A lictor, bearing on his shoulder the *fasces*, a bundle of birching rods which had once served as a symbol of royal power. Under the Republic, twelve lictors were assigned to each consul. *(British Museum, London/Scala, Florence)*

11. Posidonius – polymath and enthusiast for the Republic's global mission. *(Museo Nazionale, Naples/Fratelli Alinari)*

12. A citizen registers himself with the censor (left). A detail from the so-called altar of Domitius Ahenobarbus. *(Musée du Louvre, Paris/Scala, Florence)*

13. The grass-covered mound in the foreground is all that remains of the temple of Bellona, from where, in 82 BC, the Senate heard the screams of Sulla's prisoners as they were massacred in the nearby Villa Publica. *(Tom Holland)*

the fate of a Roman who had tasted the sweetness of glory might often be a consuming restlessness, the gnawing, unappeasable agony of an addict. So it was that Marius, even in his sixties, and with countless honours to his name, still dreamed of beating his rivals to the command of the war against Mithridates. And so it was that Sulla, even were he to win the consulship, would continue to be taunted by the example of his old commander. Just as Marius' villa outshone all others on the Campanian coast, so too did his prestige outrank that of any other former consul. Most men were confined by precedent and opportunity to holding the consulship once in their lives. Marius had held the office an unprecedented six times. He liked to claim that a fortuneteller had promised him a seventh.

No wonder that Sulla loathed him. Loathed him, and dreamed of winning the same greatness that Marius had won.

Thinking the Unthinkable

Late autumn 89 BC. Election time. Sulla left his army and headed north to Rome. He arrived there with a reputation brightly burnished by his recent exploits. First, he had forced the capitulation of all the rebel-held cities in Campania, until only Nola, bristling with her strengthened defences, had continued to hold out. Ignoring the threat that this presented to his rear, Sulla had next launched a dagger-thrust at the very heart of the rebel hinterland. Invading Samnium, he had gained a belated revenge for the Caudine Forks by ambushing a Samnite army in a mountain pass and then, having routed them, marched on the rebel capital, storming it in a brutal three-hour assault. Although Nola remained defiant, along with a few other isolated pockets of resistance, Sulla had effectively finished off the rebellion for good.

Such an achievement spoke for itself. This was just as well because that year, in the elections, there was particularly stiff competition. Supreme honour as the consulship was, it had begun to dawn on everyone that in 88 it might serve as the ticket to an even juicier prize. This, of course, was command of the war against Mithridates, a post that promised not only honour but fabulous profit as well – to say nothing of the pleasure of leaving Marius an also-ran. No wonder that Sulla wanted it so desperately – and increasingly what Sulla wanted Sulla tended to get. First, his aura as the conqueror of Samnium swept him into office. Then, a few weeks later, there was an even sweeter fulfilment: he was confirmed in the command against Mithridates. For Sulla triumph; and for Marius humiliation.

The public had little sympathy for their former favourite. Roman society was full of cruel double standards. The same moralists who warned old men that 'there was nothing of which they should more beware than the temptations of idleness and inactivity'[1] would also mock them savagely should they refuse to age gracefully. When the new consul, keen to finish off the war in Italy before heading east, hurried back to the siege of the still-defiant Nola, Marius was advised to leave for Campania too. After all, as the satirists pointed out, it would be perfectly safe for him to settle in his villa now – thanks to Sulla. Instead of making himself look ridiculous in Rome, why did Marius not just bow to the inevitable, retire to the Bay of Naples and gorge himself silly on oysters?

Marius replied to this question by starting on a very public workout. Every day there he was on the training ground, pushing himself to the limit, running, riding, practising with javelin and sword. It did not take long for crowds to start gathering, to gawp and cheer. At the same time Marius also began looking around for political support. What he really needed, of course, was a man who could propose a law to the people, transferring Sulla's command against Mithridates to himself. That, effectively, meant that he needed a tribune.

He found one in the person of Publius Sulpicius Rufus, a man blackened by subsequent propaganda as 'cruel, reckless, avaricious, shameless, and lacking in any scruples whatsoever'[2] – a rich description, considering that it most likely originated with Sulla. Whatever else he may have been, Sulpicius was not a man lacking in principle. Causes mattered to him, even to the point of destruction. Nowhere had this campaigning zeal been shown to better effect than in his lifelong advocacy of Italian rights, which still, even with the granting of full citizenship, required vigorous defence. Afraid that conservatives in the Senate were plotting to water down the enfranchisement, Sulpicius had drawn up legislation to ensure that it would be done fairly, canvassed the consuls, then presented his bill to the people. To his fury, however, both Sulla and his colleague in the consulship, Pompeius Rufus, having made what Sulpicius regarded as a commitment to support him, had opted instead to oppose the bill and ensure its defeat. Sulpicius was left nursing a bitter sense of betrayal. Previously, he had regarded Rufus as an intimate friend; now, vowing revenge, he scouted around for a fresh alliance. It was at this very moment that Marius came calling. The general and the tribune speedily reached a discreet compact. Marius agreed to support Sulpicius' legislation, while in return Sulpicius promised to propose the transfer of Sulla's command to Marius. With his hand thus strengthened, Sulpicius proceeded to reintroduce his bill. Simultaneously, his supporters took to the streets and rioting swept through the city.

News of the unrest was brought to Sulla at his camp outside Nola. Alarmed, he sped back to Rome. On his arrival he held a secret council with Pompeius Rufus, but Sulpicius, catching wind of it, led a band of his heavies to break up the meeting. In the resulting confrontation Rufus' son was murdered, Rufus himself barely escaped with his life, and Sulla, mortifyingly, had to take refuge from the mob in Marius' house. Worse humiliations were to follow. Consul though he was, Sulla now found himself powerless to resist Sulpicius' demands, for it was the tribune's mobs, not the *fasces*, who ruled Rome. Forced to agree that the pro-Italian legislation be passed and that Rufus, as payback for his treachery, be stripped of his consulship, Sulla himself appears to have been offered nothing more in exchange than the chance to continue in office and to return to the siege of Nola. At this stage there was no mention of the Mithridatic command. Sulla had no reason to doubt that his commission, at least, remained sacrosanct. All the same, returning to his camp, where the trappings of his office would have remained on magnificent and awful display, he cannot have helped but reflect bitterly upon the gap that had opened with such alarming speed between the show and the substance of his power. Such had been the damage to his prestige that only a triumphant Eastern war would ever repair it. Otherwise, far from covering him in glory, his consulship threatened to terminate his career.

For Sulla, then, as for Marius, the stakes had grown perilously high – except that Sulla, unlike Marius, was yet to realise just how high they still had to go. Then, with the dust of Rome upon him, another messenger came galloping down the road that led to Nola. Arriving among the siege works, he was brought before the consul. The messenger proved to be one of Marius' staff officers, and Sulla had only to see him to know that the news was likely to be bad. Even so, just how bad still came as a shock. There had been a plebiscite, Sulla was informed. Proposed by Sulpicius, it had been ratified by the Roman people and passed into law. By its terms, Sulla was demoted from the command against Mithridates. His replacement – inevitably – was Marius. The staff officer had come to take command of the army. Sulpicius had paid off his debt.

Sulla, first in consternation and then in mounting fury, retired to his tent. There he did some quick calculations. With him at Nola he had six legions. Five of these had been assigned to the war against Mithridates and one to the continued prosecution of the siege – in all, around thirty thousand men. Although much reduced from the numbers Sulla had commanded the previous summer, they nevertheless represented a menacing concentration of fighting power. Only the legions of Pompeius Strabo, busy mopping up rebels on the other side of Italy, could hope to rival them. Marius, back in Rome, had no legions whatsoever.

The maths was simple. Why, then, had Marius failed to work it out, and how could so hardened an operator have chosen to drive his great rival into a corner where there were six battle-hardened legions ready to hand? Clearly, the prospect that Sulla might come out of it fighting had never even crossed Marius' mind. It was impossible, unthinkable. After all, a Roman army was not the private militia of the general who commanded it, but the embodiment of the Republic at war. Its loyalty was owed to whomever was appointed to its command by the due processes of the constitution. This was how it had always been, for as long as the Republic's citizens had been going to war – and Marius had no reason to imagine that things might possibly have changed.

But Sulla did have reason: his hatred of his rival, his fury at the frustration of his ambitions and his utter belief in the justice of his case all helped him to contemplate a uniquely audacious and dreadful possibility. No citizen had ever led legions against their own city. To be the first to take such a step, and to outrage such a tradition, should have been a responsibility almost beyond a Roman's enduring. Yet it seems that Sulla, far from havering, betrayed not the slightest hesitation. All his most successful operations, he would later claim, had been the result not of a measured weighing of the odds but of a sudden flash of inspiration. Such flashes, it appeared to

Sulla, were divinely sent. Baleful cynic though he was, he was also an unusually religious man. He believed with perfect certainty that a goddess was prompting him; a great goddess, more powerful than any of the gods who might be affronted by his actions. Whatever he did, however high he reached, Sulla could be confident of the protection of Venus, who granted to her favourites both sex appeal and fortune.

How else, after all, to explain his extraordinary rise? As a man who set great store by loyalty, he had never forgotten that he owed everything to the two women who had left him their fortunes. Did this influence how he saw his relationship with Venus herself? Did he see the goddess as another woman to be seduced and worshipped, in return for all she could provide? Certainly, throughout his life, Sulla deployed his charm as a weapon, on politicians and soldiers as much as on whores. In particular, he was adept at winning the rank-and-file legionaries to his side. He could speak their language and enjoy their jokes, and he soon developed a reputation as an officer prepared to do his men a favour. When combined with his parallel reputation for extraordinary good luck, fostered over the years by a succession of military victories and daring personal escapades, Sulla's popularity with his troops was hardly a surprise.

Yet, to many, there remained something sinister about his charm. It could be read in his physiognomy. For, handsome as Sulla was, he had a violent, purple complexion, and all over his face, whenever he grew angry, mysterious white spots would appear. Medical opinion explained this disfigurement as the consequence of sexual perversion, a diagnosis that was also reckoned to confirm the persistent story that Sulla lacked a testicle. The seamy nature of such rumours had always dogged him. When Sulla had been appointed to his first campaign, Marius, as his commander, had expressed disgust at his new officer's frivolous reputation. Much later, when Sulla had more than proved his military worth, and was boasting to a nobleman of lesser achievement but greater pedigree, the nobleman would only comment that there was something not quite right about a man who had come into such wealth after being left nothing by his father. Such disquiet about Sulla's triumphs was expressed too consistently for it to be dismissed as snobbery and jealousy alone. His great victories against the Samnites, for instance, had required him to appropriate legions from their legitimate commanders, and even, on one notorious occasion, to wink at murder. In the early months of 89 BC, during the siege of Pompeii, a particularly obdurate defence had led the Roman troops to suspect their commander of treachery and lynch him. When Sulla arrived to take control of the siege from the murdered officer, he conspicuously failed to punish the mutineers, and was even rumoured to have instigated the crime himself. It says much about the ambiguous character of his reputation that such a story could not only be believed, but apparently boost his popularity with his men.

Certainly, having clubbed one officer to death, it appears that Sulla's troops had developed a taste for dispatching uppity legates. When Sulla summoned them to a meeting on the parade ground and broke the news that he had received from Rome, they immediately turned on Marius' envoy and stoned him to death. Unprompted, they then clamoured for Sulla to lead them on the capital, a demand to which Sulla delightedly acceded. His officers were so appalled by this plan that all except one resigned, but Sulla, knowing that he had already set himself beyond the pale, could no longer turn back. Leaving behind a single legion to continue the siege of Nola, he marched northwards. The news of his approach was greeted in Rome with disbelief. Some, such as Pompeius Rufus, the deposed consul, welcomed the news and hurried off to join him, but most felt only consternation and despair. Frantic embassies were sent in an attempt to shame Sulla into turning back, but to every appeal he would only answer blithely that he was marching

on Rome 'to free her from her tyrants'.[3] Marius and Sulpicius, all
too aware who were the objects of this menacing aim, desperately
sought to buy time. As Sulla approached the outskirts of Rome
they sent one final deputation, promising that the Senate would be
assembled to discuss his grievances, and that they too would attend
its meeting and be bound by its decisions. All they asked in return
was that Sulla stay camped five miles from the sacred boundary of
Rome herself.

Everyone knew that to traverse this would be a gesture of awesome and terrible significance. Rome was numinous with the
presence of gods, but there were few spaces more holy than the
pomerium, the ancient boundary that marked the furrow ploughed by
Romulus, and had not been altered since the time of the kings. To
cross it was absolutely forbidden to any citizen in arms: within the
pomerium was the realm of Jupiter, the city's guardian, and the guarantor of her peace. He was a god it was perilous to anger, so when
Sulla told Marius' envoys that he would accept their terms they
may even have believed him. But Sulla had been dissembling: no
sooner had Marius' envoys set off back for Rome than he ordered
his legions to follow, advancing in separate divisions to seize three of
the city gates. Mighty though Jupiter was, Sulla continued to rely
upon the blessings of Venus, the goddess of fortune, and a divinity –
he trusted – just as great.

As the legionaries passed over the *pomerium* and began pushing
through the narrow streets, their fellow citizens greeted them with
a hail of tiles flung down from the rooftops. Such was the ferocity
of this assault that for a moment the soldiers quailed, until Sulla
ordered that fire-arrows be shot at the roofs. As flames began to
crackle and spread down the line of the city's highways Sulla himself rode along the greatest of them all, the via Sacra, into the very
heart of Rome. Marius and Sulpicius, after a futile attempt to raise
the city's slaves, had already fled. Everywhere, mail-clad guards

took up their new posts. Swords and armour were worn outside the Senate House. The unthinkable had happened. A general had made himself the master of Rome.

It was a moment pregnant with menace. Later generations, with the benefit of hindsight, would see in it the great turning point of which the augurs had warned: the passing of an old age, the dawning of a new. Certainly, with the march on Rome of a Roman army, a watershed had been reached. Something like innocence had gone. Competition for honours had always been the lifeblood of the Republic, but now something deadly had been introduced into it, nor could its presence there, a lurking toxin, easily be forgotten. Defeat in elections, or in a lawsuit, or in a debate in the Senate – these had previously been the worst that a citizen might have had to dread. But Sulla, in his pursuit of Marius, was pushing rivalry and personal hatred to new extremes. From that moment on, the memory of it would haunt every ambitious citizen – both as a temptation and as a fear.

And naturally, having taken his fateful step, Sulla was desperate to force his advantage home. Summoning the Senate, he demanded that his opponents be branded enemies of the state. The Senate, with one nervous eye on Sulla's guards, hurriedly obeyed. Sentences of outlawry were duly pronounced on Marius, Sulpicius and ten others, including Marius' young son. Sulpicius, having been betrayed by a slave, was hunted down and murdered, but the other condemned men all escaped. Marius himself, after a series of hair-raising adventures that saw him hiding in reed beds and outfacing contract killers, eventually reached the relative safety of Africa. To that extent, Sulla's gamble had failed: the snake had been scotched, not killed. Marius had survived to fight another day. But Sulla, although he was disappointed, was not unduly alarmed. The condemnation of his great rival had been something more than just a deeply satisfying act of personal vengeance. He had also intended it to give another message: by identifying his own cause with that of the Republic, he hoped to recast his march on Rome as an action in its defence. Backed by five legions he may have been, but to Sulla legitimacy remained more important than any naked use of power. During the outlawry debate, when a venerable senator had told him to his face that a great man such as Marius should never be made a public enemy, Sulla had accepted the old man's right to dissent without demur. Whenever he could, he would behave with a similar regard towards the sensibilities of his compatriots. Far from playing the military despot, he preferred to pose as the defender of the constitution.

Nor was this mere hypocrisy. If Sulla was a revolutionary, then it was very much in the cause of the status quo. Hostile towards any hint of innovation, he had all of Sulpicius' legislation declared invalid. To replace it, he brought in laws of his own, aimed at bolstering the traditional supremacy of the Senate. Despite distaste for its *soi-disant* champion, the Senate can hardly have been averse to such measures. Yet Sulla remained caught in a dilemma. Eager to leave Italy for the Mithridatic war, but afraid of what might happen in his absence, he knew that it was vital for him to leave supporters in positions of power. Interfere too blatantly in the annual elections, however, and his claim to embody the rule of law would become laughable. As it was, he suffered the humiliation of seeing his allies failing to gain either of the consulships. True, one of the successful candidates, Gnaeus Octavius, was a natural conservative, like himself, but the second, Cornelius Cinna, had gone so far as to threaten him with prosecution. In the circumstances Sulla accepted defeat with as good a grace as he could muster. Before he would agree to the new consuls taking up their office, however, he required them to swear a public oath on the sacred hill of the Capitol that they would never overturn his legislation. Octavius and Cinna, evidently unwilling to push their luck, agreed. As he

took the oath Cinna picked up a stone and hurled it, publicly praying that if he failed to keep his word to Sulla he might similarly be
hurled out of Rome.

And with that Sulla had to be satisfied. Before he crossed from
Italy to Greece, however, he took one final measure. Wishing to
reward a faithful ally at the same time as ensuring his own security,
he arranged for the command of Strabo's legions to be transferred
to Pompeius Rufus, his colleague in the consulship of 88 BC. In fact,
far from ensuring his friend's safety, such a measure served only to
demonstrate how blind Sulla had been to the implications of his
troops' willingness to march with him on Rome. Just as Marius'
legate had done, Rufus arrived at his new army's camp armed with
a bill and nothing more. Strabo welcomed the man come to take
his place with a menacing politeness. He presented Rufus to the
troops, then absented himself from the camp – on business, he
claimed. The next day Rufus celebrated his new command by per-
forming a sacrifice. A gang of soldiers clustered round him where he
stood by the altar, and as he raised the sacrificial knife they seized
him and struck him down, 'as though he were the sacrificial offering himself'.[4] Strabo, claiming to be outraged, hurried back to the
camp but took no action against his murderous troops. Inevitably,
the rumours that had dogged Sulla in similar circumstances now
attached themselves to Strabo. There were few who doubted that
he had ordered the murder of his replacement himself.

A consul butchered by his own soldiers: Rufus' fate might seem
to confirm the doom-laden judgement of a later generation, that
after Sulla's coup 'there was nothing left which could shame warlords into holding back on military violence – not the law, not the
institutions of the Republic, nor even the love of Rome'.[5] In fact, it
illustrated the opposite. Far from following up Rufus' murder by
launching a coup of his own, Strabo held back from committing
himself to any course of action at all. Aware that with Sulla gone

from Italy he now held the balance of power, he spent the year 87 veering from faction to faction, offering his support to the highest bidder, all the while making ever more extravagant demands. Such avarice and trimming served only to compound his already massive unpopularity. Then, towards the end of the year, nemesis struck. Following his spectacular death, when the tent in which he lay dying of plague was struck by lightning, crowds mobbed his funeral procession and dragged the corpse from its bier through the mud. Without the intervention of a tribune, it would have been torn to shreds. In a society where prestige was the principal measure of a man's worth Strabo's posthumous fate was a grisly warning to anyone tempted to gamble with the interests of the state. Yet not even Strabo, grasping as he was and armed with opportunity, had thought to aim for military dictatorship. Sulla's coup had been an outrage but not, it seemed, a fatal one. The laws, the institutions of the Republic and the love of Rome still held good.

As was only natural. The Republic, in the eyes of its citizens, was something much more than a mere constitution, a political order to be toppled or repealed. Instead, hallowed by that most sacred of Roman concepts, tradition, it provided a complete pattern of existence for all those who shared in it. To be a citizen was to know that one was free – 'and that the Roman people should ever not be free is contrary to all the laws of heaven'.* Such certainty suffused every citizen's sense of himself. Far from expiring with Sulla's march on Rome, respect for the Republic's laws and institutions endured because they were expressions of the Romans' profoundest sense of their own identity. Yes, a general had turned on his own city, but even he had claimed to be doing so in defence of the traditional

---

* A claim that could have been made at any point in the Republic's long history. In fact it was made when the free state had only months to live, by Cicero in the sixth *Philippic* (19).

order. There had certainly been no revolution. For all the trauma of Sulla's march on Rome, no one could imagine that the Republic itself might be overthrown, because no one could conceive what might possibly replace it.

So it was that, even after the shocks of 88, life went on. The new year of 87 dawned with an appearance of normality. Two consuls, elected by the Roman people, sat in their chairs of state. The Senate met to advise them. The streets were empty of soldiers. Meanwhile, the man who had dared to march on Rome was disembarking in Greece. His ferocious talents, no longer turned against his own countrymen, could at last be deployed in a fitting manner. There was a war, sternest of all the Romans' traditions, to be won; enemies of the Republic to overthrow and chastise.

Sulla was marching east.

Missing the Joke

Six years earlier, in 93 BC, a Roman commissioner had paused in Athens on his way to Asia. Gellius Publicola was a man who combined a taste for Greek culture with the sensibility of a joker. Wishing to meet the philosophers for which Athens was still celebrated, he had summoned the various representatives of the squabbling philosophical schools and urged them, with a perfectly straight face, to resolve their differences. If this proved beyond their abilities, he added, then he was very graciously prepared to step in and settle their controversies for them. Forty years later, Gellius' proposal to the Athenian philosophers would still be remembered by his friends as a prize example of wit. 'How everyone roared!'[6]

Quite when the philosophers realised that Gellius was joking we are not told. Nor whether they found the joke quite so rib-tickling as Gellius himself seems to have done. One suspects that they did not. Philosophy was still a serious business in Athens. The very idea of being lectured by a bumptious Roman prankster must surely have struck the heirs of Socrates as a humiliating indignity. All the same, they no doubt laughed politely, if hollowly: Roman offers to settle squabbles had a certain ominous resonance in Greece.

And anyway, in Athens servility and arrogance had long been sides of the same coin. More than anywhere else in Greece, the sanctity of history clung to the city. The Athenians never forgot – nor let anyone else forget – that it was they who had saved Greece at the Battle of Marathon, and had once been the greatest naval power in the Mediterranean. Resplendent still upon the Acropolis, the Parthenon stood as a permanent memorial to the years of Athenian supremacy. All gone, though; long gone. In the list of the Seven Wonders of the World, composed in the century after Alexander's death, the Parthenon was conspicuous by its absence. It was too small, too out-of-date, reflecting the presumptions of an age in which empires as well as monuments had grown gigantic. Compared to the super-state of Rome, Athens was a provincial backwater. Her memories of empire were nostalgia, nothing more. Any ideas above their station, any hints that the Athenians still imagined themselves a great power, were regarded by the Romans with hilarity. During the Republic's campaigns against Macedon Athens had presumed to give her support, declaring war with a masterpiece of rhetorical invective. The Romans were not impressed. 'This was the Athenians' war against the King of Macedon, a war of words,' they sniffed. 'Words are the only weapon that the Athenians have left.'[7]

Gellius' joke was cruel because it suggested that even this last weapon might be taken away from them. As, in truth, it already had been. Whether they cared to admit it or not, philosophers, like every other legacy of the Athenian golden age, had become mere adjuncts to the service industry. Those who did particularly well out of Roman patronage had long since learned to cut the cloth of their speculations accordingly. Typical was the age's most celebrated polymath, Posidonius. Although he had studied in Athens, Posidonius was widely travelled, and rationalised what he observed in Rome's provinces – rather optimistically – as a commonwealth of man. He was a close associate of Rutilius Rufus, that upright defender of his province's interests, and evidently believed that his friend was a truer face of Rome than the *publicani* who had destroyed him. In the new order that the Republic was bringing into the world, Posidonius somehow managed to catch a reflection of the order of the universe. He argued that it was the moral duty of Rome's sub-jects to accept such a dispensation. Differences of culture and geography would soon dissolve. History was coming to an end.

Posidonius may have been expressing himself in high-flown terms, but he was only putting a gloss on what was evident enough anyway. The coming of Rome had indeed shrunk the world. It did not take a philosopher to recognise this – or to turn it to profit. The Athenian ruling classes may privately have regarded their Roman masters as bullying philistines, but they knew better than to voice such an opinion publicly. While the Romans had few compunc-tions about beggaring their defeated enemies, they had always been careful to reward their friends, and Athens had benefited accord-ingly. The juiciest prize of all had come in 165, following the final war against Macedon, during which the island republic of Rhodes had been less than full-blooded in her backing for Rome. This had been duly noted by the Senate. Rhodes had long been the major trading entrepôt in the eastern Mediterranean, and in punishing her the Romans had demonstrated that they could toy with economies to the same devastating effect that they fought on the battlefield. A toll-free harbour had been opened on the island of Delos, and presented to Athens. Rhodes had consequently seen her revenues collapse; Athens had grown rich. By the start of the first

century, so prosperous had the Athenians become that their cur-
rency, with Roman encouragement, had established itself as legal
tender throughout the Greek world. Parallel measures synchro-
nised the different systems of weights used in Italy and Athens. It
was not only Rome that benefited from the resulting trade boom.
Ships crammed with Italian commodities began to throng the harbours of Athens and Delos. The Athenian upper classes, their eyes
now firmly fixed on the world beyond their city, concentrated on
the only measure of achievement left to them – that of becoming
millionaires.

   This was not an option open to every Athenian, of course. In an
economy run by and for the super-rich the wealthier a minority of
citizens became, the more the resentments of the majority seethed.
This was true of every society in the ancient world, but in Athens –
the birthplace of democracy – perhaps uniquely so. Among the
Athenian poor, dreams of independence were indissolubly linked to
memories of the time when the power of the people had been more
than just a slogan. Nothing, of course, could have been more
designed to give big business the jitters. As it progressively tightened
its grip on government, the institutions that had once maintained
Athenian democracy were allowed to wither. However, they were
not abolished altogether because, apart from anything else, they
were good for the tourist trade. Visiting Romans enjoyed the quaint
spectacle of democracy in action. Sometimes Athens offered the
pleasures less of a museum than of a zoo.

   Then suddenly, in 88 BC, everything was turned upside down.
While the Athenian business elite watched in horror as Mithridates'
armies camped in triumph on the opposite shores of the Aegean,
their impoverished countrymen crowed in delight. The old desperate longing for freedom, so long repressed, convulsed the city.
An embassy was sent to Mithridates, who welcomed it with open
arms. An agreement was speedily reached: in return for providing

him with a harbour, Athens would have her democracy restored. The pro-Roman business classes, realising which way the wind was blowing, began to flee the city. Democracy was officially re-established, amid wild scenes of rejoicing, and even wilder scenes of slaughter. Out of the exploding class war a new government emerged, pledged to defending the city's ancient order and traditions. Athens being Athens, the revolution was led by a philosopher, one Aristion, an old sparring partner of Posidonius who did not share his rival's positive perspective on Rome. With Italy riven by war, however, and an alliance with the all-conquering Mithridates in the bag, Aristion did not expect too much trouble from the Romans. To the ecstatic Athenians, independence and democracy alike appeared secured. Then, in the spring of 87, Sulla landed in Greece.

He headed directly for Athens. Almost before they knew what had hit them, the Athenians found themselves with five vengeful legions commanded by Rome's most ruthless general camped outside their walls. Confronted by this nightmare, Aristion's only tactic was to compose rude songs about Sulla's face, comparing it with a mulberry topped with oatmeal. These would be chanted from the city walls while Aristion himself yelled obscene witticisms about Sulla and his wife, complete with extravagant hand gestures. Proof, as Posidonius commented acidly, 'that swords should never be placed in the hands of children'.[8]

Sulla, whose enjoyment of comedians had its limits, responded to Aristion with a few pointed insults of his own. He ordered the groves where Plato and Aristotle had taught to be chopped down and used to build siege engines. When an Athenian peace delegation did what Athenian peace delegations had always done and began to discourse windily on the glories of its city's past, Sulla silenced the talk with a gesture of his hand. 'Rome did not send me here to be lectured on ancient history.'[9] With this dismissal, he sent the delegates back to their city to eat boiled shoe leather, and starve. Athens' cultural capital had reached the limits of its overdraft.

When at length the city was stormed, and Sulla gave his troops licence to plunder and kill, many of the victims were suicides. They knew all too well what the fate of Corinth had been, and they dreaded the annihilation of their city. The destruction was certainly terrible: the port was obliterated and the Acropolis plundered; everyone who had served in the democratic government was executed; their supporters were stripped of the vote. The city itself, however, was not burned to the ground. Sulla, who had expressed such contempt for history, announced with a grand rhetorical flourish that he spared the living out of respect for the dead. Even as he spoke blood was spilling outwards from the city through the suburbs.

The wreckage was inherited by a government of the businessmen who had fled to Sulla when the trouble first began. They crawled back into a city from which every figleaf of independence and prosperity had been torn. Roman rule was soon confirmed beyond all doubt when Sulla, marching north from Athens, met and smashed two armies sent to Greece by Mithridates. Soon afterwards Sulla held a summit with Mithridates himself. Both men had good reason to come to an agreement. Mithridates, knowing that the game was over, was desperate to keep hold of his kingdom. Sulla, nervous of his enemies back in Italy, was eager to head home. In return for accepting controls on his offensive capability and the surrender of all the territory he had conquered, the murderer of eighty thousand Italians was rewarded by Sulla with a peck on his cheek. No one had ever emerged so unscathed from a war with the Republic before. Beaten he may have been, but Mithridates still sat on the throne of Pontus. The time would come when Rome would regret that he had not been finished off for good.

As it was, the immediate objects of Sulla's vengeance were the wretched Greeks. In the province of Asia, Roman rule was briskly reimposed. Sulla, posing as the avenger of his murdered country-men, despite the peck he had given Mithridates, applied the screws with relish. Not only were cities charged five years' back-tax, but they were expected to pay the full costs of the war, and billet the garrisons sent to oppress them. Sulla, who liked to pretend that his terms had been generous, creamed off the tribute, and in 84 headed back to Greece. Now that Athens was no longer in arms against him he could display his respect for her cultural legacy in the tradi-tional manner of victorious Roman generals – by pilfering it. The columns of the temple of Zeus were pulled down ready for trans-port to Rome. Athletes were rounded up, showpieces for Sulla's triumph, leaving the Olympic Games so denuded of its stars that only the sprint could be staged. Most gratifying of all to Sulla's sense of humour was the wholesale looting of Athenian libraries, which were stripped of their holdings. Henceforward, if anyone wanted to study Aristotle, they would have to do so in Rome. Sulla's revenge on Athenian philosophy was sweet.

Even so, his capacity for vengeance had not yet been tested to the limits. As he pointed out proudly in a letter to the Senate, in barely three years he had won back all the territory annexed by Mithridates. Greece and Asia once again acknowledged the sway of Rome. Or so it suited Sulla to pretend. In fact, he no longer repre-sented the Republic. The government he had established back in Rome had collapsed. Sulla himself had been condemned to death *in absentia*, his property razed, his family forced to flee. There was no one in the shattered East who could have doubted what Sulla's response to these insults would be. Now that Greece had been tamed, he was ready to head back home. Still trusting in his luck and the protection of Venus, Sulla prepared to embark his troops and turn his vengeance back on his native city.

Once again, Rome would have to wait his arrival, and shudder.

4

RETURN OF THE NATIVE

Sulla Redux

On 6 July 83 BC the largest and holiest building in Rome was struck by lightning. The ancient temple of Jupiter loomed on the summit of the Capitoline Hill. Here, beneath a ceiling sheathed in gold, amid trophies of statues and shields, the guardian of Rome had his shrine. Back in the distant days of the kings, excavators digging the temple's foundations had found a human head. Augurers, summoned to interpret this wonder, had explained that it foretold Rome's future as the head of the world. Who could doubt, then, that it was Jupiter who had guided the Republic to its greatness? No wonder that the Senate should choose to hold its first meeting every year in the sanctum of the god. This was where Roman power was most touched by the divine.

But now Jupiter had decided to destroy his own temple with a thunderbolt. This was not a promising omen. It hardly required the Sibylline Books to reveal that – which was just as well, since they too were going up in the blaze. But what was the cause of the god's anger? As the crowds gathered to watch the disaster, the flames billowed sparks and smoke across the Forum. This was the heart of Rome, stretching all the way from the Capitol, hill of the gods, to the Palatine, hill of power. The Forum, along with the Circus, was one of two open spaces within the city walls where Rome's citizens could mix freely. In recent years it had begun to grow pompous, cleared of market traders and lined with luxury shops, yet still, more than anywhere else in the city, it symbolised the unity of the Roman people. This had been the case since ancient times. Originally a marsh, it had been drained to provide a meeting-place for the warring inhabitants of the neighbouring hills. As such, it was where the Romans had first learned to conduct their affairs as citizens. Like the city itself, the Forum was a jumble of discordant monuments, both a museum of the Republic's history and the hub of the city's life. Lawyers pleaded their cases, bankers negotiated loans, Vestal Virgins tended their goddess's flame, and everyone came to chat or be seen. It was politics, however, that dominated the Forum. The crowds watching the destruction of Jupiter's temple would have been used to assembling at the foot of the Capitol. Here was the Comitium, where citizens gathered to hear orators address them from the Rostra, the curved speaker's plat-form made from the prows of long-ago captured ships. Immediately adjacent to it was the Curia, where the Senate met, and a little to its south the temple of Castor and Pollux, in front of which the tribunes would summon assemblies to debate and vote on laws. Along this axis of buildings and open spaces lay the great theatre of the Republic's political life, Rome's most potent expres-sion of her citizens' liberties and values. All the more portentous, then, that as the fire on the Capitol raged, it would have dyed the Forum below it an angry red. Red: the colour of Mars, the god of war and bloodshed.

Sulla was later to claim that Bellona, Mars' female equivalent, had given him advance warning of the catastrophe. Shortly after landing in Italy, one of his slaves had fallen into a prophetic trance,

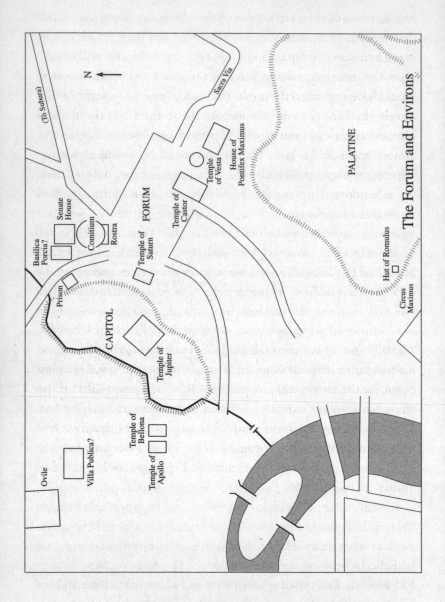

The Forum and Environs

revealing that unless victory were immediate, the Capitol would be destroyed by fire. Sulla's superstitions did not prevent him from being a master of propaganda, and this story, no doubt assiduously repeated, neatly served to blacken his rivals' cause. Certainly it would have reminded the public that Sulla, before his departure for Greece, had led the consul Cinna to the Capitol and there made him swear an oath not to attack him in his absence. Cinna had almost immediately gone back on his word. No wonder that the burning of the Capitol had come to Sulla as a godsend. From now on, as he plotted his reprisals, he could point to proof that the gods too wanted vengeance.

In fact, Cinna's original oath-breaking had been as much an act of self-defence as treachery. In the brutalised political climate that Sulla had left behind, rivalries had continued to degenerate into ever greater violence. A dispute over that perennial bugbear, the Italians' voting rights, had been sufficient to push the two consuls of 87 into open warfare. Cinna, expelled from Rome by Octavius, his colleague in the consulship, had promptly looked for ways to force a return. His first step had been to work some crowd-pleasing magic on the legion still camped at Nola, which as a result, for the second time in just over a year, had upped its siege and marched on Rome. But Cinna had conjured other allies too. The deadliest had brought not a legion but the magic of his name. After long months of exile in Africa, brooding amid the ruins of Carthage, Gaius Marius had returned.

Recruiting a personal army of slaves as he travelled through Italy, he had joined forces with Cinna, then turned on Rome. The city had fallen easily. Marius, psychotic with bitterness and rage, had launched a brutal purge of his enemies. Octavius, refusing to flee, had been hacked down where he sat in his consul's chair, and his head brought to Cinna, who displayed it in triumph on the Rostra. Other opponents of Marius had either fled or been massacred with conspicuous brutality. Meanwhile, with his gangs of slaves still rampaging through the city, the old man had finally been elected to his long-prophesied seventh consulship. No sooner had he taken up office, however, than he had abandoned himself to violent drinking bouts and nightmares. A fortnight later he was dead.

This had left Cinna as the regime's undisputed leader. With a strongman's contempt for precedent, he had maintained himself in the consulship for three consecutive years, preparing for Sulla's return. Then in 84, with Sulla poised to invade Italy, Cinna had decided to pre-empt him and take the fight to Greece. This time, however, the consul's army-camp rhetoric had let him down. His soldiers had mutinied and in the resulting disturbances Cinna himself had been murdered. Most Romans, dreading the arrival of Sulla's battle-hardened legions, must have believed that, with Cinna gone, there would be one final chance for peace. Sulla, however, contemptuously rejecting the proposals put forward by neutrals in the Senate, had refused even to contemplate reconciliation. Despite the loss of Cinna, the Marians had maintained their iron grip on power, and both sides now braced themselves for a fight to the death. Marius' own blood feud had passed to his son, a famously good-looking playboy whose lifestyle did nothing to diminish his filial loathing for his father's greatest foe. As the temple of Jupiter blazed on the Capitol, the younger Marius hurried to the scene and rescued not the statue of the god, not the prophecies of the Sibyl, but the temple treasures that would enable him to pay for more legions. A few months later he was elected to the consulship of 82. He was only twenty-six.

By now, such cavalier abuse of the constitution had become the norm. Senators who had endured years of having their ambitions blocked by Cinna and his stooges could only fume in silence at the sight of such a young man strutting around the Forum with his bodyguard of lictors. Yet, unpopular though the Marians

undoubtedly were, the alternative hardly inspired much opti-
mism. A sinister aura still clung to Sulla, the legacy of his own
protracted record of violence. No great upsurge of support greeted
his return. His claim to be restoring the Republic was treated with
at best suspicion. Armies blocked the roads to Rome and failed to
melt away.

All the same, Sulla was no longer the pariah among his peers
that he had been during his first march on Rome, back in 88, when
only a single officer had accompanied him. Five years on his
entourage was thronged with noblemen. Many of these were pursuing personal vendettas against the Marians. Pre-eminent among
them was a member of one of Rome's most celebrated families,
Marcus Licinius Crassus, whose father had led the opposition to
Marius and been executed for his pains. In the resulting purge
Crassus' brother had also been killed and the family's estates in
Italy seized. These holdings would have been considerable: Crassus'
father had combined a glittering political career with a most unsen-
atorial interest in the import–export trade. Not for nothing was
his family nicknamed 'Rich': Crassus would inherit from his father
the recognition that wealth was the surest foundation of power.
Later, he was to be notorious for claiming that until a man could
afford to maintain his own army it was impossible for him to have
too much money.[1] This was a judgement founded on youthful
experience. Fleeing his family's killers, the young Crassus had travelled to Spain, where his father's spell as governor had been
immensely profitable. Even hiding out on a remote beach the fugitive had been able to live in style, with dependants delivering
food and nubile slavegirls to his cave. Then, after several months of
subsisting on such provisions, the news of Cinna's death had
encouraged Crassus to claim his patrimony in full. Despite being a
private citizen, he had taken the unheard-of step of recruiting his
own army, a huge force of some two and a half thousand men.

Crassus had then led it round the Mediterranean, sampling alliances with various other anti-Marian factions, before finally sailing for Greece and throwing in his lot with Sulla, who, unsurprisingly, had welcomed the new arrival with open arms.

The warmest welcome of all, however, was reserved for a warlord even younger and more glamorous than Crassus. Sulla had crossed to Italy and was advancing northwards when news was brought to him that another private army had been raised on his behalf and was marching south to meet him. Since the roads were blocked by a variety of Marian forces, Sulla was nervous that the reinforcements might be wiped out, but just as he was pressing forward to their rescue there came further news: the tyro general had won a series of brilliant victories; a consular army had been put to flight. Now the army was waiting for Sulla on the road ahead, drawn up in full formation, arms glittering, faces glowing with success. Sulla, as he was meant to be, was duly impressed. Approaching the tent of the novice general, he dismounted from his horse. A young man stood waiting, his golden hair swept up in a quiff, his profile posed to look like Alexander's. He hailed Sulla as '*Imperator*' – 'General' – and Sulla then greeted him as '*Imperator*' in turn. This was an honour that it usually took even the most accomplished soldier many years to earn. Gnaeus Pompeius – 'Pompey' – was barely twenty-three.

Precocious swagger, a genius for self-promotion and an almost childlike relish for the perks of success: these were to be the defining characteristics of Pompey's rise to glory. Sulla, who indulged his protégé's vanity with an inscrutable cynicism, had his measure from the very start. He was perfectly content to flatter the young man if it helped to ensure his support. Pompey both merited and required courting. From his father, the perfidious Pompeius Strabo, he had inherited not only the largest private estate in Italy, but an aptitude for switching sides. Unlike Crassus, Pompey had no personal feud with the Marian regime. Before Sulla's arrival he had been spotted sniffing round Cinna's camp. Evidently the spectacle of its collapse into mutiny had persuaded him that Sulla would be the better man to back. Pompey always had a nose for where the richest opportunities might lie.

What he and Crassus had both realised was that civil war transformed the rules of the political game. The most ruthless and clear sighted of the younger generation had been presented with an unparalleled opportunity to leapfrog their elders. Sulla, who regarded the younger Marius as his deadliest foe, commented ruefully that as he aged his enemies grew younger. So too did his supporters. Pompey, in particular, led his army with the insouciance of a schoolboy handed a toy. To the Romans, the passions of youth were violent and dangerous, and only discipline could tame them. Pompey, however, had been given his head. '*Adulescentulus carnifex*', his enemies labelled him: 'teenage butcher'.[2] Not having had to master either custom or law during his short career, Pompey could kill without respect for either.

One man could have reined him in, of course – yet the example provided by Sulla himself was of a savagery which put even that of the 'teenage butcher' in the shade. Deliberately, it seems, he provoked one final uprising from the Samnites, massacring them whenever he had the opportunity, as though to cast himself not as a warlord but as the defender of Rome. Once again Samnium and Campania were pillaged mercilessly, and once again, for the last time in history, the Samnites strapped on their gorgeous armour and high-crested helmets and marched down into the plains. They joined a Marian cause already on the point of collapse. By 83, after a year of civil war, one consul had already fled Italy for Africa, and the other, the younger Marius, was bottled up in the hill town of Praeneste, some twenty-five miles east of Rome. The Samnites, shadow-boxing with Sulla, first attempted to march to Marius'

relief, but then, with the sudden realisation that Rome lay unpro-
tected in their rear, swung round abruptly and marched on the
capital. Sulla, taken by surprise, pursued them at frantic speed. As
the Samnites appeared within sight of Rome's walls, their commander ordered them to wipe out the city. 'Do you think that
these wolves who have preyed so terribly upon the freedoms of
Italy will ever vanish until the forest that shelters them has been
destroyed?'[3] he cried. But even as the Samnites began to mass before
the Colline Gate, the wails of women sounding in their ears from
the terrified city beyond, Sulla was drawing near. Already by noon
his vanguard of cavalry had begun to harass the enemy lines, and by
late afternoon, against the advice of his lieutenants, Sulla was ready
to throw his exhausted army into battle. All evening, and long into
the night, the struggle ebbed and flowed. Crassus shattered the
Samnite left wing, but Sulla found his own wing being broken and
his troops in danger of being crushed against the city gates. Yet still
his fortune held. Praying to the gods who had always been his protectors, he rallied his men and by dawn, when the news of Crassus'
success finally reached him, the victory was his.

The bloodbath of the Colline Gate was decisive. His enemies had
no more armies left in Italy with which to continue the war. As the
Samnite prisoners began to be rounded up Sulla was the absolute,
unquestioned master of Rome.

Sulla Felix

Three thousand prisoners were taken at the Colline Gate. A further three thousand, the Samnite reserves, surrendered on Sulla's
promise of safe conduct. No sooner had they emerged from their
stronghold, however, than they were rounded up and led off to join
the other Samnite captives. These had already been imprisoned on

the Campus Martius, the flood plain that stretched north beyond the walls of the Capitol. Even in defeat the Samnites were kept out of Rome.

Sulla's scrupulousness in this matter was ironic. Until his own legions had broken the taboo in 88 BC the only men in arms ever to have entered the city had been citizens marching in triumphal parades. Otherwise, Rome had always been off limits to the military. Since as far back as the time of the kings civilians had first had to gather on the Campus Martius – the Plain of Mars – before taking the oath that transformed them into soldiers. Here they had been ranked according to their wealth and status, for in war, as in peace, every citizen had to know his place. At the summit of the hierarchy there had been those rich enough to afford their own horses, the *equites*; below the equestrian class were five further classes of infantry; at the bottom of the heap were citizens too poor to buy even a sling and a few sling-stones, the *proletarii*. These seven classes had in turn been divided into further units, known as 'centuries'. This allowed status to be calibrated with exquisite precision. Long after 'classes' and 'centuries' had ceased to provide the basis of their army the Romans could not bring themselves to abandon so eminently satisfying a system. Instead, it remained at the heart of their political life.

Naturally, there were few citizens who did not dream of clawing themselves up the ladder, century by century, towards the uppermost rung. The higher a Roman climbed, the more fresh vistas emerged, to tempt him on further. Become an equestrian, for instance, and membership of the Senate became a sudden possibility; join the Senate and the tantalising prospect of a senior magistracy, a praetorship or even consulship, might hove into view. It was typical of the Republic that the greatest privilege it could grant one of its citizens was the chance to put himself to the vote of his fellows, and win even greater glory. Typical also that the mark of failure was to lose the class inherited from one's father.

Out on the Campus only a few structures stood on its flat and open expanse. Of these, the largest in area was an enclosure filled with barriers and aisles, of the kind used to pen livestock. The Romans called it the Ovile, or 'sheepfold'. This was where elections to the magistracies were held. The voters would be herded down the aisles in separate blocs. It was the nature of the Republic to thrive on complexity, and the organisation of these blocs varied confusingly from election to election. To vote for tribunes, for instance, the citizens would be divided into tribes. These were fabulously ancient in origin, and had been tweaked over the centuries in typically Roman manner as the Republic expanded and changed. With the enfranchisement of the Italians, they had been reorganised once again to cope with the influx of new citizens. Every member of every tribe was entitled to his vote, but since this had to be delivered in person at the Ovile the practical effect was to ensure that only the wealthiest out-of-towner could afford to travel to Rome to exercise his right. Inevitably, this served to skew the voting in favour of the rich. To most Romans, this seemed only fair. After all, the rich were the ones who contributed most to the Republic, and so it was generally conceded that their opinions should carry the greatest weight. Disproportionate voting power was yet another perk of rank.

Nowhere, however, was this principle more clearly expressed than in elections to the most senior magistracies of all. It was in these that the original functions of classes and centuries still maintained a ghostly after-life. Citizens assembled to vote for the consuls in the same way that their earliest ancestors had massed to go to war. Just as in the days of the kings, a military trumpet would be blown at daybreak to summon them to the Campus. A red flag would flutter on the Janiculum Hill beyond the Tiber, signalling that no enemies could be seen. The citizens would then line up as though for battle, with the richest at the front and the poorest at the rear. This meant that it was always the senior classes who were the first to pass into the Ovile. Nor was that their only privilege. So heavily weighted were their votes that they usually served to decide an election. As a result, there was often little point in the other classes even turning out. Not only were their votes worth a fraction of those of the equestrians, but they would only rarely be called on to register them anyway. Since they received no financial compensation for a day spent queuing outside the election pens, most of the poor must have decided that they had better things to do with their time. The equestrians no doubt agreed.

Even so, for those who could afford to succumb to election fever, the tension of voting day was one of the greatest excitements of Roman civic life. The candidates in their specially whitened togas, the milling crowds of their supporters, the tumult of yells and jeers, all contributed to the sense of occasion. Not until late in the day would heralds announce the results – at which point the successful candidates would be greeted with a great roar, and escorted amid further cheering from the Ovile towards the Capitol. Most voters chose to stay and wait for the spectacle of this climax. On a hot day, however, with clouds of brown dust scuffed up by the crowds, this might require some stamina. There were few public amenities on the Campus. Most weary voters tended to head for the Villa Publica, a walled complex of government buildings set just back from the Ovile. Here they could gossip, fan themselves and stay out of the sun.

And here it was too that Sulla, after the Battle of the Colline Gate, ordered his Samnite captives brought. They were penned beyond the arches of the central building, a square, two-storeyed reception hall, its rooms magnificently ill-suited to serve as cells for prisoners of war. The splendour of the statues and paintings that adorned these rooms reflected their decisive role in the life of the Republic, for the Villa Publica was where the hierarchies of Roman society were maintained and reviewed. Every five years a citizen had to register himself there. He also had to declare the name of his wife, the number of his children, his property and his possessions, from his slaves and ready cash to his wife's jewels and clothes. The state had the right to know everything, for the Romans believed that even 'personal tastes and appetites should be subject to surveillance and review'.[4] It was knowledge, intrusive knowledge, that provided the Republic with its surest foundations. Classes, centuries and tribes, everything which enabled a citizen to be placed by his fellows, were all defined by the census. Once the raw information had been collated by scribes, it would then be carefully scrutinised by two magistrates, who had the power to promote or demote each citizen according to his worth. The office of these magistrates, the censorship, was the most prestigious in the Republic; even more than the consulship it was regarded as the climax of a political career. So sensitive were the duties of a censor that only the most senior and reputable of citizens could be entrusted with them. The maintenance of everything that structured the Republic depended on their judgement. There were few Romans who doubted that if the census were not conducted adequately, then the entire fabric of their society would fall apart. No wonder that it was universally regarded as 'the mistress and guardian of peace'.[5]

By locking up his prisoners of war where he did, then, Sulla was once again demonstrating his taste for irony in even the grimmest of circumstances. The irony was soon to darken further. In the shadow of the Capitol, but within hearing distance of the Villa Publica, stood the temple of Bellona. Sulla sent orders to the Senate to meet him there. As they hurried to obey him, the senators would have glanced up and seen the charred ruins of Jupiter's temple on the hill high above them. It was Bellona who had warned Sulla to win his victory quickly or see the Capitol destroyed. By choosing her temple as the venue for his address to the Senate, Sulla neatly reminded his audience that he stood before them as the favourite of the gods, divinely sent to be the saviour of Rome. What this might mean in practical terms was soon to be made brutally apparent. As Sulla launched into his address, describing his victory over Mithridates, the senators began to hear the muffled sounds of shrieking from the Samnite prisoners. Sulla continued, apparently oblivious to the screams, until at last he paused and ordered the senators not to be distracted from what he had to say. 'Some criminals are receiving their punishment,' he explained dismissively. 'There is no need for worry, it is all being done on my orders.'[6]

The massacre was total. In the cramped conditions of the slaughter-house the bodies piled up high. Once the executions had been completed, the corpses were dragged across the Campus and flung into the Tiber, clogging the banks and bridges with pollution, until 'at last the river's currents cut a swath of blood through the azure open sea'.[7] The stains on the Villa Publica itself were not so easily removed. The census had been held there only three years previously. Now the rooms in which the rolls had been completed were filthy with gore. The symbolism was shocking and obvious: Sulla rarely made any gesture without a fine calculation of its effect. By washing the Villa Publica with blood he had given dramatic notice of the surgery he was planning to perform on the Republic. If the census were illegitimate, then so too were the hierarchies of status and prestige that it had affirmed. The ancient foundations of the state were unstable, on the verge of collapse. Sulla, god-sent, would perform the repairs, no matter how much bloodshed the task might require.

In its blending of superstition with the flaunting of naked power this was a vintage Sullan performance. There was no one in the Senate willing – or foolish enough – to stand up to it. Even Sulla's bitterest enemies had little choice but to acknowledge the unprecedented scale of his triumph. To Sulla himself, success had always been the surest proof of Fortune's blessing. This was why he chose to downplay his own role in the victory at the Colline Gate, and overplay that of Crassus: not because he was modest, but because, on the contrary, he wished to portray himself as Fortune's favourite – a man of destiny. Ancient writers were unclear whether to attribute this to conviction or cynicism – although in Sulla's case the two appear always to have been perfectly compatible. What is certain, however, is that by casting his victory as god-given, the man who had been the first to march on Rome, and who had devastated Italy with 'war, fire and slaughter',[8] aimed to absolve himself of all blame for the Republic's woes. This was why Sulla's exhumation of Marius' ashes, and his scattering of them into the River Anio, was an act of calculated propaganda as well as petty revenge. The death-struggle with his great rival, the very feud that had brought the Republic to its perilous pass, was reconstituted as a war in the Republic's defence. In this way alone could Sulla justify the position of supremacy that he had wrested for himself. Even Marius, in the grim insanity of his final months, had taken care to cloak himself in the tattered legitimacy of his seventh consulship. Sulla, however, was too shrewd to attempt a similar sham. He knew that there was no point in picking up the shreds of a conventional magistracy. If he were to conceal the nakedness of his power, then he would have to look elsewhere for a fitting disguise.

Before he could do that, however, he had to make absolutely certain of his victory. Leaving Rome, he headed directly for the neighbouring town of Praeneste, final stronghold of the Marian cause. On the way, the news reached him that the city had surrendered and Marius' son was dead. Rome was now without consuls. The fact that it was Sulla who had destroyed the two heads of state only served to emphasise the constitutional anomaly of his position. Sulla himself was too exultant with self-belief to care. He celebrated the scotching of his enemy's bloodline by awarding himself the title of Felix – 'The Fortunate One'. This had always been a cherished private nickname, but now Sulla decided to broadcast it publicly. By doing so, he signalled that there would be no herding of voters into the Ovile to validate his rule. Luck had brought Sulla to power, and luck – Sulla's famous luck – would save the Republic in turn. Until her favourite's work was done, and the constitution restored, Fortune was to rule as the mistress of Rome.

Her reign would prove to be savage. The casting down of the great, the raising up of the insignificant, these were the dramas in which Fortune most delighted. So too, of course, in its own way, did the Republic. Yet the constitution, subtle and finely modulated as it was, had evolved to restrain any violent change. Not for the Romans the mass executions and asset-stripping of opponents that had periodically engulfed Greek cities. Sulla, capturing Athens, had overthrown a regime dependent on precisely such tactics. Now, having captured Rome in turn, he prepared to copy them. In the practice of political terror as in so much else Athens, 'the school of Greece', could still inspire.

The death squads had fanned out through Rome even as the Samnites were being butchered in the Villa Publica. Sulla himself made no attempt to restrain them. Even his supporters, inured to bloodshed, were appalled by the resulting carnage. One of them dared to ask when the murderers would be reined in. Or at least, he added hurriedly, 'let us have a list of all those you want punished'.[9] Sulla, sardonically obliging, duly posted a list in the Forum. It featured the entire leadership of the Marian regime. All were condemned to death. Their properties were declared forfeit, and their sons and grandsons barred from standing for office. Anyone who helped to protect them was likewise condemned to death. An entire swath of Rome's political elite was summarily nominated for annihilation.

Further lists followed. Hundreds, maybe thousands, of names appeared. In a grotesque parody of the census, the names of men without Marian sympathies, but whose wealth and status made them tempting targets, began to be sneaked in. Ghouls who gathered in the Forum to inspect the lists might easily find their own names featured. Villas, pleasure gardens, swimming pools, all were now potential death warrants. Everywhere, bounty-hunters tracked down their prey. The severed heads of victims would be brought back to Rome, and Sulla, once he had inspected them and released the promised fee, might keep particularly prized specimens as trophies in his house.

Such a grisly system of accounting was easy to abuse. No one exploited it more profitably than Crassus, who had the nose for gain of a man who had suffered from confiscations himself. As the general who had saved Sulla at the Colline Gate, he was in a privileged position to throw his weight about. Gifts were duly extorted, estates snapped up cheap. At length, however, when Crassus added the name of an innocent millionaire just a little too flagrantly on to a proscription list, Sulla lost patience. In the resulting scandal relations between the two men broke down irreparably, and Sulla withdrew his favour from his former lieutenant. Crassus was already so rich that he could afford not to care.

As for Sulla, ever the master strategist, he picked quarrels only as a matter of policy. By slapping down his own ally so publicly, he could represent himself as the selfless cleanser of the Republic, washing it in blood without thought of personal gain. For all the ostentation of his shock at Crassus' avarice, however, there were few who were convinced by it. Sulla's policy had always been to cut down his enemies and build up his friends. Crassus was far too powerful and ambitious to serve as anyone's parasite, but those whom Sulla did not regard as threats were duly rewarded. Often, he would personally sell on properties at ludicrously knock-down prices. His policy was a deliberate one of ruining his opponents by enriching his supporters. 'Not until Sulla had glutted all his followers with wealth did the slaughter at last come to an end.'[10]

Generous though he was, however, the man who profited most from the proscriptions was Sulla himself. The pauper who had once been forced to doss in squalid flop-houses was now richer than any Roman in history. It so happened that during the course of the proscriptions a senator who had been condemned to death was found hiding in the house of one of his former slaves. The freedman was duly brought before Sulla to be condemned. The two men recognised each other at once. Both, long before, had shared lodgings in the same apartment block, and the freedman, even as he was hauled away to his execution, yelled at Sulla that there had once been little difference between them. He meant it as a taunt, a scream of defiance, but Sulla is unlikely to have interpreted it as such. Nothing could have better illustrated the distance he had travelled. Nothing could have better demonstrated that he was '*Felix*' indeed.

Sulla Dictator

Sulla aimed to build as well as destroy. Even as the streets of Rome ran red he talked loudly of restoring the Republic to full health. As ever with him, opportunism was the obverse of an icy conviction. The cycle of wars and revolutions through which he had hacked his way so savagely had done nothing to diminish his deeply held conservatism. Sulla had the true patrician's contempt for innovation. Far from wishing to impose some radical new model of autocracy on his fellow citizens, he looked to the past for solutions to the crisis facing Rome.

Most urgently of all, he faced the need to regularise his own position. Even with his enemies proscribed, Sulla still refused to

submit himself to the judgement of the voters. Fortunately, a
precedent for this lay conveniently close to hand. The Republic's
ancient history did indeed provide examples of citizens who had
wielded absolute power without being elected. In moments of particular crisis the authority of the consuls had sometimes been
suspended and a single magistrate nominated to take control of
the state. Such an office fitted Sulla's requirements perfectly. The
fact that it was a constitutional fossil worried him not in the slightest. By dropping heavy and menacing hints, he persuaded the
Senate to dust down the antiquated office, and appoint him to it.
The result was not only to legalise his supremacy, but to give it the
patina of tradition. After all, how could the Romans consider themselves threatened by a magistracy as authentically Republican as the
dictatorship?

In fact, though, it had always been regarded with suspicion.
Unlike the consulship, split as it was between two citizens of equal
rank, the unified powers of the dictatorship were inherently offensive to Republican ideals. This was why the office had fallen into
abeyance. Even back in the dark days of the war against Hannibal,
citizens had been appointed to it only for very short, fixed periods.
Like unmixed wine, the dictatorship had a taste that was intoxicating and perilous. Sulla, however, who enjoyed alcohol and power
equally, was proud of his head for both. He refused to accept a limit
on his term of office. Instead, he was to remain dictator until the
constitution had been 'revised'.[11] What this might mean he would
judge for himself.

A consul had twelve lictors. Sulla had twenty-four. Each one bore
on his shoulders not only the *fasces*, but also, bundled up with the
scourging rods and symbolising a dictator's powers of life and death,
an axe. Nothing could better have indicated the disproportion in
status now existing between Sulla and his fellow magistrates. He was
quick to ram home the message. No sooner had he been appointed

dictator than he ordered consular elections to be held. Both the candidates were selected by himself. When one of his own generals, the war hero who had captured Praeneste, no less, attempted to stand, Sulla warned him to back off, and then, when he refused, had him murdered publicly in the Forum. More than anyone, Sulla had reason to appreciate just how dangerous war heroes might be.

It was an irony that shadowed the entire programme of his reforms. Sulla's task as dictator was to ensure that in the future no one would ever again do as he had done and lead an army on Rome. Yet it is doubtful whether Sulla himself would have regarded this as a paradox. If, as his propaganda relentlessly insisted, he was guiltless of provoking civil war, then the fault had to lie elsewhere. And if, as his propaganda also insisted, ambition had tempted Marius and Sulpicius into endangering the Republic, then it was the corruption of the Republic's own institutions that had permitted them to thrive. Sulla was too much of a Roman to imagine that a desire to be the best might ever in itself be a crime. He certainly had no intention of suppressing his countrymen's inveterate thirsting after glory. Instead, he aimed to channel it, so that once again, rather than tearing the state to shreds, it might serve the greater glory of Rome.

The complexities, the ambivalences and the paradoxes of the constitution all infuriated the new dictator. Sulla interpreted them as loopholes, and worked hard to close them. No openings were to be left that a future Marius might exploit. Instead, ambition was to be strictly regulated. Each magistracy was to have an age threshold. Sulla, who had spent his own twenties chasing after whores, must have relished the chance to discriminate against youthful over-achievers.

Under his legislation, no one under the age of thirty would be permitted to seek election to even the most junior magistracy. This, the quaestorship, entitled a successful candidate to serve for a year as an assistant to one of the more senior magistrates, and to learn from the example of the older man. Some quaestors might even be given independent responsibilities, managing the Republic's finances, habituating themselves to the disciplines and duties of power. This was important training, for the citizen who had served as quaestor would be entitled, once he had reached his thirty-ninth birthday, to aim for a further, even more prestigious honour: the praetorship. If elected to this office, he would now, for a year, be junior in rank only to the consuls themselves. A praetor had awesome responsibilities and privileges: charged as he was with the weighty task of administering the Republic's laws, he also had the right to convene a session of the Senate, and preside over its debates. Under Sulla's new scheme of things, however, the real attraction of the praetorship was that it now served as an obligatory step on the ladder that led, rung after ordered rung, towards the consulship itself. This remained the top, the glittering prize. As always, only a few would ever win it, but the goal of Sulla's reforms was to ensure that, in the future, the victors would prove worthy of their rank. There were to be no more scandals like the career of the younger Marius. From quaestorship to praetorship to consulship, only a single path to power, and no short cuts.

The deliberate effect of this legislation was to place a premium on middle age. In this it accorded with fundamental Roman instincts. Statesmen were expected to be middle aged. Greek rulers may have portrayed themselves as preternaturally young, but the portraiture of the Republic suggests a positive relish for wrinkles, thinning hair and sagging jowls. It was no coincidence that the traditional ruling body of Rome, the Senate, derived its name from 'senex' – 'old man' – nor that senators liked to dignify themselves with the title of 'Fathers'. The ideal of an assembly rich in experience and wisdom, acting as a brake on such irresponsible elements as the young or indigent poor, was one dear to every conservative's heart. In the mythology of the Republic it was the Senate that had guided Rome to greatness, prevailing over Hannibal, breaking kings, conquering the world. Sulla, despite having trampled over the Senate at every opportunity, made the restoration of its authority the major goal of his career.

Repair work was urgently required. Civil war and proscriptions had left the august body in a parlous state. Sulla, having played a major part in the reduction of its numbers from three hundred to barely one hundred, promoted newcomers with such assiduity that by the time he had finished the Senate was larger than at any time in its history. Equestrians from all walks of life – businessmen, Italians, plunder-rich officers – were hurriedly crammed into the Senate House. Simultaneously, the opportunities for self-advancement within the Senate were also broadened. Under Sulla's reforms, the number of praetorships on offer in any one year was increased from six to eight, and of quaestorships from eight to twenty – a conscious attempt to ensure that the upper reaches of power would be regularly infused with fresh blood. The established nobility, not surprisingly, were appalled by such measures. Roman snobbery, however, was skilled at keeping newcomers in their place. Senators, like everyone else in the Republic, were bound by iron-clad rules of hierarchy. Rank structured the order in which they were called upon to speak, and junior senators rarely had the chance to speak at all. Even men who had once been outspoken critics of the Senate were no sooner promoted to the body than they found themselves silenced. Sulla, not known for his generosity towards enemies, appears to have decided that there were certain opponents it was wisest to co-opt.

Some, of course, still remained beyond the pale. The aspirations of the mob Sulla regarded with contempt. Those who represented them he regarded with naked loathing. Even as he built up the power of the Senate, Sulla emasculated the tribunate with the vindictiveness that characterised all his vendettas. He never forgot that

Sulpicius had been a tribune. Each snipping away of the tribunate's powers was a delicate act of personal revenge. To ensure that tribunes could never again propose bills attacking a consul, as Sulpicius had done, Sulla barred them from proposing bills altogether. To prevent the tribunate from attracting ambitious trouble-makers in the future, he throttled it of all potential to advance a career. With carefully nuanced malice, Sulla banned anyone who had held the office from seeking further magistracies. Quaestors and praetors might dream of the consulship, but not tribunes, not any more. Their office was to be a rung on a ladder leading nowhere. Revenge, as ever with Sulla, was sweet.

One of the ancient pillars of the constitution now lay in rubble. Even Sulla's conservative supporters in the Senate appear to have been shocked.[12] No one had ever before attempted such a work of demolition. The dictator himself cast his reforms as a restoration, the sweeping away of clutter. Yet clutter was the essence of the Republic. It spread everywhere that Sulla cared to look. It could be seen in the very appearance of Rome herself. Sulla, whose invariable response to provocation was to launch a single, rapid killer-blow against it, quickly proved himself as impatient with the urban fabric as he had been with the Marians or the tribunate. Frustrated by the city's congestion, he simply pushed back the *pomerium*, the first man to do so in the whole of Roman history. Just as coolly, he levelled the cramped but venerable Senate House, and rebuilt it to suit the proportions of his own new, inflated Senate. Not that the senators themselves displayed much gratitude. Decades later they were still mourning the original building, sanctified as it had been by the Republic's historic heroes, and complaining that 'its enlargement appeared to have shrunk it'.[13] Sulla could afford to dismiss all such moaning with a contemptuous shrug. Only on the Capitol was he inhibited by the sanctions of custom. The temple of Jupiter might have been burned to the ground, but its outline still remained. As a new temple rose from the ashes, the gigantic columns that Sulla had conveniently plundered from Athens gleamed from within the confines of the original, sacrosanct structure. Monumentalism squatted awkwardly on archaic foundations. Sulla's dictatorship could hardly have raised a more fitting memorial to itself.

Long before the completion of Jupiter's great temple, however, Sulla had resigned his office. One morning, some time late in 81 BC, he suddenly appeared in the Forum without his lictors. The man responsible for the deaths of more citizens than any Roman in history had laid aside the sanctions of supreme power, 'fearing neither the people at home nor the exiles abroad . . . Such was the extent of his daring and good luck.'[14] Once again his nerve was justified. Sulla remained a figure of dread. Only on a single occasion did anyone dare to criticise him to his face, a young man who cat-called him in the Forum; then, having failed to get a rise, he jeered him all the way home. Otherwise, the terror of Sulla's name held good.

The year after he resigned his dictatorship Sulla served as a consul; the year after that he stood down from office altogether. Relieved of formal responsibilities, he returned to the wild living of his youth. It was a lifestyle for which he had never lost his talent. As dictator, he had thrown the largest parties in Rome's history. Everyone in the city had been invited. Spit-roasts had sizzled in the streets, vintage wines had flowed from public fountains. The citizens had gorged themselves, and then, when no one had been able to eat or drink another thing, whole sides of meat had been slung with delirious wastefulness into the Tiber. As a private citizen, Sulla's parties were inevitably more intimate affairs. Whole days would be spent in drinking bouts with his old bohemian set. Dizzyingly high though he had risen, Sulla remained as loyal in his friendships as he was implacable in his feuds. Actors, dancers, down-at-heel hacks, all had been tossed crumbs from the estates of the proscribed. Those without talent had been given money never to perform again.

Those who did have talent were cherished, however much they might have passed their prime. Brutal cynic though he was, Sulla would still flatter and cosset a fading drag-queen. 'Metrobius, the female impersonator, had seen better days, but Sulla never ceased to insist that he was in love with him all the same.'[15]

Certainly, there was none of Marius' muscle-bound need to prove himself a man: no workouts on the Campus Martius for Sulla. When he retreated to his villa in Campania, he gloried in his retirement. He had restored the Republic, and the fruit of his work was peace. The crisis was over. Who could doubt, seeing Sulla in his Greek tunic, strolling with other tourists through the back streets of Naples, that the good times were back?

Yet in Italy, as in Rome, the good times had been founded on savagery and bloodshed. Not far beyond Sulla's estate rose the hills of Samnium, harrowed in a policy of deliberate extirpation. All around it, dotted across the Plain of Campania, stood cities still scarred by their resistance to Sulla. Even Naples had been stormed by his legions. Nola too, eventually, had fallen. Besieged for almost a decade, the rebel stronghold had held out until 80 BC, steeled by the same spectacle of atrocities that had persuaded other towns to incinerate themselves rather than surrender. To punish Nola, and to provide a permanent occupying force, Sulla had planted a colony of his veterans in the city, one of numerous similar settlements imposed all over Campania and Samnium. Triumphant even in his enemies' most obdurate stronghold, Sulla had celebrated by giving Nola a new and humiliating name – Colonia Felix. Only one other act of appropriation can have given him more pleasure. Just down the coast from his own estate stood Marius' celebrated villa, raised on its promontory like a military camp, a shrine to the old soldier's glory and masculine pride. Sulla sold it cheap to his daughter, Cornelia. He had always believed in rubbing salt into open wounds.

This streak of cruelty would never be forgotten, nor forgiven. Sulla had given the Romans their first glimpse of what it might mean to be the subjects of an autocrat, and it had proved a frightening and salutary one. This was a discovery that could never be unmade. After the proscriptions, no one could doubt what the extreme consequence of the Roman appetite for competition and glory might be, not only for Rome's enemies, but for her citizens themselves. What had once been unthinkable now lurked at the back of every Roman's mind: 'Sulla could do it. Why can't I?'[16]

The generation that succeeded him would have to give their own answer to that question. In doing so they would serve to define how Sulla himself was best to be judged: had he been the saviour or destroyer of the constitution? Terrible though he had proved himself to be, the dictator had also laboured hard to restore the Republic, to ensure that he would have no successor. Historians of future generations, inured to perpetual autocracy, found fantastical the idea that anyone should voluntarily have laid down supreme power. Yet Sulla had done it. No wonder that his own contemporaries found him such a baffling and contradictory figure. When he died – most probably of liver failure – no one could even agree how to dispose of his body. One consul wanted to award him a state funeral, the other to deprive him of funereal honours altogether. Fittingly, it was the threat of violence that served to resolve the debate. A huge escort of veterans assembled to bring their dead general from Campania, and the people of Rome found themselves 'as terrified of Sulla's army and his corpse as if he were still alive'.[17] No sooner had the body been laid on a huge pyre in the Campus Martius than a strong wind came gusting across the plain, whipping up the flames. And no sooner had the corpse been consumed than it started to rain.

Sulla stayed lucky to the very end.

5

FAME IS THE SPUR

A Patrician's Progress

The life of a young Roman nobleman was filled with opportunity and risk. Civil war heightened the extremes of both. Under Sulla, a young man might be plunged straight into the deep end of adult life. Some profited spectacularly. Most dazzling of all was the example of Pompey, who continued to pose and preen perfectly unruffled by Sulla's legislation against boy-wonders. Even as the dictator moved to forbid anyone under the age of thirty from holding political office, his fresh-faced lieutenant was thrashing an army of Marian die-hards in Africa, and being hailed by his troops as 'The Great'. Pompey was exceptional, however, and gloried in the fact. Others of his generation were less fortunate. Sulla's secret police respected neither youth nor pedigree. So it was, for instance, that because Marius had married into the Julians, the heir of that ancient, patrician family found himself on the run. Only nineteen, a young man whose family connections should have ensured him seamless advancement, he had to hide out in mountain haylofts and offer frantic bribes to bounty-hunters. It was an experience he would never forget. In future years he would prove himself unusually determined to master the vagaries of Fortune. No less than Pompey, the young Julius Caesar emerged from the years of Sulla's domination hardened before his time.

In this both men were only proving themselves true to their upbringings. Hardness was a Roman ideal. The steel required to hunt out glory or endure disaster was the defining mark of a citizen. It was instilled in him from the moment of his birth. The primary response of Roman parents to their babies appears to have been less tenderness than shock that anything could be quite so soft and helpless. 'An infant, like a sailor hurled ashore by savage waves, lies naked on the ground, unable to speak a word, utterly dependent on other people for his survival.'[1] To the Romans, such a condition verged on the scandalous. Children were certainly too weak to be idealised, and the highest praise a child could be given was to be compared to an adult. The result is, to modern eyes at least, a curious and frustrating gap in ancient biographies. Never do the great figures of the Republic appear chillier or more remote from us than when their earliest years are being described. We are offered portraits of them as prodigies of physical toughness or learning – stiff, priggish, implausible. Anecdotes that portray them as children rather than as mini-adults are few and far between. The greater the figure, the less adequate the portrait of his childhood is likely to appear. The early years of a man such as Caesar are effectively a blank. Any attempt to recreate them must depend, even more than is usually the case in ancient history, on supposition and generalisation. Yet the attempt is still worthwhile. The Romans were as aware as any psychologist that 'Nature displays her blueprints most clearly in a man's earliest years.'[2] Childhood was where the future citizen was made.

What, then, can we say with any certainty about the infant who would one day destroy the Republic? Gaius Julius Caesar was born on 13 July 100 BC, six years after Pompey, fifteen after Crassus. Ritual

would have surrounded him from his earliest moments. A Roman
did not become a citizen by right of birth. It was within the power
of every father to reject a newborn child, to order unwanted sons,
and especially daughters, to be exposed. Before the infant Caesar
was breastfed, his father would first have had to hold him aloft,
signalling that the boy had been accepted as his own, and was therefore a Roman. Nine days later he would have been named. Evil
spirits would have been swept out of the house with a broom. The
boy's future would have been read in the behaviour of passing birds.
A golden good-luck charm, the *bulla*, would have been placed
around the baby Gaius' neck, to stay there until he came of age
and became a full citizen.

No delay would have been permitted in preparing for that
moment. The Romans lacked a specific word for 'baby', reflecting
their assumption that a child was never too young to be toughened
up. Newborns were swaddled tightly to mould them into the form
of adults, their features were kneaded and pummelled, and boys
would have their foreskins yanked to make them stretch. Old-fashioned Republican morality and new-fangled Greek medicine united
to prescribe a savage regime of dieting and cold baths. The result of
this harsh upbringing was to contribute further to an already devastating infant mortality rate. It has been estimated that only two
out of three children survived their first year, and that under 50 per
cent went on to reach puberty. The deaths of children were constant factors of family life. Parents were encouraged to respond to
such losses with flinty calm. The younger the child, the less emotion would be shown, so that it was a commonplace to argue that 'if
an infant dies in its cradle, then its death ought not even be
mourned'.[3] Yet reserve did not necessarily spell indifference. There
is plenty of evidence from tombstones, poetry and private correspondence to suggest the depth of love that Roman parents could
feel. The rigours imposed on a child were not the result of wilful

cruelty. Far from it: the sterner the parents, the more loving they were assumed to be.

Caesar's upbringing was famously strict, and his mother, Aurelia, was accordingly remembered by subsequent generations of Romans as a model parent; so model, in fact, that it was said she had breast-fed her children. This, notoriously, was something that upper-class women rarely chose to do, despite it being their civic duty, since, as everyone knew, milk was imbued with the character of the woman who supplied it. How could a slave's milk ever compare with that of a freeborn Roman woman? Irresponsible aristocrats who handed their babies over to wet-nurses were clearly compromising their children's future. Yet still they did it. It was a clear and shocking symptom of the degeneracy of the times. Aurelia's boast that she had devoted herself to child-rearing had a proudly anachronistic ring.

And paragon of Republican motherhood that she was, no sooner had she weaned her children than she set about the business of their education. Gaius was not the exclusive focus of Aurelia's attentions. As well as her son, she had two daughters, Julia Major and Julia Minor. The Romans believed that girls had to be moulded just as much as boys. Physical as well as intellectual exercises were prescribed for both. A boy trained his body for warfare, a girl for childbirth, but both were pushed to the point of exhaustion. To the Romans, self-knowledge came from appreciating the limits of one's endurance. It was only by testing what these might be that a child could be prepared for adult life.

No wonder that Roman children appear to have had little time for play. Far fewer toys have been found dating from the Republic than from the period that followed its collapse, when the pressure to raise good citizens had begun to decline. Even so, children were children: 'As they grow older, not even the threat of punishment can keep them from playing games with all the energy they have.'[4]

Girls certainly had their dolls, since it was the custom to dedicate these to Venus as part of the rituals of marriage. Boys, meanwhile, played obsessively with spinning tops. Dice appear to have been a universal mania. At wedding parties the groom would be expected to toss children coins or nuts that could then be played for as stakes. Caesar would one day talk of rolling a die when he faced the gravest crisis of his life, and his taste for the metaphor must surely have derived from his childhood. Even throwing dice, however, he would still have been supervised by the implacable Aurelia, who was as concerned to 'regulate his behaviour when he was playing games as when he was hard at his studies'.[5] Perhaps it was from his mother, then, that Caesar first learned to practise one of his greatest skills, the art of distinguishing an acceptable risk from a heedless gamble.

If so, then it would only serve to emphasise a glaring omission in accounts of Caesar's childhood – mention of his father's influence. By supervising her son's upbringing so closely, Aurelia, model parent though she was, ran the risk of stepping on her husband's toes. The freedoms granted to Roman women may have been exceptional by the standards of the age, but the authority of a Roman father was even more so. His powers of life and death did not end with the acceptance of a child into his household. His daughters, even once they had been married off, might well remain his wards, while his sons, no matter how old they grew, no matter how many magistracies they might win, never ceased to be his dependants. There was no father quite so patriarchal as a Roman one. As was invariably the case with the Republic, however, rights brought obligations. At the census every head of a household would be asked whether he had married for the purpose of having children. It was a citizen's patriotic duty to contribute to his city's future manpower. More immediate, however, and no doubt far more keenly felt, was a father's duty to the prestige of his family.

Status in the Republic was not inherited. Instead, it had to be re-earned over each successive generation. The son who failed to equal the rank and achievements of his ancestors, the daughter who neglected to influence her husband in the interests of her father or her brothers – both brought public shame on their family. It was the responsibility of the *pater familias* to ensure that such a calamity never occurred. As a result, child-rearing, like virtually every other aspect of life in the Republic, reflected the inveterate Roman love of competition. To raise heirs successfully, to instil in them due pride in their blood-line and a hankering after glory, these were achievements worthy of a man.

Caesar's own ambitions were one day to consume the entire Republic. His father must have had some influence in fostering them. There were certain things in Rome that it took a man to teach. The young Gaius' most valuable lessons would have come not at his mother's feet but standing beside his father as he greeted political allies, or strolling across the Forum, or overhearing gossip at a senator's banquet. Only by breathing in the subtle scents of power at first hand could a boy hope to develop a nose for the Republic's manifold complexities. Caesar's father was well connected, and his name would have opened many doors. In return he would also have held an open house himself. The Romans had little concept of private space. The town house of an aristocrat was less a domestic retreat than a stage on which he could pose and be admired, a projection in stone of how he wished to be seen. Distant from the centres of power the Julians' mansion may have been, surrounded by the taverns and slums of the sloping Subura, yet it would still have provided Caesar's father with a formidable headquarters. Suitors and clients would have thronged its hallway. The relationship of such dependants to their patron constituted yet another cross-current that had to be mastered by the aspirant politician. Exploited properly, the support of clients might prove crucial to his ambitions. A Roman aristocrat was always careful to look after his own. The more influential he became, the more clients would inevitably be drawn to his flame. After 92 BC, the year in which Caesar's father became a praetor, his retinue would have begun to mark him out as a figure of consequence. But would it have been large enough to satisfy the expectations of his eight-year-old son?

These were immense. To an extent that was regarded as excessive even by Roman standards, Caesar never let slip a chance to insist on the respect due to his ancestry. His descent from Venus had been drummed into him from his earliest years. His family mansion wore the appearance of a shrine to the Julian name. Beyond a portico designed to echo the features of a temple, the walls of the atrium were hung with forbidding images, the wax death-masks of magistrates, bearing witness to the honours won by the family in the past. Painted lines connected the portraits, reaching backwards into time, towards a Trojan hero and, beyond him, a goddess. Foreign observers were in no doubt about the effect of such a spectacle on an impressionable child. 'It would be hard to imagine a more impressive scene for a youth who aspires to win fame and practise virtue.'[6] The Romans themselves described children's spirits as blazing like flames at the sight.[7] Correspondingly, however, an heir to a great mansion who proved himself unworthy of its heritage was a figure of scorn. 'It is dreadful when men can walk by it and say, "Venerable old house, dear oh dear, what a let down your current owner is!"'[8] In Caesar's case, contemplation of his family's ancient glories could only have emphasised its recent honour-famine. His father might have been a praetor, but he was not a consul. He might have been followed by a retinue of clients whenever he walked through the Forum, but he could not call on entire cities or even provinces filled with his clients, as the very greatest families could. Pompey's, for instance, *arriviste* though it may have been, was able to mobilise a swath of territories in eastern Italy. The treacherous and brutal Strabo had been an exemplary parent. It was by studying a eulogy of his father's achievements that Pompey had first learned to read. By contrast, we know nothing of the youthful Caesar's reading, only what he wrote. The themes of these compositions must have been recognised by his contemporaries as significant, else the memory of them would not have been preserved. One was written 'in praise of Hercules',[9] greatest of the Greek heroes, the secret son of Jupiter, whose achievements ultimately won him immortality. Another told the story of Oedipus.

Whatever Caesar's precise views of his father may have been – and it is perilous to argue from silence – one thing is certain: a far more impressive role-model was readily to hand. Following his year as praetor, Caesar's father was appointed to the governorship of Asia. This was a plum posting. Only some strong string-pulling behind the scenes could have fixed it. Mithridates was yet to launch his invasion, but Marius was already angling for some form of Eastern command. The sudden elevation of his in-law had the general's fingerprints all over it. As first the Italians' revolt and then civil war engulfed the Republic, Marius continued to serve as the patron of his Julian relations. Just before his death, during his bloodstained seventh consulship, he planned to shoehorn the young Caesar into the priesthood of Jupiter, a post that demanded a patrician and had been left vacant by the forced suicide of its previous incumbent. Since Caesar was only thirteen, the office had to be kept on hold for him, but already, just a child, he had been sucked directly into the vortex of the civil war.

In 84 Caesar's father died – of what we are not told. In the same year Caesar himself set aside his *bulla*, draped his body in the heavy folds of a grown man's toga and officially came of age. The consul Cinna, Rome's strongman following Marius' death, now moved fast. Caesar's priesthood was officially confirmed. The sixteen-year-old must already have cut an impressive figure, because Cinna also offered him the hand of his daughter, Cornelia. Caesar was engaged at the time, but no young man was going to miss out on the chance of having the Republic's supremo as his father-in-law. Marriage in Rome was a typically unsentimental business. Love was irrelevant, politics was all. Upper-class women, especially if they proved fertile, were prized stakes in the dice game of advancement. Because girls were far more likely to be exposed at birth than boys, there was a permanent lack of eligible fiancées. 'Spinster' is another modern word, like 'baby', with no equivalent in Latin. So keen were fathers to cash in on their daughters' marriageability that girls would typically come of age some three or four years before their brothers. The moment a girl had celebrated her twelfth birthday she could expect to be veiled behind the traditional saffron of a bride. If a wife remained her father's ward – and most wealthy women did – then her loyalty to her husband might at best prove shallow. Marriages could be formed and broken with dizzying speed, for a sudden reversal of alliances might require an equally sudden divorce. For as long as Caesar had Cornelia as his wife he could be confident of Cinna's favour. A man did not need to love his wife to prize her all the same.

When Cinna was lynched at the hands of his mutinous soldiers, however, Cornelia must suddenly have begun to seem like a liability. Once Sulla had annihilated the Marians and obliterated the last remnants of Cinna's regime, she was transformed into something even worse. As Marius' nephew and Cinna's son-in-law, Caesar was hardly likely to recommend himself to the new dictator. Even so, his name did not feature on the first proscription lists. Protégé of the Marians though he was, Caesar also had close links to Sulla. The multiform character of the Republic frequently bred contradictory loyalties. The world of the aristocracy, in particular, was a small one, and the complex web of marriage alliances could end up entangling even the bitterest rivals. Caesar's mother came from a family who had provided Sulla with some of his most influential supporters. It was an association that was to save Caesar's life.

Rather than having him killed, Sulla contented himself with depriving the young priest of Jupiter of his office, and demanding that he divorce Cornelia. Caesar, astonishingly, refused. It was this near-suicidal act of defiance that led to him fleeing Rome with a price on his head. Only the continued intercession of Aurelia's relatives finally persuaded Sulla to pardon the impudent youth. The dictator gave way with a resigned shrug and a warning that the boy had an abundance of Mariuses inside him. If Caesar resembled anyone, however, it was not Marius. The refusal to divorce Cornelia had required not only bravery, but loyalty, a strong measure of patrician hauteur and a willingness to trust to his own luck. These were qualities that Sulla, of all men, could certainly appreciate – appreciate and mistrust.

It must have been evident to Caesar that he would never be entirely safe while Sulla remained alive. He decided to head abroad, but this was not simply a retreat into exile. Now that the fast-track to political pre-eminence had been closed to him, Caesar needed to make a splendid name for himself by more conventional means. As the priest of Jupiter he would have been forbidden to ride a horse, see armed troops or even leave Rome for more than two days at a time. For a man like Caesar, a brilliant horseman, a regular at weapons practice on the Campus, restless with energy and brio, such archaic taboos would have proved stifling. His entire education had taught him to regard glory as his birthright. Now, thanks to Sulla, he had the chance to follow his desires.

They led him to Asia. Caesar travelled there as a staff officer. A political career was impossible for any Roman who had not first served as a soldier and seen at least some action. The East promised

Caesar plenty. Mithridates, the great survivor, was licking his wounds and rebuilding his power. On the Aegean island of Lesbos, the city of Mytilene still held out against the savagery of Sulla's peace terms. Everywhere there was military and diplomatic confusion. It was a situation tailor-made for a young man on the make.

Caesar appears to have made an immediate splash. Back in Rome his hyper-fashionable dress sense had raised the eyebrows of Sulla, who had commented disapprovingly on the young man's habit of wearing his belt too loosely. In the courts of Eastern kings, however, stylish dressers were much admired, and the provincial authorities were quick to realise that the patrician dandy would be ideally cut out for diplomatic missions. Caesar was accordingly dispatched to Nicomedes, the King of Bithynia – who was indeed charmed by his Roman guest. Too charmed, perhaps. Nicomedes was believed to have demonstrated his appreciation of Caesar by taking him as a lover, a scandal that was to provide Caesar's grateful enemies with gossip for decades. All the same, whatever it may have taken, his mission was a success. Not only had he kept Nicomedes sweet, but he had managed to borrow much of Nicomedes' fleet. Sailing it to Lesbos, he joined in the assault on Mytilene, where he acquitted himself with conspicuous bravery. For having saved a number of fellow citizens in battle, he was awarded a particular honour, the civic crown, a wreath of oak leaves that served as a public token of his valour. From now on, whenever Caesar entered the Circus to watch the games, even senators would have to rise to their feet to salute him. In this way he would become a familiar figure to the people, and his name widely known. His deed would be bruited throughout Rome. This was an honour of which every citizen dreamed.

But if military glory was the surest way to win the people's hearts, Caesar was far too clear sighted to imagine that it was sufficient on its own. Even though by now it was 80 BC and Sulla had laid down his dictatorship, Caesar did not hurry back to enjoy the acclamation of the Circus. Instead he remained in the East, serving with the army, studying how provincial administration worked and winning a reputation among his superiors as a safe pair of hands. Only in 78, once Sulla was safely dead, did he finally return to Rome. In a city still terrified of the dead dictator's shadow, Caesar was like a splash of colour. 'He had a talent for being liked in a way remarkable in one of his youth, and since he had an easy, man-of-the-people manner, he made himself hugely popular with the average citizen.'[10] Effortlessly charming though Caesar was, this was still a statement of political intent. Crowd-pleasers marked themselves out as *populares*. Marius had been one, Sulpicius too. Sulla's entire political programme had been an attempt to scotch the *popularis* tradition – the tradition to which Caesar regarded himself as heir.

It did not take long for him to lay claim to it publicly. The year after his return from the East he launched an audacious prosecution of one of Sulla's former officers. The regime established by Sulla still held a firm grip on power, and the officer was predictably acquitted, but Caesar's performance proved so effective that it established him overnight as one of the most admired orators in Rome. Already a war hero, seasoned in the practical politics of diplomacy and the provinces, Caesar was now also a public figure. He was not yet twenty-four.

The sheer range of Caesar's abilities, and the energy with which he developed them, marked him out as a man with a brilliant future. Greatness clearly beckoned. Even so, exceptional as he was, Caesar was not an aberration. The Republic had bred him, and it was the Republic that had channelled all his ambitions and aspirations. Despite the anarchy of the previous decade, the Romans' loyalty to their civic traditions remained unshaken. They were weary of civil war. Family honour and personal conviction might have stamped Caesar as an enemy of Sulla's settlement, but he was

not prepared to oppose it by unconstitutional means. That attempt
had already been made. No sooner had Sulla's ashes been scattered
on the wind than one of the consuls had launched an uprising
against the entire Sullan regime. The revolt had been speedily and
brutally put down. Had Caesar joined it, as he had been invited to
do, then his career would surely have been finished. All would
have been lost on a single throw. Caesar was not interested in such
odds. Instead, as generations of the aristocracy had done before
him, he readied himself for the ascent to the top, the steady
advance from post to ever more senior post. None of his youthful
achievements had any value save as foundations for such an
attempt. The Republic had always given free rein to the desire of its
citizens for glory. Far from shattering it, this was what had raised it
to its world-conquering greatness. Caesar's early career appeared to
indicate that, despite the traumas of civil war and dictatorship,
nothing had really changed.

Round and Round the Racetrack

What we describe as a greasy pole the Romans called the 'Cursus'.
This was a word with several shades of meaning. At its most basic
level it could be used of any journey, particularly an urgent one.
Among sporting circles, however, it had a more specific connota-
tion: not only a racetrack, but the name given to the chariot races
themselves, the most popular event held in the Circus Maximus,
that great sounding board of public opinion. To call a nobleman a
charioteer was an insult – little short of describing him as a gladiator or a bandit – yet there, embedded in the language of the racing
fan, the comparison persisted, a hint of what was perhaps an
unpalatable truth. In the Republic sport was political and politics
was a sport. Just as the skilled charioteer had to round the *metae*, the

turning posts, lap after lap, knowing that a single error – a clipping of a *meta* with his wheel-hub, or an attempt to round it too fast – might send his vehicle careering out of control, so the ambitious nobleman had to risk his reputation in election after election. To the cheers and boos of spectators, charioteer and nobleman alike would make their drive for glory, knowing that the risk of failure was precisely what gave value to success. Then, once it was over, the finishing line breasted, or the consulship won, new contestants would step forward and the race would start again.

'The track which leads to fame is open to many.'[11] Such was the consolatory maxim – but it was not strictly true. Because the track in the Circus was narrow, only four chariots could compete on it at a time. In elections, too, there was a similarly restricted field. Glory was not on infinite supply. Only a limited number of magistracies could be held each year. Sulla, by increasing the number of annual praetorships from six to eight, had attempted to broaden the opportunities on offer. But because he had simultaneously neutralised the tribunate and doubled the size of the Senate, his legacy was in fact one of increased competition. 'The clash of wits, the fight for pre-eminence, the toiling day and night without break to reach the summit of wealth and power'[12] – this was the spectacle that the *Cursus* provided. Over the succeeding decades it would become ever more gruelling, carnivorous and frantic.

As they had always done, established families dominated the competition. The pressure that afflicted Caesar, of belonging to a family with few consulships to its name, was no more burdensome than the pressure on a consul's son. The greater the ancient triumphs of a house, the more horrific was the idea that these might end up squandered. To an outsider, it might appear as though all a nobleman had to do was stay in his bed, 'and electoral honours would be given to him on a plate'[13] – but nothing in Rome was ever given to anyone in that way. Nobility was perpetuated not by blood

but by achievement. A nobleman's life was a strenuous series of
ordeals or it was nothing. Fail to gain a senior magistracy or –
worse – lose membership of the Senate altogether and a nobleman's aura would soon start to fade. If three generations passed
without notable successes, then even a patrician might find that he
had a name known only 'to historians and scholars, and not to the
man in the street, the average voter, at all'.[14] No wonder, then, that
the great houses so resented intruders into the Senate. The election
of *arrivistes* to the quaestorship, first and most junior of the stages on
the *Cursus*, they might just about tolerate, but access to the more
senior magistracies – the praetorship and the consulship – was ferociously guarded. This made the task of an ambitious parvenu – a
'new man', as the Romans called him – all the more arduous. Yet it
was never impossible. As old families crashed out of the race, so new
ones might find themselves in pole position to overtake. The electorate was capricious. Sometimes, just sometimes, talent might be
preferred to a celebrated name. After all, as new men occasionally
dared to point out, if magistracies were hereditary, then what
would be the point in holding elections at all?[15]

Marius, of course, provided the great example of a commoner
made good. If it were sufficiently dashing, a military career might
well provide a new man with both glory and loot. All the same, it
was hard for anyone without contacts to win a command. Rome
had no military academy. Staff officers were generally young aristocrats adept at pulling strings. Caesar would never have had the
opportunity to win his civic crown had he not been a patrician.
Even once it had been obtained, a military posting could bring its
own problems. Lengthy campaigns, of the kind that might win a
new man spectacular glory, would also keep him away from Rome.
No one on the make could afford long-term leave of absence.
Ambitious novices in the political game would generally serve their
time with the legions, and maybe even win some honourable scars,

but few made their names that way. That was usually left to established members of the nobility. Instead, for the new man, the likeliest career path to triumph in the *Cursus*, to the ultimate glory of the consulship and to seeing himself and his descendants join the ranks of the elite, was the law.

In Rome this was a topic of consuming interest. Citizens knew that their legal system was what defined them and guaranteed their rights. Understandably, they were intensely proud of it. Law was the only intellectual activity that they felt entitled them to sneer at the Greeks. It gratified the Romans no end to point out how 'incredibly muddled – almost verging on the ridiculous – other legal systems are compared to our own!'[16] In childhood, boys would train their minds for the practice of law with the same single-minded intensity they brought to the training of their bodies for warfare. In adulthood, legal practice was the one civilian profession that a senator regarded as worthy of his dignity. This was because law was not something distinct from political life but an often lethal extension of it. There was no state-run prosecution service. Instead, all cases had to be brought privately, making it a simple matter for feuds to find a vent in the courts. The prosecution of a rival might well prove a knockout blow. Officially the penalty for a defendant found guilty of a serious crime was death. In practice, because the Republic had no police force or prison system, a condemned man would be permitted to slip away into exile, and even live in luxury, if he had succeeded in squirrelling away his portable wealth in time. His political career, however, would be over. Not only were criminals stripped of their citizenship, but they could be killed with impunity if they ever set foot back in Italy. Every Roman who entered the *Cursus* had to be aware that this might be his fate. Only if he won a magistracy would he be immune from the prosecutions of his rivals, and even then only for the period of his office. The moment it ended his enemies could pounce. Bribery, intimidation, the shameless pulling of strings – anything would be attempted to avoid a prosecution. If it did come to the law courts, then no trick would be too low, no muck-raking too vicious, no slander too cruel. Even more than an election, a trial was a fight to the death.

To the Romans, with their inveterate addiction to passionate and sensational rivalries, this made the law a thrilling spectator sport. Courts were open to the general public. Two permanent tribunals stood in the Forum, and other temporary platforms might be thrown up as circumstance required. As a result, the discerning enthusiast always had a wide choice of trials from which to choose. Orators could gauge their standing by their audience share. This only encouraged the histrionics that were anyway part and parcel of a Roman trial. Close attention to the minutiae of statutes was regarded as the pettifogging strategy of a second-class mind, since everyone knew that only 'those who fail to make the grade as an orator resort to the study of the law'.[17] Eloquence was the true measure of forensic talent. The ability to seduce a crowd, spectators as well as jurors and judges, to make them laugh or cry, to entertain them with a comedy routine or tug at their heart strings, to persuade them and dazzle them and make them see the world anew, this was the art of a great law-court pleader. It was said that a Roman would rather lose a friend than an opportunity for a joke.[18] Conversely, he felt not the slightest embarrassment at displays of wild emotion. Defendants would be told to wear mourning and look as haggard as they could. Relatives would periodically burst into tears. Marius, we are told, wept to such effect at the trial of one of his friends that the jurors and the presiding magistrate all joined in and promptly voted for the defendant to be freed.

Perhaps it is no surprise that the Romans should have had the same word, '*actor*', for both a prosecutor and a performer on a stage. Socially, the gulf between the two of them was vast, but in terms of technique there was often little to choose. Rome's leading orator in the decade following Sulla's death, Quintus Hortensius Hortalus, was notorious for apeing the gestures of a mime-artist. Like Caesar, he was a celebrated fop, who 'would arrange the folds of his toga with great care and exactness',[19] then use his hands and the sweep of his arms as extensions of his voice. He did this with such grace that the stars of the Roman stage would stand in the audience whenever he spoke, studying and copying his every gesture. Like actors, orators were celebrities, gawped at and gossiped about. Hortensius himself was nicknamed 'Dionysia', after a famous dancing girl, but he could afford to brush all such insults aside. The prestige he won as Rome's leading orator was worth any number of jeers.

Naturally, there were always opponents looking to snatch his crown. It was not in the Romans' nature to tolerate any king – or queen – for very long. Hortensius' own pre-eminence had been established during the years of Sulla's dictatorship, when the law courts had been muzzled. Committed to upholding the Senate's authority, he was strongly identified with the new regime. Such was his friendship with the dictator that it was Hortensius who had delivered Sulla's funeral speech.* In the following decade his authority as a dominant member of the Senate inevitably served to buttress his legal reputation. But as the seventies BC wore on Hortensius' pre-eminence came increasingly under threat, not from a fellow member of the senatorial establishment, not even from a member of the nobility, but from a man who was an upstart in every way.

Like Marius, Marcus Tullius Cicero was a native of the small hill town of Arpinum – and, like Marius, he was filled with ambition. There the resemblance ended. Gawky and skinny, with a long, thin

---

* Almost certainly. The evidence is not entirely conclusive.

neck, Cicero was never going to make a great soldier. Instead, even from his childhood, he planned to become the greatest orator in Rome. Sent to the capital as a boy in the nineties, Cicero's precocious aptitude for rhetoric was such that the fathers of his fellow students would come to his school just to hear him declaim. The anecdote can only have derived from the infant prodigy himself, and even to the Romans – who never regarded modesty as a virtue – Cicero's conceit was something monstrous. Not unjustified, however. His vanity was as much prickliness as self-promotion. A deeply sensitive man, Cicero was torn between a consciousness of his own great talents and a paranoia that snobbery might prevent others from giving them their due. In fact, his potential was so evident that it had been spotted early by some of the most influential figures in Rome. One of these, Marcus Antonius, provided the young Cicero with a particularly encouraging role-model. Despite coming from an undistinguished family himself, Antonius' powers of oratory had succeeded in elevating him to both the consulship and the censorship, and a status as a leading spokesman of the senatorial elite. He was one of a clique of orators who dominated both the law courts and the Senate throughout the nineties, the spokesmen for an aggressive conservatism, strongly opposed to Marius and to anyone who threatened the traditional status quo. Cicero, who was always prone to hero-worship, never forgot him. Antonius and his colleagues were to prove a formative influence on what was already a passion for the Republic's ancient order. Despite the fact that it was this same order that placed so many obstacles on the path of his advancement, Cicero never wavered in his belief that it embodied the acme of constitutional perfection. During the eighties, as the Republic began its collapse into civil war, this conviction was only reinforced.

Antonius himself was murdered following Marius' *putsch* in 87 BC. His head was displayed in the Forum and his body fed to birds and dogs. The finest orators of their generation were culled along with him. The stage had now been swept clear of competition, but Cicero, unnerved by the murder of his patrons, elected to keep his head down. He spent the years of civil war studying and honing his rhetorical skills, and not until 81, when he was already in his mid-twenties, did he finally plead in his first trial. Sulla had just resigned the dictatorship, but Cicero still had to move warily. A year after his debut in the law courts he agreed to defend the son of an Umbrian landowner charged with parricide. The case was politically highly sensitive. As Cicero was to demonstrate, the murdered man's name had been illegally slipped on to a proscription list by one of Sulla's favourite freedmen, who had then trumped up the charge of par-ricide to cover his tracks. The defendant was duly acquitted. Sulla did nothing to indicate that he was in any way displeased. Cicero's reputation was made.

But not yet to his own satisfaction. Aiming for the political heights as he was, he knew that he first had to seize Hortensius' ora-torical crown. Accordingly, he threw himself into defence work, taking on other prominent cases and using the courts to test him-self to the emotional and physical limits, 'drawing on all the strength of my voice and the effort of my whole body'.[20] After barely two years of public life he found himself near breakdown. Warned by his doctors that he was putting a terminal strain on his throat, Cicero took leave of absence and headed for Greece. For six months he stayed in Athens, sight-seeing and indulging in a spot of recreational philosophy. The city still bore the scars left by Sulla's legions, but for the Romans, Athens remained inviolably the home of beauty and culture. Tourists had begun returning there even as blood was drying in the streets. Among them had been an old schoolfriend of Cicero, Titus Pomponius, a prudent refugee from the judicial murders back in Rome. Recognising the bottom of a market when he saw it, Pomponius had invested his inheritance in provincial real estate, then used the profits to fund a life of cultured leisure in the shadow of the Parthenon. Eight years later he still had not the slightest intention of returning to Rome. His friends called him 'Atticus', a nickname that suggests how distinctive his expatriate lifestyle was perceived to be. Even so, he was a straw in the wind. 'Atticus' was not the only wealthy citizen to have witnessed a decade of violence and political collapse, and decided that there might be no shame in embracing a life of secluded ease.

Sometimes Cicero was tempted to agree. He was perfectly capable of acknowledging that 'electioneering and scrabbling after office can be a wretched business'.[21] But whether his breakdown had been purely physical, or perhaps something more, he retained his passionate conviction that public life was the ideal. Leaving Athens, he crossed the Aegean to Asia. There he met Rutilius Rufus, the old enemy of the *publicani*, and still in exile fifteen years after being convicted in the most notorious scandal in Roman legal history. Rutilius was an object lesson in how dangerous it could be to uphold ancient values against the predatory greed of corrupt officials, and yet, despite his hounding, he had not despaired of the Republic. For several days the old man entertained his guest with anecdotes about the heroic figures of his youth, then sent him onwards to visit his friend, the philosopher Posidonius, on Rhodes. The great sage's conversation would have been even more motivational than that of Rutilius. Posidonius had lost none of his faith in Rome's global destiny, nor in the traditional virtues that she could bring to such a mission: 'Rugged fortitude; frugality; a lack of attachment to material possessions; a religion wonderful in its devotion to the gods; upright dealing; care and attention to justice when dealing with other men.'[22] So the list ran on. Cicero, who had always dreamed of being the most traditional kind of Roman hero, was thrilled. What was a sore throat to stand in the way of fulfilling such a destiny? By a fortunate coincidence, the world's most famous oratory clinic was also to be found on Rhodes. The rhetorician Molon, who ran it, was typical of a new breed of celebrity professors who had begun tailoring their courses to suit high achievers from Rome. Cicero was soon able to establish himself as Molon's star pupil. Having encouraged him to adopt a more restrained manner of speaking, the teacher ended up in a theatrical state of despair, lamenting that even in the field of oratory Greece had now been surpassed by Rome. Cicero, always a sucker for flattery, was delighted. 'And so I came home after two years not only more experienced,' he recalled later, 'but almost a new person. The excessive straining on my throat had gone, my style was less frenetic, my lungs were stronger – and I had even put on weight.'[23]

Energy and self-confidence now fully restored, he returned to his legal practice in the Forum, where he continued to speak for the defence. Favours were duly earned and obligations totted up. Cicero was starting to close the gap on Hortensius. At the same time he was also picking up speed in the *Cursus*. At the age of thirty, the youngest legitimate age, he was elected to the quaestorship, the most junior of the Republic's great offices, it was true, but a start all the same and, considering his background, an impressive one. The provincial from Arpinum was now not only a magistrate of the Roman people, but a member of the Senate. Assigned to Sicily, he spent a year there, attempting to put the example of Rutilius to good use, earning the respect of the provincials, and efficiently organising shipments of grain back to Rome. The brilliant young quaestor, with his customary lack of modesty, imagined that his fellow citizens would be talking of little else. Landing at Puteoli on his way home, however, Cicero was appalled to discover that no one had even realised he had been away. Typically, however, he soon managed to put the lesson to good account:

I now believe the incident benefited me more than if everyone had been offering me congratulations. I realised that the Roman people are prone to deafness, but that their eyesight is keen and observant, and so I stopped worrying what people might hear of me, but made sure that they saw me in person every day. I lived in the full glare of their observation, I was always in the Forum. Neither sleep nor the bouncer by my door ever prevented anyone from getting to see me.[24]

For those on the *Cursus*, exposure was all. A new man had to hype himself or else he was nothing. This was a lesson that Cicero would never forget.

He was now fast becoming a fixture in Rome. People who mattered were waking up to the fact that Cicero's estimation of his own talents was not merely insufferable egotism, and that his genius as an advocate was indeed something exceptional. The more this perception gathered pace, the more Cicero could begin to eye the prospect of a real breakthrough, past the staging-post of the junior magistracies and into the laps where only the aristocracy might normally be expected to advance. To achieve that, however, he would first have to establish his dominance as an orator beyond all doubt. Hortensius had to be toppled, and not only toppled, but comprehensively drubbed. His 'tyrannical rule of the law courts'[25] had to be brought to a public end.

So it was that when Cicero finally met Hortensius face to face, in a case ripe with scandal and prurient detail, the stakes could hardly have been higher. The defendant was a former governor of Sicily, Gaius Verres, and it was Cicero, breaking the habit of a lifetime, who brought the prosecution. This was a risk, but a well-calculated one. Even upon the modest record of Roman provincial administration, Verres appears to have been a spectacular blot. Treachery and greed had been the keynotes of his career. A supporter of the

Marians for as long as the Marians clung to power, he had soon sensed the way the wind was blowing, and absconded to Sulla with his commanding officer's cash box. Armed with the favour of the new regime, Verres had duly found himself launched on a series of increasingly lucrative overseas postings. Whether he was really, as Cicero was to claim, 'distinguished by nothing except his monstrous offences and his obscene wealth',[26] he certainly seems to have had an eye for ready perks – ships, disputed wills, the daughters of his hosts. Verres' real specialisation, however, was antiques. Years of pillaging the Greek world had given the Roman upper classes an immense enthusiasm for high art. Officially, this was despised as effete self-indulgence, but behind the scenes Roman grandees would chase frantically after any valuable painting or statue that was going. Now that the days of sacking Greek cities were over, the world's first art market had developed to plug the gap. Prices had duly spiralled and dealers made fortunes. Verres' own refinement had been to bring the methods of a gangster to the trade. Even as he was mass-producing fakes he was employing a team of experts, 'bloodhounds',[27] to sniff out genuine masterpieces. Verres had a talent for making offers that no one dared refuse. One provincial elder who had tried to outface the governor had been stripped naked and lashed to an equestrian statue in the town's main square. Since it had been the dead of winter, and the statue had been made of bronze, the old man had soon changed his mind. Other trouble-makers, even Roman citizens, Verres had simply had crucified.

This, then, was the man whom Cicero had decided to go after. Despite the defendant's record, he knew that the case would be no walk-over. Verres had friends in high places and a long reach. When Cicero travelled to Sicily to pursue the case in person, he found that witnesses had a suspicious tendency to fall silent or disappear. Fortunately, following his quaestorship, he had plenty of

Sicilian contacts of his own. Evidence was everywhere, even in the silence of the countryside, its farmers ruined by Verres' depredations. Clearly, as a prosecutor, Cicero relished what he found, but as an aspiring statesman he was simultaneously appalled. Verres' corruption struck at two of his most passionately held convictions: that Rome was good for the world, and that the workings of the Republic were good for Rome. This was why Cicero could argue with a perfectly straight face that the stakes in the coming trial were apocalyptic. 'There is nowhere, no matter how distant or obscure, within the boundary of the encircling Ocean, that has not suffered from the lust for oppression which drives our people on,' he warned. If Verres were not convicted, then 'the Republic will be doomed, for this monster's acquittal will serve as a precedent to encourage other monsters in the future'.[28] Magnificently over the top though all this was, there was more to it than a mere lawyerly desire to make the flesh creep. For the sake of his political ideals, and his own self-respect, Cicero had to believe what he was saying. If the *Cursus* rewarded greed rather than patriotism, and if a man such as Verres could emerge triumphant over a man such as himself, then the Republic was rotten indeed. Here was an argument that Cicero would cling to all his life: that his own success was to be regarded as the measure of the health of Rome. Genuine principle fused seamlessly with inordinate self-regard.

It did not take Hortensius long to recognise what he was up against. Rather than argue the case on Cicero's own terms, he instead sought to have the trial postponed. It was finally set for a date just before the law courts went into a lengthy recess. For the prosecution, this was a potentially devastating setback. The conventions governing an advocate's mode of address were time-consuming, and, if Cicero were to stick to them, the trial might be expected to drag on for months. The longer it continued, the more opportunities for bribery and arm-twisting Verres would have. As the trial opened the defendant had every reason to crow. Cicero, however, had prepared a devastating ambush. Rather than follow the customary rituals of the law courts, he took the unprecedented step of laying out his evidence immediately in a series of short speeches. Hortensius needed to hear only the first of these to realise that the game was up. He waived his right of reply and the trial promptly collapsed. Verres, not wanting to wait for the inevitable conviction, cut and ran with his art collection to Marseille. Cicero celebrated by publishing the full text of the speeches he would have given, no doubt nicely sharpened for pop- ular consumption, and with a few well-aimed jabs at Hortensius thrown in for good measure. The news was broadcast all over Rome: the king had lost his crown; Hortensius' rule of the law courts had been brought to a close.

Cicero's own supremacy was to last a lifetime. The advantages this brought him in terms of influence and contacts were immense. There were also more immediate spoils. At the start of his prose- cution Cicero had claimed to have no concern with personal gain. This had been disingenuous in the extreme. As Cicero would well have known, a prosecutor had the right to claim the rank of any criminal he successfully brought to justice. Verres had been a prae- tor, and so, once he had been convicted, all the perks of his status passed directly to Cicero. Among these were the right to speak in debates ahead of non-praetorian senators. For a man of Cicero's eloquence this was a crucial privilege. His oratory could now start to weave its magic not only in the law courts, but also in the very cockpit of politics.

Of course, he still had a long way to go, but he had taken great strides. 'Reflect on what city this is, on the nature of your goal, and on who you are,' his brother advised him. 'Every day, as you are walking down to the Forum, turn these thoughts over and over in your mind: "I am a new man! I want the consulship! This is Rome!"[29]

The ultimate prize was no longer an impossible dream.

The Bull and the Boy

Throughout the seventies BC the Capitol remained a building site. The great temple of Jupiter rose gradually from its ashes long after Sulla's own had been scattered on the wind. As the very grandest of the Republic's *grands projets*, it was unthinkable that such a monument should be jerry-built. Even before its completion Cicero could hail it as 'the most famous and beautiful building' in the city.[30] Just as the destruction of the previous temple had been a portent of civil war, so the new one, clearly visible to everyone who passed through the Forum, was evidence that the gods were smiling on Rome again. Peace had returned, and the Republic itself had been restored.

Or so Sulla's adherents wished everyone to believe. This was why they were so careful to keep supervision of the Capitol in their own hands. After Sulla's death, official responsibility for the temple passed to his most distinguished associate, Quintus Lutatius Catulus. He was the very embodiment of senatorial hauteur. Distinguished ancestry combined with a reputation for stern, old-fashioned integrity to win him unrivalled authority in the Senate. He was easily Sulla's most eminent heir. Yet even Catulus' loyalty had its limits. Sulla had intended to have his name immortalised on the giant architrave of the temple, but Catulus had other plans. Rather than Sulla's name, he had the temple inscribed with his own.

Catulus' reputation for austere probity does not appear to have been damaged by this act of one-upmanship. Just the opposite, in fact. The memory of Sulla was tainted and his name regarded as malign. By promoting himself at the expense of his dead leader, Catulus was effectively acknowledging this. His commitment to Sulla's legacy remained unshaken, but the way in which it had been imposed on the Republic, at the point of a sword, was an obvious embarrassment to any self-proclaimed conservative. Together with Hortensius, who was not only his closest political ally but his brother-in-law, Catulus sought to uphold a proudly backward-looking ideal, one in which a grateful Roman people would be guided towards honour and glory by the Senate. In turn, the Senate was to be guided by men like himself, embodiments of Rome's ancient order, bound by the flinty traditions of their ancestors. The Republic, however, had many different traditions, confused and confusing, and defying codification. In the past the challenge for a citizen had always been to negotiate the swirling of their cross-currents, but Sulla, having seen where they might lead, had instead sought to tame and – in some cases – to dam their flow. Like a mighty system of dykes, his legislation served to channel what had previously been unchecked. Ritual and a shared sense of duty and obligation, these were what had defined the Republic for centuries. Unwritten custom had been all. Now that was changed. Implacable traditionalists though they were, men such as Catulus were also the heirs to revolution.

Behind the embankments raised by Sulla, however, there was a constant churning pressure. The attachment of citizens to their ancient rights was not easily diverted, and legislation against the tribunate in particular was massively resented. In 75 BC, only three years after Sulla's death, the crucial law that had prohibited tribunes from holding further office was swept away. Despite a desperate manning of the dykes by Sulla's supporters, a sizeable majority of senators ended up supporting the measure. Some caved in to a violent protest movement, others were just as likely to have been influenced by personal ambition, or by feuds with opponents, or by ties of obligation, or by totally obscure factors. Motives in Rome had always been opaque. As the traditional order of the Republic began to reassert itself, so too did the old incalculability of Roman politics. Sulla's dream — that there should be a single, public conduit to power — was crumbling along with his settlement.

How was it, for instance, that even the ineffably prestige-laden Catulus might on occasions be outsmarted in the Senate by a noto-rious turncoat, Publius Cethegus? Like Verres, Cethegus had switched to Sulla just in time to save his skin. During the siege of Praeneste he had persuaded his former colleagues to surrender, then coolly turned them over to Sulla's stormtroopers for execu-tion. Thoroughbreds such as Catulus regarded him with revulsion, but Cethegus was hardly the man to care. Rather than compete for public honours, as a Roman nobleman was expected to do, he instead wheeled and dealed behind the scenes, bribing, cajoling and scheming his way to the control of a vast bloc of senators' votes. This was a political weapon that even the snootiest of aristocrats could respect. Any time an appointment needed fixing, or a bill had to be finessed, the midnight visitors would start flitting to and from Cethegus' doors.

The idea that power might be separable from glory in this way was mystifying to most Romans; disturbing too. In any election Cethegus' unsavoury reputation would have proved lethal to his hopes. His prestige was that of a lobbyist, nothing more. No Roman who aimed for the consulship could afford to keep to the disrep-utable backrooms in which Cethegus lurked. The established aristocracy might sometimes find themselves reduced to employing him, but their reluctance to emulate his career pattern spoke loudly of their disdain. Yet there was one nobleman, of high birth and overweening, almost threatening prestige, who had already long surpassed Cethegus in the dark arts of political fixing, and who had never betrayed the slightest scruples about doing so; who glided with equal facility through the shadows and the brilliant glare of public life; who 'would go to any effort, make himself amenable to anyone he came across, just so long as he obtained what he wanted'.[31] And what Marcus Crassus wanted was clear: to be the leading citizen in the state.

In the years following Sulla's death, although he was yet to win the praetorship, still less become consul, there were those who regarded Crassus as already closing in on that ambition. The row with Sulla had proved only a limited setback. Indeed, in some ways it had served to enhance Crassus' prestige. Unlike Catulus, he stood at a remove from the dictator's regime. This was how he preferred to operate, without ties or obligations to any cause except his own. Principles, to Crassus, were merely gambits in a vast and complex game, to be adopted then sacrificed as strategy required. Rather than risk leaving his fingermarks on anything, he employed proxies to test the limits on his behalf. Of such willing dependants he had an endless supply. Crassus was assiduous at cultivating men on the make. Whether he wished to help promote them to high office or merely have them serve him as patsies or ciphers, he would treat them all with the same menacing geniality, keeping open house, avoiding airs, remembering the name of anyone he ever met. In the law courts he would tirelessly plead for defendants who might later provide him with a return. A debt taken out with Crassus always came with heavy interest.

Not for nothing did he operate as the Senate's banker. Crassus had deeper funds than anyone else in Rome. Slaves, mines and real estate remained his principal investments, but he regarded no scam as too low if it would add to his coffers. Whenever a house went up in flames, Crassus would have his private fire-brigade rush to the scene, then refuse to extinguish the fire until the owner had sold him the property cheap. Prosecuted for sleeping with a Vestal

Virgin – a particularly sacrilegious crime – he could protest that he had only seduced the woman in order to snap up her property, and be believed. Despite his reputation for avarice, however, Crassus lived simply, and when his interests were not at stake he could prove notoriously mean. A philosopher, Alexander, to whom Crassus had provided grudging hospitality, would be lent a cloak for journeys then required to give it back. Alexander, as a Greek, did not have the vote. Had he been a citizen, then he would have been encouraged to borrow far more than a cloak. The more eminent his status, the more spectacularly he would have been encouraged to fall into debt. Money was easily Crassus' favourite instrument of power. The threads of gold he spun entangled the whole Republic. Little could happen in Rome of which Crassus was not immediately aware, sensitive as he was to every tremor, every fluttering of every fly caught in his web.

No wonder that he inspired in his fellow citizens a rare dread. Campaigners against Sulla's laws would violently abuse other public figures, but never Crassus. Asked why, a tribune compared him not to a spider but to a bull with hay on its horns – 'it being a custom among the Romans', as Plutarch explains, 'to tie hay round the horns of dangerous bulls, so that people who met them might be on their guard'.[32] Such respect was what Crassus most craved. More clearly than anyone else in Rome, he had penetrated to the heart of the lesson of the civil wars: that the outward trappings of glory were nothing compared to pre-eminence among the people in the know. In a society such as the Republic, where envy and malice always followed fast on greatness, supremacy was a perilous status. Only if it inspired fear without undue resentment could it hope to endure. In the art of preserving such a balance Crassus ruled supreme.

Yet, to his chagrin, he found himself overshadowed by one rival to whom the laws of political gravity appeared simply not to apply. The show-stealer, as ever, was Pompey. Where Crassus manoeuvred to enjoy the substance of power, Pompey never ceased to enjoy the glitter and clamour of its show. But by play-acting the general he rapidly became the genuine thing, and not merely a general, but the darling of Rome. The 'teenage butcher' had an innocent's charm. 'Nothing was more delicate than Pompey's cheeks,' we are told: 'whenever he felt people's eyes on him, he would go bright red.'[33] To the public, such blushes were an endearing reminder of their hero's youth, of the boyish modesty that appeared all the more estimable when set against the unparalleled arc of his rise. What citizen had not dared to imagine himself doing as Pompey had done, seizing the chance for glory with both hands and soaring towards the stars? The Romans' tolerance of his career betrayed the depth of their crush. Far from provoking their jealousy, Pompey enabled them to live out – however vicariously – their deepest fantasies and dreams.

Pompey's superstardom was something that even Sulla had been forced to respect. No one else had tested the limits of the dictator's patience quite like Pompey, the spoiled and favoured son. After routing the Marian armies in Africa he had crossed back to Italy and refused a direct order to disband his legions – not with any intention of toppling Sulla's regime, but because, like a small child with his eye on a new and glittering treat, he had wanted a triumph. Sulla, either in mockery or admiration, had agreed to confirm his protégé in the title awarded him by his troops: 'Magnus' – 'The Great'. The granting of the supreme honour of a triumph, however, to a man who was not even a senator, had given him pause. Pompey, typically, had met condescension with impudence. 'More people worship the rising than the setting sun,'[34] he had told the ageing dictator to his face. Sulla, wearily, had at last given way. Pompey, no doubt blushing becomingly, had duly ridden in triumph through the streets, the spoils of his victories preceding him, cheered to the hilt by his adoring fans. And not even twenty-five.

After an excitement like that, the grind of a conventional political career was unappealing. No slogging after quaestorships for Pompey the Great. Having helped Catulus to put down the armed revolt that had followed Sulla's death, he had then pulled his favourite stunt of refusing to disband his troops. Again, this had not been with any intention of carrying out a coup himself, but because he had been enjoying himself too much as a general to be prepared to give up his legions. Instead, he had demanded to be sent to Spain. The province was still infested with Marian rebels, and the Senate, in confirming Pompey's command, had not been merely surrendering to blackmail. The war against the rebels promised to be deeply unglamorous, with plenty of hazards and few rewards. Catulus and his colleagues had been glad to see Pompey go.

Crassus, too, must have hoped that his young rival was riding for a fall. Once again, however, Pompey was to prove himself insufferably successful. Gruelling though the war did indeed prove to be, the rebel armies were gradually subdued. Crassus, who never ceased to regard Pompey's title of Magnus as a joke, began to hear it used ever less ironically by everyone around him. In 73 BC, the year in which Crassus became praetor, Pompey was busy extinguishing the final embers of rebellion, and settling Spain to his own immense advantage. In the province that had provided Crassus with his first army, Pompey was now securing a client base as well. Soon he would be returning to Rome, trailing clouds of glory, his army of seasoned veterans at his back. No doubt he would demand a second triumph. After that, who could tell?

Crassus, faced with a threat like Pompey, appears to have re-evaluated his strategy. Immense though his own prestige was, it remained half in the shadows. Now was the time to move into the full glare of public approbation. Crassus was no Cethegus. He knew perfectly well that power without glory would always be limited, especially in competition with a rival such as Pompey. He needed a smashing victory of his own, and fast. But where? And against whom? Suitable enemies were in frustratingly short supply.

And then suddenly, like a storm out of the blue, his opportunity arrived.

The Shadow of the Gladiator

That midsummer of 73 there was a breakout from a gladiatorial school in Campania. Like shellfish and luxury accommodation, such schools had become increasingly big business in the region. Gladiators were very much a home-grown speciality. Long before the arrival of Rome on the scene, tombs across Campania and Samnium had been the settings for duels between armed warriors, staged in honour of the spirits of the ever-thirsty dead. Even as the rituals of blood-spilling began to be commercialised by a growing Roman interest in them, gladiators continued to dress in the style of Samnite warriors, complete with brimmed helmets and ungainly, bobbing crests. As time went by, and Samnite independence faded into history, so the appearance of these fighters came to seem ever more exotic – like that of animals preserved from extinction in a zoo.

To the Romans themselves, the whiff of the foreign that clung to gladiatorial combat was always a crucial part of its appeal. As the Republic's wars became ever more distant from Italy, so it was feared that the martial character of the people might start to fade. In 105 BC the consuls who laid on Rome's first publicly sponsored games did so with the specific aim of giving the mob a taste of barbarian combat. This was why gladiators were never armed like legionaries, but always in the grotesque manner of the Republic's enemies – if not Samnites, then Thracians or Gauls. Yet this spectacle of savagery, staged in the Forum, the very heart of Rome, inspired emotions of admiration as well as loathing and contempt. The upper classes might like to pretend that the games existed for the benefit of the *plebs*, but the example of a gladiator's courage could affect anyone. 'Even when they have been felled, let alone when they are still standing and fighting, they never disgrace themselves,' enthused the sophisticated Cicero. 'And suppose a gladiator has been brought to the ground, when do you ever see one twist his neck away after he has been ordered to extend it for the death-blow?'[35] Here, in the gesture of a vanquished foreign slave, was the embodiment of everything that the Romans most admired.

Distorted though the reflection may have been, the gladiator held up a mirror to the watching crowd. He enabled the Romans to witness the consequence of their addiction to glory in its rawest, most extreme and most debased form. The difference between a senator campaigning for the consulship and a gladiator fighting for his life was only one of degree. A Roman was brought up to thrill to the spectacle of both. In a society such as the Republic, fascination with the violence of the arena came naturally. The more excessive its gore-spattered theatricality, the more the Romans found themselves craving it. But the carnage also served them as a deadly warning. Gladiatorial combat was evidence of what might happen once the spirit of competition was given free rein, once men started to fight each other not as Romans, bound by the restraints of custom and obligation, but as brutes. Blood on the sand, corpses dragged away on hooks. Should the frameworks of the Republic collapse, as they had almost done during the years of civil war, then such might be the fate of everyone, citizen as well as slave.

Here, then, was another reason why the training schools tended to be concentrated in Campania, at a safe distance from Rome. The Romans could recognise the savagery in the soul of the gladiator and feared to have it harboured it in their midst. In the summer of

73, even though the number on the run was well below a hundred, the Romans still sent a praetor to deal with them, along with an army of three thousand men. The fugitives having taken refuge on the slopes of Vesuvius, the Romans settled down to starve them out. Gladiators, however, knew all about lunging at an opponent's weak spot. Finding the slopes of the volcano covered with wild vines, they wove ladders out of the tendrils, then descended a precipice and attacked the Romans in the rear. The camp was captured, the legionaries routed. The gladiators were immediately joined by further runaways. Leg irons were melted down and forged into swords. Wild horses were captured and trained, a cavalry unit formed. Spilling out across Campania, the slaves began to pillage a region only just starting to recover from Sulla's depredations. Nola was besieged yet again, and looted. Two further Roman armies were routed. Another praetor's camp was stormed. His *fasces* were captured, and even his horse.

What had begun as a makeshift guerrilla force was now forming itself into a huge and disciplined army of some 120,000 men. Credit for this belonged to the leader of the original break-out, a Thracian named Spartacus. Before his enslavement he had served the Romans as a mercenary, and combined the physique of a gladiator with shrewdness and sophistication. He recognised that if the rebels stayed in Italy, it would be only a matter of time before their outraged masters annihilated them, so in the spring of 72 he and his army began to head for the Alps. They were pursued by Gellius Publicola, the humorist whose joking at the expense of Athenian philosophers had so amused his friends years before, and who had just been elected to the consulship. Before he could engage with Spartacus, however, the slaves met with the Roman forces stationed to guard the northern frontier, and destroyed them. The route over the Alps, and to freedom, now stood wide open. But the slaves refused to take it. Instead, meeting and brushing aside Gellius'

army, they retraced their steps southwards, back towards the heart-
lands of their masters and everything they had previously been
attempting to escape.

The Romans were perplexed by this *volte face*. One explanation
they offered for it was overconfidence: 'the slaves were stupid, and
foolishly laid too much confidence in the huge numbers who were
flocking to join their force'.[36] In fact, it would have been hard for
the rebels not to have been overwhelmed by the discovery of just
how many other slaves there were in Italy. Human beings were not
the least significant portion of the wealth to have been plundered by
the Republic during its wars of conquest. The single market established by Roman supremacy had enabled captives to be moved
around the Mediterranean as easily as any other form of merchan-
dise, and the result had been a vast boom in the slave trade, a
transplanting of populations without precedent in history.
Hundreds of thousands, perhaps millions, had been uprooted from
their homelands and brought to the centre of the empire, there to
toil for their new masters. Even the poorest citizen might own a
slave. In rich households the labour glut obliged slave-owners to
think up ever more exotic jobs for their purchases to specialise in,
whether dusting portrait busts, writing invitations or attending to
purple clothes. By their very nature, of course, such tasks were
recherché. The work of most slaves was infinitely more crushing.
This was particularly the case in the countryside, where conditions
were at their worst. Gangs were bought wholesale, branded and
shackled, then set to labour from dawn until dusk. At night they
would be locked up in huge, crowded barracks. Not a shred of pri-
vacy or dignity was permitted them. They were fed the barest
minimum required to keep them alive. Exhaustion was remedied
by the whip, while insubordination would be handled by private
contractors who specialised in the torture – and sometimes execution – of uppity slaves. The crippled or prematurely aged could

expect to be cast aside, like diseased cattle or shattered wine jars. It hardly mattered to their masters whether they survived or starved. After all, as Roman agriculturalists liked to remind their readers, there was no point in wasting money on useless tools.

This exploitation was what underpinned everything that was noblest about the Republic – its culture of citizenship, its passion for freedom, its dread of disgrace and shame. It was not merely that the leisure which enabled a citizen to devote himself to the Republic was dependent upon the forced labour of others. Slaves also satisfied a subtler, more baneful need. 'Gain cannot be made without loss to someone else':[37] so every Roman took for granted. All status was relative. What value would freedom have in a world where everyone was free? Even the poorest citizen could know himself to be immeasurably the superior of even the best-treated slave. Death was preferable to a life without liberty: so the entire history of the Republic had gloriously served to prove. If a man permitted himself to be enslaved, then he thoroughly deserved his fate. Such was the harsh logic that prevented anyone from even questioning the cruelties the slaves suffered, let alone the legitimacy of slavery itself.

It was a logic that slaves accepted too. No one ever objected to the hierarchy of free and un-free, merely his own position within it. What the rebels wanted was not to destroy slavery as an institution, but to win the privileges of their former masters. So it was that they would sometimes force their Roman prisoners to fight as gladiators: 'Those who had once been the spectacle became the spectators.'[38] Only Spartacus himself appears to have fought for a genuine ideal. Uniquely among the leaders of slave revolts in the ancient world, he attempted to impose a form of egalitarianism on his followers, banning them from holding gold and silver and sharing out their loot on an equal basis. If this was an attempt at Utopia, however, it failed. The opportunities for violent freebooting were simply too tempting for most of the rebels to resist. Here, the Romans believed, was another explanation for the slaves' failure to escape while they had the chance. What were the bogs and forests of their homelands compared to the temptations of Italy? The rebels' dreams of freedom came a poor second to their greed for plunder. To the Romans, this was conclusive evidence of their 'servile nature'.[39] In fact, the slaves were only aiming to live as their masters did, off the produce and labour of others. Even on the rampage they continued to hold a mirror up to Roman ideals.

It was no wonder that the Romans themselves, who could recognise efficient looting when they saw it, should have begun to panic. With the defeat of Gellius' army, and the Republic's other legions all serving abroad, the capital suddenly found itself perilously exposed. Crassus, who had not boasted of being rich enough to raise his own army for nothing, now made his move. His supporters in the Senate were mobilised. After a furious debate the consuls were stripped of their two legions, and Crassus was awarded sole command. The new generalissimo immediately launched a recruiting drive, quadrupling the size of the forces at his disposal. Having won the chance to establish himself as the saviour of the Republic, he did not intend to waste it. When two of his legions, in direct contradiction of his orders, engaged with Spartacus and suffered yet another defeat, Crassus' response was to resurrect the ancient and terrible punishment of decimation. Every tenth man was beaten to death, the obedient along with the disobedient, the brave along with the cowardly, while their fellows were forced to watch. Military discipline was reimposed. At the same time, a warning was sent to any slaves tempted to join Spartacus that they could expect no mercy from a general prepared to impose such sanctions upon his own men. Ruthless as Crassus was, he never did anything without a fine calculation of its effect. At a single brutal stroke the property-grubbing millionaire had transformed his image into that of the stern upholder of old-fashioned values. As Crassus would have been perfectly aware, the traditions of Roman discipline always played well with the voters.

With his authority now firmly established, Crassus moved to ring-fence the capital. Spartacus responded by retreating further south. He knew that this was where he was most likely to find new recruits. Leaving behind the town-dotted prosperity of central Italy, his army began to pass through a dreary succession of vast estates. On the plains all was desolate save for toiling chain-gangs, while across the uplands there was no one to be met with save for the occasional foreign slave driving huge flocks or herds across otherwise empty ranches. What had once been a landscape of flourishing towns and villages was now '*Italiae solitudo*' – 'the wilderness of Italy'. Driving the rebels further southwards through this desolation, and away from Rome, Crassus finally succeeded in penning them in the very heel of the peninsula. By now winter was starting to close in, and to ensure that his quarry could not escape, Crassus raised a barricade stretching from shore to shore. Spartacus found himself trapped. Two despairing attempts were made to storm the legionaries' ditch and wall. Both were repulsed, to Crassus' immense relief, for he, like his quarry, was starting to grow desperate. Time was running out. An enemy far more threatening than Spartacus was looming on the horizon. After five years in Spain, Pompey was on his way home.

When Spartacus learned of this he attempted to capitalise on Crassus' discomfiture by offering to negotiate. Crassus contemptuously refused. Spartacus responded by crucifying a Roman prisoner in full view of the barricades. All day long the screams of the dying man were borne on the icy wind to his fellow citizens. Then, as evening darkened and snow began to gust, Spartacus made a third attempt to force the barricades. This time he broke free. Fleeing Crassus, he began to zigzag northwards. Crassus, with one eye on the rebels and the other on the ever-nearing Pompey, followed him at a frantic speed, picking off stragglers in a series of escalating clashes. At last the rebels were cornered again, and Spartacus turned and prepared to fight. Ahead of his marshalled men, he stabbed his horse, spurring the possibility of further retreat, pledging himself to victory or death. Then the slaves advanced into battle. Spartacus himself led a desperate charge against Crassus' headquarters, but was killed before he could reach it. The vast bulk of the rebels' army perished alongside their general. The great slave uprising was over. Crassus had saved the Republic.

Except that, at the very last minute, his glory was snatched from him. As Pompey headed south with his legions towards Rome he met with five thousand of the rebels, fugitives from Spartacus' final defeat. With brisk efficiency he slaughtered every last one, then wrote to the Senate, boasting of his achievement in finishing off the revolt. Crassus' feelings can only be imagined. In an attempt to counteract Pompey's glory-hogging he ordered all the prisoners he had captured to be crucified along the Appian Way. For over a hundred miles, along Italy's busiest road, a cross with the body of a slave nailed to it stood every forty yards, gruesome billboards advertising Crassus' victory.

To most Romans, however, the war against Spartacus had been an embarrassment. Compared to Pompey's achievement in slaughtering thousands of tribesmen in a far-off provincial war, Crassus' rescue act in Rome's backyard was something to forget. This is why, even though both men were voted laurel wreaths, Crassus had to be satisfied with a second-class parade, touring the streets of Rome not in a chariot but on foot. No pavement-pounding for Pompey, of course. Nothing but the best for the people's hero. While Pompey, preening like a young Alexander, rode in a chariot pulled by four white horses, his trains of loot and prisoners snaking ahead of him through the streets, his adoring fans going wild, Crassus could only watch, and fume.

All the same, he was careful not to let his resentment show. Cheering crowds, however gratifying in themselves, were only means to an end, and that end, for Crassus, was always the substance of power. Infinitely more than a triumph, he wanted the consulship. With elections fast approaching, he performed a characteristically adroit somersault by suggesting to his great rival that they run on a joint ticket. Pompey, as nervous of Crassus' political skills as Crassus was of Pompey's popularity, at once agreed. Both men were duly elected unopposed.

Pompey was thirty-six when he became his country's head of state, well below the minimum age set by Sulla. Uniquely for a consul, he had never even been a senator. Nervous about making gaffes, he had to ask a friend to write him a bluffer's guide to the Senate House. Even so, for all his inexperience, Pompey was not the man to go tiptoeing around. Dash was what had raised him to the pinnacle of military glory, and dash was what he brought to the battlefields of politics. No sooner had he become consul than he introduced a bill to unmuzzle the tribunate and restore to it all the ancient privileges abolished by Sulla. The cornerstone of the dead dictator's legislation was thereby casually demolished, and a colourful, and potentially destabilising, element restored to the Republic's political life. The crowds, who had been demanding just such a measure for almost a decade, went delirious once more.

This time round, however, Crassus shared equally in their applause. Not wishing to miss out on the credit for giving the people back their ancient rights, he had been careful to co-sponsor the reform. Even Catulus, sensing the way the wind was blowing, had withdrawn his opposition. Not that this implied senatorial approval of Pompey. Far from it. His greatness, and the irregular nature of his consulship, remained deeply offensive to the traditionalist leaders of the Senate. This enabled Crassus, whose own consulship was entirely legal, to present himself as their champion.

As he was always happiest doing, he chose to hedge his bets. With one hand he splashed out on huge public banquets and free supplies of grain for the poor, while with the other he poured poison into his fellow senators' ears, abusing Pompey as a dangerous demagogue and manoeuvring to block off any further crowd-pleasing measures. As a result, rather than working together for the good of the Republic, as consuls were supposed to do, Pompey and Crassus were soon openly at each other's throat.

Nothing excited the crowds in an arena more than to see a duel between two gladiators armed with different weapons and skills. The most popular form of combat set a swordsman, magnificently armoured with breastplate and helmet, against a nimble-footed trident-carrier, whose aim was to entangle the swordsman in the meshes of a net. Pompey and Crassus provided a similar spectacle: two opponents so different, yet so evenly matched that neither could establish an advantage over the other. Rather than providing the Romans with entertainment, however, the duel shocked and disturbed them. Slaves might fight to the death, but not the consuls of the Roman people. A gladiator might slash the throat of a defeated opponent, but for one of the two heads of state to finish off his fellow was an affront to every ideal of the Republic. Ultimately, Pompey and Crassus seem to have realised that they were both being equally damaged by their feud. Towards the end of their year in office, as they were presiding at a public assembly in the Forum, a citizen suddenly interrupted them and asked for permission to relate a dream. It was granted. 'Jupiter,' the citizen announced, 'appeared to me, and told me to announce in the Forum that the consuls should not lay down their office until they have become friends.'[40] There was a long pause. Then Crassus crossed to Pompey and took his hand. He praised his rival. The two were reconciled.

The episode sounds suspiciously like a put-up job, but that makes it no less significant. A decade after Sulla's death, the idea that anyone might repeat what he had done, and establish a primacy over the state, still filled the Romans with horror. Powerful as Pompey and Crassus both were, neither could afford to be seen as more powerful than the other. This was the lesson that the Republic, even as it instilled in its citizens the desire to be the best, still insisted upon. Achievement was worthy of praise and honour, but excessive achievement was pernicious and a threat to the state. However great a citizen might become, however great he might wish to become, the truest greatness of all still belonged to the Roman Republic itself.

6

A BANQUET OF CARRION

The Proconsul and the Kings

To the Romans, it was the intoxicating quality of power that made it so dangerous. To command the affairs of one's fellow citizens and to lead them into war, these were awesome responsibilities, capable of turning anybody's head. After all, what else had the Republic been founded upon if not this single great perception – that the taste of kingly authority was addictive and corrupting? Except, of course, that with Rome now the mistress of the world and the arbiter of nations, the authority of her consuls far exceeded any king's. All the more reason, then, to insist on the checks that had always hedged about their office.

And yet – the growing extent of the Republic's reach confronted the Romans with a dilemma. Now that they were the citizens not of a small city state but of a superpower, the demands on their attention appeared limitless. Wars flared up everywhere. The more distant and intractable the enemy, the greater the logistical demands upon the consuls. In extreme circumstances, this left the Senate with little choice but to appoint a magistrate who could take their place, who could be, as the Romans put it, '*pro consule*'. As the Republic's empire expanded throughout the second century BC so recourse to proconsuls had become ever more common. By the nature of their duties, they might find themselves campaigning for a period far longer than the conventional single year. Pompey, for instance, had spent five years in Spain. The war was duly won, but not without raising conservative hackles back in Rome. Pompey's grandstanding only confirmed the Senate in its distaste for extravagant commissions of proconsular power. The situation in Spain had been desperate, but elsewhere, if Rome's interests were not immediately threatened, then senators might prefer to tolerate any amount of low-level anarchy rather than grant one of their peers a licence to clear it up.

Such was the situation with the province of Asia. There, the war against Mithridates had left a legacy of misery and chaos. The cities groaned under punitive exactions; the social fabric was nearing collapse; along the frontier, petty princelings snarled and snapped. Over the wounds of the ruined province Roman flies buzzed eagerly, not only ambitious young officers like Julius Caesar, but also the agents of the *publicani*, ruined by Mithridates, now drawn back by the scent of fresh blood. Despite everything, Asia remained Rome's richest province – and this was precisely what prevented the Senate from imposing an equitable settlement on the region. Who could be trusted to administer it? No one had forgotten the last proconsul appointed to deal with trouble in the East. Even over his own supporters, Sulla cast a warning shadow.

All the same, everyone in Rome was aware that the war against Mithridates was a job left unfinished. Eager to return to Italy and win the civil war, Sulla had consciously forfeited the Republic's right to full vengeance: his decision to spare the butcher of eighty thousand Italians when he could have destroyed him had been an act of pure expediency. It particularly rankled with those who felt themselves to have been implicated in the policy. This was why the officers left behind by Sulla continued to launch periodic raiding missions against Mithridates, trying to provoke him into a response. It was also why the senatorial establishment, led by those arch-Sullans Catulus and Hortensius, refused to ratify the peace treaty that their own generalissimo had signed. When Mithridates' envoys travelled to Rome they were fobbed off with the excuse that the Senate did not have the time to see them. For month after month the ambassadors were left to stew.

All of which left Mithridates in no doubt that the Romans wished to see him toppled. Not that he had ever given up on his own ambitions. Asia appeared as full of rich pickings as it always had. Away from the prying eyes of Roman observers, Mithridates was slowly rebuilding his offensive capability, which had been shattered by the sanctions imposed by Sulla. This time round he looked abroad, to his enemy, for inspiration. Jewelled armour and gilded weapons were out, Roman-style discipline and efficiency were in. Mithridates began to arm his infantry with the *gladius*, the short, double-edged Spanish sword that the legionaries had adopted a century or so before. The savage injuries inflicted by this weapon, used as it was to stab and strike at the vital organs, had always provoked a particular horror in the East. Now Mithridates aimed to make it his own.

To this end, in the summer of 74 BC he approached the Marian rebels in Spain and secured their assistance in equipping and training his army. The news, when it leaked out, caused outrage and horror in Rome. The Republic was never so dangerous as when it believed that its security was at stake. The Romans rarely went to war, not even against the most negligible foe, without somehow first convincing themselves that their pre-emptive strikes were defensive in nature. Mithridates, of course, was no negligible foe. Asia once again seemed at genuine risk. Such was the groundswell of outrage that the authorisation of an Eastern command at last became inevitable. But still the perilous question had to be answered: to whom?

In 74 the Sullan establishment retained sufficient control over the Senate to veto anyone too potentially overweening. This ruled out Pompey, who at this stage was in any case still embroiled in Spain, and Crassus, preoccupied as he was with his campaign for the praetorship. Fortunately for Catulus and his allies, one of their own was serving as consul that year. Lucius Lucullus was the most able and impressive of all the great noblemen who had attached their stars to the dictator and his settlement. His career, however, had been tumultuous from the start. He came from an ancient family chiefly celebrated for bad marriages and feuds. His mother had been insatiably unfaithful, and his father had indulged in a series of vendettas that had culminated in his prosecution and exile. Lucullus had inherited the blood-feud, and first made a name for himself by taking to court the man who had convicted his father. Such implacability was to prove an enduring feature of his character. It could translate all too easily into stiffness, for Lucullus was not blessed with the common touch, and rather than attempt to buy popularity, he was grimly content to be regarded as aloof and stingy. But he was also a humane and highly cultivated man, a philosopher and historian, steeped in Greek culture and possessing a genuine concern for the well-being of Rome's subjects. Inveterate in his hatreds, he was also passionate in his loyalties and beliefs. He was particularly devoted to Sulla and his memory. It was almost certainly Lucullus who had been the one officer prepared to accompany Sulla on his first march on Rome. During the war against Mithridates he had balanced his duty to his general's commands and his desire to protect the wretched Greeks with integrity and skill. Subsequently, he was the dedicatee of the dictator's memoirs, the executor of his will and the guardian of his children. Unlike Pompey or Crassus, Lucullus could be trusted to stay true to his dead friend.

The Sullan establishment was therefore quick to mobilise in his support. Other powerful factions also moved to back him. Just before winning the consulship, Lucullus had married into the very grandest of Rome's patrician dynasties. The Claudii were notorious for their arrogance and waywardness, but they could also boast half a millennium of high achievement, a record of consistency without parallel in the Republic. No family had more portrait-masks in its hall, or more hereditary clients, or more fingers in lucrative foreign pies. The prestige of the Claudii was such that it could transform even an aristocrat of Lucullus' pedigree into a frantic social climber. So eager had he been to make a Claudian match that he had even agreed to forgo a dowry. His wife, in the best tradition of Lucullan brides, had soon proved herself fabulously unfaithful, but Lucullus must have calculated that she was a price worth paying to have the Claudii on his side. Not that his in-laws were any less hard-headed in their own calculations. The head of the family, Appius Claudius Pulcher, had only recently inherited that position on the death of his father, and had two brothers and three sisters to provide for, as well as his own ambitions. Sublimely imperious and opportunistic as he was, Appius could recognise that Lucullus was his likeliest ticket to a glamorous career in the East. The baby of the family, Publius Clodius, also had military aspirations. He had just turned eighteen, the traditional age for a young Roman to start his service as a soldier. Clodius, like Appius, had his eyes fixed on the glory trail.

Before they and their brother-in-law could set out for Asia, however, Lucullus still had to be confirmed in his command. Even with the backing of both Catulus and the Claudii, he found that a majority of senators remained against him. Desperate, he realised that there was no alternative but to put out the feelers to the Senate's arch-fixer, Publius Cethegus. Too proud to do so directly, Lucullus opted for the lesser evil of seducing Cethegus' mistress, and persuading her to bring her lover on board. The ploy worked:

Cethegus began to spin and strongarm in Lucullus' favour. His bloc of tame senators was brought into play and the deadlock was broken. Lucullus was finally given his command.

With him went his consular colleague Marcus Cotta. This was either a compliment to Mithridates' fearsome reputation or, more likely, a sign that the Senate could still not quite bring itself to entrust the war to a single man. Whatever the reason for it, the arrangement rapidly backfired. While Lucullus prepared to invade Pontus, Cotta managed to lose an entire fleet to Mithridates, then narrowly avoided losing his army as well, and ended up ignominiously blockaded in a port on the Bosphorus. Mithridates was now within striking distance of the province of Asia. To the indignation of his men, Lucullus loyally aborted his own invasion and swung back to the rescue of his incompetent colleague. At the news of his approach, Mithridates raised the siege, not to retreat but to launch a full-blown invasion of Asia itself. He had every reason to feel confident: his new model army had already put paid to one consul and it outnumbered Lucullus' five legions by almost four to one. Mithridates must have thought that he had every chance of once again sweeping the Romans into the sea.

Lucullus, however, refused to take the bait. Instead of staking all on a frontal engagement, he harried the Pontic army, cutting off its food supplies, 'making its stomach the theatre of war'.[1] With the coming of winter, Mithridates was forced to retreat, leaving behind him the wreckage of his siege engines and thousands of his men. Then, in the spring of the following year, Lucullus struck again. This time he was able to launch his invasion of Pontus undistracted by events in his rear. Over the next two years he systematically destroyed Mithridates' grip on power. By 71 BC virtually the whole of the kingdom was in Lucullus' hands, and a new province stood ready to be absorbed into the Romans' empire. The war against Mithridates appeared to have been brought to a triumphant close.

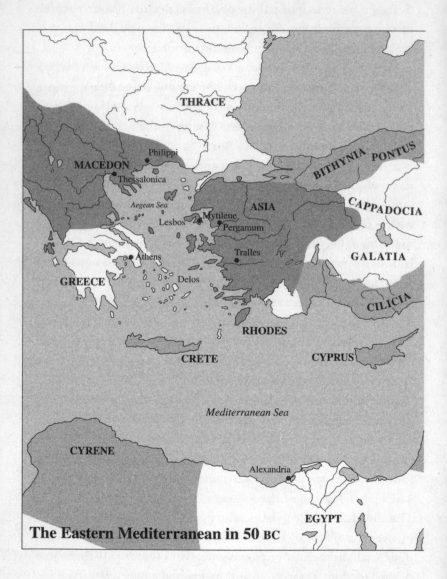

The Eastern Mediterranean in 50 BC

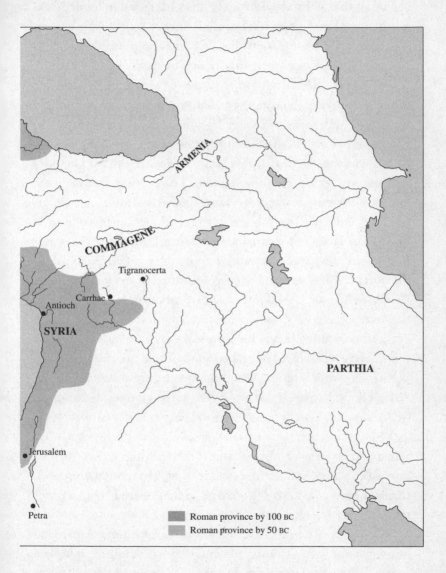

Roman province by 100 BC
Roman province by 50 BC

Except that Mithridates himself, unyielding still in his defiance, had managed to slip through Lucullus' fingers. A man with such an instinct for self-preservation that he had conditioned his body to tolerate poison was never going to accept defeat lightly. Instead, dodging every Roman attempt to capture him, he crossed the mountains to neighbouring Armenia, where he threw himself on the mercy of its powerful king, Tigranes. Lucullus promptly dispatched Appius to demand Mithridates' surrender. This was the first official mission that Rome had sent to Armenia, a kingdom that had rarely disturbed the Republic's calculations before, for it had always been remote from Rome's sphere of influence, and its rise to prominence had been only a recent phenomenon. In little more than a decade Tigranes had established himself as the dominant power in what is now Iraq, adopting the grandiloquent title of the 'King of Kings' and all the gorgeous ritual of an Oriental court. Wherever he rode he was attended by four client kings, puffing as they ran to keep pace with his horse. Whenever he sat the same kings stood waiting beside his throne, ready to hop like slaves to their master's bidding. Naturally, none of this flummery cut the slightest ice with Appius. When he met Tigranes he treated the King of Kings as the Claudii always treated everyone – with supercilious disdain. Tigranes, not used to being sneered at by anyone, still less by foreigners in their early twenties, was outraged. He refused to hand over Mithridates. The diplomatic chill further intensified when Appius, in defiance of all international niceties, turned his nose up at the gifts that Tigranes offered him and contemptuously accepted only a single cup.

So it was that Lucullus, without any official authorisation, found himself at war with a country of which few back in Rome had even heard. Despite the lateness of the season he acted with his customary decisiveness. Braving the floods of the Euphrates, he struck eastwards. His target was Tigranocerta, a city that the Armenian king had not only lovingly built from scratch, but honoured with his own royal name. At the news that his showpiece capital was under siege, Tigranes came storming to its relief. This was exactly what Lucullus had been banking on, despite the fact that he was now further from Rome than any Roman general in history, and that his legions were, as usual, vastly outnumbered. Tigranes himself, when he saw the pitiable size of the force opposed to him, joked that the Romans 'were too many to be an embassy, and too few to be an army'.[2] The royal quip provoked much sycophantic mirth, but the smile was soon to be wiped from Tigranes' face. In one of the most stunning victories in the annals of the Republic, Lucullus not only annihilated the Armenian army, but stormed Tigranocerta and literally took it to pieces. With their customary brutal efficiency, the Romans stripped the city bare, Lucullus taking the royal treasures, his men everything else. Then the city was levelled. Tigranes, a fugitive within his own kingdom, was powerless to intercede. Of the splendid monuments and palaces that the King of Kings had so recently erected to his glory barely a brick was left.

But the destruction – and the profit – were not as total as they might have been. By the accepted rules of war, Lucullus would have been perfectly justified in enslaving the defeated population. Instead he set them free. Most had been forcibly transported to Tigranocerta, and by sending them back to their homes Lucullus aimed to foster separatist movements across Tigranes' kingdom. It was a policy that combined shrewdness and humanity in equal measure. No Roman ever questioned that the defeated should pay for the privilege of being conquered, but Lucullus combined an eye for plunder with a strong sense of *noblesse oblige*. He certainly did not regard himself as an agent of slave-dealers or *publicani*, breeds for whom he had nothing but aristocratic contempt. Already, before setting out on the war against Tigranes, he had moved to deal with the blood-sucking that had disfigured Asia for so long. Interest rates had been slashed. The more scandalous abuses of the money-lenders had been banned. Regulation had been rigorously imposed. As a result, the indemnities that had left the Greek cities of Asia mortgaged to the hilt had at last begun to be paid off. Within a bare four years they would all be cleared.

The ancient ideals of the aristocracy had always provided the Republic's empire with its conscience, but in the figure of Lucullus the traditional paternalism of a senator combined with a radical new interpretation of Rome's globalising mission. His passion for Greek culture enabled him to see clearly that Roman rule had no long-term future in the East unless the Greeks were given at least a stake in it. The clemency shown to the population of Tigranocerta had reflected a consistent policy. In Pontus Lucullus had not only spared Greek cities that held out against him, but paid for their restoration once they had been stormed. By refraining from their obliteration, he invested in their future and the empire's own security and long-term health.

Naturally, this did nothing to quieten the howls of indignation back in Rome. Debt relief for provincials was not a popular policy with big business. For as long as his provincial record remained one of brilliant success, Lucullus was unassailable, but the storming of Tigranocerta marked the high point of his career, and from that moment on he became ever more vulnerable to attacks on his command. Breathtaking though his victory over Tigranes had been, he had failed in his primary objective: Mithridates remained on the loose. Throughout the following year of 68 BC, Lucullus found himself on a wild-goose chase through the badlands of Armenia, harried by an enemy that now knew better than to meet him face to face. Increasingly, his triumphs seemed to be melting in his grasp. Back in Rome the financial lobby no longer had any qualms about unleashing their tame politicians on him. Various tribunes began to strip Lucullus of his provinces one by one, snapping at him like wolves on the trail of a wounded beast. In Pontus the irrepressible Mithridates popped up with yet another army and won a series of quick victories over the Roman garrisons. Meanwhile, Lucullus himself was bogged down far away from the field of these disasters, in southern Armenia, vainly attempting to bring the war against Tigranes to a satisfactory close. The strategically important city of Nisibis was captured, and Lucullus prepared to hunker down there for the winter. But the gravest threat to his position no longer came from Tigranes. Instead, as he was soon to discover, it would emerge from within his own camp.

During that winter of 68 Lucullus was surrounded by soldiers who had been with him for six years. Subject to merciless discipline, paid the barest minimum required to keep them alive, they had been marched across mountains and over deserts, zigzagging backwards and forwards, for over a thousand miles. To many of them – and some had been serving in the East for almost two decades – home must have seemed the haziest of memories. Yet all dreamed of returning there. It was why they fought: not merely to test themselves, in the approved Roman manner, against the savagery of the enemy and the fear of a violent death, but to reclaim a status that poverty had caused them to lose. The regard of his fellow citizens was as much of an obsession for the outcast as it was for the rich. Only war enabled him to demonstrate what even the most snobbish acknowledged, that 'there is no condition so base that it cannot be touched by the sweetness of glory'.[3] And – of course – of loot.

The armies of the Republic had not always been filled with penniless volunteers. When the citizens assembled for elections on the Campus Martius, ranked strictly according to their wealth, they were preserving the memory of a time when men of every class had been drafted, when a legion had indeed embodied the Republic at war. Ironically, in those nostalgically remembered days, only those without property had been excluded from the levy. This had reflected deeply held prejudices: among the Romans, it was received wisdom that 'men who have their roots in the land make the bravest and toughest soldiers'.[4] The horny-handed peasant, tending to his small plot, was the object of much sentimental attachment and patriotic pride. Unsurprisingly, for the Republic had become great on his back. For centuries the all-conquering Roman infantry had consisted of yeoman-farmers, their swords cleaned of chaff, their ploughs left behind, following their magistrates obediently to war. For as long as Rome's power had been confined to Italy, campaigns had been of manageably short duration. But with the expansion of the Republic's interests overseas, they had lengthened, often into years. During a soldier's absence, his property might become easy prey. Small farms had been increasingly swallowed up by the rich. In place of a tapestry of fields and vineyards worked by free men, great stretches of Italy had been given over to vast estates, the 'wilderness' through which Spartacus had marched. Of course, it was not truly a wilderness, being filled with chain-gangs – but it lacked free-born citizens. The sight of 'a countryside almost depopulated, with a virtual absence of free peasants or shepherds, and no one except for barbarian, imported slaves',[5] was what had shocked Tiberius Gracchus into launching his reform project. He had warned his fellow citizens that the foundations of their military greatness were being eroded. Every peasant who lost his farm had meant a soldier lost to Rome. To generations of reformers, the miseries of the dispossessed had seemed a portent of the entire Republic's doom. The crisis in Italian agriculture was so overwhelming as to prove virtually intractable, but the crisis in military recruitment, at least, had begged an obvious reform. In 107 Marius had bowed to the inevitable: the army was opened to every citizen, regardless of whether he owned property or not. Weapons and armour had begun to be supplied by the state. The legions had turned professional.

From that moment on, possession of a farm was no longer the qualification for military service, but the reward. This was why, when the first mutterings of mutiny began to be heard in the winter of 68, the whispers were all of how Pompey's veterans, merely for fighting rebels and slaves, were already 'settled down with wives and children, in possession of fertile land'. Lucullus, by contrast, was starving his men of loot. The charge was patently untrue – Tigranocerta had fallen and been plundered only the previous year – but it was widely believed. After all, was Lucullus not notoriously mean? Had he not prevented the Greek cities back in Pontus from being looted? Were his men not 'wasting their lives roaming across the world, with no reward for their service save the chance to guard the wagons and camels of Lucullus, and their freight of gold and gem-encrusted cups'?[6]

Discipline in the professionalised legions was even more merciless than it had been in the citizen levies of the past. Sentiments of mutiny were not lightly articulated. Fortunately for the resentful soldiery, however, there was a spokesman ready to hand. To Lucullus, his identity could not have come as more of a betrayal. The young Clodius Pulcher, unlike his elder brother Appius, had not been entrusted with flamboyant foreign missions. Nor had he been given the rapid promotion that he believed, as a Claudius, was his god-given right. Piqued by the perceived disrespect, Clodius had been waiting for the opportunity to stab his brother-in-law in the back. His revenge, when it came, was brazen. The patrician scion of Rome's haughtiest family began to present himself as 'the soldier's friend'.[7] His rabble-rousing had an immediate and devastating effect: Lucullus' entire army went on strike.

Withdrawing their labour had always been the ultimate – indeed, the only – sanction available to disgruntled plebeians. In a camp on the very limits of civilisation, far from the frontiers of the empire, let alone from Rome herself, the primordial history of the

Republic was once again replayed. But the world in which the mutineers staged their strike was no longer that of their ancestors. Their
own interests were almost the least of what was at stake. Not only
was the mutiny hopelessly entangled with the snarl of aristocratic
rivalries, but it was imperilling a vast swath of territories, contain-
ing millions of Rome's subjects, and sending reverberations
throughout the whole of the East. This was the potential greatness
of a proconsul, that even in the hour of catastrophe the whole
world might seem filled by the shadow-play of his downfall. As the
legionaries sat on their weapons the news was brought to them
that Mithridates had returned to Pontus and reclaimed his kingdom. And Lucullus, the aloof and haughty Lucullus, went from
tent to tent, taking the hand of each soldier like a suppliant, and the
tears streamed down his cheeks.

The War against Terror

In the months following his soldiers' strike, as Lucullus struggled to
deal with Mithridates and mutineers simultaneously, a rare smile
would have been brought to his face by the news that Clodius had
been taken prisoner by pirates. 'The soldier's friend' had been quick
to abscond from Lucullus' camp. Heading west, he had arrived in
Cilicia, a Roman province on the south-eastern Turkish coast.
Another of his brothers-in-law, Marcius Rex, the husband of
Clodius' youngest sister, was the governor there. Marcius, who disliked Lucullus and was perfectly happy to cock a snook at him, had
rewarded the young mutineer with the command of a war fleet. It
was while out on patrol with this that Clodius had been seized.

Capture by pirates had recently become something of an occu-
pational hazard for Roman aristocrats. Eight years previously Julius
Caesar had been abducted while en route to Molon's finishing

school. When the pirates demanded a ransom of twenty talents, Caesar had indignantly claimed that he was worth at least fifty. He had also warned his captors that he would capture and crucify them once he had been released, a promise that he had duly fulfilled. Clodius' own dealings with pirates were to contribute less flatteringly to his reputation. When he wrote to the King of Egypt demanding the ransom fee, the response was a derisory payment of two talents, to the immense amusement of the pirates and the fury of the captive himself. The final circumstances of Clodius' release were lost in a murk of scandal. His enemies – of whom there were many – claimed that the price had been his anal virginity.

Whatever the rewards it was capable of bringing them, however, kidnapping was only a sideline for the pirates. Calculated acts of intimidation ensured that they could extort and rob almost at will, inland as well as at sea. The scale of their plundering was matched by their pretensions. Their chiefs 'claimed for themselves the status of kings and tyrants, and for their men, that of soldiers, believing that if they pooled their resources, they would be invincible'.[8] In the nakedness of their greed, and in their desire to make the whole world their prey, there was more than a parody of the Republic itself, a ghostly mirror-image that the Romans found unsettling in the extreme. The shadowiness of the pirates' organisation, and their diffuse operations, made them a foe unlike any other. 'The pirate is not bound by the rules of war, but is the common enemy of everyone,' Cicero complained. 'There can be no trusting him, no attempt to bind him with mutually agreed treaties.'[9] How was such an adversary ever to be pinned down, still more eradicated? To make the attempt would be to fight against phantoms. 'It would be an unprecedented war, fought without rules, in a fog';[10] a war that appeared without promise of an end.

Yet for a people who prided themselves on their refusal to tolerate disrespect, this was a policy of unusual defeatism. It was true that the rocky inlets of Cilicia and the mountain fastnesses that stretched beyond them were almost impossible to police. The area had always been bandit country. Ironically, however, it was Rome's very supremacy in the East that had enabled the pirates to swarm far beyond their strongholds. By hamstringing every regional power that might pose a threat to its interests, and yet refusing to shoulder the burden of direct administration, the Republic had left the field clear for the triumph of brigandage. To people racked by the twin plagues of political impotence and lawlessness, the pirates had at least brought the order of the protection racket. Some towns paid tribute to them, others offered harbours. With each year that passed the pirates' tentacles extended further.

Only once, in 102, had the Romans been provoked into tackling the menace head on. The great orator Marcus Antonius, Cicero's hero, had been dispatched to Cilicia with an army and a fleet. The pirates had quickly fled their strongholds, Antonius had proclaimed a decisive victory, and the Senate had duly awarded him a triumph. But the pirates had merely regrouped on Crete, and they soon returned to their old haunts, as predatory as before. This time round the Republic chose to turn a blind eye. An all-out war against the pirates promised to be as hopeless as ever, but there were also powerful interest groups in Rome that positively encouraged inactivity. The more that the economy was glutted with slaves, the more dependent it became on them. Even when the Republic was not at war this addiction still had to be fed. The pirates were the most consistent suppliers. At the great free port of Delos it was said that up to ten thousand slaves might be exchanged in a single day. The proceeds of this staggering volume of trade fatted pirate captain and Roman plutocrat alike. To the business lobby, profit talked louder than disrespect.

Many Romans, particularly in the upper reaches of the aristocracy, were naturally appalled by this blot on Rome's good name.

Lucullus was merely the boldest to take a stand against it. But the
Senate had long been in bed with the business classes. It was for this
reason, perhaps, that the most far-sighted critic of the Republic's
hunger for human livestock was not a Roman at all, but a Greek.
Posidonius, the philosopher who had celebrated the Republic's
empire as the coming of a universal state, recognised in the monstrous scale of slavery the dark side of his optimistic vision. During
his travels he had seen Syrians toiling in Spanish mines, and Gauls
in chain-gangs on Sicilian estates. He was shocked by the inhuman
conditions he had witnessed. Naturally, it never crossed his mind to
oppose slavery as an institution. What did horrify him, however,
was the brutalising of millions upon millions, and the danger that
this posed to all his high hopes for Rome. If the Republic, rather
than staying true to the aristocratic ideals that Posidonius so
admired, permitted its global mission to be corrupted by big business, then he feared that its empire would degenerate into a
free-for-all of anarchy and greed. Rome's supremacy, rather than
heralding a golden age, might portend a universal darkness.
Corruption in the Republic threatened to putrefy the world.

As an example of what he feared, Posidonius pointed to a series of
slave revolts, of which that of Spartacus had been merely the most
recent. He might just as well have cited the pirates. Bandits, like
their prey, were most likely to be fugitives from the misery of the
times, from extortion, warfare and social breakdown. The result,
across the Mediterranean, wherever men from different cultures
had been thrown together, whether in slave barracks or on pirate
ships, was a desperate yearning for the very apocalypse so feared by
Posidonius. Rootlessness and suffering served to wither the worship
of traditional gods, but it provided a fertile breeding ground for
mystery cults. Like the Sibyl's prophecies, these tended to be a
fusion of many different influences: Greek, Persian and Jewish
beliefs. By their nature, they were underground and fluid, invisible

to those who wrote history – but one of them, at least, was to leave a permanent mark. Mithras, whose rites the pirates celebrated, was to end up worshipped throughout the Roman Empire, but his cult was first practised by the enemies of Rome. Mysterious threads of association bound him to Mithridates, whose very name meant 'given by Mithra'. Mithras himself had originally been a Persian deity, but in the form worshipped by the pirates he most resembled Perseus, a Greek hero, and one from whom Mithridates, significantly, claimed descent. Perseus, like Mithridates, had been a mighty king, uniting West and East, Greece and Persia, orders far more ancient than the upstart rule of Rome. On Mithridates' coinage there appeared a crescent and a star, the ancient symbol of the Greek hero's sword. This same sword could be seen in the hand of Mithras, plunging deep into the chest of a giant bull.

In a distortion of the original Persian myth, the bull had become the symbol of the Great Antagonist, the Principle of Evil: was this how the pirates saw Rome? The cloak of secrecy that veiled their mysteries makes it impossible to know for sure. What is certain, however, is that the alliance between the pirates and Mithridates, which was very close, went far beyond mere expediency. And what is equally certain is that the pirates, preoccupied with plunder as they were, also saw themselves as the enemies of everything embodied by Rome. No opportunity was wasted to trample upon the Republic's ideals. If a prisoner was discovered to be a Roman citizen, the pirates would first pretend to be terrified of him, grovelling at his feet and dressing him in his toga; only when he was wearing the symbol of his citizenship would they lower a ladder into the sea and invite him to swim back home. Raiding parties would deliberately target Roman magistrates and carry off the symbols of their power. Because Antonius had abducted treasures to lead in triumph through Rome, the pirates struck back by seizing his daughter from her villa on the coast. These were carefully calculated outrages, reflecting a shrewd awareness of Roman psychology. They struck at the very essence of the Republic's prestige.

Honour, naturally, demanded a response – but so too, increasingly, did commercial self-interest. Roman business, having sponsored a monster, now began to find itself menaced by its own creation. The pirates' growing command of the sea enabled them to throttle the shipping lanes. The supply of everything, from slaves to grain, duly dried to a trickle and Rome began to starve. Still the Senate hesitated. Such had been the growth in piracy that it was clear that nothing less than a Mediterranean-wide command would prove sufficient to deal with it. This, to many senators, seemed to be a proconsulship too far. In the end, a second Marcus Antonius, the son of the great orator, was awarded the command in 74 BC, but his chief qualification was certainly not any hereditary talent for fighting pirates. Rather, it was his very incompetence that recommended him – as it was waspishly observed, 'it is no great deal, the promotion of those whose power we have no cause to fear'.[11] Antonius' first measure was to indulge in some lucrative freebooting of his own off Sicily; his second to be roundly defeated by the pirates off Crete. Roman prisoners were bound in the fetters that they had brought to chain the pirates, then left to dangle from the yardarms of the pirates' ships.

Even this bobbing forest of gibbets was not to be the most humiliating symbol of superpower impotence. In 68 BC, as Lucullus was striking east against Tigranes, the pirates responded by launching an attack against the very heart of the Republic. At Ostia, where the Tiber met the sea, barely fifteen miles from Rome, the pirates sailed into the harbour and burned the consular war fleet as it lay in dock. The port of the hungry capital went up in flames. The grip of famine tightened around Rome. Starving citizens took to the Forum, demanding action on the crisis and the appointment of a proconsul to resolve it – not a paper tiger like Antonius, but a man who could get the job done. Even now, the Senate dug in its heels. Catulus and Hortensius understood perfectly well who their fellow citizens wanted. They knew who was waiting in the wings.

Ever since his consulship, Pompey had been deliberately lying low. His displays of modesty, like all his displays, were carefully staged for their effect. 'It was Pompey's favourite tactic to pretend that he was not angling for the things which in fact he wanted the most',[12] a shrewd gambit at the best of times, but especially so when his ambitions aimed as high as they did now. Instead of vaunting himself, he had adopted Crassus' stratagem of employing proxies to do the boasting on his behalf. Caesar was one of these, a lone voice in favour of Pompey in the Senate – less out of any great enthusiasm for Pompey than because he could see clearly how the dice were going to fall. Now that Sulla's reforms had been rolled back, the tribunes were back in play. Not for nothing, during his consulship, had Pompey restored their ancient powers. The tribunes had helped him to dismantle Lucullus' command, and it was a tribune, in 67 BC, who proposed that the people's hero be given a sweeping licence to deal with the pirates. Despite an impassioned appeal from Catulus not to appoint 'a virtual monarch over the empire',[13] the citizens rapturously ratified the bill. Pompey was granted the unprecedented force of 500 ships and 120,000 men, together with the right to levy more, should he decide that they were needed. His command embraced the entire Mediterranean, covered all its islands, and extended fifty miles inland. Never before had the resources of the Republic been so concentrated in the hands of a single man.

In every sense, then, Pompey's appointment was a leap into the dark. No one, not even his supporters, quite knew what to expect. The decision to mobilise on such a scale had in itself been a gesture of despair, and the pessimism with which the Romans regarded even their favourite's prospects was reflected in the length of his commission: three years. As it proved, to sweep the seas clear of pirates, storm their last stronghold and end a menace that had been tormenting the Republic for decades took the new proconsul a mere three months. It was a brilliant victory, a triumph for Pompey himself and an eye-opening demonstration of the reserves of force available to Rome. Even the Romans themselves appear to have been a little stunned. It suggested that no matter how hesitant their initial response to a challenge might be, there was still no withstanding them should their patience be pushed too far. Campaigns of terror were containable. Rome remained a superpower.

Yet, even though Pompey's victory had demonstrated once again that the Republic could do pretty much as it pleased, there was none of the savagery that had traditionally been used to drive that lesson home. In a display of clemency quite as startling as his victory, Pompey not merely refrained from crucifying his captives, but bought them plots of land and helped to set them up as farmers. Brigandage, he had clearly recognised, was bred of rootlessness and social upheaval. For as long as the Republic was held responsible for these conditions, there would continue to be a hatred of Rome. Yet it hardly needs emphasising that the rehabilitation of criminals was not standard Roman policy. Perhaps it is significant that Pompey, midway through his campaign against the pirates, should have found the time to visit Posidonius on Rhodes. We know that he attended one of Posidonius' lectures and then spoke privately with him afterwards. Since it was not the role of philosophers to challenge Roman prejudices, but to give them an intellectual gloss, we can be certain that Pompey would have heard nothing that he did not want to hear – but Posidonius must have helped him, at the very least, to clarify his opinions. Posidonius himself was deeply impressed with his protégé. In Pompey he believed that he had finally found the answer to his prayers: a Roman aristocrat worthy of the values of his class. 'Always fight bravely', he advised the parting proconsul, 'and be superior to others', a pithy admonition from Homer that Pompey was delighted to accept.[14] This was the spirit in which he pardoned the pirates. So it was that the town where he settled them was titled Pompeiopolis: his mercy and munificence were to contribute eternally to the greatness of his name. Stern in war, gracious in peace, it was no wonder that Posidonius could hail him as the hero of the hour.

But Pompey, greedy as ever, wanted more. It was not enough to be the new Hector. From his earliest days, teasing his quiff in front of the mirror, he had dreamed of being the new Alexander. Now he was determined to seize his chance. The East lay all before him, and with it the prospect of glory such as no Roman citizen had ever won before.

The New Alexander

One day in the spring of 66 BC Lucullus watched a cloud of dust rise up on the horizon. Although he was camped by the side of a wood, the plain that stretched before him was parched and treeless. When he finally made out an endless line of troops emerging from the dust, he saw that the lictors of the commanding general had wreathed their rods in laurel, and that the leaves were dry. His own lictors rode out to greet the new arrivals, and in a gesture of welcome handed over fresh laurel. In exchange they were given the faded wreaths.

By such a sign did the gods confirm what everyone already knew. Since the mutiny the winter before Lucullus had found his authority withering by the day. Barely on speaking terms with his men, and certainly unable to trust them in combat, he had dragged his army in slow retreat back from Armenia. Licking his wounds in the uplands west of Pontus, he had been forced to watch helplessly as Mithridates entrenched himself once again in his old kingdom. Yet this was not the worst agony. Lucullus' replacement was the very man who had always most hankered after his proconsulship, and who had connived with the financiers and their tame tribunes to hack away at his command.

In the aftermath of the victory over the pirates there had been few prepared to stand in the way of Pompey the Great. The majority of the Senate, recognising a winner when they saw one, had abandoned their qualms and voted to award him further, and even more unprecedented, powers. Not only was he to command the largest force ever sent to the East, but he was given the right to make war and peace as he chose, on the spot. Lucullus, by contrast, had been left with nothing. Plenty of his erstwhile allies, including two former consuls and a raft of ancient names, had eagerly signed up to serve with the new proconsul. Lucullus, watching as his fresh laurel wreaths were handed over to Pompey's lictors, would have recognised a host of impeccably aristocratic faces in his enemy's train. Did they meet his gaze or, embarrassed, look away? Triumph, failure – both, to the Romans, provided an irresistible spectacle.

Unsurprisingly, the meeting between Lucullus and Pompey, conducted with chilly politeness at first, soon degenerated into a slanging match. Pompey jeered at Lucullus for his inability to finish off Mithridates. Lucullus retorted with a bitter description of his replacement as a carrion bird maddened by blood, only ever settling on the carcasses of wars fought by better men. The abuse turned so violent that the two generals finally had to be pulled apart, but it was Pompey who was the proconsul and could therefore land the killer-blow. He stripped Lucullus of his remaining legions, then continued on his way, leaving Lucullus to nurse his injured dignity, and depart, a private citizen again, on the long road back to Rome.

Even so, his insult had been the more wounding. Events were to confirm his boast that he had broken the backs of both Mithridates and Tigranes, and in Pompey's eagerness to fix on his prey there was indeed something of the scavenger smelling blood upon the wind. For the last time Mithridates was swept from his kingdom. As usual he vanished into the mountains, but even though he evaded his pursuers yet again, all he had left to menace them now was a phantom, his name. Tigranes, recognising overwhelming force when he saw it, and having no wish to take to the mountains himself, hurried to accommodate himself to Pompey's dispensation. Arriving at the Roman camp, he was forced to dismount and hand over his sword. Proceeding on foot to where Pompey was waiting, he removed his royal diadem, then knelt in his gold and purple to grovel in the dust. Before he could prostrate himself, however, Pompey had taken his hands and raised him back up to his feet. Mildly, he invited the King to sit by his side. Then, in a polite tone, he began to set out the peace settlement. Armenia was to become a Roman dependency. Tigranes was to hand over his son as a hostage. In return he would be permitted to retain his throne, but not much else. The wretched King hurriedly assented to the terms. To celebrate, Pompey then invited Tigranes to his field tent to dine. This was the very model of a Roman general's behaviour: after the ruthless assertion of the Republic's might, the gracious gifting of scraps from the table.

Pompey's genius for posing had found its perfect stage in the East. Acutely conscious that the eye of history was upon him, the great man rarely did anything without angling his profile towards it. As Alexander had done, he had even brought a tame historian with him, to chronicle every act of heroism, every magnanimous deed. He fought campaigns as he handled kings, with half an eye to providing sensational copy. It was not enough to thrash recalcitrant Orientals. He had to tangle with poisonous snakes, hunt after Amazons, push eastwards towards the great ocean that encircled the world. And all the while, uninhibited by finicky cavils from the

Senate, he could fuss with territories as though they were counters on a gaming board, rearranging them as he pleased, handing out crowns, abolishing thrones, the still-boyish master of the fate of millions.

Not that Pompey ever forgot that he was a magistrate of the Roman people. After all, a citizen was only as great as the glory he brought to the Republic. Pompey's proudest boast would be that 'he had found Asia on the rim of Rome's possessions, and left it in the centre'.[15] His humbling of kings, his disposal of kingdoms, his far-flung campaigns at the edge of the world, all had this achievement as their strategic goal. When Pompey raised Tigranes from the dust, he did so as the stern protector of the Republic's interests. The scene would otherwise have lacked its heroic glow. The flummery of kingship was all very well for impressing barbarians, but its only true value was to serve as a backdrop to the free-born virtues of Rome. No wonder that Pompey's apeing of Alexander, however much it might provoke the contemptuous snorts of rivals like Crassus, was so relished by the vast majority of his fellow citizens. They could instinctively recognise it for what it was: not a display of impatience with the Republic, but, on the contrary, an affirmation of its superior dignity and worth.

For the memory of Alexander's greatness had always served the Romans as a reproach. Even worse, it provided an inspiration to their foes. In the East the model of kingship established by Alexander had never lost its allure. For more than a century it had been neutered and systematically humiliated by Rome, yet it remained the only credible system of government that could be opposed to the republicanism of the new world conquerors. Hence its appeal to monarchs, such as Mithridates, who were not even Greek, and hence, most startling of all, its appeal to bandits and rebellious slaves. When the pirates had called themselves kings, and affected the gilded sails and purple awnings of monarchy, this had not been mere vanity, but a deliberate act of propaganda, as public a statement as they could make of their opposition to the Republic. They knew that the message would be read correctly, for invariably, whenever the order of things had threatened to crack during the previous decades, rebellion had been signalled by a slave with a crown. Spartacus' communism had been all the more unique for the fact that the leaders of previous slave revolts, virtually without exception, had aimed to raise thrones upon the corpses of their masters. Most, like the pirates, had merely adopted the trappings of monarchy, but there were some who had brought the fantastical worlds of romances to life, and claimed to be the long-lost sons of kings. This, in a world ruled by a republic, was what revolution had come to mean. The royal pretensions of slaves fed naturally into the swirling undercurrents of the troubled age, the prophecies, which Mithridates' propaganda had exploited so brilliantly, of the coming of a universal king, of a new world monarchy, and the doom of Rome.

So when Pompey presented himself as the new Alexander, he was appropriating a dream shared by potentate and slave alike. If any Roman was qualified to appreciate this, it was Pompey himself. The conqueror of the pirates, and the patron of Posidonius, he would have been perfectly aware of the menacing links that existed between kingship and revolution, between the uppitiness of Oriental princelings and the resentments of the dispossessed. Having stamped out the threat of piracy, it was now his aim to stamp out similar threats wherever they smouldered throughout the East. One realm in particular appeared to invite his intervention. For decades Syria had served as a breeding ground for anarchy and violent visions of apocalypse. During the first great slave revolt against Roman rule, in Sicily back in 135, the leader of the revolt had even called his followers 'Syrians' and himself 'Antiochus', the latter a title filled with resonance. Kings of that name had once ruled a great empire, a successor to that of Alexander himself, stretching at its height to the gates of India. Those glory days were long gone. Tolerated by the Republic precisely because it was weak, all that was left to the dynasty was its heartland of Syria. Even that, in 83, had been stolen by Tigranes, and it was only Lucullus, resuscitating what had appeared beyond all hope of resurrection, who had placed an Antiochus back on the Syrian throne. Pompey, glad of the chance to reverse anything that his predecessor had done, pointedly refused to recognise the new king. But personal spite, while it may have added relish to this decision, did not explain it. Antiochus was both too enfeebled and too dangerous to be permitted to survive. His kingdom was in chaos, a focal point for social revolution, while the glamour of his name continued to cast its hypnotic and subversive spell. If Syria were left as it was, a festering sore on the flank of Rome's possessions, then there was the constant danger that its poison might infect a new Tigranes, a new generation of pirates or rebellious slaves. This, to Pompey, was intolerable. Accordingly, in the summer of 64, he occupied Antioch, the capital of Syria. Antiochus, the thirteenth king of that name to have held the throne, fled into the desert, where he was ignominiously murdered by an Arab chieftain. The wraith of his kingdom was dispatched to its grave at last.

In its place a new empire was rising. Rather than the Senate's traditional isolationism, Pompey embodied a new doctrine. Wherever Roman business interests were threatened, the Republic would intervene — and, if need be, impose direct rule. What had once been a toehold in the East was now to be a great tract of provinces. Beyond them was to stretch an even broader crescent of client states. All were to be docile and obedient, and all were to pay a regular tribute. This, henceforward, was what the *pax Romana* was to mean. Pompey, who had won his proconsulship with the backing of the financial lobby, had no intention of repeating Lucullus' error by treading on its toes. But while he was happy to identify himself with its interests, he was also careful not to appear its tool. The age of unbridled exploitation was over. Bureaucracy was no longer to be uninhibitedly laissez-faire. In the long run, as even the business lobby had come to recognise, this was a policy that promised just as many pickings as before. It was certainly in no one's interest to kill off geese that were laying such splendid golden eggs.

The great achievement of Pompey's proconsulship was to demonstrate that the concerns of business could truly be squared with the ideals of the senatorial elite. It established a blueprint for Roman rule that was to endure for centuries. It also, not coincidentally, raised Pompey himself to a pinnacle of glory and wealth. The client-rulers who swelled the train of Rome also swelled his own. In the autumn of 64 Pompey headed south from Antioch to bag a few more. His first target was the fractious kingdom of Judaea. Jerusalem was occupied. The Temple, despite desperate resistance, was stormed. Pompey, intrigued by reports of the Jews' peculiar god, brushed aside the protests of the scandalised priests and passed into the Temple's innermost sanctum. He was perplexed to find it empty. There can be little doubt as to whom Pompey thought was more honoured by this encounter, Jehovah or himself. Not wishing to aggravate the Jews any further, he left the Temple its treasures, and Judaea a regime headed by a tame high priest. Pompey then marched south, aiming to strike across the desert for Petra, but he was never to reach the rose-red city. Midway he was halted by dramatic news: Mithridates was dead. The old king had never given up on his defiance, but when even his son turned against him and blockaded him in his chambers, Rome's arch-enemy had been cornered at last. After vainly attempting to poison himself he had finally been dispatched by one of the few things to which he had not cultivated an immunity, the sword point of a loyal guard. Back in Rome the news was greeted with ten days of public thanksgiving.

Pompey himself, after announcing the news to his cheering legions, sped back to Pontus, where Mithridates' body had been brought by his son. Not caring to inspect the corpse, Pompey contented himself with rifling through the dead king's belongings. Among them he found a red cloak that had once belonged to Alexander. Looking ahead to his triumph, he promptly tried it on for size.

Few would have denied that it was his by right. His achievements stood comparison with any in the history of Rome. Yet as the great man prepared to head for home at last, the East finally pacified, his immense task done, there were few of his fellow citizens who did not find themselves unsettled by the prospect of his return. His wealth was beyond the dreams of avarice – even of Crassus himself. His glory was so dazzling as to blot out every rival. Could a Roman become the new Alexander while also remaining a citizen? In the last resort only Pompey himself could answer this question – but there were plenty, as they waited for him, prepared to fear the worst. Much had happened in Rome during Pompey's five-year absence. Once again, the Republic had found itself in the grip of crisis. Only time would tell whether Pompey's homecoming would help resolve it, or lead to a crisis greater still.

7

THE DEBT TO PLEASURE

Shadows in the Fishpond

While Pompey lorded it over the East the man he had replaced indulged himself with the most flamboyant sulk in history.

Lucullus had every reason to feel peeved. His enemies, not content with having had him dismissed from his command, continued to goad him on his return to Rome. Most vindictively of all, they blocked his triumph. In doing so they cheated him of the ultimate tribute that the Republic could pay to one of its own. Driven through the grateful streets, borne on the clamour of deafening applause and acclamation, a general on the day of his triumph became something more than a citizen, something more even than a man. Not only was he dressed in the gold and purple of a king, but his face was painted red like the holiest statue in Rome, that of Jupiter in the great temple on the Capitol. To partake of the divine was a glorious, intoxicating, perilous thing, and during the few brief hours when it was permitted a general became a spectacle of wonder and edification. To the Roman people who lined the streets to cheer him, he was living reassurance that ambition might indeed be sacred, that in struggling to reach the top, and to achieve great things, a citizen was fulfilling his duty to the Republic and to the gods.

Few could doubt that the victor of Tigranocerta merited such an honour. Even Pompey, stripping Lucullus of his legions, had left him a few thousand men for his triumphal procession. Yet in the Republic there was nothing so awe inspiring that it was not also touched by the sordid day-to-day. Those who had profited from intrigue – as Lucullus had done when he had first won his pro-consulship – might expect to suffer from it too. These were the rules by which every politician played. The sniping of enemies was proportionate to the stature of a man. The prospect of what Lucullus might achieve as a civilian filled his opponents with fear, just as it inspired his allies with high hopes. Behind the scenes assorted grandees did what they could to reverse the opposition of the tribunes, and see that Lucullus was granted his triumph, but however genuine their outrage, and however loud their cries of scandal, they had their own selfish reasons for campaigning on his behalf. No friendship in Rome was ever entirely devoid of polit-ical calculation.

But Catulus and his supporters, who had been relying upon Lucullus to take his place as a leader of their cause, were to be dis-appointed. With humiliation following upon humiliation, something inside Lucullus appeared to have snapped. The man who had spent six gruelling years in pursuit of Mithridates was by now drained of enthusiasm for combat. He abandoned the political battlefield to others, and surrendered himself instead, with all the ostentation he could muster, to pleasure.

In the East, as a triumphant assertion of the Republic's greatness, Lucullus had ripped apart the palaces and pleasure-gardens of Tigranes until not a trace of them had remained. Now, returned to Italy, he set about surpassing all the wonders he had destroyed. On a ridge beyond the city walls he built a park on a scale never before witnessed in Rome, a riot of follies, fountains and exotic plants, many of them brought back from his sojourn in the East, including a souvenir from Pontus, most enduring of all his legacies to his homeland, the cherry tree. At Tusculum his summer villa was extended until it spread for miles. Most spectacularly of all, along the Bay of Naples, where Lucullus had no fewer than three villas, he built gilded terraces on piers, fantastical palaces shimmering above the sea. One of these same villas had belonged to Marius, the very estate to which the old general had refused to retire, dreaming of yet more campaigns, yet more triumphs. Lucullus, who had bought the villa for a record price from Sulla's daughter, seemed determined to transform it and everything else he owned into monuments to the vanity of ambition. His extravagances were deliberately raised to be offensive to every ideal of the Republic. Once, he had lived by the virtues of his class. Now, retiring from public life, he trampled on them. It was as though, embittered by the loss of first power and then honour, Lucullus had turned his contempt upon the Republic itself.

In place of a triumph he instead flaunted his fabulous appetites. Sulla, to celebrate his victories, had feasted the whole of Rome, but Lucullus, with a greater expenditure of gold, positively revelled in private – and even solitary – excess. Once, when he dined alone and his steward provided him with a simple meal, he cried out in indignation, 'But Lucullus is feasting Lucullus today!'[1] The phrase was widely repeated, amid much shaking of heads, for nothing was more scandalous to the Romans than a reputation for enjoying *haute cuisine*. Celebrity chefs had long been regarded as a particularly pernicious symptom of decadence. Back in the virtuous, home-spun days of the early Republic, so historians liked to claim, the cook 'had been the least valuable of slaves', but no sooner had the Romans come into contact with the fleshpots of the East than 'he began to be highly prized, and what had been a mere function instead came to be regarded as high art'.[2] In a city awash with new money and with no tradition of big spending, cookery had rapidly become an all-consuming craze. Not only cooks but ever more exotic ingredients had been brought into Rome on a ceaseless flood of gold. To those who upheld the traditional values of the Republic, this mania threatened a ruin that was as much moral as financial. The Senate, alarmed, had accordingly attempted to restrain it. As early as 169 the serving of dormice at dinner parties had been banned, and later Sulla himself, in a fine show of hypocrisy, had rushed through similar laws in favour of cheap, homely fare. All mere dams of sand. Faddishness swept all before it. Increasingly, millionaires were tempted to join their cooks in the kitchens, trying out their own recipes, sampling ever more outlandish dishes. This was the crest of the wave that Sergius Orata had ridden to such lucrative effect, but oysters did not lack for rivals in the culinary stakes. Scallops, fatted hares, the vulvas of sows, all came suddenly and wildly into vogue, and all for the same reason: for in the soft-ness of a flesh that threatened rapid putrescence yet still retained its succulence, the Roman food snob took an ecstatic joy.

Most treasured, most relished, most savoured of all were fish. So it had always been. The Romans had been stocking lakes with spawn for as long as their city had been standing. By the third century BC Rome had come to be ringed by ponds. Freshwater fish, however, because so much easier to catch, were far less prized than species found only in the sea – and as Roman gastronomy grew ever more exotic, so these became the focus of intensest desire. Rather than remain dependent upon tradesmen for their supply of turbot or eel, the super-rich began to construct salt-water ponds. Naturally, the prodigious expense required to maintain these only added to their appeal.

The extravagance of it all was justified by the ancient principle that a citizen should subsist off the produce of his land. Roman nostalgia for the countryside cut across every social boundary. Even the most luxurious of villas also served as farms. Inevitably, among the urban elite, this tended to encourage a form of play-acting that Marie-Antoinette might have recognised. A favourite affectation was to build couches in a villa's fruit store. A particularly shameless host, if he could not be bothered to grow and harvest his own fruit, might transport supplies from Rome then arrange them prettily in his store for the delectation of his guests. Pisciculture had a similarly unreal quality. Self-sufficiency in fish came at a staggering price. As agriculturalists were quick to point out, homemade lakes 'are more appealing to the eye than to the purse, which they tend to empty rather than fill. They are expensive to build, expensive to stock, expensive to maintain.'[3] The claim that fish-breeding had anything to do with economy became increasingly impossible to justify. In 92 BC a censor, no less, a magistrate elected to maintain the Republic's stern ideals, had burst into tears at the death of a lamprey. He had grieved, it was reported, not for a ruined supper but 'as though he had lost a daughter'.[4]

Thirty years later the craze had reached epidemic proportions. Hortensius, rather than even contemplate eating one of his beloved mullets, would send to Puteoli if he ever needed fish for his table. As one of his friends commented wonderingly, 'You would sooner get him to let you take his carriage-mules from his stable and keep them, than remove a bearded mullet from his fish-pond.'[5] In pisciculture, as in every other form of extravagance, however, it was Lucullus who set the most dazzling standards of notoriety. His fish-ponds were universally acknowledged to be wonders, and scandals, of the age. To keep them supplied with salt water, he had tunnels driven through mountains; and to regulate the cooling effect of the tides, groynes built far out into the sea. The talents that had once been devoted to the service of the Republic could not have been more spectacularly, or provocatively, squandered. '*Piscinarii*', Cicero called Lucullus and Hortensius – 'fish fanciers'. It was a word coined half in contempt and half in despair.

For Cicero, with the acuity of a man who wanted desperately all that Lucullus was busy throwing away, could penetrate to the heart of the mania for fish-ponds. It spoke of a sickness in the Republic itself. Rome's public life was founded on duty. Defeat was no excuse for retiring from the commitments that had made the Republic great. The cardinal virtue for a citizen was to hold one's ground, even to the point of death, and in politics as in warfare one man's flight threatened the entire line of battle. Cicero, despite having seized Hortensius' oratorical crown, had no wish to see his rival retire. The new man closely identified himself with the principles for which great aristocrats such as Hortensius and Lucullus had always stood. As he drew, step by careful step, ever closer to the supreme prize of the consulship, so it appalled him to see men he regarded as his natural allies sitting by their fish-ponds, feeding their bearded mullets by hand, leaving the Republic to twist in the wind.

But for Hortensius, as for Lucullus, the consciousness of having been bested, of holding only second place, was a burning agony. The orator's retirement was not as total as the proconsul's, but it was, in its own way, just as pointed. Increasingly, the law courts in which Hortensius had been so publicly routed by Cicero came to serve him as a stage for his eccentricities. A man who had brushed against his toga and damaged the arrangement of the folds was prosecuted for insulting behaviour. Just as flamboyantly, in the middle of a trial Hortensius moved for an adjournment, explaining that he wished to hurry back to his estate and supervise the irrigation of his plane trees with vintage wine. His opponent on this occasion, as on so many others, was Cicero. Wild extravagance was one arena in which the parvenu could hardly compete.

So it was that the ancient Roman yearning for glory turned pathological. Lucullus, splitting mountains for the benefit of his fish, and Hortensius, serving peacocks for the first time at a banquet, were both still engaged in the old, familiar competition to be the best. But it was no longer the desire for honour that possessed them. Instead it was something very like self-disgust. Lucullus, we are told, squandered his money with every appearance of contempt, treating it as though it were something 'captive and barbarian', to be spilled like blood.[6] No wonder that his contemporaries were appalled and perplexed. Not properly understanding his condition, they explained it as madness. Ennui was an affliction unknown to the Republic. Not so to later generations. Seneca, writing in the reign of Nero, at a time when the ideals of the Republic had long since atrophied, when to be the best was to risk immediate execution, when all that was left to the nobility was to keep their heads down and tend to their pleasures, could distinguish the symptoms very well. 'They began to seek dishes,' he wrote of men such as Lucullus and Hortensius, 'not to remove but to stimulate the appetite.'[7] The fish-fanciers, sitting by their ponds and gazing into their depths, were tracing shadows darker than they understood.

Party People

Self-indulgence did not have to be a stigma of defeat. What to great noblemen were the honeyed venoms of retirement might well to others promise opportunity. A few short miles down the coast from Lucullus' villa at Naples stood the fabled beach resort of Baiae. Here, out into the glittering blue of the bay, stretched gilded pier after gilded pier, cramping the fish, as the humorists put it. To the Romans, Baiae was synonymous with luxury and wickedness. A holiday there was always a source of guilty pleasure. No statesman would ever willingly admit to spending time in a town so notorious, yet every season Rome would empty of the upper classes as they headed south to its temptations. It was this that made Baiae such a hot spot for the upwardly mobile. Whether at its celebrated sulphur baths or over a dish of the local speciality, purple-shelled oysters, the resort offered precious entrées into high society. Baiae was a party town, and the strains of music and laughter were forever drifting through the warm midnight air, borne from villas, or the beach, or yachts out in the bay. No wonder that the place drove moralists apoplectic. Wherever wine flowed and clothes began to be loosened, traditional proprieties might start to slip too. A handsome social climber who had barely come of age might find himself talking on familiar terms to a consul. Deals might be struck, patronage secured. Charm and good looks might secure pernicious advantages. Baiae was a place ripe with scandal, dazzling in its aspect but forever shadowed by rumours of corruption: wine-drenched, perfume-soused, a playground for every kind of ambition and perversion, and – perhaps most shockingly of all – for the intrigues of powerful women.

The queen of Baiae, and the embodiment of its exclusive, if faintly sleazy, allure, was the eldest of the three Claudian sisters, Clodia Metelli. Her eyes, dark and glittering, had the ox-like appearance that invariably made Roman men go weak at the knees, while her slang set trends for an entire generation. The very name she adopted, a vulgar contraction of the aristocratic 'Claudia', reflected a taste for the plebeian that would influence her youngest brother to spectacular effect.[8] To affect a lower-class accent had long been a mark of the *popularis* politician – Sulla's enemy Sulpicius, for instance, had been notorious for it – but now, with Clodia, plebeian vowels became the height of fashion.

Naturally, in a society as aristocratic as that of the Republic, it required blue blood to make a trend out of slumming – Clodia, by virtue of marriage as well as breeding, stood at the heart of the Roman establishment. Her husband, Metellus Celer, came from

the only family capable of rivalling the prestige and arrogance of the
Claudii themselves. Fabulously fecund, the Metelli cropped up
everywhere, often on opposing sides. So it was, for instance, that
while one of the Metelli loathed Pompey so passionately that he had
come within a whisker of attacking the proconsul with a full war
fleet, Clodia's husband spent much of the sixties BC on active service as one of Pompey's legates. The great lady herself no doubt
endured this separation with equanimity. Her primary loyalty was
to her own clan. The Claudii, in contrast to the Metelli, had always
been famously close; in the case of Clodius and his three sisters,
notoriously so.

It was Lucullus, embittered and determined on the ruin of his in-
laws, who had first made the rumours of incest public. On his
return from the East he had openly accused his wife of sleeping
with her brother and divorced her. Clodius' eldest and dearest sister,
who had let him into her bed when he had been a small boy, nervous of night-time fears, inevitably found her own name blackened
by such a charge as well. In Rome censoriousness was the mirror-
image of a drooling appetite for lurid fantasy. Just as it endlessly
thrilled Caesar's contemporaries to think of him as the bed partner
of the King of Bithynia, so the pleasure that Clodius' enemies
took in the accusations of incest against him never staled. No smoke
without fire – and there must have been something unusual
about Clodius' relations with his three sisters to have set tongues
wagging. Throughout his career, he was to display a taste for pushing experience to the edge, and so it is perfectly possible that the
gossip-mongers knew what they were talking about. Just as plausibly, however, the rumours could have been fuelled by the uses to
which Clodia put her status as a society beauty. 'In the dining room
a cock-teaser, in the bedroom an iceblock':[9] this gallant description of her by a former lover suggests the care with which she
exploited her sexual appeal. For any woman, even one of Clodia's

14. The eyes of the dead were always imagined as gazing at an aristocratic Roman, inspiring him to rival the great deeds of his family's past. Here a toga-clad worthy clutches two heavy portrait busts – often identified as ancestral, although this is not certain. The head of the statue originally came from a separate sculpture. Late first century BC.

(Museo Capitolino, Rome/Fratelli Alinari)

15. Charioteers competing in the *cursus*. *(Museo Nazionale, Naples/Scala, Florence)*

16. Gladiators fighting in the arena at Pompeii, while spectators brawl outside. The mural dates from the first century AD: more than a century after Spartacus, gladiators continued to be big business in Campania. *(Museo Nazionale, Naples/Scala, Florence)*

17. The quiff and smirk of power: Pompey the Great. *(Ny Carlsberg Glyptotek, Copenhagen)*

18. Legionaries with shields and coats of mail (centre). A detail from the so-called altar of Domitius Ahenobarbus, first century BC, probably illustrating the soldiers' discharge from service. To end up 'settled down with a wife and children, in possession of fertile land' was every legionary's dream. *(Musée du Louvre, Paris/Scala, Florence)*

19. On his return from the East in 66 BC, Lucullus filled his gardens overlooking the Campus Martius with the cuttings of empire. Pleasure parks became one of the most prized attributes of greatness. This scene is from Augustus' villa at Prima Porta, near Rome.
(Museo Nazionale Romano, Rome/Scala, Florence)

20. Fish – both as provender and pets, a supreme Roman passion. As with his gardens, so with his 'fish-fancying', Lucullus became notorious for carrying the craze to excess.
(Museo Nazionale, Naples/Scala, Florence)

21. To the Roman super-rich, a villa on the bay of Naples had long been the ultimate must-have property, and to those who could not afford one, an object of fantasy and desire. Piers stretched so far out into the sea that it was said the fish felt cramped, while on the shore fantastical landscape gardening might dig out tunnels and raise up hills.
(Museo Nazionale, Naples)

22. 'Let arms yield rank to the toga of peace.' Cicero never let anyone forget his boast that in 63 BC, with the defeat of Catiline's 'conspiracy', he had saved the Republic. *(Museo Capitolino, Rome/Fratelli Alinari)*

23. Showdown in the Senate House. Cicero denounces a blackguardly Catiline, as imagined by Cesare Maccari in 1888 – one of a number of his frescoes in the seat of the modern Italian senate. *(Palazzo Madama, Rome/Scala, Florence)*

24. The temple of Castor in the Forum. In 58 BC, the year of his rumbustious tribunate, Clodius demolished its steps, and transformed it into a para-military headquarters.
(*Art Archive*)

25. To Roman men, the fact that women might meet to celebrate mysterious religious rites was endlessly titillating. In this mural from the Villa of Mysteries at Pompeii, a sense of the sacred is powerfully blended with the erotic – hinting, perhaps, at what inspired Clodius to desecrate the rites of the Good Goddess in 62 BC.
(*Art Archive*)

26. A funerary bust, traditionally held to be that of Cato. In 59 BC, the year of Caesar's consulship, Cato was the spearhead of the resistance to the triumvirate of Caesar, Pompey and Crassus. *(Museo Vaticano, Rome/Fratelli Alinari)*

'The Dying Gaul'. The statue is larger than life – fittingly, for ever since the sacking of Rome by Gallic warbands in the fourth century BC, the threat from Gaul never ceased to cast its shadow over the Republic. In the year following his consulship, what better way was there for Caesar to make his mark than by launching a pre-emptive strike against the barbarians to the north? *(Museo Capitolino, Rome/Art Archive)*

rank, dabbling in politics was a high-wire act. Roman morality did not look kindly on female forwardness. Frigidity was the ultimate marital ideal. It was taken for granted, for instance, that 'a matron has no need of lascivious squirmings'[10] – anything more than a rigid, dignified immobility was regarded as the mark of a prostitute. Likewise, a woman whose conversation was witty and free laid herself open to an identical charge. If she then compounded her offences by engaging in political intrigue, she could hardly be regarded as anything other than a monster of depravity. Seen in such a light, the charges of incest against Clodia were hardly surprising. Indeed, they marked her out as a player in the political game.

Misogyny alone, however, savage and unrelenting though it was, does not entirely explain the vehemence of the abuse that society hostesses such as Clodia provoked. Women had no choice but to exert their influence behind the scenes, by stealth, teasing and seducing those they wished to influence, luring them into what moralists were quick to denounce as a feminine world of gossip and sensuality. To the already ferociously nuanced world of male ambition, this added a perilous new complication. The qualities required to take advantage of it were precisely those that had always been most scorned in the Republic. Cicero, not one of life's natural party animals, listed them in salacious detail: an aptitude for 'debauchery', 'love affairs', 'staying up all night to the din of loud music', 'sleeping around' and 'spending cash to the point of ruin'.[11] The final, clinching disgrace, and the ultimate mark of a dangerous reprobate, was to be a good dancer. In the eyes of traditionalists nothing could be more scandalous. A city that indulged a dance culture was one on the point of catastrophe. Cicero could even claim, with a perfectly straight face, that it had been the ruin of Greece. 'Back in the old days,' he thundered, 'the Greeks used to stamp down on that kind of thing. They recognised the potential deadliness of the plague, how it would gradually rot the minds of its citizens with pernicious manias and ideas, and then, all at once, bring about a city's total collapse.'[12] By the standards of that diagnosis, Rome was in peril indeed. To the party set, the mark of a good night out, and the city's cutting-edge craze, was to become ecstatically drunk and then, to the accompaniment of 'shouts and screams, the whooping of girls and deafening music',[13] to strip naked and dance wildly on tables.

Roman politicians had always been divided more by style than by issues of policy. The increasing extravagance of Rome's party scene served to polarise them even further. Clearly, it was an excruciating embarrassment for traditionalists that so many of their standard-bearers had themselves succumbed to the temptations of luxury: men such as Lucullus and Hortensius were ill-placed to wag the finger at anyone. Even so, the ancient frugalities of the Republic still endured. Indeed, for a new generation of senators, the backdrop of modish excess made them appear more, not less, inspiring. Even as it wallowed in gold, the Senate remained an instinctively conservative body, reluctant to glimpse a true reflection of itself, preferring to imagine itself a model of rectitude still. Politicians able to convince their fellow senators that this was more than just a fantasy might accrue considerable prestige. Sternness and austerity continued to play well.

It is hard otherwise to explain the remarkable authority of a man who in the mid-sixties BC had only just turned thirty, and held no office higher than the quaestorship. At an age when most senators would sit in respectful silence to listen to their seniors, Marcus Porcius Cato had a voice that boomed out across the Senate House floor. Rough and unadorned, it appeared to sound directly from the rugged, virtuous days of the earliest Republic. As an officer, Cato had 'shared in everything he ordered his men to do. He wore what they wore, ate what they ate, marched as they marched.'[14] As a civilian, he made a fashion out of despising fashion, wearing black because the party set all sported purple, walking everywhere, whether in blazing sunshine or icy rain, despising every form of luxury, sometimes not even bothering to put on his shoes. If there was more than a hint of affectation about this, then it was also the expression of a profoundly held moral purpose, an incorruptibility and inner strength that the Romans still longed to identify with themselves, but had rather assumed were confined to the history books. To Cato, however, the inheritance of the past was something infinitely sacred. Duty and service to his fellow citizens were all. Only after he had fully studied the responsibilities of the quaestorship had he been prepared to put himself up for election. Once in office, such was his probity and diligence that it was said he 'made the quaestorship as worthy of honour as a consulship'.[15] Plagued by a sense of its own corruption as it was, the Senate was not yet so degenerate that it could fail to be impressed by such a man.

To the grandees of the previous generation in particular, Cato served as an inspiration. They were quick to see in him the future of the Republic. Lucullus, for instance, eager to hand on his torch to a successor, chose to celebrate his divorce by marrying Cato's half-sister. His new bride was an improvement on the old one only in the sense that her affairs were not incestuous, but the unfortunate Lucullus, once again saddled with a party girl for a wife, forbore for years to divorce her, out of respect for Cato. This did not mean that Cato himself was prepared to extend any special favours to his brother-in-law; far from it. If he believed that the good of the Republic was at stake, he would prosecute Lucullus' friends, and indeed take on anyone whom he believed required a lesson in virtue. On occasions he even went so far as to lecture Catulus. Cato was not prepared to take part in the intrigues that everyone else took for granted, a display of inflexibility that would often baffle and infuriate his allies. Cicero, who admired Cato deeply, could nevertheless bitch that 'he addresses the Senate as though he were living in Plato's Republic rather than the shit-hole of Romulus'.[16] Such criticism seriously underestimated Cato's political acumen. Indeed, in many ways his strategy was the polar opposite of Cicero's, who had made an entire career out of testing the limits of compromise. Cato moved to the rhythms of no one's principles but his own. Drawing his strength from the most austere traditions of the Republic, he fashioned himself into a living reproach to the frivolities of his age.

It was a deliberate tactic on Cato's part to make his enemies, in comparison to his own imposing example, appear all the more vicious and effeminate. Chasing after women and staying out drunk were not expressions of machismo to the Romans; the very opposite, in fact. Indulgence threatened potency. Gladiators, in the week before a fight, might need to have their foreskins fitted with metal bolts to infibulate them, but citizens were supposed to rely on self-control. To surrender to sensuality was to cease to be a man. Just as domineering women such as Clodia might be portrayed as vampires, 'sapping'[17] the appetites of those who succumbed to their charms, so gilded rakes like Clodius were savaged as creatures less than women. With unwearying relish, the same charge was repeated time and again.

Yet for all that this abuse reflected deeply held prejudices, there was something nervy and shrill about it. No Roman ever bothered striking at an enemy he did not fear. The signs of effeminacy were also the signs of knowingness, of superiority, of savoir faire. Fashion served the function it has always done: of distinguishing those who followed it from the common herd. In a society as competitive as the Republic this gave it an obvious and immediate appeal. Rome was filled with ambitious young men, all of them desperate for marks of public status. To be a member of the smart set was to sport precisely such marks. So it was that fashion victims would adopt secret signals, mysterious gestures such as the scratching of the head with a single finger. They grew goatees; their tunics flowed to the ankles and wrists; their togas had the texture and transparency of veils and they wore them, in a much-repeated phrase, 'loosely belted'.[18]

This, of course, was precisely how Julius Caesar had dressed in the previous decade. It is a revealing correspondence. In the sixties as in the seventies, Caesar continued to blaze a trail as the most fashionable man in Rome. He spent money as he wore his toga, with a nonchalant flamboyance. His most dandyish stunt was to commission a villa in the countryside and then, the moment it had been built, tear it down for not measuring up to his exacting standards. Extravagance such as this led many of his rivals to despise him. Yet Caesar was laying down stakes in a high-risk game. To be the darling of the smart set was no idle thing. The risk, of course, was that it might result in ruin – not merely financial, but political too. It was noted by his shrewder enemies, however, that he never let his partying put his health at risk. His eating habits were as frugal as Cato's. He rarely drank. If his sexual appetites were notorious, then he was careful to choose his long-term partners with a cool and searching caution. Cornelia, his wife, had died back in 69 BC and Caesar, looking for a new bride, had fixed his eye on Pompeia, the granddaughter of Sulla, no less. Throughout his career, Caesar was to prove himself keenly aware of the need for good intelligence, and this was as evident in his selection of mistresses as in his choice of a wife. The great love of his life was Servilia – who just happened to be the half-sister of Cato, and therefore the sister-in-law of Lucullus. Just for good measure, she was also Catulus' cousin. Who knows what family confidences Servilia may have whispered into her lover's ear?

No wonder that Caesar's enemies grew to be wary of his resources of charm. Just as he thought nothing of blowing a fortune on a single pearl for Servilia, so he mortgaged his future to seduce his fellow citizens. More outrageously than anyone had ever done before, he translated the party spirit into the dimension of public life. In 65 BC, at the age of thirty-five, he became aedile. This was not a magistracy that it was obligatory for would-be consuls to have held, but it was popular all the same, because aediles were responsible for the staging of public games. As such, it was an opportunity tailor-made for a showman such as Caesar. For the first time, gladiators were adorned in silver armour. Glittering magnificently, over three hundred pairs of them fought it out for the entertainment of the citizenry. The display would have been even more dazzling had not Caesar's enemies rushed through legislation to limit the numbers. Senators could recognise a shameless bribe when they saw it. They also knew that no bribes were ever offered without an expectation of a return.

In the great game of personal advancement Caesar's profligacy was a high-risk but deliberate gambit. His enemies might condemn him as an effeminate dandy, but they also had to acknowledge him as an increasingly heavyweight political contender. Caesar himself, every so often, would rub their noses in this fact. As aedile, he was responsible not only for the games, but for the upkeep of public places. One morning Rome woke to find all the trophies of Marius, long a non-person, restored. The Sullan establishment was appalled. After Caesar had coolly admitted his responsibility, Catulus went so far as to accuse him of assaulting the Republic with a battering ram. Caesar, playing the innocent, responded with outrage himself. Had Marius not been just as great a hero as Sulla? Was it not time for the rival factions to bury the hatchet? Were they not all citizens of the same republic, after all? The mob, assembling in Caesar's support, roared out its answer: 'Yes!' Catulus was left to splutter impotently. The trophies stayed in place.

Episodes such as this served to demonstrate that the *popularis* tradition, scotched but not destroyed by Sulla, was starting to revive. It was a striking achievement – but it came at a cost. For the *plebs*, who idolised Caesar, his munificence was the key to his appeal, but his enemies could reasonably hope that it might also prove to be his downfall. Just as Cato was famous for his austerity, so Caesar was notorious for his debts. Everyone knew that a moment of reckoning would have to come. It duly arrived in 63 BC. Caesar, looking to break into the front rank of the Senate once and for all, and to colour his loose-belted image with a touch of more traditional prestige, chose to stake his entire career upon a single election. The post of Rome's high priest, the *pontifex maximus*, had just become vacant. This was the most prestigious office in the Republic. The man elected to it held it until he died. Quite apart from the immense moral authority it bestowed, it also came with a mansion on the via Sacra, in the Forum. If Caesar became *pontifex maximus*, then he would be, literally, at the centre of Rome.

His opponent in the election was none other than that grandest of all grandees, Quintus Lutatius Catulus. Under normal circumstances, Catulus would have considered himself a shoo-in. The very fact of Caesar's candidature was a scandal. *Pontifex maximus* had always been considered a post suitable for a distinguished former consul, and emphatically not for a politician on the make. Caesar, however, was not the man to be put off by a minor detail of tradition like that. Instead, he opted for his invariable strategy when confronted by a problem: he threw money at it. The electors were bribed on a monstrous scale. By now Caesar had stretched his credit to the limit. On the day that the result of the election was due to be announced he kissed Aurelia goodbye, then told her, 'Mother, today you will either see me as high priest or I will be heading into exile.'[19]

As it proved, he would indeed be moving from the Subura – not into exile, but to his new mansion on the via Sacra. Caesar had pulled it off. He had been elected high priest. Once again, his extravagance had paid spectacular dividends. He had dared to gamble for massive stakes – against the status quo and the most ancient traditions of the Republic itself – and he had won.

Caelius' Conspiracy

There were plenty who gambled and did not win. Caesar's strategy of conspicuous extravagance was perilous. The promise of future greatness was staked against ruin. Money might be squandered, but never potential. Lose an election, fail to gain a lucrative posting, and a whole career might come crashing down.

It was no wonder that the provincial aristocracy, even as they fostered the ambitions of their sons, should also have slightly dreaded them. To send an heir to Rome was a calculated risk. Young men were easy prey to money-sharks. If a father were prudent, he would attempt to find patrons in the capital, mentors who might not only instruct his son in the labyrinthine ways of the Republic, but also protect him from the city's many seductions. Particularly for families who had never held office in Rome, it was essential to secure the best. So it was, for instance, that when a banker by the name of Caelius Rufus succeeded in obtaining for his son the sponsorship of not only Crassus but Cicero too, the young Caelius was immediately marked out as a brilliant prospect. This in turn – ironically – served to secure him massive credit. When the usurers came swarming, Caelius welcomed them with open arms. Handsome, witty and buccaneering, the young man was soon developing a lifestyle far in excess of his allowance. He was too ambitious to neglect his education, but even as he studied under his two guardians he was simultaneously establishing a reputation as one of the three best dancers in Rome. New circles were opening to him – circles in which Cicero tended not to move. As he became ever more of a fixture on the party scene, Caelius began to fall under the spell of a whole new order of acquaintance.

And in particular of a louche patrician by the name of Lucius Sergius Catilina – Catiline. Caesar was not the only man to have founded a career on wild extravagance, nor was he the only aristocrat to have a chip on his shoulder about the bare walls of his atrium. Catiline's great-grandfather had been a celebrated war hero, fighting against Hannibal with a prosthetic iron hand, but politically his ancestors had been an embarrassment. Even so, although there had been no consul in the family for almost four hundred years, Catiline's patrician status provided him with cachet. He could pass muster, for instance, with the rigorously snobbish Catulus. Their friendship had been literally sealed with blood. Back in the dark days of the proscriptions, Catiline had helped Catulus to punish his father's murderer. The wretched man had been whipped through the streets to where the tomb of Catulus' father stood, his bones smashed with rods, his face mutilated, and only then put out of his misery by decapitation. To Catulus, this savagery had been a grim act of filial piety, a blood-offering to his father's restless soul. Catiline had had no such excuse. After the murder he had brandished the severed – and supposedly still breathing – head back through the streets of Rome. Even by the standards of the civil war this was regarded as repellent behaviour. Although nothing was ever proved in a court of law, charges of murder, to say nothing of adultery and sacrilege, were to dog Catiline for the rest of his career. True, his sinister reputation was not always a handicap: among more raffish circles it combined with his stylishness and approachability to make him into a figure of menacing glamour. But while this served to provide him with a considerable constituency, it also placed him in a tactical bind. 'His main appeal he targeted at the young':[20] how long could Catiline continue to do this without alienating allies such as Catulus, let alone the majority of senators who already mistrusted him?

In an attempt to square the circle he turned to Crassus for help – or so at least the political gossip had it. No one could be sure, of course. Crassus' manoeuvrings were invariably veiled in shadow. But one thing could be certain: Crassus, in the sixties BC, was a worried man. Once again he was faced with the prospect of being trumped by Pompey. Not only would his old rival soon be returning at the head of a seasoned army, but he would be stupefyingly wealthy: for the first time in his political career Crassus was threatened with losing his status as the richest man in Rome. No wonder that he was frantic to shore up his support. Catiline, with huge ambitions and even huger debts, must surely have struck him as well worth a punt.

It was not merely that Crassus was looking to have a tame consul elected. Catiline also promised other pickings. He was popular wherever the margins of political life were at their seamiest: among the bands of upper-class delinquents brawling in the Subura; among the salons of scheming, dissipated women; among the indebted, the disappointed and the impatient; in short, wherever respectability tipped over into the disreputable. For the abstemious Crassus, a former consul, such a world was clearly out of bounds, although Cicero commented waspishly that he would dance in the Forum if it would win him a legacy.[21] That was as may be – but for as long as Crassus had Catiline as his creature, fishing in the murky waters of the underworld, glad-handing the salons, scheming with radicals in late-night bars, it was the proxy whose dignity was on the line.

It is impossible to distinguish what Caelius' precise role was in all this. It is conceivable, of course, that he had first met Catiline through the agency of Crassus, whose dark political skills Caelius had been studying at first hand. It is even possible that Cicero was responsible for the introduction. In 65 BC a rapacious spell as the governor of Africa had finally caught up with Catiline, when Clodius, back in Rome from the East, and eager to make a mark in the law courts, charged him with extortion. At the same time Cicero, the new man, was nerving himself for an attempt on the consulship. He knew that Catiline was planning to stand as well, and so briefly considered defending him in his forthcoming trial, hoping that the two of them might then run for office the following year on a joint ticket. Catiline, however, turned down the offer with a sneer of patrician contempt. The trial held few fears for him. Sure enough, he was speedily acquitted, possibly with the collusion of Clodius, almost certainly with the assistance of hefty bribes from Crassus. He was now free to run for the consulship of 63 BC. Catiline and Cicero would be going head to head.

Caelius was by his guardian's side throughout the election campaign. For a young politician who was himself a new man it must have been an intoxicating experience. The election was the most unpredictable in years. Cicero's whole career had been a preparation for it, but Catiline, just as desperate, was attempting to make good four centuries of family failure. Snobbery formed the basis of his entire campaign. It was conducted in open alliance with another nobleman, Antonius Hybrida, a man so debauched and thuggish that it was hard to believe that he was the son of Cicero's great hero, Marcus Antonius. Confronted by two such disreputable candidates, the aristocracy took a deep breath, held their noses, and voted for the least bad option. So too, with a good deal more enthusiasm, did the equestrian classes. Cicero won by a mile. Hybrida beat Catiline to a distant third place.

For any patrician, this would have been a humiliation. For Catiline, it threatened disaster: his debts were submerging him, and Crassus, in particular, would have no interest in sponsoring a loser. Yet Catiline had not abandoned all hope. As Cicero, draped in his purple-bordered toga, guarded by his lictors, a consul of the Roman people at last, began his year in office, so Catiline licked his wounds and plotted his comeback. His credit would last him until another election, and so he continued to borrow, lavishing everything on bribery. At the same time, rather than concealing the scale of his debts, he started to boast about them openly. This was a staggering risk, but, in the circumstances, one he had to take. The misery of indebtedness percolated far beyond the gilded seediness of his own circle. Italy seethed with the resentments of the oppressed, whether in the festering tenements of Rome or on barren farmland, where Sulla's veterans, mortgaged to the hilt, scratched at dust and recalled the fat days of civil war. At private meetings Catiline began to promise the poor that he would be their champion. After all, as he pointed out, 'Who was best qualified to be the leader and stan-dard-bearer of the desperate, if not a man who was bold and desperate himself?'[22]

Cicero, who had been keeping a careful eye on Catiline, was only too willing to take such incendiary talk at face value. Was it possible, he began to wonder, that, having attained the honour of the con-sulship, he might now be granted the even more glorious honour of saving the Republic from revolution? The prospect filled him with a mixture of consternation and dizzied delight. He and Catiline, stalking each other, both had a vested interest in raising the stakes, in making the flesh of their respective audiences creep. But when at last the two men confronted each other openly in the Senate House, Catiline allowed his loathing of the tongue-wagging upstart opposite to push him into a fatal act of bravado. 'I can see two bodies,' he commented, not quite enigmatically enough, 'one thin but with a large head, one huge, but headless. Is it really so ter-rible if I offer myself to the body which is lacking a head?'[23] His fellow aristocrats, the 'large head' of Catiline's riddle, were omi-nously unamused. Wrapped in metaphor or not, revolutionary sentiments did not go down well in the Senate House. Catiline had effectively just lost himself a second successive election. Cicero, patrolling the Campus Martius on polling day, made sure to wear a breastplate beneath his toga, and made even more sure that the voters could glimpse it. As the results were announced and Catiline's defeat became known, so the usurers flocked to pick at his corpse.

Like Caesar campaigning to be *pontifex maximus*, Catiline had staked everything on a single throw. He had gambled that it was possible to play Janus, showing one face to the senatorial and equestrian elite, the other to the poor, the indebted, the dispossessed. The gamble had failed. But if the establishment had turned its back on Catiline, then the underworld had not. He had stirred up hopes perhaps greater and more desperate than he knew. In the countryside, where peasants were starting to arm themselves with scythes and rusty swords, in Rome, where demonstrations were increasingly boiling over into riots, even in the Senate itself, where losers in the great game of advancement chafed against their debts and disappointments, talk of revolution still burned like sparks in the air. And there, sharing in the wild talk, was Marcus Caelius.

Why? Were the young man's debts already so prodigious that he was prepared to risk all his hopes of legal advancement by taking part in revolution? Or was it the excitement, the whisperings of conspiracy, that tempted him? Or idealism? A fervour for Catiline's cause certainly appears to have radicalised many brilliant young men. Generational tensions were more than capable of setting father against son. One senator preferred to kill his heir rather than see him consorting with Catiline, despite the fact that, like Caelius, the young man had been 'outstandingly talented, well read, and good looking'.[24] Even Cicero was forced to admit that Catiline was 'still capable of maintaining the loyalties of many fine men by putting on a show of moral fervour'.[25] So Caelius may have continued to support him for either the basest or the noblest of reasons, or a mixture of the two. But there is a further possibility: it is conceivable that Caelius may not have been supporting Catiline at all. Headstrong as he was, he was also more than capable of a calculating cynicism. Perhaps he was providing his guardian with a pair of well-placed eyes.

Cicero certainly still needed well-placed spies. Following Catiline's failure in the election, the consul's forebodings of revolution had become increasingly alarmist. People were starting to demand proof. And then, just as nervousness was turning to mockery, a packet of letters was suddenly delivered to Cicero's house. They set out Catiline's plans for a wholesale massacre. The man who handed over these incriminating documents was none other than Crassus. He claimed that they had been handed in to his doorkeeper by an 'unknown man'.[26] When Cicero read the letters out to the Senate the following morning, panic gripped the city. A state of emergency was declared, and the Republic entrusted to Cicero's hands. Crassus, having publicly shopped his protégé, slunk back into the shadows. In reading accounts of this improbable story it is hard to avoid the conclusion that Catiline was not the only conspirator in that autumn of 63. Who might the 'unknown man' have been? We know of only one person who was simultaneously an intimate of Cicero, Crassus and Catiline. That person was Caelius.

Wild speculation, of course. Any or all of the above explanations are possible. But it is not sufficient to blame a lack of sources alone for the mystery. It also reflects something fundamental about the Republic itself. The longing of the Romans for glory, which burned brightly within them and lit their city and indeed their entire empire with its flame, also cast flickering and treacherous shadows. Every ambitious politician required the skills of a conspirator. When Cicero met Catiline for the last time, face to face in the Senate House, he dissected his enemy's manoeuvrings with forensic brilliance, exposing them to the full scorching glare of his outrage, picking over the details of the conspiracy to such effect that Catiline fled Rome that very night. Ever after Cicero was to regard this as his finest hour, 'a pinnacle of immortal glory',[27] as he modestly expressed it. The image of himself as the dauntless protector of the Republic, a patriot pure and simple, would provide him with the touchstone for the rest of his career. It was a perspective that Catiline, unsurprisingly, failed to share. Before leaving Rome he had written to Catulus, still protesting his innocence, bitterly complaining that he had been manoeuvred into exile. Heading north, ostensibly towards retirement in Marseille, he had in fact turned aside to take command of a ragbag army of peasants and war veterans. Meanwhile, back in Rome, more spine-tingling details of his plots, fed to the Senate at judicious intervals, had started to emerge: Gauls in the north of Italy were to rise in savage revolt; slaves were to be freed; the city itself was to be put to the torch. The whole of Rome was engulfed by hysteria. Cicero was the hero of the hour. Yet a few dissenting voices could still be heard. The crisis had been manufactured, they whispered. Catiline had been right. It was Cicero who had pushed him into his revolt, Cicero and his vainglory, Cicero the upstart, greedy for fame.

Of course, as is invariably the way with conspiracy theories, hard proof was lacking. No one was on hand to subject Cicero to the kind of grilling that he himself had given Catiline. The truth remained obscured behind a haze of disinformation. It was certainly evident that Cicero had employed dirty tricks to smoke out his enemy, but how much further than that he might have gone was impossible to say. Yet, in a sense he would have been less a Roman had he not schemed to push his enemy over the edge. Every consul dreamed of stamping his term of office with glory. That was how the game of self-advancement was played. Cicero may not have behaved according to the standards of his own propaganda, but then again – apart from Cato – who ever did?

And it was Catiline, after all, who had first upped the stakes. The civil war had shown how quickly violence could escalate. In a society as competitive as Rome's even to talk of forcing short cuts through the constitution was perilous, like tossing a flame on to a tinder box. This explains why Cicero was so anxious to erect firebreaks around Catiline. He feared that if the conspirators were not isolated, then the conflagration might quickly spread out of control. Sure enough, no sooner had Catulus accepted that Catiline had indeed been plotting to destroy the Republic than he was attempting to finger Crassus and, just for good measure, Caesar too. Cicero may have had his own suspicions on that account, but Catulus' move was precisely the kind he was desperate to avoid. He had no wish to see a man like Crassus backed into a corner.

On 5 December, with panic-stricken rumours growing wilder by the hour, he convened a crisis meeting of the Senate. All the conspiracy's ringleaders in Rome had been identified and arrested, he announced. Neither Crassus' nor Caesar's name appeared on the list. Even so, the great debate that followed was at least as much about the hatreds and ambitions of the various speakers as it was about the conspiracy itself. At stake was the issue of what to do with Catiline's henchmen. Many were of good family, and it was forbidden by the severest laws of the Republic to execute any citizen without a proper trial. But did the state of emergency entitle Cicero to waive this sacred injunction? Caesar, still nervous that the hysteria might sweep him away, proposed the novel idea that the conspirators should be imprisoned for life; Cato, opposing him, demanded their execution. Here, in the clash between these two men so matched in talent, so opposite in character, was the opening salvo of a struggle that would eventually convulse the Republic. For now, it was Cato who emerged triumphant. A majority in the

Senate agreed with him that the safety of Rome was more important than the rights of individual citizens. And besides, who ever
heard of imprisonment as a punishment? The conspirators were
sentenced to death.

Among their number was a former consul. Watched by a confused and frightened crowd, he was led through the Forum, Cicero
by his side, bristling with grim self-importance, four other senators
following in quick succession. With the shadows of twilight deepening over the city, the five prisoners were lowered into the
blackness of an underground cell. Here they were garrotted. Cicero,
emerging from the gloom, tersely announced their deaths to the
crowd. Many in the Forum were friends of the executed men, and
they now slunk away, but throughout the rest of the city the news
was greeted with an explosion of applause. A blaze of torches illumined the road that led from the Forum up to Cicero's house. As
the consul climbed it he was escorted by a phalanx of the greatest
names in Rome. All acclaimed him as the saviour of his country.
Surely, not even in his wildest dreams could the provincial from
Arpinum ever have imagined such a day.

What had impressed his colleagues was not merely that he
appeared to have saved the Republic, but that he had done so with
comparatively little bloodshed. Cicero himself remained desperate
to preserve a fire-wall around the conspiracy. He refused, for
instance, to investigate his fellow consul, Antonius Hybrida, despite
the fact that Hybrida had been one of Catiline's closest friends.
Cicero bribed his colleague with the governorship of Macedon, a
rich province that would more than enable him to pay off his debts,
and command of the war against Catiline. Since Hybrida was not
merely suspected of double-dealing with the rebels, but was also a
coward and an alcoholic to boot, this provoked much unease. Allies
of Pompey began to press for the great man's recall. This in turn
provoked an eruption of outrage from Cato, who announced that

he would rather die than see Pompey given an Italian command. But if anyone had genuinely stood in Pompey's way, it was Cicero. The prospect of a Rome pushed into armed factions, their rivalry escalating into ever greater violence, degenerating in the end into open civil war, this had been his ultimate nightmare. Nothing would have provided Pompey with a more perfect excuse to intervene with his legions. It was in this sense that Cicero had indeed saved the Republic, less from Catiline, perhaps, than from itself.

In the summer of 62 BC, just a few bare months before Pompey was due back in Italy, Catiline's makeshift army was finally cornered and destroyed. Hybrida, succumbing to a diplomatic illness, spent the entire battle in his tent, then scuttled off to Macedon, to extract his blood-money but otherwise lie low. He was not alone in beating a tactical retreat from Rome. Humbler players in the conspiracy were also slipping away. Among them was Caelius. He travelled to Africa, where his father had extensive business holdings, staffed with protective subordinates. But Caelius had far from abandoned his political career. For a year he served in Africa as an aide-de-camp to the province's newly appointed proconsul, and did so very successfully. Whatever Caelius' precise role in the conspiracy had been, his future still lay all before him. He had seen enough of public life to know that nothing in it was for ever. Alliances might buckle, twist and be reversed. The heroes of one year might be the villains of the next. In the blink of an eye the political landscape might be utterly transformed.

And so it would soon dramatically prove.

Scandal

Early every December women from the noblest families in the Republic would gather to celebrate the mysterious rites of the Good

Goddess. The festival was strictly off limits to men. Even their statues had to be veiled for the occasion. Such secrecy fuelled any number of prurient male fantasies. Every citizen knew that women were depraved and promiscuous by nature. Surely a festival from which men were banned had to be a scene of lubricious abandon? Not that any male had ever dared take a peek to confirm this thrilling suspicion. It was one of the idiosyncrasies of Roman religion that even those who sniggered at it also tended to regard it with awe. Men, just as much as women, honoured the Good Goddess. She was one of the divine protectors of Rome. Clearly, should her rites be profaned, the sacrilege might threaten the security of all.

In the winter of 62 BC the matrons had particular reason to pray for the Good Goddess's favour. Catiline was dead, but fears and rumours still gusted through the Forum. After a leisurely saunter on the tourist trail around Greece, Pompey had finally arrived on the Adriatic coast. It was said that he would be crossing to Italy before the end of the month. What would it be like for other ambitious noblemen, having to live like pygmies in the shadow of Pompey the Great? It was a question of particular concern to the two women who presided over the rites of the Good Goddess: Aurelia, Caesar's mother, and Pompeia, his wife. The *pontifex maximus* himself, although he had provided his mansion for the occasion, was naturally not present. Along with every other male in his household, free and slave alike, Caesar had withdrawn for the night.

The mansion began to fill with incense, music and great ladies. Now, for a few brief hours, it was the city's women who held the safety of Rome in their hands. There was no longer any call for them to skulk in the shadows, afraid of prying eyes. Yet one of Aurelia's maids, looking for some music, observed a flute-girl who was doing exactly that. She approached her; the flute-girl shrank away. When the maid demanded to know who she was, the flute-girl shook her head, then mumbled Pompeia's name. The maid

shrieked. Dressed in a long-sleeved tunic and breastband the
stranger might have been, but the voice had been unmistakably
male. Uproar ensued. Aurelia, frantically covering up the sacred
statues of the goddess, suspended the rites. The other women went
in search of the impious intruder. They finally found him, hidden in
the room of one of Pompeia's maids. Off came the veil of the bogus
flute-girl to reveal . . . Clodius.

  Such at least was the story that immediately swept like wildfire
around Rome. Gossip convulsed the city. Friends and enemies of
Clodius alike huddled to swap the salacious details. If sporting a
goatee or touching the head with a finger could be considered
marks of effeminacy, then Clodius, by dressing up in women's
clothes and gatecrashing a sacred ritual, had clearly taken offensiveness to a whole new level. Overnight he became the toast of
every loose-belted dandy and the bogey of every conservative in
Rome. Caught in the middle, deeply embarrassed by the affair, was
Caesar. Naturally, he had to affect outrage. Not only had Clodius
violated the pontifical house, but it was also rumoured that he had
been planning to violate Pompeia herself. Cuckolded Roman husbands had been known to set their slaves on adulterers, to beat
them, rape them, even castrate them; at the very least Caesar
would have been justified in dragging Clodius through the courts.
But the *pontifex* had an image problem: despite his elevated religious status, he remained a topic of fevered gossip himself, the rake
who had been labelled 'a man for every woman, and a woman for
every man'.[28] For Caesar to adopt the tone of the moral majority
might open him to even greater ridicule, quite apart from making
an enemy of Clodius and alienating the fast set who were his natural supporters. After all, he was planning to run for the
consulship within a couple of years. Clodius was far too well connected, and capricious, to risk offending. In the end Caesar resolved
his dilemma by divorcing Pompeia, but refusing to say why:

'Caesar's wife must be above suspicion'[29] was his single, Delphic comment. Then, before anyone could press him further, he slipped away to Spain, where he was due to serve as governor. It was a measure of his eagerness to be away from Rome that he arrived in his new province before the Senate had even had time to confirm his appointment.

Caesar's departure did nothing to dim the obsession with the scandal. The continuing hysteria that surrounded Clodius' stunt submerged even the news of Pompey's arrival. This, contrary to most people's fears, passed off without any great alarms. Rather than marching on Rome, the returning proconsul dismissed his army, then headed for the capital 'unarmed, with no one to escort him save a few intimate friends, for all the world as though he were returning from a holiday abroad'.[30] Pompey's shows of simplicity were always ostentatious. The crowds who lined the route of his progress duly cheered themselves hoarse. His rivals back in Rome, however, were less easily impressed. Now that they no longer needed to fear Pompey they could concentrate on the far more pleasurable activity of cutting him down to size. To everyone's delight, his first public speech was a flop. Pompey's blend of pomposity and false modesty presented his enemies with an irresistible target. When he complacently commended the Senate for suppressing Catiline, Crassus was immediately up on his feet, praising Cicero to the skies, lauding him in ludicrously exaggerated terms, claiming that he never looked at his wife or home without thanking Cicero for their continued existence. Cicero himself, completely failing to recognise the irony, was thrilled. He had always idolised Pompey, and to be praised like this in the great man's presence was heaven. Yet even he had to acknowledge that his hero, listening to Crassus' speech, had appeared a little 'peeved'.[31]

This was hardly surprising. Pompey had recently been hearing a good deal from Cicero. The previous year, while he had still been in

Greece, a huge letter had thudded on to his reading desk, a book-length self-promotion in which the former consul had presumed to compare his achievements to those of the new Alexander. Pompey's response had been withering. For Cicero, whose conceit still veiled gnawing insecurities, the cold dismissal by his hero had been deeply hurtful. He consoled himself with the thought that Pompey was jealous, but the rebuff had wounded not merely his vanity, but his entire vision of the future of Rome. As was so often the case with Cicero, the two went hand in hand. Yes, it was he who had saved the Republic, but, as he modestly acknowledged, he could never have done it without the support of his fellow citizens. The year of his consulship had been their, as well as his, finest hour. Surely this sense of common purpose could be maintained? What was a republic, after all, if not a partnership of interest and justice? Naturally, Cicero himself, as 'the saviour of his country', would have to remain at the helm, but he graciously accepted that other leading figures, Pompey especially, would also have their parts to play. All citizens – senators, equestrians and poor alike – would live in harmony. Self-interest would be subordinated to the interests of Rome.

As a manifesto, of course, this was a vision of cloud-cuckoo-land. It was hardly as though Cicero himself had been immune to ambition. Liberty – and the opportunity for an outsider to win the consulship – would be stifled by a society in which everyone knew his place. It was a paradox that was to torture Cicero all his life. His blueprint for the future, however impractical, was the product of much agonised reflection. Cicero was proud to consider himself the heir of the Republic's noblest traditions. Chief among these was the age-old balance between ambition and duty. Should this be upset, then criminals might start to hack their way to the top, and tyrants to emerge. Catiline had been foiled – but he was bound to have successors. It was essential that they too be destroyed. After all, what hope was there for the Republic if the great were not the good?

The passion with which Cicero held such opinions did not encourage him to look indulgently on Clodius' prank. Surely only a Catiline in the making could have committed such a shocking offence? Adding to Cicero's mounting excitement was his sense that, just as it had done in the glory days of his consulship, the Senate was closing ranks. Despite the fact that there was no law against gatecrashing the goddess's rites, a powerful groundswell of opinion was starting to move in favour of declaring it a crime. A vote was taken. It was agreed that Clodius should be brought to trial. The size of the majority reflected not only genuine outrage, but, as ever in Rome, the venom of personal hatreds. Clodius did not lack for enemies. Chief among those, of course, was Lucullus. It took a special occasion to drag him from his fish-ponds. One of these had been his triumph, back in 63, which Cicero, as consul, had finally succeeded in authorising. Lucullus had used the event as an opportunity for point-scoring. His accounts had been carried on huge billboards through the streets, stating precisely how much he had paid his soldiers – the princely sum of nine hundred and fifty drachmas each. Clearly, the dagger-blow of the mutiny had not ceased to ache. Now, two years later, Lucullus eagerly re-emerged. He could smell Clodius' blood. Preparing for the trial, he rehearsed all his old resentments: the mutiny, the incest of his wife. He also persuaded Hortensius to bestir himself and lead the prosecution. A formidable array of witnesses began to be assembled. Notable among these was Aurelia. Whatever the qualms of her son, she was more than willing to confirm that, yes, she had seen Clodius in her house on the fateful night.

But Clodius had powerful friends of his own. Leading his defence was one of the most illustrious figures in the Senate, a former consul no less, Gaius Scribonius Curio. Following standard procedure, Curio had no sooner accepted the case than he set about manufacturing an alibi for his client. An equestrian was found who was prepared to testify that Clodius had spent the day of the Good Goddess's rites with him, ninety miles away from the scene of the supposed crime. It was now up to Hortensius to trump this evidence. It did not take him long. A witness was found for the prosecution, and a most impressive one too. It turned out that on the day of the festival of the Good Goddess Cicero had been with Clodius, not ninety miles away, but in the heart of Rome.

Would he testify to this effect, however? For all Cicero's horror at Clodius' alleged behaviour, it was still an agonising decision. There had been no history of enmity between the two men. During Cicero's consulship Clodius had even served as one of his bodyguards. More than that, they were now neighbours. Cicero had recently gone up in the world – literally so. Following his consulship he had bought a splendid house on the Palatine, mortgaging himself to the hilt in order to do so, but feeling that his new status more than justified the expense. He was, after all, the saviour of the Republic. From the portico of his poplar-shaded mansion he could now look down at the Forum, the most exclusive view in the world. The neighbours included not only Clodius, but his glamorous sister. Cicero was proud of his intimacy with Rome's haughtiest family, so much so, in fact, that his wife accused Clodia of angling to seduce him.

According to gossip, Cicero was nagged so relentlessly about this that he decided to testify against Clodius merely to win some peace. His wife should have saved her breath. In the final reckoning an opportunity to line up with the cream of the senatorial elite was simply too tempting for Cicero to resist. His appearance duly caused a sensation. As he stepped forward to give his evidence the baying of Clodius' supporters rose in a crescendo. Gangs imported from the slums had been milling around the Forum for weeks, intimidating Clodius' enemies, marshalled by the son of Clodius' advocate, a young man dismissed by Cicero as 'Curio's little daughter',[32] but a reckless, dangerous opponent all the same. On this occasion, however, his tactics backfired. Nothing served to bolster Cicero's courage more than the feeling that he was the star of a show. As the jurors rallied to form a human shield around him, he gave his evidence in a clear, unshaken voice. The next day a crowd gathered outside his house to roar their approval. Clodius' conviction appeared to have been sealed. The jurors asked for bodyguards in turn.

But stalwart in defence of Cicero though they had been, they were to acquit themselves less impressively when over the next couple of days a mysterious slave began knocking at their doors. Offers of cash were dangled before them, and the favours of women or upper-class boys as they preferred. The flagrancy of this approach reaped a decisive reward. Clodius was acquitted by thirty-one votes to twenty-five. His enemies exploded with fury. Catulus, meeting one of the jurors, asked him sulphurously, 'Was this why you wanted a bodyguard, then? To make sure that your bribes would be safely guarded?'[33]

For all the grandees – Lucullus especially – Clodius' acquittal was a bitter blow. For Cicero, however, it was a disaster. Lacking the resources of a Catulus or Hortensius, he now found himself confronted by an enemy whom even Caesar had been reluctant to provoke. In the weeks following the trial he did not help matters by baiting Clodius in the Senate with a succession of ill-considered sallies. What had originally been an animosity typical of many relationships in Rome now rapidly began to spiral into a full-blown blood-feud. Clodius may not have been Cicero's equal as a wit, but in the nursing of vendettas he was soon to prove himself without peer.

To Cicero himself, personal catastrophe was always a crisis for the whole of Rome. On other occasions, however, he would have acknowledged that the savagery of political life was the index of its liberty. Fortunes rose, fortunes fell; alliances were forged, alliances fell apart. These were the rhythms of a free republic. The fact that the gloss of his consulship was rapidly vanishing may have been upsetting to Cicero, but it was a source of quiet satisfaction to most of his colleagues. Achievement in Rome was valued, but excessive greatness was feared. Many could share in power, but no one man could rule supreme. Only Sulla had done that – and he had soon retired.

What reason was there to think that this would ever change?

8

TRIUMVIRATE

Cato's Gambit

On 28 September 61 BC Pompey the Great rode for the third time in a triumph through Rome. Even by his own standards it was a show of unparalleled magnificence. At its heart, naturally, was the conquering hero himself. For the benefit of spectators who did not have grandstand views, a huge portrait bust was carried in the procession, fashioned entirely out of pearls. Its predominant feature was an immaculate quiff. This was the same hairstyle Pompey had displayed in his first triumph, eighteen years previously. The role of boy wonder had proved a hard one to let slip. So sensitive was Pompey about his age that he had even arranged for his triumph to start on the day before his birthday — his forty-fifth. Not that this was a detail he chose to broadcast. Sporting the cloak as well as the quiff of Alexander, he had no wish to appear as mutton dressed as lamb. Alexander had famously died young, at the age of thirty-two. Pompey had already spent a whole decade being thirty-four.

Only with a career of short cuts behind him could a Roman have suffered a mid-life crisis of this nature. Most of Pompey's countrymen yearned for their forties. Middle age was the prime of a citizen's life, and for the upper classes a time when they could at last run for the consulship. To the Romans, the cult of youth appeared unsettling and foreign, a delusion to which kings in particular were prone. Greek potentates were forever attempting to hold back the years, whether by preserving their youth in images of marble or by raising pompous monuments to themselves. A Roman was expected to know better. After all, what was the lifeblood of the Republic if not the onward passage of time? Each year magistrate gave way to magistrate, and the man who relived his term of office excessively, as Cicero did, became a figure of ridicule. As water was used to dilute wine, so time was relied upon to dissipate the headiness of glory. The Romans, precisely because they had a deeper thirst for honour than any other people in the world, were the more alert to its perils. The sweeter it tasted, the greater the risk of intoxication. The limit of a magistracy was set at a year, but of a triumph at one or two days. The procession ended, the feast consumed, the trophies hung in the temples of the gods, all that was left behind was litter in the streets. For the Romans, the truest monuments to glory were fashioned not of marble but of memories. Spectacle, if it were not to be an insufferable affront to civic values, had to be fleeting, ephemeral, just like the authority of the magistrate who sponsored it. Forbidden great architecture, the Romans made an art form out of festival instead.

Never did their city appear more like the capital of an empire than when its shabbiness was transformed into a realm of fantasy. Whole theatres might be raised, adorned with marble columns, their floors made of glass or gilded floorboards, filled with bronze statues and dazzling *trompe l'oeils* – and yet the theatres themselves were merely sets. Thrown up to stage a festival, they would be torn down brutally the moment it had finished. Only once, back in 154, had the censors licensed the construction of a permanent theatre, but even as it was nearing completion, prominent at the base of the

Palatine, opinion in the Senate had hardened against it and it had been dismantled, block by block. The result, still apparent nearly a century later, was a powerful incongruity: Rome, mistress of the world, lacked what even the most provincial towns in Italy possessed: a theatre built of stone.

To many citizens, this remained a source of pride, an emphatic demonstration of republican virtue and a guarantee of that 'peculiar manliness which has always distinguished the Roman people'.[1] To others, it was an embarrassment. Pompey, for instance, swaggering his way around the East, had resented being upstaged by the splendours of Greek architecture, regarding it as an affront to his own prestige and that of Rome. Having looted everything from wine-coolers to balsam trees for his triumph, he had rounded off his pilfering by having sketches drawn of the great theatre of Mitylene, planning to build a copy of it, 'only larger and more magnificent'.[2] Even as the debris from his triumph was being swept up, Pompey's labourers were moving in on the Campus Martius. Flat, empty and close to the Forum, nothing more tempting to a developer could have been imagined – and Pompey had never been good at resisting temptation. The monumentalism of his plans was obvious from the start. He claimed, disingenuously, that he was building a temple to Venus and that the seats were designed as steps leading upwards to the shrine, but nobody was fooled. Once again, as had happened throughout Pompey's career, precedent was being trampled with cavalier abandon. Not that Pompey himself was remotely bothered. The money being spent was his own, after all. What else should he spend his fortune on if not a gift to the Roman people?

Most of the Roman people, unsurprisingly, agreed. But while Pompey's admirers thrilled to the gargantuan scale of their hero's generosity, his peers in the Senate did not. There, particularly in its upper reaches, suspicion was deepening to the point of paranoia. It was noted that the foundations of the new theatre stretched almost to the Ovile. The completed complex would tower above the voting pens. Elections would be held literally in Pompey's shadow. The Republic itself seemed in danger. This was the cry that had always united the aristocracy against over-reachers, and so it did again now. Catulus, long the leading critic of Pompey's unconstitutional career, had died shortly after Clodius' trial, perhaps driven into his grave by the result, but Cato remained unbending as the champion of tradition, and he was more than ready to take on Pompey. In association with the inveterately envious Crassus he constructed an unshiftable bloc of opposition to Pompey's interests, reducing the great general, in the midst of all his glory, to a sudden, startled impotence. The Senate refused to ratify his settlement of the East. His veterans were denied the farms they had been promised. Even his victory over Mithridates was sneered at by Cato as 'a war against women'.[3]

Pompey reacted with hurt and perplexity. Had he not conquered 324 different nations? Had he not doubled the size of Rome's empire? Why did the Senate refuse to give him his due? Illegal in his methods he may have been, but in his aims he was the very model of convention. Far from aiming at a monarchy, as his enemies darkly hinted, Pompey longed for nothing more than to be accepted into the bosom of the establishment. He had his own insecurities. His family was not an ancient one. The prestige of a man such as Cato, whose achievements were a fraction of his own, gnawed at him, and inspired in him an envious respect. Even when his own reputation had been at its highest, on his return from the East in 62 BC, Pompey had demonstrated an almost puppyish desire to know that Cato respected him in turn. He had gone so far as to divorce his wife, despite the fact that she was the sister of his close ally, Metellus Celer, and announced that he and his son would marry Cato's two nieces. Naturally, since he was now Rome's most eligible bachelor, Pompey had assumed that Cato was bound to give his permission. So too had the prospective brides, but no sooner had the two girls excitedly started making their wedding plans than their uncle had told them to save their breath. Cries of joy had turned to tears. Not a woman in the household had failed to take their side. Cato, however, was hardly the man to be swayed by tantrums. 'Pompey should know', he pronounced dismissively, 'that I will not be outflanked via the bedroom of a girl.'[4] The embarrassed suitor was left looking sleazy and underhand, with nothing to show for the affair save the enmity of the insulted Metellus. Once again Cato's unerring eye for the moral high ground had enabled him to seize the tactical heights as well. Pompey, floundering ever more badly in unfamiliar terrain, began to be worn down by his enemy's constant sniping. By the spring of 60 he seemed almost to have given up the battle. The great man did nothing all day, Cicero confided to Atticus, except sit in wistful silence, 'and gaze at the toga which he wore in his triumph'.[5]

Whatever the satisfaction that Cato took in such reports, however, he remained on his guard. Even amid the wreckage of his political fortunes Pompey remained a formidable foe. It was clear to everyone that if he wanted to break the logjam that Cato and Crassus had so skilfully constructed, then he would need an ally in the consulship, and not just any ally, but a heavyweight capable of facing down Cato. There was one obvious candidate for this role, but in the spring of 60 he was far away, in Spain.

Caesar, to most people's surprise, had been making a great success of his spell as governor. The loose-belted dandy had proved a natural general. A dashing little war in what is now northern Portugal had not only enabled him to recoup many of his debts, but had led the Senate to award him a triumph. Even these successes, however, paled in comparison to the news of Pompey's deepening predicament. Caesar could recognise the chance of a lifetime when he saw it. To seize it, however, he would have to hurry. Candidates for the consulship had to declare themselves in Rome by the start of July. Abandoning his province before his successor had even arrived, and travelling at his customary breakneck pace, Caesar made it to the Campus just in time. There, however, amid the clamour and dust of Pompey's building work, he had to halt. Until he had celebrated his triumph he remained officially under arms, and therefore forbidden to enter Rome. Caesar installed himself in the Villa Publica, then hurriedly applied for the right to stand for the consulship by proxy – a request that the Senate, with a day to spare, appeared perfectly content to grant.

Cato, however, was not. Knowing that a vote would have to be taken before sunset, he rose to his feet and spoke long into the night. A furious Caesar found himself having to choose between his triumph and the consulship. He can hardly have hesitated. Unlike Pompey, he had never had any problem in distinguishing the substance from the shadow of power. He entered Rome and a race that he knew was his to win.

Cato and his allies knew it too. In their battle with Pompey this was a sudden and alarming twist. The fact that Caesar could rely not only on Pompey's backing but on his own immense popularity served to make him doubly a threat. Having failed to block his old enemy's entrance into the race, Cato now moved hurriedly to neutralise the effects of his anticipated victory. The most urgent requirement was to ensure the election of a sound second consul, one who could be relied upon to counteract Caesar's measures. Money from Pompey's limitless fortune was already flooding the electorate: it was obvious that he would be spending whatever it took to buy up both consulships. Cato's chosen candidate was his son-in-law, an earnest and somewhat plodding senator by the name of Marcus Bibulus, who suddenly, to his delight, found himself cast as the saviour of the Republic. The full weight of Pompey's enemies swung behind him. So grave did the situation appear to Cato that he was even prepared to turn a blind eye when Bibulus, going head to head with Pompey's agents, began to hand out bribes himself.

The money proved to have been well spent. In the elections Caesar came first in a landslide, but Bibulus scraped into second place. So far so good for Cato – but now that he had countered Pompey's manoeuvrings he also had to block Caesar's own ambitions. The military talents of the consul-elect had been widely noted. To Cato, the prospect of allowing such a glory-hunter anywhere near another province was intolerable. But how to stop him? Every consul, once he had completed his term of office, was appointed to a governorship as a matter of course. But why, Cato began pointing out, when there was so much unrest near to home, should the consuls of 59 be dispatched to the empire's outer reaches? After all, more than a decade after Spartacus' defeat, Italy remained infested with bandits and runaway slaves. Why not, just for one year, make the consuls responsible for their extermination? The Senate was persuaded. The proposal became law. Rather than a province, Caesar could now look forward to policing Italian sheepfolds.

Austere though he was, Cato was evidently not without a sense of humour. It was a dangerous move, of course, to make a man such as Caesar into the butt of a joke, but Cato, by doing so, was priming a trap. If Caesar refused to accept the Senate's decision, then he would have to rely on force to reverse it; he would be branded a criminal, a second Catiline; Pompey's name too would be besmirched by association, and his programme stymied for good. Cato's strategy had always been to identify himself with the constitution and corner his enemies into playing the role of wreckers. Ruthless and bold as Caesar was, how far would he dare to go? Any violent extremes would be met by a formidable coalition. At Caesar's elbow his fellow consul promised him unwearying opposition: Bibulus had spent a lifetime being overshadowed by his glamorous rival and loathed him accordingly. In the Senate Cato's allies formed a strong and cohesive majority. Crassus, with his powerful bloc, could surely be relied upon as well: if there was one constant in the world of Roman politics it was that Crassus would be on the opposite side of everything to Pompey. Perilous as the contest promised to be, Cato could feel grimly confident of victory. As he had to be – for he had chosen to use the Republic, and its very stability, as his stake.

From the start, then, crisis menaced the fateful year of Caesar's consulship. The mood of the Senate as it assembled to hear the new consul for the first time was jittery, mistrustful. Caesar, surpassingly gracious, sought to charm his audience, but Cato, obdurate as ever, refused to be charmed. When Caesar presented a moderate and carefully reasoned bill for the settlement of Pompey's veterans up he rose in kneejerk opposition. On and on he talked, repeating his favourite tactic, until Caesar cut it short by giving the nod to his lictors. As Cato was led away, the seats of the Senate House began to empty. Caesar demanded to know why the senators were leaving. 'Because I'd rather be with Cato in prison', one of them spat back, 'than in the Senate House with you.'[6] Caesar, hiding his fury, was forced to back down. Cato was released. Eyeball to eyeball the two men had gone – and Caesar had blinked.

Or so it appeared. In fact, it soon became clear that Caesar's retreat had been merely tactical. Abandoning the Senate House altogether, he took the campaign for his land bill directly into the Forum. As he did so, Rome began to fill with Pompey's veterans. Caesar's enemies found themselves increasingly disconcerted by this menacing backdrop. So flustered did Bibulus become that he committed the supreme gaffe of telling the voters that he cared nothing for their opinion. Cato, watching, must have buried his face in his hands. All the same, he still believed that Caesar was bluffing. It was true that a bill passed by the people would have the full force of the law, but even so, to go against the stated wishes of the Senate was the tactic of a gangster. If Caesar persisted with it, then his credit among his colleagues would be destroyed and his career would be over. Surely no one could be so criminal as to court such a fate.

Caesar's game plan, however, was soon to become all too clear. In the run-up to the vote on the bill he paraded his celebrity supporters. Few could have been surprised when Pompey stepped forward to argue in favour of the settlement of his veterans, but the identity of the second speaker came as a thunderbolt. Throughout a career of slipperiness and opportunism, Crassus had remained constant to a single principle: opposition to Pompey's goals. Even that, it now appeared, had been a principle too far. Crassus justified his U-turn as the action of a statesman, performed in the interests of the Republic – but everyone knew that he had never made a selfless move in his life. In his cold and calculating soul not even the pleasure of hatred, it appeared, could compete with the passion for power. The pre-eminence that he had never quite been able to obtain on his own was now within his grasp. Cato, outflanked, found all his defences being turned. It quickly began to dawn on him that, while Pompey and Caesar on their own might have been withstood, the addition of Crassus to their alliance made his enemies the effective masters of Rome. The three men would be able to carve up the Republic as they pleased, ruling as a troika, a 'triumvirate'. No wonder that Caesar had appeared so blithely self-assured.

Cato and Bibulus threw themselves into a desperate rearguard action to halt the passage of the land bill. On the day of the public vote Bibulus appeared in the Forum to announce that he had observed unfavourable omens in the sky, and that the vote would therefore have to be suspended. The response of the *pontifex maximus* to this news was to have a bucket of dung emptied over Bibulus' head. No sooner had the hapless consul begun wiping the excrement from his eyes than he found that a bodyguard formed of Pompey's veterans was beating up his lictors and smashing his *fasces*. Amid a chorus of jeers, Bibulus and Cato were then bundled from the Forum, after which the vote was taken and the land bill duly passed. To perform the lucrative task of administering it, a commission was established, headed by – who else? – Pompey and Crassus. Finally, to set the seal on his victory, Caesar demanded that the Senate swear to obey the new law. Intimidated and disoriented, his opponents meekly complied. Only two men held out. One of these was Metellus Celer, by now dangerously ill, but still with sufficient strength to continue his defiance of the man who had so grievously insulted his sister. The other, inevitably, was Cato. Both were finally persuaded to give way by Cicero, who pointed out that their exile would hardly serve to help their cause: 'You may not need Rome, but Rome will need you.'[7]

Yet even as Cato braced himself to carry on the fight he could not help but reflect with bitterness on his own role in the crisis. By pushing Caesar and Pompey to the extremes, and failing to anticipate the full depths of Crassus' cynicism, he had done much to precipitate the coup. 'The three-headed monster'[8] had been smoked out into the open, and now that it no longer had to keep to the shadows it was able to scavenge unfettered. Pompey had his settlement of the East ratified, Crassus toyed profitably with the tax laws, while Caesar scouted around for a proconsular command. He settled on the governorship of two provinces, Illyricum in the Balkans and, directly on the northern frontier of Italy itself, Gallia Togata, 'Toga-Wearing Gaul'. The only consolation for senators concerned at the thought of Caesar being awarded three legions virtually on Rome's doorstep was the fact that neither of his two provinces offered much scope for flamboyant conquests. Then suddenly, in the spring, Metellus Celer succumbed to his illness and

Caesar was given the opportunity to lay his hands on a third province – for Metellus' death had not only removed a thorn from Pompey's side, but left Transalpine Gaul, on the far side of the Alps, without a governor. This was a province temptingly menaced by any number of barbarians, and Caesar snaffled it up eagerly. The term of his command, for all three provinces, was set at a stupefying five years. The new proconsul was promised a rich feast of glory indeed.

For Cato, this represented an especially bitter defeat. The shattered fragments of his coalition were powerless to oppose it. When hatred for Pompey tempted Lucullus out of retirement one last time he was treated with such dismissive hostility by Caesar that he broke down and begged for mercy on his knees. That so great and haughty a man should have abased himself was shocking to everyone: perhaps, in the tears he shed before Caesar, there was an early symptom of the senile dementia that would progressively destroy him until his death two years later. If so, then the darkening of Lucullus' mind would have seemed to Cato a grim portent of the enfeeblement of the Republic. It was a sickness to which he was determined he would not succumb himself.

No true citizen could endure to be a slave. This was a truth written in the blood of Rome's history. After the bucket of excrement had been poured over his head, Bibulus had turned to his fellow consul, loosed the folds of his shit-bespattered toga, and bared his throat. Caesar, amused, had ducked the invitation to cut it – but, for all the melodrama of Bibulus' gesture, it had served to restore to him his honour. Cato and his allies had no qualms about offering themselves for martyrdom. The consul immured himself in his house, playing the refusenik to great effect for the remainder of the year, while Cato took the challenge directly into the Forum, daring his enemies to do their worst. Both men courted intimidation and violence. Not only did they succeed in casting a shadow of illegality over Caesar's legislation, but they ruined the image of the triumvirate behind it. No more telling blow in the propaganda war could have been struck. Caesar, for the sake of his career, had been prepared to play fast and loose with the constitution, but neither Pompey nor Crassus wished to be regarded as a rapist of the Republic. As far as they were concerned, they were playing by the rules: that complex, unwritten skein of precedents that bound every player in the political game. The powerful had been joining together in syndicates since the earliest days of the Republic. So it was, for instance, that when Caesar wished to solidify his alliance with Pompey he did so in the most traditional manner possible: by giving him the hand of his daughter. Cato, however, with the moral authority of a man who had refused to take a similar step, immediately denounced him as a pimp. Insults such as this drew blood. Although Crassus, Macavity-like as ever, evaded much of the abuse, Caesar and Pompey both grew steadily more reviled. They kept their grip on the reins of power, but that, for a Roman aristocrat, was never enough. He also had to be respected, honoured, loved.

For Pompey, unpopularity was especially hard to bear. The man who had spent a lifetime basking in the adoration of his fans now found himself 'physically twisted' by the loss of his prestige, 'moping miserably, racked with indecision'. So pathetic was the sight that Cicero told Atticus he believed that 'only Crassus could enjoy it'.[9] Naturally, the smirking of his old enemy did nothing to improve Pompey's mood. The alliance between the two men came increasingly under strain. Neither Crassus, scanning around for fresh carcasses to pick at, nor Pompey, morose with resentment and self-pity, felt any loyalty to the other. Within months of the emergence of the three-headed monster, two of the three heads were snapping viciously at each other. Cato, observing the spectacle with stern satisfaction, could begin to hope that the Republic might be saved after all.

True, there remained the menace of the third head. Caesar had Gaul waiting for him. A war there, which he was almost bound to start, would provide him with an unparalleled opportunity to rebuild his reputation. All the same, Cato's tactics had inflicted permanent damage on Caesar too. He would leave behind him in Rome a legacy of hatred and fear. No matter how much glory he won in Gaul, and no matter how much gold, a hard core of opponents would continue to regard him as a criminal. For as long as Caesar remained a proconsul he was safe from prosecution – but he could not remain in Gaul for ever. The five years would pass, and at the end of them Cato would be waiting, ready to move. Justice demanded it, as did the needs of his country. If Caesar were not destroyed, then force would be seen to have triumphed over law. A republic ruled by violence would barely be a republic at all.

Clodius Raises the Stakes

The winter festival of the crossroads, the Compitalia, had always been an excuse for riotous celebrations. To the poor, crammed into the maze of back alleys that snarled off every shopping street in Rome, the opportunity to band together, to honour the gods who protected their neighbourhood, was a precious one. But to the rich, it spelled trouble. The Senate, impatient with anything that appeared to challenge its authority, had spent the sixties BC legislating the Compitalia virtually out of existence. The local trade associations, the *collegia*, which had traditionally organised street parties during the festival, had been the particular focus of senatorial suspicion. In 64 they had been banned altogether. The festival itself had been left to wither and die.

By 59, the Compitalia had become so drained of menace that Cicero could regard it as nothing more than a pleasant backdrop to a stroll. His old friend Atticus was over from Greece, and in January, to celebrate the festival, Cicero suggested that they tour the city's crossroads together. The two men had much to discuss. It was the first month of Caesar's consulship. A few weeks previously Cicero had been approached by an agent of the triumvirate. Would he be interested, the agent had asked, in joining forces with Caesar, Pompey and Crassus? Cicero had failed to appreciate this offer for what it was, a chance to rule Rome – but even had he done so, he would surely still have turned it down. He was the conqueror of Catiline, after all. How could he possibly take part in a conspiracy against the Republic? The rule of law was precious to him – even more precious than his personal safety. Cicero, who was not a fearless man by nature, knew that his decision had left him dangerously exposed. Just think, he told Atticus wistfully, what he had turned his back on: 'reconciliation with my enemies, peace with the great unwashed, a leisured old age'.[10]

All the same, his nerves cannot have been too badly on edge, else he would never have suggested a tour of the crossroads. It had been in the cramped maze of Rome's alleyways that Catiline had sought to foster revolution, and three years after his death the spectres of debt and hunger still stalked the festering streets. As Cicero and Atticus negotiated their way through the filth they could hardly have failed to notice the signs of want. The aristocracy was not entirely oblivious to the sufferings of the poor. Cicero himself, when it suited him, might make eloquent common cause with what he privately disparaged as the 'mob'. Others went well beyond words. The senator responsible for doubling the distribution of subsidised grain in Rome had been none other than that pillar of the establishment Marcus Cato. Of course, even while promoting welfare, he had made sure to appear as stern and rectitudinous as ever. He did not, as Caesar did, seduce his fellow citizens, make them feel loved. Differences between politicians were a matter less of policy than of image. It would have been as insulting for Cato to be labelled a demagogue as for a matron to be confused with a whore.

This was why crossroads, which were notoriously the haunt of both rabble-rousers and prostitutes, were rarely frequented by the respectable; they were good for the occasional day out, perhaps, but nothing more than that. An association with crossroads could be grievously damaging to a citizen's good name – or to his wife's. Clodia Metelli, for instance, had found herself stuck with the mortifying nickname of 'Lady Copper-Bit',[11] after the low-rent hookers who plied their trade on street corners. One spurned lover described her as selling herself 'on crossroads and back-alleys',[12] while another sent her a purse filled with copper coins. Clodia was susceptible to these slanders because of her reputation for promiscuity and her raffish sense of fashion, but slang was not the limit of her taste for gangster chic. Disrespect was invariably punished. Humiliations were answered in kind. The humorist responsible for the gift of coppers had soon had the smile wiped off his face. Publicly beaten and gang-raped, it was he who had been used like a whore.

On no one did Clodia's glamorous blend of style and violence have a more profound influence than her younger brother. What would have been fatal to the career of a conventional politician was grasped by Clodius as a potential lifeline. He badly needed one. Acquitted of impiety he might have been, but his prospects had been severely damaged by the exposés of his trial. For a member of the Republic's most arrogant family, the discovery of how little support he commanded from his own class had been a wounding humiliation. As Lucullus could vouch, Clodius was as sensitive to personal affronts as he was imaginative in finding ways to avenge them. Cold-shouldered by the Senate, he began to play up to the slums. The poor, like every other class of Roman, were easily dazzled by snob appeal, and Clodius had both star quality and the popular touch to excess: a man capable of provoking a mutiny in defence of his wounded honour was clearly a demagogue of genius. Even so, Clodius would need to be elected tribune before he could hope to marshal the mob – and therein lay a problem. How could a man who was patrician to his fingertips hold an office reserved exclusively for plebeians? Only by becoming a plebeian himself – a move so unorthodox that it would require a public vote to secure his adoption into a plebeian family, which in turn would need to be sanctioned by a consul. This, in 59, effectively meant Caesar, a man well aware of Clodius' talent for making trouble. The time might come when the triumvirate would find a use for his antics; but in the meanwhile Caesar was content to leave the would-be tribune to stew.

All of which Atticus, a fixture at Clodia's dinner parties and therefore privy to Claudian gossip, was well placed to pass on to his friend. Cicero duly breathed a deep sigh of relief. Yet even with Clodius muzzled he found that the past kept on slipping its leash. One particular embarrassment was his former colleague as consul, Antonius Hybrida. After a corrupt and inept spell as governor of Macedon, the Catilinarian turncoat had just resurfaced in Rome. Also back in town, eager to make a mark, and to obscure his own involvement with Catiline, was the precocious Marcus Caelius. On both counts Hybrida presented him with an irresistible target. In April 59 Caelius brought a prosecution. He savaged the defendant in a brilliantly witty speech, portraying him as a disgrace to the Republic, whose twin policies as governor had been to grope slave-girls and spend his whole time drunk. But Cicero, for the defence, failed to enjoy his protégé's jokes. He had no fondness for Hybrida, but knew that the conviction of his former colleague, the man whose army had brought about Catiline's final demise, would have ominous implications for himself. His rushed execution of the conspirators had not been forgotten, nor, by many, forgiven. When

Hybrida was duly convicted the slums erupted in cheering. Bunches of flowers appeared on Catiline's grave.

For Cicero, the disaster of Hybrida's conviction was compounded by a fatal miscalculation. During the trial, in the course of a bad-tempered speech, he had dared to attack the members of the triumvirate by name. Caesar, aggravated by this buzzing of dissent, promptly moved to silence it. The means was ready to hand. Within hours of the speech having been given, Clodius had been declared a plebeian. Cicero, panicking, bolted from Rome. Hunkered down in a villa on the coast, he bombarded Atticus with frantic letters, begging him to milk Clodia for news of her brother's intentions. Then, towards the end of the month, venturing out on to the Appian Way, he ran into a friend coming from Rome who confirmed for him that, yes, Clodius was indeed standing for election to the tribunate. But if that were the bad news, then there was also some good. Clodius, it appeared, mercurial as ever, had already turned on Caesar. This immediately set Cicero to building castles in the air. Perhaps his two enemies, consul and prospective tribune, might end up destroying each other? A week later and Cicero was cheerleading for Clodius. 'Publius is our only hope,' he confided to Atticus. 'So yes, let him become a tribune, please, yes!'[13]

Even by Cicero's standards this was a startling turnaround. Yet in a city seething with machinations no feud could ever be reckoned eternal. Nothing better illustrated this than the identity of the friend who had met Cicero on the Appian Way. Curio, Clodius' closest political ally, was every bit as unprincipled and volatile as his friend. Since orchestrating the intimidation of Cicero at Clodius' trial he had continued to blot his reputation with scandal. His relationship with Hybrida's nephew, a rugged, handsome young man by the name of Mark Antony, had become the talk of Rome. Even by the standards of the time the scale of their debts was regarded as shocking. It was whispered that Antony, despite his bull-neck and muscle-bound body, dressed as a woman to play the role of Curio's wife. When the two men had been banned from seeing each other Curio had smuggled his friend in through his father's roof – or so the scandal-rakers claimed.* Then, in the year of Caesar's consulship, gossip and disapproval had abruptly turned to praise. Curio, far too arrogant to cringe before anyone, raised the morale of the entire Senate by his flamboyant defiance of Caesar. There was no more talk of him now as 'Curio's little daughter'. Instead, his recklessness was hailed as the courage of a patriot. Respectable senators saluted him in the Forum. The circus greeted him with rapturous acclaim.

These were marks of honour that any citizen might desire. In the shadow cast by the triumvirate Curio's defiance illumined the Republic. It was certainly no idle fantasy for Cicero to hope that Clodius might be tempted to share in his friend's glory. Yet fantasy it was soon to prove. Clodius had recognised, far more cynically and penetratingly than anyone else, the full scale of the opportunities presented by the crisis. For the moment at least the mould of the Republic had been shattered. Clodius, who rarely came across an orthodoxy without flaunting his contempt for it, was perfectly suited to this new climate of lawlessness. Rather than take a stand against the triumvirate, he prepared not merely to emulate their methods but to push them to new extremes. After all, with a conventional political career closed off to him, he had nothing to lose. Clodius was not interested in the bleating praise of men like Cicero. What he wanted, like any member of his arrogant, high-reaching

---

* To be specific, Cicero, sixteen years later, in the *Philippics*. Truth was rarely allowed to stand in the way of Cicero's talent for invective. All the same, it does appear at least possible that Antony's relationship with Curio had been sufficiently intimate to justify a whiff of scandal.

family, was power. Win that and the marks of honour would surely follow soon enough.

His plan was simple: seduce the mob and seize control of the streets. So criminal, so outrageous was this policy that in more settled times surely not even Clodius would have dared conceive it. With the events of Caesar's consulship, however, the fatal toxin of violence had been reintroduced to the Republic, and its poison was spreading fast. The triumvirate wished to maintain its stranglehold; the conservatives in the Senate wished to break free; both sides needed an ally prepared to dirty his hands. Clodius, promoting himself as just such a man, began alternately to woo and menace the two sides. 'Selling himself now to this client,' Cicero sneered, 'now to that'[14] – a whore, just like his sister. But Clodius' capriciousness disguised a savage sense of focus. In his ambitions, if not his loyalties, he was utterly constant. He wished to prove himself worthy of his family name. And in addition, of course, he wished to see Cicero destroyed.

In December Clodius took up his tribunate. He had prepared for the moment with great care. A raft of legislation was immediately laid before the people. The bills were crowd-pleasers all. Most blatantly eye-catching was a proposal to replace the subsidised grain supplies established by Cato with a free monthly dole. The slums duly seethed with gratitude, but Clodius had no illusions that this counted for much in itself. Of all the many treacherous foundations upon which a nobleman might build a career, none was more shifting than the affections of the poor: just as discipline made an army, so the lack of it made a mob. But what if a way could be found to mobilise the slums? This was the question that Clodius, surreptitiously, had introduced in the form of an innocuous-sounding second bill. He proposed that the Compitalia be restored to its full glory; the *collegia* too. All across the vast sprawl of Rome, wherever there were crossroads, the banned clubs would be reformed.

Clodius, with his gangster swagger, had always cut a dash as their patron. Now, if the law could only be passed, they would be bound to him for ever. Wherever there was a crossroads he would have a private gang.

This was a potentially massive innovation. Indeed, so massive an innovation was it that the Senate entirely failed to recognise it as such. The idea that a nobleman and the poor might have intimate bonds of obligation was entirely alien to the Roman mind, nor could anyone even conceive what the consequences might be. As a result, Clodius found it easy to force through the measure. He dealt with what limited opposition there was contemptuously, by twisting arms and greasing palms. Even Cicero was bought off. Using Atticus as a go-between, Clodius promised not to prosecute him over the executions of the conspirators, and Cicero, after much havering, agreed in return not to attack his enemy's bills. In early January 58 the legislation was passed. On the same day Clodius and his heavies occupied the temple of Castor, a convenient stone's throw away from the centre of the Forum. Here was where the *collegia* were to be organised. The space around the temple began to fill with tradesmen and artisans from the crossroads, chanting Clodius' name and jeering at his opponents. The steps to the temple itself were demolished, leaving the podium as a fortress. The *collegia* were restructured on paramilitary lines. The threat of violence grew ever more palpable in the air. Then, suddenly, the storm broke. When one of Caesar's lieutenants was arraigned for prosecution and appealed to the tribune for help, Clodius' gangs piled in, mugging the judge where he sat and smashing up the court. The trial itself was permanently abandoned. As an exercise in controlled thuggery, its success appears to have exceeded the expectations of even Clodius himself.

It certainly prostrated Cicero. Not only had his deadliest enemy revealed an alarming talent for organised violence, but he had also publicly aligned himself with the interests of Caesar. Since the end of his consulship, the new governor of Gaul had been lurking beyond the city's boundary, keeping track of events in Rome. Now he watched on in studied silence as Clodius prepared for his revenge. Trampling on the spirit, if not the letter, of his agreement with Cicero, the tribune brought forward yet another bill. Dressed up as a statement of stern republican principle, it proposed that any citizen guilty of putting another to death without trial should be sent into exile. There was no need to mention names. Everyone knew its target. With this deft push, Cicero was sent slithering and slipping towards the brink.

Scrabbling desperately to haul himself back, he grew his hair, put on mourning and toured the streets. Clodius' gangs dogged him, hurling abuse, stones and shit. Hortensius, trying to rally to his old rival's support, was cornered and almost lynched. Wherever Cicero looked, he found the escape routes blocked. The consuls, respectable senators who would normally have stood up for him, had been bribed with lucrative provincial commands. The Senate was cowed. Caesar, when Cicero brought himself to grovel in the proconsul's tent, was apologetic, but shrugged his shoulders and said that there was nothing he could do. Perhaps, he suggested silkily, Cicero might care to reconsider his opposition to the triumvirate and take a post on the governor's staff in Gaul? No matter how desperate Cicero's plight, that would have been a humiliation too far. Even exile was preferable to abject dishonour. Briefly, Cicero thought of fighting back, of organising street gangs of his own, but he was dissuaded by his friends. It was Hortensius, still covered in scars and bruises, who advised him to cut his losses and go. Stunned by the scale and suddenness of the catastrophe, taunted by the jeering from the pickets outside his house, contemplating the ruin of a lifetime's achievement, Cicero numbly prepared for his departure. Only in the dead of night did he at last dare steal out from his house. Travelling on foot to avoid attention from Clodius' gangs, he slunk through the streets towards the city gates. By dawn he was safely on the Appian Way. Behind him, as the morning hearth fires began to be lit, Rome shimmered and then vanished beneath a haze of brown smoke.

As the news began to spread through the waking city, Clodius was as stunned as everyone else. In an ecstasy of triumphalism his mobs surged up the Palatine and occupied Cicero's house. The wretched exile's mansion, his pride and joy, the most visible and public mark of his rank, was trashed. Then the demolition men moved in. Watched by a packed Forum, the house was torn to pieces, block by block, while next to it, casting the rubble in its imposing shadow, Clodius' mansion stood proud and inviolate. Just in case this act of vengeance was mistaken for mob violence, rather than the justified punishment of an enemy of the people, the tribune rushed through yet another bill, formally condemning Cicero by name. On the building site where the criminal's mansion had once stood, a temple to Liberty was raised. The remaining land was annexed by Clodius himself. All was transcribed on to a tablet of bronze, which the tribune, stern-faced, then carried to the Capitol and placed on public display. Here they were to stay for eternity, testifying to his glory, and to Cicero's crimes.

No wonder that the struggle for pre-eminence in the Republic was growing so savage, when the rewards could be so sweet.

Caesar's Winning Streak

As Cicero dragged himself disconsolately from Rome, into an exile that would ultimately see him holed up in Macedon, Caesar headed north. Now that the end-game between the great orator and Clodius appeared to have played itself out, the governor of Gaul could no longer afford to linger on in the outskirts of the capital.

Throughout the Alps trouble was threatening. German war bands had begun to flood across the Rhine, and waves from the incursions were already lapping against the Roman frontier.

Caesar, travelling as usual at a furious speed, headed directly for the point of maximum pressure. Eight days after leaving Rome he arrived in Geneva. Just beyond Lake Leman a vast and menacing wagon train was parked on the border. The Helvetians, natives of the Alps, had tired of their mountain home and wished to strike out west. The new governor, recognising a golden opportunity when he saw it, played for time. First, he announced to the tribesmen that he would consider their request to pass through Roman territory – then promptly sealed off the border. Five extra legions, two of them recruited from scratch, were force-marched to man it. The Helvetians, finding the frontier blocked, began to skirt its length, their long wagon train lumbering westwards, 360,000 men, women and children on the march. Caesar shadowed them, passing across the frontier and into free Gaul. Taking the Helvetians by surprise, he ambushed their rearguard and then, when the tribesmen attacked Caesar in turn, defeated them a second time in a ferocious battle. The survivors sued for terms. Caesar ordered them back home.

It had been a stunning victory – and thoroughly illegal. The previous year sweeping new measures had come into effect, specifically designed to regulate abuses by provincial governors and restrain their ambitions. Their author had been none other than Caesar himself. Now, by picking a fight with a tribe not subject to the Republic, on territory not ruled by the Republic, he had flagrantly broken his own law. His enemies back in Rome were quick to point this out. In time, Cato would even propose that Caesar be handed over to the tribes he had assaulted. To many in the Senate, the Gallic adventure appeared both unwarranted and unjust.

Not to most citizens, however. One man's war criminal was another man's hero. Barbarian migrations had always been the stuff

of Roman nightmares. Whenever wagons began rumbling across
the north, the reverberations would echo far away in the Forum.
The Republic had no fiercer bogeyman than the pale-skinned,
horse-maned, towering Gaul. Hannibal might have ridden up to
Rome's gates and flung his javelin over them, but he had never
succeeded in capturing the seat of the Republic. Only the Gauls had
managed that. Way back, at the beginning of the fourth century BC,
a barbarian horde had burst without warning across the Alps, sent
a Roman army fleeing from it in panic, and swept into Rome. The
Capitol alone had remained sacrosanct, and even that would have
fallen had not the sacred geese of Juno alerted the garrison to a
surprise attack. When the Gauls, having slaughtered, looted and
burned at will, had withdrawn as suddenly as they had come, they
had left behind them a city resolved never again to endure such
indignities. This was the steel that had enabled Rome to become the
mistress of the world.

Even three centuries later, however, memories of the Gauls
remained raw. Every year guard-dogs would be crucified, a posthumous punishment of the dogs who had failed to bark on the
Capitol, while Juno's geese, as an ongoing reward for their ancestors' admonitory honking, were brought to watch the spectacle on
cushions of purple and gold. A more practical measure was the
setting aside of an emergency fund, to be used only in the event of
a second barbarian invasion. Even now that the Republic was a
superpower this was regarded as an eminently sensible precaution.
When men lived not as citizens but halfway to beasts there could be
no knowing when their savagery might not suddenly erupt. Within
living memory a nation of giants, three hundred thousand of them,
it was reckoned, had appeared suddenly from the wastelands of the
north, destroying everything in their way, subhuman monsters
from the icy rim of the world. Their men had eaten raw flesh; their
women had attacked legionaries with their bare hands. Had Marius,

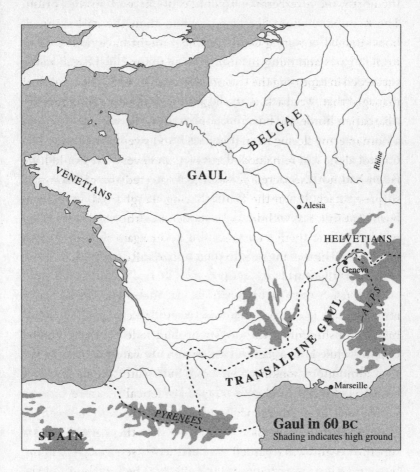

Gaul in 60 BC
Shading indicates high ground

in two brilliant victories, not managed to annihilate the invaders, then Rome, and the world with her, would surely have come to an end.

Scares on this scale were not quickly forgotten. No wonder that most citizens, when they heard the news of the Helvetians' defeat, cared nothing for the laws that might have been broken to achieve it. After all, what greater duty did a proconsul have than to secure the safety of Rome? Caesar himself scrupulously refuted the charge of glory-hunting. The security of his province, and Italy too, had been at stake. For as long as there were restless tribes beyond the Roman frontier, ignorant of the conventions of civilised behaviour, the danger would persist. By this logic, familiar to generations of Romans, the assault on the Helvetians could be reckoned an act of self-defence. So too Caesar's ongoing campaign – for having dispatched the Helvetians back to their homeland, to serve as a buffer between the Germans and his province, he had next swung east to attack the Germans themselves. The fact that their king had been given the official title of 'friend of the Roman people' cut no ice with Caesar. The Germans were successfully provoked into offering battle, defeated, then driven back across the Rhine. There, in the dark, dripping woods, they were welcome to lurk, but not near Caesar's province – nor anywhere in Gaul.

Already the two were being elided. That winter of 58–57 BC, rather than withdrawing his legions back into his province, Caesar left them billeted a hundred miles north of the frontier, deep in the territory of a supposedly independent tribe. Once again, an illegal measure was justified by the proconsul as an act of forward defence. This was an argument that may have satisfied public opinion back in Rome, but it did nothing to ease a mounting sense of outrage in Gaul itself. The full implications of Caesar's new policy were by now starting to hit home. What precisely would satisfy the Romans' desire for a defensible frontier? If the Rhine to the east, then why not the Channel to the north, or the Atlantic coast to the west? Across frozen forests and fields, from village to village, from chieftain's hall to chieftain's hall, the same rumour was borne: the Romans were aiming 'to pacify all Gaul'.[15] As warriors burnished their glittering, jewel-wrought shields, and striplings, eager to prove themselves ready for battle, forded ice-sheeted streams with full armour on their backs, so rival tribes sought to patch up their differences. Free Gaul prepared itself for war.

As did Caesar. He was not the man to tolerate anti-Roman agitation. It made no difference whether a tribe had been defeated or was free, the Republic demanded respect, and honour required that a proconsul instil it. Having provoked the Gauls into defiance, Caesar now felt perfectly justified in smashing it. That winter he recruited two more legions. High-handedly, and without any reference to the Senate, he had already doubled the number of troops originally allocated to his province. When winter thawed to spring and Caesar left camp, he had an army of eight legions, some forty thousand men, by his side.

He would need every last one. Heading due north, Caesar was venturing into territory never before penetrated by Roman forces. It was shadow-haunted, sinister, dank with mud and slaughter. Travellers whispered of strange rites of sacrifice, performed in the dead of oaken glades, or by the side of black-watered, bottomless lakes. Sometimes, it was said, the nights would be lit by vast torches of wickerwork, erected in the forms of giants, their limbs and bellies filled with prisoners writhing in an orgy of death. Even at the feasts for which the Gauls were famous, their customs were barbarous and repulsive. The ubiquitous Posidonius, who had travelled through Gaul in the nineties BC, taking notes wherever he went, observed that duels were common over the best cuts of meat, and that even when warriors did get round to feasting they would not lie down to eat, as civilised men did, but would sit and let their straggling moustaches drip with grease and gravy. Blank-eyed spectators of these scenes of gluttony, and a spectacle even more repellent, were the severed heads of the warriors' enemies, stuck on poles or in niches. So universally were these used as decorations in Gaulish villages that, Posidonius confessed, he had almost grown used to them by the end of his trip.[16]

To the legionaries, marching ever further north along pitted, winding tracks, peering nervously through the endless screens of trees, it must have appeared that they were entering a realm of utter darkness. This was why, on their shoulders, they bore stakes as well as spears. The camp they built after every day's march, always identical, night after night, provided them not only with security against ambushes, but also a reminder of civilisation, of home. In the midst of barbarism, a forum and two straight streets would be laid out. The sentries, peering out into the blackness from behind the palisade, would have the comfort of knowing that behind them, at least, there was a corner of a foreign field that was temporarily Rome.

Yet what appeared impossibly barbarous to the legionaries had already been synthesised and fed through Caesar's intelligence machine. Their general knew precisely where he was heading – and it was not into the unknown. Caesar may have been the first to lead the legions beyond the frontier, but there had been Italians roaming through the wilds of Gaul for decades. In the second century BC, with the establishment of permanent Roman garrisons in the south of the country, the natives of the province had begun to develop a taste for their conquerors' vices. One, in particular, had gone straight to their heads: wine. The Gauls, who had never come across the drink before, had not the slightest idea how to handle it. Rather than diluting it with water, as the Romans did, they preferred to down it neat, wallowing in drunken binges, and 'ending up so inebriated that they either fall asleep or go mad'.[17] Merchants, who found this style of consumption highly lucrative, had begun to foster it as widely as they could, travelling far beyond the limits of the Roman province, until soon enough the whole of Gaul had grown sodden with liquor. Naturally, with a market of alcoholics to exploit, the merchants had begun to inflate their prices. Since their ability to do this depended on the natives not cultivating their own vineyards, the Senate, ever savvy when it came to fleecing foreigners, had made it illegal to sell vines to 'the tribes beyond the Alps'.[18] By Caesar's time the exchange rate had stabilised at a jar of wine for one slave, which, at least as far as the Italians were concerned, made for a fabulously profitable import–export business. The slaves could be sold on for a huge mark-up, and the extra manpower available to Roman viticulturists enabled ever more gallons of wine to be produced. It was a virtuous circle that kept everyone – apart from the slaves, of course – happy. The Gauls stayed sozzled, and the merchants grew rich.

Caesar, in daring to imagine that he could impose himself upon a country as vast, warlike and independent as Gaul, was perfectly aware how much he owed to Italian exporters. It was not only that they provided him with spies. The Germans, having witnessed the effect of wine on the Gauls, had gone so far as to 'ban it from being imported into their own country, because they think it makes men soft'.[19] Quarrelsome too. Wine was more precious to Gallic chieftains than gold. Tribes were endlessly raiding each other for slaves, depopulating the countryside with their razzias, breeding bestial, debilitating rivalries – all of which made them easy prey for a man such as Caesar. Even when his spies reported that a confederation numbering 240,000 had been formed against him, he was unperturbed. This was despite the fact that the tribes in his way belonged to the Belgae, the people who, because 'they were furthest removed from the civilisation and luxury of the Roman province, and were least often visited by merchants importing the kind of goods which lead to effeminacy',[20] were reckoned the bravest in Gaul. Caesar struck against them hard, with all the steel-armoured efficiency he could bring to bear. The further north he advanced, the more the Belgic alliance fragmented. Tribes who submitted were treated with ostentatious generosity. Those who resisted were wiped out. Caesar's eagles were duly planted on the coast of the North Sea. At the same time messengers came to him from Publius Crassus, the dashing young son of the triumvir, with news that the legion under his command had received the submission of all the tribes in the west. 'Peace', Caesar wrote in triumph, 'had been brought to the whole of Gaul.'[21]

The news was received ecstatically back in Rome. In 63 Pompey had been granted ten days of public thanksgiving. Now, in 57, Caesar was awarded fifteen. Not even his bitterest enemies could deny the stunning nature of his achievements. After all, nothing that enhanced the prestige of the Republic could be reckoned a crime, and Caesar, by teaching the Gauls to honour its name, had brought into the orbit of Rome people previously lost in the darkness of barbarism. As one of his old opponents gushed in the Senate, 'regions and nations unreported to us in books, or in first-hand accounts, or even by rumours, have now been penetrated by our general, our army, and the arms of the Roman people'.[22] Rejoice indeed!

Yet, for Caesar, there could be no relaxing. Deep and devastating though his incursion had been, a single raid had hardly been sufficient to reduce Gaul to the status of a province. For now, the country was prepared to acknowledge Caesar's prestige, but supremacy, among a people as inveterately competitive and quarrelsome as the Gauls, was founded on treacherous sands. And so it was too, of course, in Rome. This was why Caesar, even in the damp forests of the north, still had to keep one eye firmly fixed on the political battlefield in the capital. Events in Rome did not stand still just because he was absent. Much had already changed. Nothing better illustrated this than the identity of the man who had stood up in the Senate to propose the thanksgiving for Caesar's achievements in Gaul. After a bitter exile of eighteen months Cicero had returned to Rome.

Pompey Throws Again

In the dark days before his flight into exile the frantic orator had gone grovelling to Pompey as well as to Caesar. Cicero had long despaired of his idol's failings, but he had never entirely given up on him. Despite Pompey's evident complicity in the outrages of Caesar's consulship, Cicero had continued to hope against hope that all might yet be well, and the great man be won back to the cause of legitimacy. Pompey, for his part, had been flattered to play the role of Cicero's patron, and had even condescended to warn Clodius against pushing his vendetta too far. There had been a certain pathos in this gesture: at a time when his popularity was in free fall, and he was being booed for the first time in his life, Pompey had found in Cicero's hero-worship a welcome reminder of the good old days. Desperate to unburden his doubts and frustrations, he had even confessed to the orator that he regretted his role in the triumvirate – a revelation that Cicero, in high excitement, had immediately passed on to all his friends. Inevitably, Caesar had got wind of it – and been confirmed in his view that Cicero would have to go. Pompey, forced to choose between his father-in-law and his trusting friend, had reluctantly acquiesced. As Clodius' persecution of Cicero reached its violent climax, so he had retired in embarrassment to his country villa. Refusing to take the hint, Cicero had pursued him there. He had been informed by the doorman that no one was at home. Pompey, unable to face an interview with the man he had betrayed, had slipped out through the back.

With Cicero safely gone, the great man was plunged into a renewed bout of brooding. Equivocations did not sit well with his self-image. He was still no nearer to squaring the impossible circle that had tormented him since his return from the East. He wanted the respect and admiration of his peers, and the supreme authority to which he believed his achievements entitled him – but he could not have both. Now, having made his choice, he found that power without love had a bitter taste. Spurned by Rome, Pompey turned for comfort instead to his wife. He had married Caesar's daughter, Julia, for the chilliest of political motives, but it had not taken him long to grow helplessly smitten with his young bride. Julia, for her part, gave her husband the adoration without which he could not flourish. Surrendering to their mutual passion, the couple began to spend more and more time secluded in a love nest in the country. Pompey's fellow citizens, unaccustomed as they were to displays of conjugal affection, sniggered in prurient disapproval. Here was true scandal. The public resentment of Pompey began to grow tinged with scorn.

No one was more sensitive to this changing wind of opinion than Clodius. He had a good nose for weakness, and began to wonder whether Pompey, for all the glamour of his reputation and his loyal veterans, might not perhaps be a man of straw – a hunch far too tempting not to be put immediately to the test. Aware that nothing would prove more vexatious to Pompey than a renewed assault on his settlement of the East – the issue which, after all, had forced him into the fateful alliance with Crassus and Caesar in the first place – Clodius went straight for the jugular. Prince Tigranes, the son of the King of Armenia, was still in Rome as a hostage, eight years after his father had handed him over to Pompey as a guarantee of good behaviour. Clodius not only abducted the Prince from under the great man's nose, but then, to add injury to insult, put him on a boat bound for Armenia. When Pompey tried to seize back his hostage, his supporters were set upon and beaten up. The establishment, far from taking Pompey's side, relished the spectacle of his impotent rage. This, of course, was precisely what Clodius had been banking on. Even as his gangs were rampaging through the streets, he found himself basking in the glow of the Senate's approval.

Not that Clodius, given the opportunity to humiliate an enemy, had ever needed much encouragement. As with Cicero, so now with Pompey, he could smell blood. His gangs duly went into a feeding frenzy. Whenever the unhappy Pompey ventured into the Forum he would be greeted with a chorus of jeers. This was no idle matter. One of the most ancient laws of the Republic defined the chanting of abuse as akin to murder. By the light of such tradition Clodius was issuing death-threats, and Pompey was unnerved accordingly. He had never before been the object of such mockery. His passion for his wife provoked particular hilarity. '"What's the name of the sex-mad general?"' Clodius would yell. '"Who touches the side of his head with his finger?" . . . And after each question, he would make a signal to the mob by shaking out the folds of his toga, and his gangs, like a trained chorus, would scream out the answer in unison: "Pompey!"'[23]

'Who touches the side of his head with his finger?' For a man given to dressing up as a dancing-girl to accuse Rome's greatest general of effeminacy took some nerve. This was all the more so because many of his most intimate circle were also embroiled in sex scandals. Mark Antony, moving on from his affair with Curio, had begun sniffing around Clodius' much-loved wife, Fulvia, a breach of the codes of friendship that would soon see the two men threatening to kill each other. Similar trouble was also brewing over a woman to whom Clodius was even more passionately devoted. Following his triumphant prosecution of Hybrida, Marcus Caelius had celebrated by renting a luxury apartment from Clodius on the Palatine. There he had met Clodia. Witty, handsome and famous for his rhythm, Caelius had proved to be just the widow's type. The ambitious Caelius had needed no encouragement to take up with a Claudian, and Clodia, with her husband barely cold, was evidently in the mood for consolation. Of course, her idiosyncratic style of mourning could not help but raise eyebrows. The affairs of the great lady remained a topic of abiding interest to Rome's scandal-rakers, and a favourite theme of abusive sloganeering in the Forum. But no matter what was chanted against him and his sister, Clodius was always able to drown it out. Charges of immorality only pro-voked him to ever more furious denunciations of his own. The outrageous hypocrisy of it all only added to the fun. And so the abuse of Pompey and his lechery continued.

Of course, Clodius being Clodius, he could not resist seeing just how far the intimidation could be pushed. In August, as Pompey was crossing the Forum to attend a meeting of the Senate, a clat-tering of metal on stone rang out from the temple of Castor. One of Clodius' slaves had pointedly dropped a dagger. Pompey, believing his life to be in danger, at once retreated from the Forum and bar-ricaded himself behind his front door. Clodius' gangs pursued him and set up camp outside. The tribune threatened to do to Pompey what he had already done to Cicero: seize his mansion, level it and build a temple to Liberty in its place. Pompey, unlike Cicero, did not bolt and run, but he found himself blockaded, unable to leave his house – a staggering reversal for the greatest man in the Republic. Again the Senate watched on in smug satisfaction. Crassus, with whom Clodius had been careful to remain on excellent terms, nat-urally shared in the general smirking. For Clodius himself, it was an intoxicating, scarcely believable moment of triumph. Champion of the aristocracy, patron of the slums, he appeared to be the master of Rome.

But only fleetingly. By testing the opportunities provided by street violence to the very limits, Clodius had blazed a trail that others were already preparing to follow. In December 58 Clodius' term of office came to an end. Among the new tribunes was a gruff and brutal Pompeian, Titus Annius Milo. Encouraged by his patron, Milo formally indicted Clodius for employing violence, an open-and-shut case if ever there was one. Clodius, by appealing to his brother Appius, who was praetor that year, managed to have the charge suppressed, and ordered his gangs to ransack Milo's house in revenge. But the new tribune, backed by the infinite resources of Pompey, and aware that he was dead meat unless he met violence with violence, refused to be intimidated. He began to recruit gangs of his own, not, as Clodius had done, by bribing amateurs from the slums, but by importing well-armed, well-trained heavies from Pompey's estates and buying up gladiators to steel their ranks. At a stroke, Clodius' monopoly on street violence ended, a challenge to which the former tribune rose with predictable gusto. The gang warfare escalated daily. Soon, it had become so brutal that all government institutions in the Forum, including the law courts, had to be suspended. Day after day, across the public places of Rome, the tides of anarchy ebbed and flowed.

By such desperate measures did Pompey impose himself and his authority back upon a city in which for months he had been kept under virtual house arrest. Yet the Senate, as well as the streets, had to be bent to his will, and Clodius, the arrogant, impossible Clodius, given a taste of his own medicine. The obvious means for achieving that was even then wringing his hands in high-flown misery across the Adriatic. Pompey, having refused to exert himself to save Cicero the year before, now began touring Italy, drumming up support for the exile's return. Clients in the countryside and provincial towns were ordered to Rome. All through the summer of 57 they flooded into the capital. Meanwhile, Caesar, far away in Gaul, had been persuaded to give his reluctant approval to Cicero's recall, and a vote in the Senate also backed it, by 416 to 1.

The dissenting voice had, inevitably, belonged to Clodius. In August the long-awaited public vote was finally held in the Campus Martius. Clodius, attempting to disrupt it, was seen off with contemptuous ease by Milo, whose gangs stood on guard all day by the Ovile. So confident was Cicero of the result that he had already set sail for Italy as the vote was being held, and he was brought the news of his official recall as he waited in Brundisium. His progress from then on, with Tullia, his adored and much-missed daughter by his side, was like a dream come true. Cheering supporters lined the Appian Way. As he approached Rome the crowds streamed out to greet him. Applause followed him wherever he went. 'I did not simply return home,' he observed modestly, 'but ascended to the sky.'[24]

But not even Cicero was conceited enough to doubt that the real triumph had been Pompey's. More than ever, the orator's old, familiar boasting had a shrillness bred of fear. Every Roman found it an agony to owe another man a favour, and Cicero now owed Pompey and Caesar his career. Hence his gushing in the Senate House. As well as leading the praise for Caesar's conquests, he found himself proposing that Rome's entire corn supply be put into Pompey's hands. The motion was passed, but only once Clodius, with hateful logic, had pointed out to the Senate House its precise implications: Pompey would be able to bribe the starving slums with bread, while Cicero, the self-proclaimed scourge of demagoguery, now stood revealed as its agent. The bare-faced effrontery of these accusations did not make them any less true. Cicero duly spluttered and squirmed.

The exchange in the Senate House had served notice that Clodius felt not remotely chastened by his enemy's return. When Cicero succeeded in persuading Rome's priests that his mansion on the Palatine could be restored to him without offence to the goddess Liberty, Clodius resorted to naked terrorism. Cicero's workmen were driven from the building-site; his brother's house was set on fire; Cicero himself was assaulted on the via Sacra. At the same time the street fighting between Clodius and Milo reached a new pitch of violence, and the two gang leaders, each openly threatening to murder the other, also attempted to pursue each other through the courts. Once again, Milo indicted Clodius on a charge of using violence, and once again, by pulling strings in the Senate, Clodius wriggled free. In February 56, with a hypocrisy remarkable by even his standards, Clodius brought an identical charge against Milo. Cicero and Pompey, rallying to their man's cause, prepared to speak in Milo's defence. The spectacle of his three deadliest enemies lined up against him threw Clodius into a frenzy. As Pompey rose to speak the Forum seethed with catcalls and jeers. Clodius, from the prosecutor's bench, began cheering on his gangs. As he had done before, he stood and tugged on his toga, giving cues to his supporters as they chanted abuse. Soon they were spitting at Milo's strongarms, then throwing fists and stones. Milo's gangs fought back. Clodius himself was dragged off the rostra, and a full-scale battle broke out. Amid the pandemonium, the trial itself was abandoned.

Pompey, shaken and bruised, retired from the Forum pale with fury. He was in no doubt who the mastermind behind the riot had been – and it was not Clodius. For three years Pompey had been in a syndicate with Crassus, and still he was quick to blame his old nemesis for every debacle. On this occasion, however, his suspicions appeared well founded. Ever since autumn 57, and his appointment as Rome's grain commissar, Pompey had been angling for another Eastern command. So too had Crassus. Until the riot, mutual self-interest had kept their rivalry in the shadows, but Clodius, typically, had ripped aside the veil. 'Who's after a trip east?' he had bellowed to his gangs. 'Pompey!' the gangs had thundered back in reply. 'Who do we all want to go instead?' The answer had been deafening, and calculated to give Pompey apoplexy: 'Crassus!'[25] A few days later Pompey told Cicero that he blamed his partner in the triumvirate for the riot, for Clodius, for everything. He then confided, just for good measure, that Crassus was plotting to have him killed.

The news spread like wildfire. The triumvirate was finished. That much, at least, seemed clear to everyone. If anyone did express surprise, it was only that the syndicate had lasted so long. After all, as surely as the seasons passed, so too did the grip of great men upon power. In that spring of 56 BC the thaw seemed general throughout the Republic. Old enemies of the triumvirate – Bibulus, Curio – began to stir, stretch their limbs, wake from hibernation. In the Senate the riot in the Forum was officially condemned as 'contrary to the interests of the Republic',[26] and the responsibility for it pinned not on Clodius but on Pompey. This insult to his honour needled the great man into another vast explosion of temper, and, inevitably, he blamed Crassus. But although this may briefly have served to cheer him up, the evidence of his unpopularity with the entire Senate was now too glaring to be ignored. All his dearest ambitions – to bask in the praise and respect of his peers, to lead a brilliant second command to the East – stood revealed as hopeless fantasies. For Pompey the Great, it appeared, the glory days were over. As his fury subsided he plunged into a massive sulk.

The scent of his failure hung like carrion-perfume over Rome. In the Senate scavengers whined and snarled with excitement. With Pompey wallowing helplessly in the shallows, attention next turned to the prospects for beaching a second big beast. Caesar's enemies knew that there would never be a better opportunity to finish him off. Three years they had been waiting – and now, at last, one of them moved in for the kill.

Courage came easily to Lucius Domitius Ahenobarbus. In his case it was indistinguishable from an arrogance so pronounced as to verge on stupidity. Obscenely rich, obscenely well bred, he was a man described by Cicero, who was sensitive to such things, as having been born a consul-designate. In that spring of 56, Domitius prepared to claim his birthright. A brother-in-law of Cato, a blood-enemy of Pompey, who had executed Domitius' brother in the dark days of the civil war, there could be no doubting where his loyalties would lie. In announcing that he would stand for the consulship, he openly declared that, if elected, he would have Caesar's command declared invalid. As a replacement, naturally, he proposed himself. Transalpine Gaul had been conquered by his grandfather and he regarded it as his by hereditary right. At his back the establishment bayed its approval. First Pompey; now Caesar – surely the over-reachers, the would-be tyrants, were doomed?

Four and a half centuries of the Republic's history said that they were. Tradition was stronger than any triumvirate. One man slipped, another took his place. This was how it had always been. Let Pompey, Caesar and their successors be eclipsed. Whatever happened, the Republic would endure.

Or so everyone assumed.

9

THE WINGS OF ICARUS

Crassus Loses his Head

As the triumvirate splintered, others, lower down the food chain, were engaged in desperate struggles of their own. At the beginning of April, Marcus Caelius was brought to trial. His colourful past did not bear close scrutiny. Certainly, the prosecution had no problem in alleging a vast range of vices and crimes, including – most shockingly of all – an assault on a deputation of ambassadors and the murder of its leader. What gave the trial its whiff of scandal, however, was a further charge: that Caelius had attempted to poison his lover, Clodia Metelli. Clearly the relationship had not been going well.

Not that the prosecutors ever even alluded to it. Because the details of the affair promised to be as damaging to Caelius as to Clodia, they had calculated that the defence team would be equally as discreet. But they had reckoned without Cicero. Relations with his old pupil had long been rocky, but the opportunity to launch a full-frontal assault on Clodia had been too good to miss. Rather than draw a veil over the affair, Cicero instead chose to make it the focus of his entire defence. 'Suppose a woman who has lost her husband throws her house open to every man who needs sexual release, and publicly lives the life of a prostitute, suppose she thinks nothing of going to parties given by total strangers, suppose she carries on like this in Rome, in her pleasure-gardens, and among the orgy-set at Baiae,' he thundered, 'then do you really think it would be scandalous and disgraceful for a young man such as Caelius to have picked her up?'[1] Of course not! After all, she was only a street-walker, and therefore fair game! The jurors, listening to Rome's queen of chic being eviscerated in this manner, were titillated and appalled. What they failed to notice was that Cicero, by going after his enemy's sister, had obscured all the really serious charges against his client beneath a froth of innuendo. The strategy proved to be gratifyingly successful: Caelius was acquitted. Cicero could purr with satisfaction at a hatchet-job well done.

So dazzling had the performance been that it quite put in the shade a speech delivered at the trial by Caelius' other guardian. Not that this would have concerned Crassus. He had never been one for pyrotechnics. He had no need of them. His purpose in coming to Caelius' rescue had been to protect his investment in the young man's future; a goal duly achieved, and at minimal political cost to himself. True, he had been privy to the demolition of Clodia, but even Clodius, rarely reticent in defence of his family's honour, knew better than to lash out at Crassus. Subtle and understated in his methods he may have been, a man of whispered hints and promises rather than open threats, yet he remained the most menacing figure in Rome. Now at last, in the spring of 56, Crassus was preparing to test just how far that menace would carry him. Even as he spoke at Caelius' trial his mind was elsewhere. A political master-stroke was being prepared.

The previous month Crassus had travelled to Ravenna, a town just beyond the frontier of Roman Italy, inside Caesar's province of Gaul. Two other power-brokers had been waiting there for him.

One had been Caesar himself, the other Clodius' haughty eldest brother, Appius Claudius. Following a secret conference between the three men Crassus had returned to Rome, while Appius, staying with Caesar, had headed west. In mid-April the two conspirators arrived in the frontier town of Lucca. So too, heading north from Rome, did Pompey. A second conference was held. Again, its precise terms remained mysterious, but news of the meeting itself had spread so quickly that Pompey, arriving for it, had been accompanied by two hundred senators. More than a hundred bundles of *fasces* could be seen propped up in the Luccan streets. Senators on the make, their nostrils filled with the scent of power, scrabbled for advancement. To their more principled colleagues back in Rome, the clamouring of these aristocratic petitioners delivered an ominous message. Once again, authority appeared to be draining away from the Senate. Perhaps the triumvirate was not dead, after all?

And yet it seemed barely credible that Pompey and Crassus could have patched up an alliance a second time. What compact could they possibly have reached? And what of Caesar's role in the murky business? What was he after now? One of the first to find out was Cicero. Chastened by his experience of exile, he no longer had any illusions that he could hold out against the combined might of the triumvirate. Against Clodius and Clodia, yes, but not against those who were infinitely his superior 'in resources, armed force, and naked power'.[2] When Pompey leaned on him he crumpled. Vulnerable and nervy, eloquent and respected, Cicero made a perfect tool. He was put to work straight away. That summer he had to stand up in the Senate House and propose that the provinces of Gaul, which Domitius Ahenobarbus had been eyeing so hopefully, remain Caesar's, and his alone. Domitius, taken aback by this *volte-face*, exploded with fury. What was Cicero up to? Why was he arguing for something that he had once condemned as outrageous? Had he no shame? In private such questions left Cicero sick with misery. He knew that he was being exploited, and hated himself for it. In public, however, he paraded the ingenious argument that by changing sides he was in fact displaying statesmanship. 'Standing rigid and unchanging has never been considered a great virtue in the Republic,' he pointed out. Far from trimming, he was merely 'moving with the times'.[3]

No one was much convinced – Cicero himself least of all. Maudlin with self-contempt, he tried to cheer himself up by indulging in the one constant he had been left, his blood-feud with Clodius. High on the Capitol, the bronze tablet celebrating his exile was still on public display. Accompanied by Milo, Cicero took it down, removed it and hid it in his house.* Clodius not only had the nerve to denounce him for unconstitutional behaviour, a complaint upheld by Cato at his most sententious, but also erected billboards on the Palatine advertising a long list of Cicero's crimes. Even among the shifting sands of the Republic there were some things that never changed.

Yet even as their dog-fight twisted this way and that, the two men found themselves joined by more than mutual hatred. Appius had decided that it was time he became consul: hence his trips to Ravenna and Lucca to meet the triumvirs. In return for their backing in the elections for 54 he had offered them the support of himself and his youngest brother. For Pompey in particular, who had spent two years being harried and humiliated by Clodius, this was a rich prize indeed. The inimitable talents of Rome's greatest rabble-rouser were now the triumvirs' to do with as they pleased. Just as Cicero had been employed as the tool of Caesar's interests, so Clodius was put to work serving those of Pompey and Crassus.

---

* Or destroyed it, the evidence is unclear.

Orders went out to his network of tribunes and gang-leaders. A campaign of intimidation was launched, its aim to secure the postponement of the consular elections for 55. The violence, as it tended to do whenever Clodius was involved, quickly escalated. A band of senators attempted to block his entry into the Senate House; Clodius' supporters responded by threatening to burn the Senate House to the ground. Meanwhile, the elections had still not been held, and all the while Rome was filling with the triumvirs' clients, including a great flood of Caesar's veterans, given special leave from Gaul. Outraged senators put on mourning. Horrible suspicions crowded their minds. At last the question that had been buzzing around Rome for months was put openly to Pompey and Crassus, both of whom had been attempting, in their most statesmanlike manner, to stay above the fray. Were they planning to stand for the consulship of 55? Crassus, slippery as ever, answered that he would do whatever was best for the Republic, but Pompey, pinned down by insistent questioning, finally blurted out the truth. The carve-up that had enabled them to bury their rivalry stood revealed to the world.

Opposition was instantaneous and implacable. The two candidates were taken aback. Having postponed the elections in order to fill the city with Caesar's veterans, they now began to panic that they might still not win. Midnight visits were paid to the homes of rival candidates. Muscles were flexed, arms twisted. Only Domitius refused to stand down. By now it was January. For the first weeks of 55 there had been no consuls at all, and elections could no longer be postponed. Hours before the voting pens opened, in the dead of night, Domitius and Cato attempted to stake a place on the Campus Martius. There they were surprised by armed thugs who killed their torchbearer, wounded Cato, and put their men to flight. The next day Pompey and Crassus duly secured their second joint consulship. Even now they had not finished with their election rigging. When Cato won a praetorship Pompey had the result declared void. The aedileships were shamelessly parcelled out to supporters; so much so, in fact, that the Campus erupted into fresh violence. This time Pompey was caught in the thick of it and his toga splashed with blood.

The sodden garment was taken back to his home, where his pregnant wife was waiting anxiously for news. When Julia saw the blood-caked toga she fainted with shock and her baby was lost. No one could be surprised that the sight of Pompey the Great spattered with the gore of his fellow citizens should have resulted in his wife's miscarriage. By such signs did the gods make their judgements known. The Republic itself was being aborted. Cicero, writing in confidence to Atticus, joked miserably that the triumvirs' notebooks were no doubt filled with 'lists of future election results'.[4] To their peers, the criminality of Pompey and Crassus was so naked as to appear sacrilegious. Whereas before, in 59, they had employed Caesar as their proxy, now it was they who were staining the sacred office of the consulship. And to what end? Surely they had already both won glory enough? Why, merely to secure the consulship for a second time, had they resorted to such violent and illegal extremes?

The answer was not long in coming, and even Pompey and Crassus had the grace to be embarrassed by it. When a tame tribune came forward with a bill that would give the consuls five-year commands in Syria and Spain the two men affected innocent surprise, but no one was fooled. The more closely the terms of the bill were inspected, the more dismaying they appeared. The two proconsuls were to have the right to levy troops, and declare war and peace, without reference to the Senate or the people. A separate bill awarded identical privileges to Caesar, confirming him in his command and extending it for a further five years. Between them, the three members of the syndicate would now have direct control of twenty legions and Rome's most critical provinces. The city had often echoed to cries of 'tyranny' – but never, surely, with such justification as now.

From its earliest days the nightmare that its own ideals might turn against it had haunted the Republic. 'It is disturbing', Cicero reflected, 'that it tends to be men of genius and brilliance who are consumed by the desire for endless magistracies and military commands, and by the lust for power and glory.'[5] An ancient insight. The Romans had always appreciated that everything they found most splendid in a citizen might also be a source of danger. This explained why, over the centuries, so many limits upon the free play of ambition had evolved. Laws and customs, precedents and myths, these formed the fabric of the Republic. No citizen could afford to behave as though they did not exist. To do so was to risk downfall and eternal shame. Pompey and Crassus, true Romans, understood this in their blood. It was why Pompey could conquer by land and sea, and yet yearn for the respect of a man like Cato. It was why Crassus could be the most feared man in Rome, and yet choose to veil his power behind shadows. Now, however, their scruples were no longer sufficient to restrain them. After all, in order to win his second consulship, Pompey had almost had Cato killed. And Crassus, during the debate on his proconsular command, grew so heated that he punched a senator in the face.

Indeed, it was generally observed, in that summer of 55, just how excitable this formerly discreet man had become. Crassus had turned voluble and boastful. When he won the governorship of Syria by lot he could not stop talking about it. Even had he not been in his sixties such behaviour would have been regarded as unseemly. Suddenly, people were laughing at him behind his back. This had never happened before. The more that Crassus stepped into the full glare of unpopularity, the more his sinister mystique began to fade. He found himself being jostled by mobs, and even, on occasions, having to turn tail and beg Pompey for protection. With such humiliations did the Roman people punish Crassus for his betrayal of the Republic. When the time finally came for him to depart for his province no celebrations accompanied him, no cheering crowds. 'What a villain he is!'[6] Cicero exclaimed, gloating over the shabbiness of Crassus' departure. But the lack of a rousing send-off was not the worst. As the proconsul clattered out through the city gates on to the Appian Way he found a tribune waiting for him by the side of the road. Earlier, the same man had attempted to arrest Crassus, a stunt contemptuously brushed aside. Now he was standing by a brazier. Clouds of incense rose from it, drifting across the tombs of ancient heroes, perfuming the winter breeze. Gazing at Crassus, the tribune began to chant. The words were archaic, barely comprehensible, but their portent was perfectly clear: Crassus was being cursed.

To such an accompaniment, then, did he set out from Rome on his Eastern command. Nothing could better have reminded him of the high price he had paid to secure it. What had previously been dearest to Crassus, his prestige, was shot to pieces. No wonder, during his consulship, that he had betrayed signs of nerves. Yet these were not, as his enemies hinted, evidence of senility or a loosening grip. In the ledger of Crassus' mind, costs and benefits were still being balanced as cynically as ever. Only a prize beyond compare could have persuaded him to sacrifice his credit in the Republic. Syria on its own would hardly serve as recompense. In exchange for his good name Crassus wanted nothing less than the riches of the world.

In the past he had mocked such fantasies. His bitter rival, during his third and most grandiloquent triumph, had been followed by a giant float representing the globe. Yet Pompey the Great had been too nervous of the role of Alexander to indulge in it wholeheartedly, too respectful of the traditions of his city. Crassus, understanding this, and confirmed in his contempt for Pompey's braggadocio, had originally felt no need to play the world conqueror himself. But then Caesar had taken up the role. In the space of two short years he had won himself wealth to rival Pompey's. Crassus, chill and calculating, had not been slow to recognise the implications of this. Travelling to Ravenna, reaching his compact with Pompey and Caesar, mounting his brutal election campaign, he had been prompted by a mingling of greed and fear, of rampant avarice, and of a dread of being left behind. More clearly perhaps than either of his partners in crime, he had glimpsed an unsettling new order. In it a few high-achievers – maybe two, but Crassus hoped three – would wield a degree of power so disproportionate to that of their fellow citizens that Rome herself would be placed in their shadow. After all, if the Republic were the mistress of the world, then for men who dared seize control of it, and marshal its resources as they pleased, what limits could there be? The sky, perhaps – but nothing lower.

In the spring of 54 BC Crassus arrived in his new province and advanced to its eastern frontier. Beyond the River Euphrates a great trunk road stretched across flat desert until it passed into the glare of the horizon and could be seen no more. But Crassus knew where it led. Peering into the rising sun, he could glimpse, in his imagination, the haze of spices, the glint of onyx, cornelian and pearls. There were many fabulous reports of the riches of the East. It was said that in Persia there was a mountain formed entirely of gold; that in India the whole country was defended by 'a wall built of ivory';[7] and that in China, the land of the Seres, silk was woven by creatures twice the size of beetles. No man of intelligence could believe such ludicrous stories, of course, but the fact that they were told served to illustrate an indubitable and glittering truth: the proconsul who made himself master of the Orient would have wealth beyond compare. No wonder that Crassus gazed east and dreamed.

Of course, if he were to plant the standards of the Roman people upon the shores of the Outer Ocean, then he would first have to deal with the barbarians at his door. Immediately beyond the Euphrates stood the kingdom of Parthia. Not much was known about it, except that the natives – like all Orientals – were effeminate and deceitful. Lucullus and Pompey had both signed peace treaties with them – an inconvenient detail that Crassus had not the slightest intention of respecting. Accordingly, in the summer of 54 he crossed the Euphrates and seized a number of frontier towns. The Parthians indignantly demanded his withdrawal. Crassus refused. Having procured his war, however, he was content to bide his time. The first year of his governorship he spent in profitable looting. The Temple in Jerusalem, and many others, were stripped bare. 'Days were spent hunched over the measuring scales.'[8] Thanks to his careful accounting, Crassus was able to recruit an army truly worthy of his ambitions: seven legions, four thousand light infantry, as many horsemen again. Among the cavalry – an exotic touch – were a thousand Gauls. Their commander was Crassus' youngest son, Publius, who had served with such success under Caesar and now looked to repeat his dashing exploits for his father. All was ready. In the spring of 53 Crassus and his army crossed the Euphrates again. The great adventure had begun.

At first the emptiness appeared to mock the scale of Crassus' preparations. Ahead of his army, to the east, nothing could be seen save the haze of the heat. Then, at length, the advance guard came across hoofprints, the tracks of what appeared to be a large cavalry division. These turned aside from the road and vanished into the desert. Crassus decided to follow them. Soon the legions found themselves marching across a desolate plain with not a stream, nor even a blade of grass, in sight, only scorching dunes of sand. The

Romans began to wilt. Crassus' ablest lieutenant, a quaestor by the name of Cassius Longinus, urged his general to turn round, but Crassus, so skilled at making strategic retreats in the political arena, would not hear of it now. On the legions advanced. Then came the news for which their general had been hoping. The Parthians were near, and not just a cavalry division, but a large army. Eager to ensure that the enemy did not escape him, Crassus ordered on his legions. They were now in the heart of the baking, sandy plain. They could make out horsemen ahead of them, shabby and dusty. The legionaries locked shields. As they did so, the Parthians dropped aside their robes to reveal that both they and their horses were clad in glittering mail. At the same moment, from all around the plain, came the eerie sound of drums and clanging bells, a din 'like the roaring of wild predators, but intermingled with the sharpness of a thunderclap'.[9] To the Romans, it seemed barely human, a hallucination bred from the shimmering heat. Hearing it, they shuddered.

And all that long day was to have the pattern of a bad dream. The Parthians fled every effort to engage them, fading like mirages across the dunes, but armed, as they wheeled and galloped away, with steel-tipped arrows, which they fired into the sweating, parched, immobile ranks of legionaries. When Publius led his Gauls in pursuit, they were surrounded by the enemy's heavy cavalry and wiped out. Publius himself was decapitated, and a Parthian horseman, brandishing the head on a spear, galloped along the ranks of Romans, jeering them and screaming insults at Publius' father. By now the legions were surrounded. All day long the Parthians' deadly arrows rained down upon them, and all day long, doggedly, heroically, the legions held out. With the blessed coming of dusk the shattered remnants of Crassus' great expedition began to withdraw, retracing their steps to Carrhae, the nearest city of any size. From there, under the resourceful leadership of Cassius, a few straggling survivors made their way back across the Roman frontier.

They left behind them twenty thousand of their compatriots dead
on the battlefield, and ten thousand more as prisoners. Seven eagles
had been lost. Not since Cannae had a Roman army suffered such
a catastrophic defeat.

Crassus himself, stupefied by the utter ruin of all his hopes, was
lured by the Parthians into a parley. Having tricked so many, he
now found himself tricked in his turn. Caught up in a scuffle, he
was struck down. Death spared Crassus a humiliating ordeal.
Baulked of their prey, the Parthians inflicted it instead on an impersonator drawn from the ranks of their prisoners. Dressed as a
woman, escorted by lictors whose rods were adorned by money-
bags, and axes by legionaries' heads, followed by jeering prostitutes,
the captive was led in a savage parody of a triumph. Clearly, the
Parthians knew more of Roman military traditions then the
Romans had known of theirs.

Meanwhile, the head of the real Crassus had been dispatched to
the court of the Parthian king. It arrived just as a celebrated actor,
Jason of Tralles, was singing a scene from Euripides' great tragedy,
The Bacchae. By a gruesome coincidence, this was a play that featured a severed head. Jason, with the quick thinking of a true
professional, seized the gory trophy and cradled it in his arms, then
improvised an apt soliloquy. Unsurprisingly, the spectacle of
Crassus as a prop in his own tragedy brought the house down.

For a man who had aimed so high and been brought so low, no
more fitting end could have been devised.

The sky, after all, had not proved the limit.

Ad Astra

It was an article of faith to the Romans that they were the most
morally upright people in the world. How else was the size of their

empire to be explained? Yet they also knew that the Republic's greatness carried its own risks. To abuse it would be to court divine anger. Hence the Romans' concern to refute all charges of bullying, and to insist that they had won their empire purely in self-defence. To people who had been flattened by the legions, this argument may have appeared laughable, but the Romans believed it all the same, and often with a deadly seriousness. Opposition to Crassus' war against Parthia, for instance, had been bitter. Everyone knew that there had been no excuse for it save greed. The blood-soaked sands of Carrhae showed that the gods had known this too.

All the same, Crassus was not the only man to have dreamed of pushing Rome's supremacy to the limits of the world. Something was changing in the mood of the Republic. Globalising fantasies were much in the air. The globe itself could be found on coins as well as triumphal floats. The old suspicion of empire was fading fast. Overseas commitments, it appeared, could be made to work. Even the most conservative elements in the Senate were coming to accept this. In 58 Cato had left Rome for the island of Cyprus. His mission was to annexe it. Originally, he had been violently opposed to such a policy, not least because it had been proposed by Clodius, who planned to use revenues from Cyprus to fund his extravagant corn dole. But when the tribune, with typically malevolent cunning, had proposed that his most upright opponent be sent to administer Rome's new possession, and the Senate had enthusiastically agreed, Cato had felt duty bound to go. Arriving in Cyprus, he had exercised his duties with his customary scrupulousness. The Cypriots had been given peace and good government, and the Roman people the old ruler's treasure. Cato had returned home loaded with silver and a library of account books. So delighted had the Senate been by the honest dealings it found transcribed within them that it had awarded Cato the privilege of wearing a toga edged with purple – an extravagance that Cato had sternly turned down.

Even so, he was proud of what he had achieved in Cyprus – not only for the Republic, but for the provincials themselves. It appeared to him self-evident that the rule of an upstanding Roman administrator was vastly preferable to the squalid anarchy that had prevailed in Cyprus before his arrival. Here was a portentous development: the Senate's most unbending traditionalist squaring Rome's ancient virtues with her new world role. Greek intellectuals, of course, had long been pushing for this – as Cato would well have known, for he was a keen scholar of philosophy, which he studied with the seriousness he brought to all he did. It was Posidonius, every Roman's favourite guru, who had argued that subject peoples should welcome their conquest by the Republic, since it would contribute towards the building of a commonwealth of man. Now the Romans themselves were latching on to the same argument. Assumptions that would have been unthinkable even a few decades previously were becoming commonplace. Enthusiasts for empire argued that Rome had a civilising mission; that because her values and institutions were self-evidently superior to those of barbarians, she had a duty to propagate them; that only once the whole globe had been subjected to her rule could there be a universal peace. Morality had not merely caught up with the brute fact of imperial expansion, but wanted more.

It helped, of course, that the empire brought colour and clamour to Rome, the news of conquests from strange, far-distant lands, the flooding of gold through her streets. Throughout the sixties BC the Romans had associated such pleasures with the name of Pompey. Now, in the fifties, they could enjoy them again, courtesy of Caesar. Even in the dankest reaches of Gaul, the proconsul never forgot his audience back at home. He lavished his attentions on them. He had always taken pleasure in spending money on other people – it was one of the qualities that made him loved – and now, at last, that money was his own. Gallic plunder flowed south.

Caesar was generous to everyone: his friends, anyone he thought might prove useful, and the whole of Rome. Preparations began to be made for a huge extension of the Forum, one that could hardly fail to keep his name on everybody's lips. But if Caesar aimed to woo his fellow citizens with gargantuan complexes of marble, he also wished to entertain them, to have them thrill to the glamour of his exploits. His dispatches were masterpieces of war reporting. No Roman could read them without feeling a rush of excitement and pride. Caesar knew how to make his fellow citizens feel good about themselves. As so often before, he was putting on a show – and as an arena he had the entire, spectacular expanse of Gaul.

Of course, in March 56 BC, had it not been for his quick thinking and diplomatic skills, he might have lost it to Domitius Ahenobarbus. The risk had forced him to move fast. It had been Caesar who had suggested the meetings at Ravenna and Lucca with Crassus and Pompey. He had felt no particular jealousy of the ambitions of his two partners in the triumvirate. As far as he had been concerned, they could have whatever they wanted, just as long as he was allowed another five years as governor of Gaul.

While Caesar saw to the diplomacy at Ravenna and Lucca that would secure this, he knew that he was urgently needed in Britanny. A legion had been stationed there for the winter, and, with food supplies running low, its commander had been forced to send out foraging parties. Straying into the territory of a local tribe, the Venetians, some requisition officers had been kidnapped. The Venetians themselves, who had been forced to hand over hostages to the Romans the previous autumn, had hopefully suggested a swap, but while this was an offer that might have seemed reasonable enough to them, it had betrayed a woeful misunderstanding of their enemy. In their innocence the Venetians had assumed that the Romans were playing by the accepted rules of tribal warfare, in which hit-and-run raids and ambushes, tit-for-tat skirmishes and hostage-taking, were all taken for granted. To the Romans, however, such tactics were terrorism, and punishable as such. Caesar prepared to teach the Venetians a devastating lesson. Because they were a maritime power, he ordered one of his ablest officers, Decimus Brutus, to construct a war fleet. The Venetian ships, taken by surprise, were wiped out. The tribe had no choice but to surrender. Its elders were executed and the rest of the population sold as slaves. Caesar, who normally prided himself on his clemency, had decided on this occasion 'to make an example of the enemy, so that in future the barbarians would be more careful about respecting the rights of ambassadors'[10] – by which, of course, he meant his requisition officers. The double-speak betrayed his real agenda. The Gauls had to be woken up to a new reality: from now on it was Caesar who would be setting the rules. Tribal squabblings and rebellions were things of the past. The country was to be at peace – a peace policed and upheld by Rome.

The brutal punishment of the Venetians had its desired effect. That winter, the mood throughout Gaul was one of sullen submission. Most tribes had still not measured themselves against the Romans, but rumour had done its work, and it was now widely known that the terrifying newcomers had proved themselves invincible wherever they had been met in combat. Only into the dense forests of Germany, it appeared, had the news failed to penetrate. In the spring of 55 BC, two tribes made the mistake of crossing the Rhine into Gaul. Caesar's patience with fractious natives was by now wearing thin. The invaders were summarily wiped out. Then, in order to deliver the barbarians beyond the Rhine an unmistakable warning, Caesar crossed the river himself. He did this not in a boat – a mode of transport that struck him as 'beneath his dignity'[11] – but over a specially constructed bridge. The engineering brilliance required to build it spoke as loudly of Roman power as did the bristling discipline of the legions who crossed it: the Germans on the far bank took one look at the monstrous wooden structure rising out of the rushing currents and melted into the woods. These, the fabled forests of Germany, were the subject of many tall tales. They were said to be the haunt of strange monsters, and to stretch so interminably that a man could walk for two months and still not leave them behind. Caesar, peering into their murk, had no intention of putting such stories to the test: leaving the Germans to cower in the shadows, he burned their villages and crops, then crossed the Rhine back to Gaul. The bridge, constructed with such skill and effort, he ordered to be pulled down.

Caesar had always had a penchant for spectacular acts of demolition. After all, only a decade previously he had levelled his new villa and thereby made himself the talk of Rome. The iron-bodied general who always snatched his soldier's rations in the saddle, who was capable of inspiring whole legions with his courage, who shared every rigour and hardship that he imposed upon his men, sleeping on frozen ground wrapped only in his cloak, was still the flamboyant Caesar of old. The tastes he had indulged as a rake, for excitement and grand gestures, now infused his strategy as a proconsul of the Roman people. As ever, he looked to dazzle, to overawe. The building and levelling of a bridge across the Rhine had served only to whet his appetite for even more spectacular exploits. So it was that no sooner had Caesar crossed his men back into Gaul than he was marching them northwards, towards the Channel coast and the encircling Ocean.

Set within its icy waters waited the fabulous island of Britain. It was as drenched in mystery as in rain and fog. Back in Rome people doubted whether it existed at all. Even traders and merchants, Caesar's usual sources of information, could provide only the sketchiest of details. Their reluctance to travel widely through the island was hardly surprising. It was well known that barbarians

became more savage the further north one travelled, indulging in
any number of unspeakable habits, such as cannibalism, and even –
repellently – the drinking of milk. To teach them respect for the
name of the Republic would be an achievement of Homeric proportions. For Caesar, who never let anyone forget that he could
trace his ancestry back to the time of the Trojan War, the temptation was irresistible.

In his report to the Senate he sought to justify an attack on
Britain by claiming that the natives had come to the help of the
rebellious Venetians, and that, anyway, the country was rich in
silver and tin. This was not entirely convincing – for if either motive
had really been uppermost in Caesar's mind, then he would have
given himself an entire season's campaigning in the island. As it
was, the Roman fleet did not set sail until July. It was indeed to
prove a journey back in time. Waiting for the invaders on the
Kentish cliffs was a scene straight out of legend: warriors careering
up and down in chariots, just as Hector and Achilles had done on
the plain of Troy. To add to the exotic nature of it all, the Britons
wore peculiar facial hair and were painted blue. So taken aback
were the legionaries that they stood cowering in their transport
boats until finally a standard-bearer, clutching his eagle to him,
plunged into the waves alone and started wading towards the shore.
His comrades, shamed into action, piled into the water after him.
After some messy fighting a beach-head was established. Some
more battles were fought, some villages burned, and some hostages
taken. Then, with bad weather closing in, Caesar had his men pack
up and sail back to Gaul.

Nothing remotely concrete had been achieved, but in Rome the
news that an army of the Republic had crossed both the Rhine and
the Ocean caused a sensation. True, a few inveterate spoilsports
such as Cato pointed out that Caesar was now exceeding his brief
more monstrously than ever and charged him with war crimes.

Most citizens were in no mood to care. Even the lack of plunder did little to dampen the general mood of wild enthusiasm. 'It's now definite that there isn't an ounce of silver in the whole of Britain,' Cicero reported a few months later, 'nor any prospect of loot apart from slaves. And even then,' he added sniffily, 'it's hardly as though you'd expect a slave with a decent knowledge of music or literature to emerge from Britain, is it?'[12] But his tone of amused hauteur fooled no one. Cicero was as excited as anyone, and in 54, when there was a second summer of campaigning across the Channel, he followed events with a feverish interest. So did everyone else: Rome was agog for news. In their impact on a waiting public Caesar's expeditions to Britain have been aptly compared to the moon landings: 'they were an imagination-defying epic, an achievement at once technological and straight out of an adventure story'.[13] Few doubted that the entire island would soon be forced to bow to the Republic's supremacy. Only Cato was immune to the war fever. He shook his head and warned sombrely of the anger of the gods.

And sure enough, Caesar had indeed pushed too far, too fast. As he crossed the Thames in search of the frustratingly elusive Britons, his agents brought him ominous news: the harvest in Gaul had failed; rebellion was threatening; Caesar was needed back in person immediately. There had already been one violent storm in the Channel, and the legionaries lived in terror of a second destroying their fleet and marooning them for the winter. Caesar decided to cut his losses. A face-saving treaty was patched up with a local chieftain. The dream of reaching the ends of the world had to be put on hold. Although he disguised the painful truth as well as he could from his fellow citizens, Caesar had over-reached himself. At stake now was not the conquest of Britain, but the very future of a Roman Gaul.

That winter and the following summer danger came from various tribal uprisings, isolated bushfires of rebellion. The garrison of one legionary camp was ambushed and wiped out – almost seven thousand men were lost. Another was laid under siege and only rescued by Caesar himself in the nick of time. The proconsul, nervous that the flames of rebellion might spread, was everywhere, crisscrossing the country, stamping out the sparks. Sometimes he would leave the Gauls themselves to do the fire-fighting, handing over the territory of rebellious tribes to their neighbours to plunder as they pleased. Divide and rule – the policy still held good. Summer 53 BC passed and still there had been no general conflagration. Caesar began to relax. The previous year he had been forced to campaign throughout the winter, but not now. The new year found him in Ravenna planning for the end of his governorship and a glorious return to Rome. To his anxious fellow citizens, he announced – yet again – the pacification of Gaul.

That January of 52 BC the snow never stopped falling. In the mountain passes it lay especially thick. Caesar's legions, stationed in the far north of the country, were cut off from their general. But bad weather was soon to be the least of their problems. Despite the snow, the Gauls were perfectly able to make contact with one another. Across the lowlands of the country war bands were massing. Seemingly against the odds, a great horde of tribes in northern and central Gaul had begun to negotiate a compact, burying their differences in the face of the common foe. The organiser of this alliance, and its undisputed leader, was an imposing nobleman by the name of Vercingetorix. 'As a commander, he displayed the utmost attention to detail and discipline, for he was determined to whip waverers into shape.'[14] These were qualities that even Caesar could respect, as well he might – for they were the qualities of a Roman. Vercingetorix hated the invaders, but he had studied them assiduously, determined to master the secrets of their success. When he ordered every tribe to send him a specified quota of troops, he was emulating the methods of Roman administrators and tax collectors, the agents of an order that spanned Gaul and far beyond. The world was shrinking. Win or lose, the Gauls could not hope to alter that. Their new unity was bred of both desperation and the global reach of Rome. It was Caesar who had taught the Gauls what it meant to be a nation. Now that achievement threatened to destroy him.

Or so it seemed. In fact, although an alliance of Gallic tribes was precisely what Caesar had spent six years desperately working to avoid, it also offered him a tantalising opportunity – a chance to crush resistance once and for all. As he always preferred to do, he went directly for the jugular. With Vercingetorix's army massing on the border of the old Roman province, threatening the Republic's rule over the whole of Gaul beyond the Alps, Caesar sped towards the centre of the revolt. To do this, he had to breast passes covered in two metres of snow, and gallop with only the smallest escort through the wilds of enemy territory. His daring was rewarded. He succeeded in joining with his legions. But now Caesar too was cut off from Italy. The Romans were starving, for Vercingetorix had persuaded his allies to burn their supplies rather than allow the hated enemy to seize them. Desperate for food, Caesar succeeded in storming one city but was repulsed from another, his first defeat in open combat after six years as proconsul. The news encouraged even more tribes to throw in their lots with Vercingetorix. Some of Caesar's lieutenants began to despair: they advised their general to try to fight his way back to safety, to preserve what he could from the ruin, to abandon Gaul.

Caesar refused. 'It would have been shameful and humiliating'[15] – and therefore unthinkable. Whatever his own doubt and weariness, his outward show of confidence remained as sovereign as ever. In Caesar's energy there was something demonic and sublime. Touched by boldness, perseverance and a yearning to be the best, it was the spirit of the Republic at its most inspiring and lethal.

No wonder that his men worshipped him, for they too were Roman, and felt privileged to be sharing in their general's great adventure. Battle-hardened by years of campaigning, they were in no mood to panic now at the peril of their situation. Their faith in Caesar and their own invincibility held good.

When Vercingetorix, presuming otherwise, attempted to finish them off, Caesar's troops inflicted heavy losses on his cavalry and forced them to withdraw. Deciding to wait for reinforcements, Vercingetorix withdrew to the town of Alesia – a stronghold north of modern-day Dijon, and so impregnable that it had never before been captured. Caesar, rarely one to be impressed by precedent, straight away put it under siege. A huge line of earthworks, almost fifteen miles long, imprisoned Vercingetorix and his men within the town. Alesia had food sufficient for thirty days, but thirty days passed, and still the siege held firm. The Gauls began to starve. Vercingetorix, determined at all costs to maintain the strength of his warriors, settled on the grim expedient of expelling from Alesia anyone unable to fight. Women and children, the old and the sick, all were driven from the town walls. Caesar, however, refused to let them pass, or even, although they begged him, to take them as slaves. Instead, determined to shame Vercingetorix into letting the refugees back into Alesia, he left them huddled in the open, where they ate grass, and slowly died of sickness or the cold.

Then at last came the news for which Caesar had been bracing himself. Two hundred thousand Gauls were hurrying to their leader's rescue. Immediately, Caesar ordered a second line of fortifications to be built, this time facing outwards. Wave after wave of screaming, sword-slashing warriors broke against the defences. All day, the Roman ramparts held. Dusk brought a respite – but not the end of the ordeal. The Gauls had been testing the Roman blockade, searching out its weakest point – and they had found it. To the north of the town, where two legions had established their camp, a hill directly overlooked the fortifications, and it was from here, at dawn, that the war bands pressed their attack. Filling in the trenches, they swarmed over the palisades, while ahead of them, in the Romans' rear, came the answering war-cries of Vercingetorix's men. The legionaries, trapped between this pincer, fought back with desperate ferocity. Both sides knew that the decisive moment was at hand. The Romans – just – managed to hold their lines. Even as the Gauls, seeking to pull down the palisade with hooks, heaved and cheered at the splintering of watchtowers, so, from the legionaries manning the gaps, there rose an answering cheer. In the distance, at the top of the hill overlooking their position, they had caught a flash of scarlet: their general's cloak. Caesar, who had spent all the day galloping along the line of fortifications, yelling encouragements to his men and following the rhythms of the desperate struggle, had finally decided to commit his last reserves. Having slipped out unnoticed from the fortifications, and taking the Gauls utterly by surprise, the Roman cavalry charged down the hill. The legionaries, swords stabbing, advanced from the ramparts to meet them. Now it was the turn of the Gauls to be caught in a pincer movement. The slaughter was terrible, the Roman triumph total. Vercingetorix's men, hearing the death-screams of their countrymen, withdrew back into Alesia. Outnumbered by the army he was besieging, and vastly outnumbered by the army that had been besieging him in turn, Caesar had defeated both. It was the greatest, the most astonishing, victory of his career.

The next morning Vercingetorix rode out from Alesia in glittering armour and knelt at his conqueror's feet. Caesar, in no mood to be merciful, had him loaded with chains and thrown into prison. The war was not yet over, but it was already won. The victory had come at a terrible cost. Between the walls of Alesia and the Roman palisade lay the emaciated corpses of women and children. Above them were the bodies of warriors cut down by the legions, and beyond them, piled around the outer fortifications, stretching away from Alesia for miles, were innumerable corpses, the limbs of horses and humans horribly tangled, their bellies swollen, their blood fertilising the muddy fields, the slaughter-ground of Gallic liberty. And yet Alesia had been only a single battle. In all, the conquest of Gaul had cost a million dead, a million more enslaved, eight hundred cities taken by storm – or so the ancients claimed.[16]

These are near-genocidal figures. Whatever their accuracy – and there are historians prepared to accept them as plausible[17] – they reflected a perception among Caesar's contemporaries that his war against the Gauls had been something exceptional, at once terrible and splendid beyond compare. To the Romans, no truer measure of a man could be found than his capacity to withstand grim ordeals of exhaustion and blood. By such a reckoning, Caesar had proved himself the foremost man in the Republic. He had held firm to the sternest duty of a citizen: never to surrender, never to back down. If the cost of doing so had been warfare on a scale and of a terror rarely before experienced, then so much more the honour, for both himself and Rome. In 51 BC, the year after Alesia, when Caesar resolved to make an example of another rebellious city by chopping off the hands of everyone who had borne arms against him, he could take it for granted that 'his clemency was so well known that no one would mistake such a severe measure for wanton cruelty'.[18] He was right. Caesar was indeed famous – among the Romans – for his clemency. But he was even more famous for his love of glory – and in such a cause the whole of Gaul and beyond had been made to bleed.

Ultimately, however, the great task was done and there was peace. The Republic owed Caesar much. Surely, with his term of office now drawing to its finish, there would be magnificent honours waiting for him in Rome. The acclamation of his grateful fellow citizens, a splendid triumph, high office once again? After all,

who could justly refuse any of these to Caesar, the conqueror of
Gaul?

After almost a decade away he was ready to head for home.

Weeping for Elephants

In Rome, of course, there remained one man of greater renown and
wealth than even Caesar. Pompey the Great lived in no one's
shadow. Certainly not that of Caesar, a man whom Pompey had
always regarded as his protégé. Naturally, in the condescending
manner that befitted Rome's premier general, he took pride in his
father-in-law's achievements — but nothing more. The idea that
Caesar might rival him, let alone surpass him, never crossed the
great man's mind.

Some tried desperately to open his eyes. Back in 55 BC, while
Crassus was preparing for his expedition to the East and Caesar, far
away in Gaul, was turning his thoughts to Britain, an unexpected
visitor had come knocking on Pompey's door. Cato had just been
through a bruising few months. In January, attempting to block the
second consulship of Pompey and Crassus, he had been badly
beaten up by Pompey's heavies. Since then, he had campaigned
tirelessly and courageously against the granting of five-year commands to the two consuls, but again to no avail. Now Pompey
wanted Caesar to have an identical command. Cato, swallowing
his pride, had come to beg his adversary to reconsider. Could he not
see that he was raising up a monster on his shoulders? The time
would come when he would no longer have the strength to throw
off Caesar, or to bear his weight. When that happened both men
would totter, locked in a death-clinch, and collapse. And the
Republic? Beneath the weight of two such colossi, the Republic
would surely be flattened into dust.

Pompey rejected the appeal. In 55, of all years, he could feel sublimely confident of his power and good fortune. On the Campus Martius, where workmen had been labouring for years at his great theatre, the scaffolding had finally come down. Revealed to the astonished eyes of the Roman people was the most stupendous complex of buildings in their city's history. Set within a beautiful park, it comprised not only an auditorium, but a public portico, a chamber for the Senate and a new house for Pompey himself. Surmounting it all was the temple to Venus, the device by which Pompey had been able to justify its construction in the first place, and that he trusted would serve to protect it for ever from the levelling instincts of jealous rivals.

This was a sensible precaution, for the entire complex stood as an exercise in provoking jealousy. No expense had been spared. In the gardens rare plants bore upon their aromas a soothing reminder of Pompey's conquest of the East. In the portico gold-woven curtains hung between the columns, while in the background streams ran gently murmuring from countless fountains. Diaphanously draped goddesses, posing coyly in the shade, added to the ambience of what established itself overnight as the most romantic spot in Rome. All the statues and paintings were celebrated masterpieces, carefully selected by Atticus, that knowledgeable connoisseur, and a board of other experts, for Pompey had wished his displays to have the imprimatur of absolute quality. The most imposing piece of all, however, was not an antique, but a specially commissioned statue of Pompey himself. Strategically placed in the new Senate House, it ensured that even when the great man was absent his shadow would fall across the proceedings.

What need was there for the sponsor of such magnificence to go haring after barbarians in order to prove himself? True, in the north of his allocated province of Spain there were savages still waiting to be tamed, but these were small fry, hardly worthy of a world conqueror's attention. Not that Pompey wished to forfeit his command, or the legions that came with it. Rather, he planned to govern Spain from a distance, through the agency of lieutenants. Let Crassus go and fight the Parthians, and Caesar the Gauls – Pompey had already triumphed over three continents. Now, with his theatre completed, his many victories on behalf of the Republic could be restaged as spectacular entertainments. No travelling to the limits of the globe for Pompey the Great. Rather, at his command, the limits of the globe would meet in Rome.

And they would take on bestial form. Back in his twenties, as a precocious young general, Pompey had taken time out from pulverising Libyans to go lion-hunting. 'Even the wild animals that live in Africa', he had pronounced, 'should be taught to respect the strength and courage of the Roman people.'[19] Along the frontiers of the Republic's empire, beyond the light of the legionary's flickering campfire, lions stalked the night as they had done since the creation of the world, primordial symbols of terror, preying on man's ease of mind. Yet now, in his fifties, wishing to celebrate the dedication of his theatre, Pompey could order them brought to his theatre – and it was done. And not only lions. A century later, fleets weighed down with ravening exotica would be seen as the perfect symbol of the Republic's new global reach. 'The padding tiger, shipped in a golden cage, lapping at human blood, applauded by the crowds.'[20] So wrote Petronius, Nero's master of ceremonies, summing up an age.

It was important to Pompey's purpose that the savagery of his imports serve to edify as well as entertain. This was why animals were rarely kept in zoos. Only by displaying them in combat, the monstrous matched with the human, could Pompey instruct his fellow citizens in what it took to be the rulers of the world. Sometimes the lesson was too much for the citizenry to bear. When twenty elephants, an unprecedented number, were attacked by spearmen, their trumpetings of distress so harrowed the spectators that everyone in the theatre began to weep. Cicero, who had been in the audience, puzzled over this. How was it possible, he wondered, that a spectacle so impressive had afforded so little delight?

He analysed his own feelings. The violence, rather than thrilling him, had left him numb. Prisoners being savaged by lions, proud and magnificent wild creatures being skewered on spears: neither seemed the kind of entertainment to afford a cultured man much pleasure. Yet if one thing had depressed Cicero about the entertainments above all others, it had been their scale. The slaughter of the twenty elephants had been merely the climax of what he freely acknowledged to have been 'the most lavish and magnificent show of all time'[21] – an unparalleled display of the Republic's greatness. Pompey had filled his theatre with wonders from every corner of the empire: not only lions, tigers and elephants, but leopards, lynxes, rhinoceroses and stag-wolves, to say nothing of the mysterious cephos,* a creature from Ethiopia with the hands and feet of a man, so rare that it was never seen in Rome again. And yet Cicero, a citizen passionately proud of his city's achievements, the most articulate spokesman for Rome's global destiny that the Republic had ever produced, was left bored and oppressed by his hero's games: 'If these are sights which must be seen, then you have seen them many times.'[22] Pleasure and excitement had both been dulled by excess. Cicero could no longer identify with the emotions that Pompey wished him to feel. Games designed to glorify the Republic served to glorify only the sponsor himself. Gazing humbly down upon the carnage, spaced around the theatre, were fourteen statues, each one representing a nation conquered by Pompey.[23] Marble and blood combined to create an extravaganza of

---

* The cephos is generally assumed to have been a species of baboon. Pliny the Elder, 8.28.

self-promotion unmatched in the Republic's history. Never before
had the Romans been made to feel quite so inferior to a man who
was, after all, a citizen just like them. Was this why the distress of
the elephants had moved them more deeply than the mastery of
the spearmen? At the end of the games, rather than cheering 'the
general and the lavish display which he had laid on especially to
honour them, they rose to their feet, and, through their tears,
called down curses upon his head'.[24]

Of course, the Roman people were fickle: their anger with
Pompey rarely lasted for long. Yet their suspicions – of his greatness,
of his generosity – remained. Pompey's games had been staged in
September 55 BC; weeks later his fellow citizens went to the polls.
Despite – or perhaps because of – the new theatre complex looming massively in the background, they delivered its sponsor a
pointed rebuff. The previous year Pompey had blocked the candi-
dacies of Domitius Ahenobarbus and Cato; now, for the year 54,
both men were elected – Domitius as consul and Cato as praetor.
True, there was one candidate backed by Pompey who did secure
election, and to the consulship, no less – but Appius Claudius,
despite his role as one of the conspirators at Lucca, was hardly a reli-
able ally. Imperturbable and self-serving, he did no one's bidding but
his own. He might not have built a theatre, but he had breeding,
and that, in his own opinion, counted for much more.

The results brought home to Pompey the full ambiguity of his
position. By any reckoning he was the first citizen in the Republic.
He had just completed his second consulship; he was the governor
of Spain, the commander and general of its army; his generosity was
the wonder of Rome. Yet the more he sought to consolidate his
power, the more it seemed to slip through his fingers. Every effort
that he made to secure pre-eminence brought a matching defeat.
Increasingly criminal in his methods, Pompey remained conform-
ist in his dreams. The consulships of Appius and Domitius, both of

them notorious for their arrogance, mocked the insecurities of the arriviste. So too, and even more cruelly, did the praetorship of Cato. This infuriating, obdurate, extraordinary man had no legions, no great wealth with which to bribe his fellow citizens. In rank he was not even the equal of a consul, let alone of Caesar or Pompey. Yet he wielded an authority hardly less than that of either. Even as senators took their seats in Pompey's theatre, or surreptitiously accepted presents from Gaul, they still identified themselves with Cato, with his principles and beliefs. Over the years he seemed to have become the embodiment of legitimacy – almost of the Republic itself. Caesar, far away in Gaul, could afford to scoff at such pretensions. But Pompey, who in his heart of hearts still yearned for Cato's approval, could not.

Such approval now appeared as remote as ever. The brutality of Pompey's actions in seizing the consulship would not lightly be forgiven. His army remained a standing menace. Nor did Pompey have the slightest intention of giving up so much as a single legionary. Yet even as he persisted in intimidating the establishment he clung to his hope of winning its heart. For the citizens of a republic such as Rome, loneliness was a bewildering, almost incomprehensible state. Only outlaws – or kings – could truly know it. This was why Pompey, no matter how violently he offended his peers, still wooed them. He had been loved too long, too ardently, not to crave and need love still.

It was a cruel irony, then, that even as he returned to his improbable courtship of the Senate his personal life, which had been so happy and such a comfort to him, should suddenly have darkened. In August 54 BC his adored wife Julia went into labour. Again she miscarried, but this time she did not survive the loss of her baby. Her husband and father were left equally devastated. For Caesar, however, grief was compounded by alarm. The love that both he and Pompey had felt for Julia had provided the two men with a bond strong enough to survive any number of political tensions. Now that bond was gone. Caesar, preoccupied with rebellions in Gaul, was desperate not to have his position back in the capital weakened. He needed Pompey more than Pompey needed him, and both men knew it. For a while their shared bereavement would continue to unite them, but not for ever. How long would Pompey stay single? His eligibility was a valuable asset – far too valuable not to be exploited. His return to the marriage market would give him unanticipated room for manoeuvre. And that, of course, was precisely what unsettled his partner so much.

Yet Pompey was still hemmed in by obligations. For as long as the menacing figure of Crassus remained on the horizon, he would remain nervous of offending Caesar. Mutual fear, not affection, was what had provided the triumvirate with its cement. No one partner could stand up to the other two. This was why, in carving up the Republic's empire, the three conspirators had been so careful to interlock their power bases. By doing so they aimed to defend themselves from one another as much as from their common foes. But then, a year after Julia's death, midway through 53 BC, the news arrived from Carrhae that Crassus was dead. For Caesar this was a second devastating blow, but it is unlikely that Pompey shed many tears. After all, what sweeter measure of success could there be than the failure of a rival? Let the Roman people shudder – the Parthian victory would serve to remind them that victories against Eastern barbarians could never be taken for granted. Should the situation on the frontier turn really ugly, then Pompey's fellow citizens would know where to turn. But even if – as happened – the Parthians did not press their advantage into Syria, Pompey could still stretch his limbs and exult in a novel feeling. A malign presence had been exorcised from his life. Never again would it shadow him, cabin him, torment him. Crassus was no more.

Now, suddenly, everything seemed to be moving Pompey's way. Sleaze had begun to corrode the moral authority of the Senate. The consulship of Appius and Domitius had ended amid high outrage when the two men were accused of accepting bribes to fix the forthcoming consular elections. Four candidates had been standing and all four were indicted. Amid escalating rumours of ever more shady deals, the elections had to be postponed for six months. For Domitius, and the cause of senatorial respectability for which he had been the spokesman, the scandal was a particular calamity. As Cicero cattily pointed out, Appius had no reputation to lose, 'but his colleague is left a broken reed, utterly discredited'.[25] Such was the turmoil that it seemed only one man could restore order. Pompey's lapdogs began to mutter that he should be made dictator. When Cato, to no one's surprise, exploded at the suggestion, Pompey ostentatiously turned down the offer. But still the whisperings would not be silenced. They could be heard throughout the feverish, troubled capital: in the Senate House, the Forum, the slums. The Republic was collapsing. A strongman was needed. Only Pompey would do. Pompey himself kept his peace, looked modest, and bided his time.

It was the perfect strategy. As the sense of crisis steadily deepened, the mood in the Republic began to turn brutal as well as fetid. In his desperation to find a forceful counterweight to Pompey, Cato had settled upon an extraordinary choice. His favoured candidate for the consulship of 52 was none other than Clodius' old sparring-partner, the turbulent street-brawler Milo. Once a ferocious partisan of Pompey, Milo had been unceremoniously dumped by the great man, and was therefore happy to throw his lot in with Cato and his plans. Pompey warned his former protégé to stand down, and when Milo refused threw his weight behind rival candidates. But his fury was, of course, nothing compared to that of Milo's deadliest enemy. For three years Clodius had been on his best behaviour, attempting to rebrand himself as a sound and sober statesman, but the prospect of having Milo as a consul was too much. Like a reformed alcoholic reaching for a bottle, Clodius returned to the streets. His old gangs were resurrected. In reply Milo bought up the gladiator schools. As 53 BC drew to a close, Rome descended into anarchy. So too did the Republic. For the third time in four years elections were postponed, this time because the presiding official had been knocked out by a brick. With all public business in abeyance, club-wielding mobsters roamed the streets, while law-abiding citizens cowered where they could.

It seemed that things could hardly become any worse. Then, on 18 January 52 BC, they did. Clodius and Milo met face to face on the Appian Way. Taunts flew; one of Milo's gladiators flung a javelin; Clodius was struck in the shoulder. His bodyguards hauled their wounded leader to a nearby tavern, but Milo's heavies, following in pursuit, overpowered them. Clodius himself was slung out of the tavern on to the road, where he was speedily finished off. There, by the side of a shrine to the Good Goddess, his corpse was left mangled and naked in the dust. It appeared that the goddess had at last had her revenge.

But Clodius' friends claimed differently. After his body had been found and brought back to Rome, the news of his murder spread quickly from crossroad to crossroad. The slums began to echo with wails of lamentation. Soon crowds were massing outside Clodius' mansion on the Palatine. Fulvia showed them the gashed body of her husband, carefully pointing out each wound. The mob howled in misery and rage. The next day the corpse of the people's hero was borne from the Palatine, across the Forum, and laid on the rostra. Meanwhile, in the neighbouring Senate House benches were kicked over, tables smashed, clerical records plundered. Then, on the floor of the chamber, a pyre was raised. Clodius was laid upon it. A torch was brought. More than thirty years had passed since the destruction of Jupiter's temple on the Capitol, warning the Roman people of coming catastrophe. Now, once again, the Forum was lit a violent red. In the flickering glare battles between the partisans of Clodius and those of his murderer reached a new and intoxicating pitch of savagery. Still the flames raged, and as the Senate House crashed into blackened ruin they spread to a neighbouring monument: the Basilica Porcia. Here was where Rome's first permanent law court had been built – by an ancestor of Cato, no less. In a spectacle loaded with pointed and deliberate symbolism, it too was consumed. That night, when Clodius' partisans feasted in honour of their dead leader, they did so amid the ashes of the Senate's authority.

Now at last Pompey's moment had come. Even Cato, gazing at the charred shell of his ancestor's monument, had to accept that. Anything was preferable to anarchy. He still could not bring himself to accept a dictatorship, but proposed as a compromise that Pompey should serve for the year as sole consul. The paradoxical nature of such an office was indication enough of the monstrous nature of the times. The Senate met in Pompey's theatre, and on Bibulus' motion invited the great man to rescue the Republic. Pompey obliged with brisk and military efficiency. For the first time since the civil war, armed troops were marched into Rome. The gangs of Clodius and Milo proved no match for Pompey's legionaries. Milo himself was speedily put on trial. Since the charge was the murder of Clodius, Cicero leapt at the chance to defend him. It was his hope, in such a cause, to deliver the speech of his life. His opportunity came on the last day of the trial. That morning he crossed from his mansion on the Palatine to the law courts. Eerie and unprecedented silence cloaked the city. All the shops had been boarded up. Guards had been posted on the corner of every street. Pompey himself was stationed beside the law courts, surrounded by a wall of troops, the sun glinting off the steel of their helmets – and this in the Forum, the very heart of Rome. Cicero, taken aback by the spectacle, lost his nerve. His speech was delivered, we are told by one source, 'without his customary assurance'.[26] Others claimed that he could barely stammer so much as a word. Milo was found guilty. He left that same week for exile in Marseille. Other ring-leaders of the mob violence were similarly served. In the space of barely a month peace had been restored to Rome.

Even Cato had to acknowledge that Pompey had done well, though he did so with his customary gracelessness. When Pompey took him aside to thank him for his support, Cato sternly retorted that he had not been supporting Pompey, but Rome. 'As for advice, he would happily give it in private, if asked, and if he were not asked, then he would give it anyway in public.'[27] Disguised as a slap in the face as this offer was, Pompey accepted it gratefully. Even since his return from the East a decade before he had been waiting for such a moment. However begrudgingly, Cato had acknowl-edged his status as first citizen. At long last, Pompey appeared to have power and respect together.

No wonder that when Caesar, that same new year, having racked his brains to come up with a suitable bride for his partner, had finally proposed his own great-niece Octavia, Pompey had turned down the offer. He had not meant to signal the end of his friendship by this rebuff, merely that it could not be taken for granted. Now that he had been restored to respectability in the eyes of the senatorial estab-lishment, there were bidders for his hand who could offer more than Caesar. Pompey had been eyeing up the daughters of the crème de la crème for a while. One in particular had caught his connois-seur's eye. The death of young Publius Crassus at Carrhae had left his wife Cornelia a widow. Beautiful and cultivated, she also happened to be exquisitely well connected. The pedigree of her father, Quintus Caecilius Metellus Pius Scipio Nascia, was sonorously reflected in the roll-call of his names. The fact that Metellus Scipio himself was a vicious nonentity, pre-eminent at nothing save the staging of pornographic floor shows, mattered not the slightest. What did matter was the fact that he was the head of the Metelli, closely related to any number of impressive patricians, and descended from the same Scipios who had defeated Hannibal and captured Carthage. Cornelia's own delights were an added bonus. Taking a break from cleaning up the streets of Rome, Pompey decked himself out in wedding garlands. It was the fifth occasion on which he had done so. This time round he was twice the age of his new bride. He brushed aside all the predictable jeers. Married life suited him. Above all, it provided him with a salve for his grief over Julia. The happy couple were soon scandalously in love.

A man in the arms of a woman such as Cornelia could know himself to be in the very bosom of the aristocracy. It was a sweet fulfilment, made all the sweeter by the fact that Cato, the man who had pronounced Pompey unworthy of his niece's hand, had himself once been jilted by Cornelia's mother. Old rancours ran deep, and there was no love lost between Cato and Metellus Scipio. Even so, when Pompey pronounced that the state of emergency in Rome had been brought under control and invited his father-in-law to serve as consul with him for the remainder of 52 BC, Cato could hardly object. After all, Pompey was behaving with impeccable regard for the constitution. The Republic had been sick, and now it was restored. All was just as it had been in the past.

Pompey's fellow citizens were desperate to believe this. Even those who had long been suspicious of his ambitions now had their own reasons for acknowledging his pre-eminence. Haughty aristocrats who had seen what Pompey had been able to achieve on behalf of that grand pornographer Metellus Scipio had begun to moderate their disdain. Cato might still clap his hands over his ears whenever Pompey said anything unconstitutional, but in general, and for the first time, he was prepared to give his old opponent a hearing. And then, of course, there was Caesar. In Gaul, amid the blood and smoke of Alesia, Pompey's partner still looked to him for friendship. Many different interests, many of them irreconcilably opposed – and yet all of them looking for support to a single person.

This was unprecedented in the history of the Republic. No wonder that Cicero found himself marvelling at Pompey's 'abilities and good fortune, which have enabled him to achieve what nobody else has ever done'.[28] Yet even as the great man exulted in his primacy, each faction competing for his favours was manoeuvring to destroy the others, and force Pompey to identify with them alone. Who was exploiting whom? This was a question that had barely begun to be resolved. Yet it would be soon enough – to the point of destruction and beyond.

Mutually Assured Destruction

The art of theatre-building did not come to an end with the construction of Pompey's marble monster. If anything, it rose to new heights of rococo ingenuity, as ambitious noblemen competed to lay foundations not of stone but deep within the affections of the Roman people. Most extraordinary of all was a theatre built by Curio, the brilliant young intimate of Clodius. In 53 BC Curio's father had died. Curio had been in Asia at the time, on provincial duties, but even before his return to Rome he had begun drawing up plans for a series of truly spectacular funeral games. When the theatre that had been designed to stage them was finally unveiled, the audience found to their excitement that they too were to be a feature of the show. Two different stages had been built, complete with banks of seats, both precariously balanced on a revolving pivot. Two plays could be performed simultaneously, and then, at midday, when the acting was done, there would be an immense cranking of machinery, the theatres would revolve, lock together and form a single stage. 'This was where the gladiators would battle, even though the Roman people themselves, as they spun round in their seats, were in far greater peril than the gladiators.' More than a century later the elder Pliny could only shake his head in astonishment at the design. 'And yet that was not the most amazing thing!' he exclaimed. 'Even more incredible was the madness of the people. There they sat, perfectly content, in seats which were treacherous and liable to collapse!'[29]

Here, it might have been thought, in a city as sensitive to omens as Rome, was a wonder pregnant with menace. To later generations, the identification of the Republic with Curio's amphitheatre – so splendid, so unstable – must have been an obvious one to make. Indeed, it is surely the reason why the memory of it was preserved. But if any of the spectators who risked their necks clambering into the stalls were aware of the portentous nature of what they were doing, then the record of it has failed to survive. The mood of the Republic was fretful, but not apocalyptic. Why would it have been otherwise? Rome's system of government had endured for almost five hundred years. It had won her a greatness so surpassing that not a king in the world had been able to withstand her. Above all, it gave to every citizen the measurement of himself, the reassurance that he was not a subject or a slave, but a man. A Roman could no more conceive of the Republic's collapse than he could imagine himself an Egyptian or a Gaul. Fearful of the gods' anger he may have been, but not to the point of dreading the impossible.

So there was no one to read in the creaking of Curio's theatre an approaching cataclysm. Just the opposite: to the voters, it ground out a familiar rhythm. Curio had his eye on a tribunate. His theatre was designed not only to honour his dead father, but to advance his ambitions. In that cause, as had become the fashion despite the tears over Pompey's elephants, the blood of exotic animals had to be spilled. Curio specialised in panthers, a taste he shared with Caelius, who was always badgering contacts in the provinces for more. Both men knew how important it was to cut a dash with the electorate. As Caesar had done before them, they gambled with their futures by running up monstrous debts. Once this might have branded them as lightweights. Now it marked them out as rising stars.

So too did other, more time-tested talents. The Republic still swirled as violently as it had ever done with ambitions, hatreds and intrigues, but Curio and Caelius were both skilled in negotiating such treacherous currents, knowing when to hold fast and when to tack to fresh winds. Principle rarely blinded them to personal advantage. Their own relationship was a case in point. Each could recognise a useful ally in the other, despite the fact that during the perilous days after Clodius' murder, when the Republic had appeared on the verge of anarchy, they had been on opposite sides. Curio, Clodius' oldest ally, had remained faithful to the memory of his dead friend, and indeed proved such a comfort to Clodius' widow Fulvia that the two of them ended up marrying. Caelius, by contrast, had continued his feud with Clodia and her brother with implacable gusto, and in 52 BC, when he was tribune, used the full resources of his office to serve as cheerleader for Milo. A year later, however, when Caelius found himself particularly short of panthers, Curio thought nothing of slipping him twenty of his own. As it had always been, bet-hedging remained a politician's wisest course.

Except that, on the gravest and most insoluble problem of the day, this was becoming ever more tricky. Ironically, it was Caelius himself who had brought the issue to a head. Midway through 52 the news had reached Rome of Caesar's victory at Alesia. The city had been full of dark forebodings about the situation in Gaul, and so the realisation that war bands of vengeful barbarians would not be sweeping southwards after all was greeted with an immense outpouring of relief. Twenty days of thanksgiving were voted by the

Senate, while Caelius, in his role as tribune, proposed a comple-
mentary bill of his own. By its terms Caesar was to be awarded a
unique privilege: rather than being obliged to arrive at Rome in
person to stand for the consulship – as he had had to do, for
instance, in the previous decade – he was to have the right to run
for election while remaining in Gaul. All nine of Caelius' colleagues
in the tribunate backed this proposal. The bill duly became law.

But this hardly settled the matter. Instead, it served to open a
division in the Senate that was to widen with each passing month,
polarising opinion in a way that was to grow steadily more dangerous, until it would finally yawn so unbridgeably that the entire
Roman people would find themselves teetering on the edge of a
fatal abyss. At the heart of the crisis lay the simple fact that Caesar,
if he were permitted to progress seamlessly from Gaul to a second
consulship, would at no stage be a private citizen. This, to many,
was intolerable – for only a private citizen could be brought to trial.
No sooner had Caelius' bill been passed than Cato was fulminating
against it. The criminal actions of Caesar's first consulship had been
neither forgotten nor forgiven. For almost a decade his enemies
had been waiting for the opportunity to bring him to account.
Now that the chance was nearing they had no intention of being
denied their prey.

There were plenty who tried to reconcile the irreconcilable.
Caelius, in bringing his bill, had been prompted by Cicero, who
counted himself as a friend of both Caesar and Cato. Of course,
too – and far more crucially – did Pompey. For a precarious few
months he had succeeded in balancing the interests of his old ally
and a host of Caesar's opponents, Cato not least. Having at last won
for himself the undisputed pre-eminence he had always craved,
Pompey had no wish to see it threatened by having to choose
between rival blocs of his supporters. Yet no matter how deter-
minedly he closed his eyes to it, the dilemma refused go away. In

the debate on Caesar's future neither side would accept any hint of a compromise. Both believed themselves utterly, implacably in the right.

For Caesar himself, still wading through the mud and slaughter of Gaul, it was an outrage that he, a proconsul of the Roman people, should be obliged to guard his back against the machinations of petty stay-at-homes like Cato. For almost a decade he had been exerting himself titanically in the cause of the Republic – and was he now, as his reward, to face the ignominy of a trial? Milo's conviction offered a grim precedent of what might happen to him: the Forum ringed with steel, the defence intimidated, the conviction hurried through. Once he had been found guilty in a court of law, Caesar's great achievements would help him not a whit. To the cheering of pygmies who had never in their lives rallied an ambushed legion, or planted an eagle beyond the icy northern seas, or defeated in one battle two colossal hordes of barbarians, he would be forced into exile, to spend the rest of his life in the company of men such as Verres, his expectations withering to nothing in the sunshine of Marseille.

Yet the more that Caesar vaunted the exceptional nature of his claims, the more disgusted his many enemies became. Unspoken behind his demands lay the menace of his army, swollen by illegal levies and battle-hardened in the fire of his adventuring. If Caesar were to return home as consul, then he would have no problem in ramming through legislation that would secure farms for his veterans, and a reservoir of armed strength for himself that would put even Pompey in the shade. Rather than permit that, Cato and his allies were prepared to go to any lengths. Interminable disputes over Caesar's command began to dominate the Senate's every session. How many legions should he be permitted to keep? When should a successor be nominated? When should Caesar himself have to stand down? 'You know the form,' drawled Caelius to

Cicero. 'Some decision will be reached about Gaul. Then someone stands up and complains about it. Then someone else stands up in turn . . . and so it drags on – a long, elaborate game.'[30]

Yet arcane though the debate frequently appeared, Caelius' yawns of boredom were an affectation. He was as penetrating an analyst of folly and ambition as anyone in Rome, and he was starting to recognise what was threatening: a catastrophe so appalling as to seem almost beyond belief. What had begun as a feud of the kind that had always existed in the Republic – indeed, had formed the essence of its politics – was now spreading a contagion of bitterness and antagonism far beyond the ranks of the two rival factions. Cato, determined to destroy Caesar once and for all, was repeating his favourite tactic by spurning all hint of compromise, seeking to isolate his enemy, arraying legitimacy and the name of the Republic itself against him. Caesar, for his part, was flooding Rome with bribes, wooing and cajoling his fellow citizens with all his effortless powers of charm. Most still wished to remain neutral. It was not their quarrel. Yet such were the stakes, they could not help but be caught up on the swell and wash of the arguments. Day by day, month by month, the Roman people were dividing into two. An ill-omened phrase, rarely spoken of as a foreboding since the dark days of Sulla, began to be whispered again: civil war.

Not that anyone truly believed that this could happen. Win over Pompey and win the argument – such was the expectation. The great man himself, desperately struggling to maintain control of the situation, vacillated. Still not wishing to alienate either side, he gave to Caesar with one hand and took away with the other. The problem with this strategy, as Caelius pointed out, was that 'he lacks the cunning to keep his real views out of sight.'[31] Those views, by the summer of 51 BC, were coming ever more clearly into focus. Cato's grisly warnings were having their effect. Since Caesar's ultimate sanction was his army, this could not help but strike Pompey as a challenge to himself. Honour and vanity alike obliged him to dig in his heels. Rome's greatest general could not appear to be nervous of the legions of Gaul. At the end of September he finally delivered an unambiguous verdict: Caesar should give up his command the following spring. This would be months before the consular elections, and provide Cato, or anyone else, with plenty of time to bring a prosecution. And what if Caesar put up a tribune to veto such a proposal and still sought to win the consulship while keeping hold of his army? Pompey was asked. The answer was softly spoken, but delivered with unmistakable menace: 'You might as well ask, What if my son chooses to raise a stick against me?'[32]

Now at last the rupture between the two old allies was in the open. Pompey, the son-in-law, had claimed the fearsome rights of a Roman father over Caesar. The conqueror of Gaul was to be treated – and presumably punished – like a rebellious child. Since this was an attack as much upon Caesar's self-regard as upon his interests, it was doubly unforgivable. But if he were to stay in the fight, then he would need fresh supporters. Above all, he would need a tribune, a heavyweight with the nerve and spirit to stand up to proposals that now had the full muscle of Pompey behind them. Unless they could be vetoed, Caesar knew that he was finished.

But when the results of the elections for 50 BC were announced it appeared that his fortunes had taken a further turn for the worse. Ablest and most charismatic of the new tribunes was none other than Curio, reaping due reward for his spectacular theatre. He had been the darling of the Roman people for almost a decade, ever since the summer of Caesar's consulship. Then, still in his twenties, he had dared to defy the menaces of the consul and been cheered for it in the streets. In the ensuing nine years the bad blood between the two men had worsened. As a result there could be no doubt who had most to fear from the energies of the combustible new tribune. Surely now, people began to hope, Caesar would have to back down? Surely the crisis might be abating?

That winter, as Rome shivered, it certainly appeared so. The city, it struck Caelius, was numb with cold and lethargy. Most surprisingly of all, Curio's tribunate had nothing to show for itself. As Caelius wrote to Cicero, in a tone of half regret, 'it's deep frozen'. But midway through his letter he suddenly had to eat his words: 'I take back everything I wrote above, when I said that Curio was taking things coolly – because, to be sure, he's suddenly started turning up the temperature – and how!'[33] The news was astonishing, barely believable. Curio had swung behind his old enemy. The man who had confidently been expected to take the side of Cato and the constitutionalists had done just the opposite. Caesar had his tribune after all.

It was a sensational ambush. Caelius himself attributed his friend's *volte-face* to irresponsibility, but that, as he would later recognise, was unfair. Others were to assume that Curio had been bought with Gallic gold, which was probably closer to the mark, but again did not tell the whole story. In fact, the tribune was playing a classic game. By working to outflank Cato's obstructions, he hoped to do for Caesar what Caesar himself had done for Pompey – and to reap similar rewards. It was hardly principled, but Curio was doing nothing that had not been sanctioned by centuries of similar sharp practice.

Nor was Cato, nor was Pompey. Nor even was Caesar. Throughout the centuries of the Republic's history, its great men had sought to win glory, and to do their enemies down. Nothing had changed over the years save the scale of opportunities on offer and the scope for mutual destruction that they had brought. To the Romans of a later age, mourning the death of their freedom, this was to be tragically clear. 'By now,' wrote Petronius of the Republic's last generation, 'the conquering Roman had the whole world in his hand, the sea, the land, the course of the stars. But still he wanted more.'[34] And because he wanted more, he took more; and because he took more, he wanted more. It was almost impossible for appetites so monstrous to be sated within the ancient limits of custom or morality. Pompey and Caesar, Rome's greatest conquerors, had won resources for themselves beyond all the imaginings of previous generations. Now the consequences of such obscene power were becoming grimly apparent. Either man had the capability to destroy the Republic. Neither wished to do so, but deterrence, if it were to have any value, obliged both to prepare for the worst. Hence Caesar's recruitment of Curio. So high were the stakes, and so finely poised the equilibrium of power, that the activities of a single tribune, Caesar hoped, might prove sufficient to tip the balance of terror – to make the difference between peace with honour and catastrophe beyond recall. So Curio trusted too.

But their enemies remained as determined as ever to call their bluff. As Curio vetoed their every effort to prise Caesar away from his command, demands began to be made of Pompey that he should make good his boasts of forcing the proconsul to back down. Pompey responded by taking to his bed. Whether his illness was diplomatic or not, it certainly convulsed Italy with anxiety. In every town, the length and breadth of the country, sacrifices were offered up for the great man's preservation. The invalid, unsurprisingly, was gratified in the extreme. By the time he finally emerged from his sickroom, he felt a perfect confidence in his popularity. He had been given the reassurance he needed to prepare for the ultimate sanction of war. When a nervous supporter asked what forces he would be able to put into the field should Caesar do the unthinkable and march on Rome, Pompey smiled calmly and told him not to worry. 'I only have to stamp my foot, and all over Italy legionaries and cavalry will rise up from the ground.'[35]

But many were not so sure. To Caelius, it appeared self-evident that Caesar's army was incomparably superior to anything that Pompey could muster. 'In peacetime,' he wrote to Cicero, 'while taking part in domestic politics, it is most important to back the side that is in the right – but in times of war, the strongest.'[36] Nor was he alone in this cynical judgement. Behind it lay the same calculation arrived at by Curio: that support for Caesar might offer a short cut to power. Hungry for immediate pickings, an entire generation was turning away from the cause of legitimacy. Between the fast set and the senior statesmen of the Senate, draped in the dignity of their offices and years, there had always been tensions, but now, amid all the war talk, the mutual contempt was widening into something truly ominous.

A bitter election, with that snooty epitome of the establishment Domitius Ahenobarbus on one side and the young Mark Antony on the other, made it obvious to all. Amid the smog and forebodings of an oppressive summer, Hortensius had died, leaving behind him the largest private zoo in Italy, ten thousand bottles of wine, and an augurate. With the Republic seemingly lurching towards disaster, it was certainly no time to tolerate a vacancy in the augural college – for whenever Rome's magistrates, whether by studying the flight of birds, or the pattern of lightning, or the eating habits of sacred chickens, sought to interpret the will of the gods and prescribe how best their anger could be appeased, it was the augurs who would confirm that the correct ruling had been made. Since the office was immensely prestigious, Domitius naturally regarded it as his by right. His young opponent disagreed. True, a hint of the disreputable still clung to the rake who had cohabited so outrageously with Curio and tangled with Clodius over the affections of his wife, but Antony had come a long way since the wild days of his youth. Serving in Gaul, he had covered himself in glory, and now, back in Rome, was fêted as one of Caesar's most brilliant officers. Domitius, with the full weight of the senatorial establishment behind him, remained overwhelmingly the favourite, but Antony, at Alesia and elsewhere, had grown used to seeing off high odds. So he did again now. In a famous victory, worthy of being set beside Caesar's own election as *pontifex maximus*, he won the augurate. Domitius was left incandescent with fury, and the chasm between the two factions in the Republic grew a little wider still.

It seemed by now that every skirmish thrown up in political life was having a similar effect. The vast majority of citizens who cared for neither side, or for both, were in despair. 'I'm fond of Curio,' wailed Cicero, 'I wish to see Caesar honoured in the manner which is his due, and as for Pompey, I would lay down my life for him – all the same, what really counts with me is the Republic itself.'[37] But there was nothing that he or anyone who thought like him could do. Spokesmen for peace were increasingly dismissed as appeasers. The rival factions were embracing their doom. It was as though, peering over the edge, vertigo was tempting them to jump. The thrill of a bloodlust was ripe in the winter air, and the talk was all of war.

In December 50 BC one of the two consuls, Gaius Marcellus, travelled in the full pomp of his office to Pompey's villa in the Alban Hills. His colleague, having begun the year as an anti-Caesarian, had been persuaded, much like Curio, and no doubt for similar motives, to switch sides – but Marcellus, spurning all overtures, had remained implacable in his hostility to Caesar. Now, with only days left in office, he felt that the time had come to put some more steel into Pompey's backbone. Watched by an immense number of senators and a tense, excited crowd, Marcellus handed his champion a sword. 'We charge you to march against Caesar,' he intoned sombrely, 'and rescue the Republic.' 'I will do so,' Pompey answered, 'if no other way can be found.'[38] He then took the sword, along with the command of two legions at Capua. He also set about raising fresh levies. All of which was illegal in the extreme – an embarrassment predictably made much of by Caesar's supporters. Caesar himself, stationed menacingly at Ravenna with the 13th Legion, was brought the news by Curio, who by now had finished his term and had no wish to stay in Rome to suffer prosecution, or worse. Meanwhile, back in the capital, his place as tribune had been taken by Antony, who occupied himself throughout December by launching a series of blood-curdling attacks on Pompey and vetoing anything that moved. As the tension heightened, the deadlock remained.

Then, on 1 January 49 BC, despite the stern opposition of the new consuls, who were both, like Marcellus, virulent anti-Caesarians, Antony read out a letter to the Senate. It had been hand-delivered by Curio and penned by Caesar himself. The pro-consul cast himself as the friend of peace. After a lengthy recitation of his many great achievements he proposed that both he and Pompey lay down their commands simultaneously. The Senate, nervous of the effect that this might have on public opinion, suppressed it. Metellus Scipio then stood up and dealt the death-blow to all the final, flickering hopes of compromise. He named a date by which Caesar should surrender command of his legions or be considered an enemy of the Republic. This motion was immediately put to the vote. Only two senators opposed it: Curio and Caelius. Antony, as tribune, then promptly vetoed the bill.

For the Senate, that was the final straw. On 7 January a state of emergency was proclaimed. Pompey immediately moved troops into Rome, and the tribunes were warned that their safety could no longer be guaranteed. With a typically melodramatic flourish, Antony, Curio and Caelius disguised themselves as slaves, and then, hiding in wagons, fled north towards Ravenna. There, Caesar was still waiting with his single legion. The news of Pompey's emergency powers reached him on the tenth. Immediately, he ordered a detachment of troops to strike south, to seize the nearest town across the frontier, inside Italy. Caesar himself, however, while his men were setting out, passed the afternoon by having a bath, then attending a banquet, where he chatted with guests as though he had not a care in the world. Only at dusk did he rise from his couch. Hurrying in a carriage along dark and twisting byways, he finally caught up with his troops on the bank of the Rubicon. There was a moment's dreadful hesitation, and then he was crossing its swollen waters into Italy, towards Rome.

No one could know it at the time, but 460 years of the free Republic were being brought to an end.

10

WORLD WAR

Blitzkrieg

In Gaul, against the barbarians, Caesar had preferred to stab hard and fast wherever he was least expected, no matter what the risks. Now, having taken the supreme gamble of his life, he aimed to unleash the same strategy against his fellow citizens. Rather than wait for his full complement of legions to arrive from Gaul, as Pompey had expected him to do, Caesar decided instead to rely upon the effects of terror and surprise. Beyond the Rubicon there was no one to oppose him. His agents had been busy softening up Italy with bribes. Now, the moment he appeared before them, the frontier towns opened their gates. The great trunk roads to Rome were easily secured. Still no one advanced from the capital. Still Caesar struck on south.

News of the blitzkrieg was carried to Rome upon crowds of refugees. The effect of their arrival was to send fresh refugees streaming out of the city itself. Invasions from the north stirred ancestral nightmares in the Republic. Cicero, as he followed the reports of Caesar's progress with obsessive horror, wondered, 'Is it a general of the Roman people we are talking about, or Hannibal?'[1]

But there were other ghosts abroad too, from a more recent period of history. Farmers working in the fields beside the tomb of Marius reported sightings of the grim old general, risen from his sepulchre; while in the middle of the Campus Martius, where Sulla's corpse had been consumed, his spectre was glimpsed, intoning 'prophecies of doom'.[2] Gone was the war fever, so glad and confident only a few days before. Panicky senators, who had been assured by Pompey that victory would be a walkover, were now starting to calculate whether their names might not soon be appearing on Caesar's proscription lists. The Senate rose and, as one body, besieged their generalissimo. One senator openly accused Pompey of having deceived the Republic and tempted it into disaster. Another, Favonius, a close friend of Cato, jeered at him to stamp his foot and produce the legions and cavalry he had promised.

But Pompey had already given up on Rome. The Senate was issued with an evacuation order. Anyone staying behind, Pompey warned, would be regarded as a traitor. With that he headed south, leaving the capital to its fate. His ultimatum made final and irreparable the schism in the Republic. Every civil war cuts through families and friendships, but Roman society had always been especially subtle in its loyalties, and contemptuous of brute divisions. For many citizens, a choice between Caesar and Pompey remained as impossible as ever. For some, it was particularly cruel. As a result all eyes were upon them. What, for instance, was a man such as Marcus Junius Brutus to do? Earnest, dutiful and deep-thinking, yet heavily committed to both rivals, his judgement would carry special weight. Which way would Marcus Brutus choose to leap?

There was much to encourage him into Caesar's camp. His mother, Servilia, had been the great love of Caesar's life, and it was even claimed that Brutus himself was their love child. Whatever the truth of that rumour, Brutus' legal father had been one of the young Pompey's many victims during the first civil war, and so it was widely assumed that he was bound to favour the old flame of his mother over the murderer of her husband. But Pompey, once the 'teenage butcher', was now the champion of the Republic, and Brutus, an intellectual of rare probity and honour, could not bring himself to abandon the cause of legitimacy. Attached to Caesar he may have been, but he was even closer to Cato, who was both his uncle *and* his father-in-law. Brutus obeyed Pompey's orders. He abandoned Rome. So too, after a night of havering and hand-wringing, did most of the Senate. Only the barest rump remained. Never before had the city been so emptied of its magistrates. Barely a week had passed since Caesar's crossing of the Rubicon, and already the world had been turned upside down.

Pompey, of course, could argue that there were sound military reasons for the surrender of the capital – and so there were. Nevertheless, it was a tragic and fatal mistake. The Republic could not endure as an abstraction. Its vitality was nourished by the streets and public places of Rome, by the smoke rising from age-blackened temples, by the rhythms of elections, year on year on year. Uprooted, how could the Republic remain true to the will of the gods, and how were the wishes of the Roman people to be known? By fleeing the city the Senate had cut itself off from all those – the vast majority – who could not afford to pack up and leave their homes. As a result, the shared sense of community that had bound even the poorest citizen to the ideals of the state was betrayed. No wonder that the great nobles, abandoning their ancestral homes, dreaded looters and the fury of the slums.

Perhaps, if the war proved to be as short as Pompey had promised it would be, then none of this would matter – but it was already becoming clear that only Caesar had any hope of a lightning victory. Even as Pompey retreated south through Italy his pursuer was gathering pace. It seemed that the scattered legions summoned to the defence of the Republic might suffer the same fate as

Spartacus' army, pinned down in the peninsula's heel. Only complete evacuation could spare them such a calamity. The Senate began to contemplate the unthinkable: that it should reconvene abroad. Provinces had already been allocated to its key leaders: Sicily to Cato, Syria to Metellus Scipio, Spain to Pompey himself. Henceforward, it appeared, the arbiters of the Republic's fate were to rule not in the city that had bestowed their rank upon them, but as warlords amid distant and sinister barbarians. Their power would be sanctioned by force, and force alone. How, then, were they different to Caesar? How, whichever side won, was the Republic to be restored?

Even those most identified with the cause of the establishment showed themselves tormented by this question. Cato, contemplating the results of his greatest and most ruinous gamble, did nothing for his followers' morale by putting on mourning and bewailing the news of every military engagement, victory as well as defeat. Neutrals, of course, lacked even the consolation of knowing that the Republic was being destroyed in a good cause. Cicero, having obediently abandoned Rome on Pompey's orders, found himself disoriented to the point of hysteria by his absence from the capital. For weeks he could do nothing save write plaintive letters to Atticus, asking him what he should do, where he should go, whom he should support. He regarded Caesar's followers as a gang of cutthroats, and Pompey as criminally incompetent. Cicero was no soldier, but he could see with perfect clarity what a catastrophe the abandonment of Rome had been, and blamed it for the collapse of everything he held dear, from property prices to the Republic itself. 'As it is, we wander about like beggars with our wives and children, all our hopes dependent upon a man who falls dangerously ill once a year, and yet we were not even expelled but *summoned* from our city!'[3] Always the same anguish, the same bitterness, bred of the wound that had never healed. Cicero already knew what his fellow senators were soon to learn: that a citizen in exile was barely a citizen at all.

Nor, with Rome abandoned, was there anywhere else to make a stand. The one attempt to hold Caesar ended in debacle. Domitius Ahenobarbus, whose immense capacity for hatred embraced Pompey and Caesar in equal measure, refused point blank to retreat. He was inspired less by any grand strategic vision than by stupidity and pig-headedness. With Caesar sweeping through central Italy, Domitius decided to bottle himself up in the crossroads town of Corfinium. This was the same Corfinium that the Italian rebels had made their capital forty years before, and memories of that great struggle were not yet entirely the stuff of history. Enfranchised they may have been, but there were plenty of Italians who still felt themselves alienated from Rome. The cause of the Republic meant little to them – but not so that of Caesar. After all, he was the heir of Marius, that great patron of the Italians – and the enemy of Pompey, the partisan of Sulla. Old hatreds, flaring back to life, doomed Domitius' stand. Certainly, Corfinium had no intention of perishing in his defence: no sooner had Caesar appeared before its walls than it was begging to surrender. Domitius' raw levies, confronted by an army that by now comprised five crack legions, were quick to agree. Envoys were sent to Caesar, who accepted their capitulation gracefully. Domitius raged, but in vain.

Hauled before Caesar by his own officers, he begged for death. Caesar refused. Instead he sent Domitius on his way. This was only seemingly a gesture of mercy. For a citizen, there could be no more unspeakable humiliation than to owe one's life to the favour of another. Domitius, for all that he had been spared to fight another day, left Corfinium diminished and emasculated. It would be unfair to dismiss Caesar's clemency as a mere tool of policy – Domitius, if their positions had been reversed, would surely have had Caesar put to death – but it served his purposes well enough. For not only did it satisfy his own ineffable sense of superiority, but it helped to reassure neutrals everywhere that he was no second Sulla. Even his bitterest enemies, if they only submitted, could have the assurance that they would be pardoned and spared. Caesar had no plans for proscription lists to be posted in the Forum.

The point was jubilantly taken. Few citizens had the pride of Domitius. The levies he had recruited, to say nothing of the people whose town he had occupied, had no hesitation in rejoicing at their conqueror's leniency. News of the 'Pardon of Corfinium' spread fast. There would be no popular uprising against Caesar now, no chance that Italy would swing behind Pompey and come suddenly to his rescue. With Domitius' recruits having crossed to the enemy, the army of the Republic was now even more denuded than it had been, and its sole stronghold was Brundisium, the great port, the gateway to the East. Here Pompey remained, frantically commandeering ships, preparing for the crossing to Greece. He knew that he could not risk open battle with Caesar, not yet – and Caesar knew that if only he could capture Brundisium, he would be able to finish off the war at a stroke.

And so now, for both sides, began a desperate race against time. Speeding south from Corfinium, Caesar was brought the news that half of the enemy's army had already sailed, under the command of the two consuls, but that the other half, under Pompey, still waited crammed inside the port. There they would have to remain, holed up, until the fleet returned from Greece. Caesar, arriving outside Brundisium, immediately ordered his men to sail pontoons to the harbour mouth and throw a breakwater across the gap. Pompey responded by having three-storey towers built on the decks of merchant ships, then sending them across the harbour to rain missiles down on Caesar's engineers. For days the struggle continued, a desperate tumult of slingshot, heaving timbers and flames. Then, with the breakwater still unfinished, sails were spotted out to sea.

Pompey's fleet was returning from Greece. Breaking through the harbour mouth, it docked successfully, and the evacuation of Brundisium was at last able to begin. The operation was conducted with Pompey's customary efficiency. As twilight deepened the oars of his transport fleet began to plash across the harbour's waters. Caesar, warned by sympathisers inside the city, ordered his men to storm the walls – but they broke into Brundisium too late. Out through the narrow bottleneck left them by the siegeworks, Pompey's ships were slipping into the open night. With them went Caesar's last hope of a speedy resolution to the war. It was barely two and a half months since he had crossed the Rubicon.

When dawn came it illumined an empty sea. The sails of Pompey's fleet had vanished. The future of the Roman people now waited not in their own city, nor even in Italy, but beyond the still and mocking horizon, in barbarous countries far from the Forum or the Senate House or the voting pens.

As the Republic tottered, so the tremors could be felt throughout the world.

Pompey's Victory Feast

The East, unlike Rome, was familiar with kings. The stern subtleties of republicanism meant little to people who could conceive of no form of government save monarchy, and might on occasion even worship their sovereigns as divine. To the Romans, naturally, this superstition appeared contemptible. All the same, their magistrates had long been awarded their own elevated places in the pantheons of their subjects: their praises had been wafted to the heavens upon dense clouds of incense, their images placed in the temples of strange gods. For the citizen of a republic in which jealousy and suspicion accompanied every parade of greatness, these were heady pleasures – but also perilous ones. Rivals back in Rome were quick to denounce any hint of regal delusion. 'Remember you are a man'* – this was the warning whispered by a slave into Pompey's ear at the moment of his most godlike felicity, when the conqueror of the East had ridden in his triumph for the third time through Rome. His enemies, however, had been unwilling to leave a message so vital to the future health of the Republic merely to a slave. Such had been their envy of Pompey that they had deployed all their machinations against him, and thereby driven him into the arms of Caesar. Now those same enemies were his allies in exile. Huddled in Thessalonica, the Senate had to try to swallow its resentment of Pompey's godlike reputation. After all, they needed it to get them back home.

Fortunately for his cause, the credit of the new Alexander still held good. Even as he stripped the Eastern provinces bare of legions, Pompey sent out imperious summonses to the various potentates he had settled or confirmed on their thrones. The enthusiasm with which these client kings rallied to him suggested that it was Pompey, rather than the Republic, who had been keeping the gorgeous East in fee. Joining the legions of citizen soldiers in Greece were any number of bizarre-looking auxiliaries, led by princes with glamorous and exotically un-Roman names: Deiotarus of Galatia, Ariobarzanes of Cappadocia, Antiochus of Commagene. No wonder that Pompey, to whose training camp near Thessalonica these panjandrums flocked, began to appear in the light less of a Roman proconsul than of an Eastern king of kings.

Or so Domitius sneered. It was a typically abusive insult from a man whose defeat at Corfinium had done nothing to improve his temper. Yet it struck a chord. A whiff of the Oriental had long

---

* This celebrated phrase is found only in much later sources, but even if it is apocryphal, it is entirely true to the spirit and the values of the Republic.

attached itself to the great man. Behind his back Cicero had once called him 'Sampsiceramus', a barbarously syllabled name suitable to a Persian despot. But this had been satire, and affectionately meant. Now, fretting miserably still in Campania, Cicero no longer saw the joke. It seemed to him that the champion of the Republic was growing altogether too Mithridatic for comfort. He confessed to Atticus that Pompey had revealed to him his strategy for bringing Caesar to his knees, and that it was a terrible one. The provinces were to be occupied; the grain supplies cut off; Italy left to starve. Then carnage. 'From the very first, Pompey's plan has been to plunder the whole world, and the seas too, to whip up barbarian kings into a frenzy, to land armed savages on our Italian shores, and to mobilise vast armies.'[4] Here, from the pen of the Republic's most eloquent spokesman, was an echo of prophecies at least a century old. Cicero's imaginings had caught an apocalyptic fever long endemic among Rome's subject peoples. Had not the Sibyl foretold that Italy would be raped by her own sons? And Mithridates himself that a great monarch armed with the dominion of the world would emerge triumphant from the East? No wonder, then, when men back in Italy heard news of Pompey's preparations that they shuddered, despairing of the Republic.

Yet fear of one warlord did little to bolster the image of the other. True, Caesar had a genius for propaganda: he had succeeded brilliantly in quashing fears that he might be planning a bloodbath, and he was assiduous in identifying his own rights with those of a traduced and outraged people. Even so, his mastery of spin could not obscure the fact that he was guilty of the highest treason. In late March, when Caesar finally entered Rome, he found the city sullen and unwelcoming. No matter how many doles of grain he promised the Roman people, they refused to be charmed. The rump of the Senate left in the capital was even less accommodating. When Caesar formally summoned them to hear his self-justifications, hardly anyone showed up.

From those few who had appeared Caesar demanded the right to seize Rome's emergency funds. After all, he pointed out, there was no longer any need to fear a Gallic invasion, and who could be more deserving of the treasure than himself, the conqueror of Gaul? The senators, cowed and nervous, appeared ready to give in. Then a tribune, Caecilius Metellus, had the nerve to impose his veto. Caesar's patience gave out. No defence of the rights of the people now. Instead, troops entered the Forum, the temple of Saturn was broken open, the public treasure was seized. When the stubborn Metellus persisted in trying to block this sacrilege Caesar lost his temper again. He warned the tribune to stand aside or be cut down. For nine years Caesar had been accustomed to having his every order obeyed, and he did not have the time or the temperament to moderate this habit of command now. Metellus stood aside. Caesar took the gold.

It was with relief that he returned, after two frustrating weeks in Rome, to his army. As usual he was in a hurry to press on. There were Pompeian legions active in Spain, a fresh campaign to be won. Behind him, in charge of the fractious capital, he left an amenable praetor, Marcus Lepidus. The Senate was completely bypassed. The fact that Lepidus himself was of the very bluest blood, as well as being an elected magistrate, did little to disguise the unconstitutional nature of this appointment. Naturally, there was outrage. Caesar ignored it. The appearance of legality mattered to him, but not so much as the reality of power.

For those who were not Caesar, however, for those who relied upon the law as the bulwark of their liberty and the guarantor of their traditions, all was now confusion. What was an honourable citizen to do? No one could be sure. Old route maps were proving to be treacherous guides. Civil war made of the Republic a disorienting labyrinth, one in which familiar highways might turn suddenly into culs-de-sac, and cherished landmarks into piles of rubble.

Cicero, for instance, having finally screwed up the courage to scuttle for Pompey's camp, still found himself lost. Cato, taking him to one side, told him that his coming had been a terrible mistake and that he would have been 'more useful to his country and friends staying at home, and remaining neutral'.[5] Even Pompey, when he found out that Cicero's only contributions to the war effort were defeatist witticisms, publicly wished that he would go over to the enemy. Instead, Cicero sat in lugubrious impotence and moped.

But such despair was the privilege of a wealthy intellectual. Few citizens could afford to indulge it. Most sought other ways of making order out of the chaos of the times. There was nothing more upsetting to a Roman than to feel deprived of fellowship, of a sense of community, and rather than endure it he would go to any extreme. But in a civil war to what could a citizen pledge his loyalty? Not his city, nor the altars of his ancestors, nor the Republic itself, for these were claimed as the inheritance of both sides. But he could attach himself to the fortunes of a general, and be certain of finding comradeship in the ranks of that general's army, and identity in the reflected glory of the general's name. This was why the legions of Gaul had been willing to cross the Rubicon. What, after nine years' campaigning, were the traditions of the distant Forum to them, compared to the camaraderie of the army camp? And what was the Republic, compared to their general? There was no one capable of inspiring a more passionate devotion in his troops than Caesar. Amid all the confusion of war it had become perhaps the surest measure of his greatness. Arriving in Spain to take on three veteran Pompeian armies in the summer of 49 BC, he was able to push his soldiers to the extremes of exhaustion and suffering, so that, within months, the enemy had been utterly vanquished. No wonder, when backed by such steel, that Caesar dared to scorn the limits placed on other citizens, and even sometimes those on flesh and blood. 'Your spirit', Cicero would later tell him, 'has never been content within the narrow confines which nature has imposed upon us.'[6] But nor were the spirits of the men who followed his star: his legions, he boasted, 'could tear down the heavens themselves'.[7]

Here, in the mingling of the souls of Caesar and his army, was the glimpse of a new order. Ties of mutual loyalty had always provided Roman society with its fabric. So they continued to do in time of civil war, but increasingly purged of old complexities and subtleties. Simpler to follow the blast of a trumpet than the swirl of contradictory obligations that had always characterised civilian life. Yet these same obligations, comprised as they were of centuries of taboos and traditions, were not lightly to be set aside. Without them the Republic, at least as it had been constituted for centuries, would die. The checks and balances that had always served to temper the Romans' native love of glory, and divert it into courses beneficial to their city, might soon fall away. An ancient inheritance of customs and laws might be forever lost. Already, in the first months of the civil war, the ruinous consequences of such a catastrophe could be glimpsed. Political life still subsisted, but as a grisly parody of itself. The arts of persuasion were increasingly being abandoned as resorts to violence and intimidation took their place. The ambitions of magistrates, no longer dependent upon votes, could now be paid for with their fellow citizens' blood.

No wonder that many of Caesar's partisans, freed of the restraints and inhibitions of tiresome convention, should have grown intoxicated by a world in which it appeared that there were no limits to what they might achieve. But some reached out too far, too fast – and paid the price. Curio, as dashing and impetuous as ever, led two legions to disaster in Africa; disdaining to flee, he died alongside his men, who perished packed so tightly around him that their corpses were left standing like sheaves of corn in a field. Caelius, still fatally addicted to intrigue, returned to his political roots and attempted to force through Catiline's old programme of cancelling debts. When he was expelled from Rome he raised a pro-Pompeian revolt in the countryside, only to be captured and killed; a squalid end. Antony, alone of the three friends who had fled to Caesar, managed not to stumble. This reflected not any great sure-footedness but rather a preoccupation with other concerns. Even though Caesar had left him in command of Italy, Antony devoted most of his energies to billeting a harem of actresses on senators, vomiting in the popular assembly, or – a favourite party trick – dressing up as the wine god Dionysus and driving a chariot hitched to lions. Yet in the field there was no more natural soldier, and Caesar could forgive steel and élan any amount of vulgarity. Hence Antony's rapid promotion. He was an officer worthy of the men he commanded. When Caesar finally took the fight to Pompey in early 48 BC, crossing the Adriatic in the dead of winter, Antony dodged storms and the Pompeian fleet to bring him four extra legions as reinforcements. As the two rival armies sparred nervously with each other, jabbing here, feinting there, he was always in the thick of the action, dashing, tireless, the most glamorous and discussed man on either side.

But something of the monstrous and sinister energy of their general appeared to have imbued all of Caesar's soldiers. It was as though, like the spirits of the dead, they could subsist on the lifeblood of their foes. Caesar's old adversary Marcus Bibulus, in command of Pompey's Adriatic fleet, had 'slept out on board ship, even in the bitterness of winter, pushing himself to the limits, refusing to delegate, anything to get to grips with his enemy',[8] but still Caesar had succeeded in running his blockade, and had left the shattered Bibulus to expire of a fever. When Pompey, in the war of attrition that followed, aimed to starve his opponents into submission, Caesar's legions dug up roots and baked them into loaves. These they flung over the enemy barricades as symbols of defiance.

No wonder that Pompey's men found themselves 'terrified of the ferocity and toughness of their enemy, who seemed more like a species of wild animal than men';[9] nor that their general, when he was shown one of the loaves baked by Caesar's soldiers, ordered the news of it suppressed.

But Pompey himself, in private, was reassured. He knew that no men, not even Caesar's, could subsist on roots for ever. Backed by Cato, who continued to mourn the death of every citizen, no matter from which side, he waited for Caesar's army to fall to pieces. His strategy appeared to be paying off when Caesar in July 48 BC, bruised by a stinging reversal in the no man's land between the two armies, suddenly abandoned his position on the Adriatic coast and marched east. Now was the moment when Pompey, had he truly been the tyrant of Cicero's forebodings, could have sailed for Italy unopposed – but he preferred to spare his native land the horrors of invasion. Instead, he too abandoned his fortifications on the coast. Leaving only a small garrison behind under the command of Cato, he set off eastwards after Caesar. Dogging his adversary's every twist and turn, he emerged from the wilds of the Balkans into northern Greece. Here, around the city of Pharsalus, was flat, open land, perfect for a battle. Caesar was desperate to force a decisive engagement, and drew up his legions within sight of Pompey's camp. Pompey refused to take the bait. He knew that in everything that counted – money, food supplies, support of the natives – time was on his side. For days Caesar continued to offer battle. For days Pompey remained within his camp.

But in his council of war tempers were fraying. The senators in Pompey's train, impatient for action, wanted Caesar and his army wiped out. What was wrong with their generalissimo? Why would he not fight? The answer was all too readily to hand, bred of decades of suspicion and resentment: 'They complained that Pompey was addicted to command, and took pleasure in treating former consuls and praetors as though they were slaves.'[10] So wrote his not unsympathetic adversary, who could give orders to his subordinates as he pleased and not be jeered at for it. But this was because Caesar, whatever he pretended otherwise, was not fighting as the champion of the Republic. Pompey was. To him, it was a title that meant everything. Now his colleagues, as jealous of overweening greatness as they had always been, demanded that he demonstrate his fitness to lead them by bowing to the wishes of the majority – let him crush Caesar once and for all! Pompey, reluctantly, gave way. The orders went out. Battle was to be joined the following day. Pompey the Great, by staking his own and the Republic's future upon a single throw, had finally proved himself a good citizen.

But that night, as his fellow senators ordered victory banquets prepared and decked their tents with laurel, and quarrelled over who should inherit Caesar's high priesthood, Pompey had a dream. He saw himself entering his great theatre on the Campus Martius, climbing the steps that led to the temple of Venus, and there, to the cheers and applause of the Roman people, dedicating the spoils of all his many victories to the goddess. It was enough to make him wake up in a cold sweat. Other men might have been cheered by such a vision, but Pompey remembered that Caesar was descended from Venus, and so he dreaded that all his laurels and greatness were on the point of being lost to him for ever, and becoming his rival's.

And so it proved. The next morning, despite outnumbering the enemy more than two to one, it was Pompey's army that was shattered and rolled back. Their opponents had been ordered not to throw their javelins, but to keep them as spears, aiming and stabbing them at the faces of the enemy cavalry, who were noblemen all, and vain of their good looks. Caesar, once the dandy nonpareil himself, had formulated the perfect tactic. Pompey's cavalry turned and fled. Next, his loosely armed slingers and archers were cut down. Domitius, leading the left wing, was killed as his legions buckled. Caesar's men, outflanking Pompey's line of battle, then attacked from the rear. By midday the battle was over. That evening it was Caesar who sat down in Pompey's tent and ate the victory meal prepared by Pompey's chef, off Pompey's silver plate.

But as twilight deepened and stars began to blaze in the burning August night, he rose and returned to the battlefield. All around him were piles of Roman dead, and the cries of the wounded echoed across the plain of Pharsalus. 'They were the ones who wanted this,'[11] said Caesar, in mingled bitterness and grief, surveying the slaughter-ground. But he was wrong. No one had wanted the slaughter. That was the tragedy. Nor was it concluded yet. Caesar's victory had been shattering, but the agony of the Republic appeared no nearer to a resolution. Rome and the world had fallen into the conqueror's hands. So it seemed. But what was he to do with them? What could he do? After the cataclysm, how and what was Caesar to rebuild?

To the remnants of Pompey's army, he displayed his celebrated clemency. Of those who accepted it, no one gave him greater joy than Marcus Brutus. After the battle Caesar had ordered a special search to be made for the son of his old flame, fearing for his safety. Once Brutus had been found unscathed, he was welcomed into the ranks of Caesar's most intimate advisers. This was an appointment made of personal affection, but also calculation. Brutus was a widely respected man, and Caesar hoped that his recruitment might encourage other, more die-hard opponents to seek a similar reconciliation. He would not be entirely disappointed. Cicero, who had not been at Pharsalus, having stayed behind with Cato on the Adriatic coast, was one of those who decided that the war was as good as over. It almost cost him a lynching – only the intervention of Cato prevented him from being run through by a Pompeian sword. Cato himself, naturally, refused to countenance any thought of surrender. Instead, embarking with his garrison, he set sail for Africa. This alone ensured that the war would continue. As a mark of his indomitability, Cato announced that not only would he continue to grow his hair and beard in mourning, but that he would never again lie down to eat. For a Roman, this was a grim resolution indeed.

And then, of course, there was Pompey. He too remained on the loose. After Pharsalus he had galloped out of the back gates of his camp to the Aegean coast, and from there, avoiding the bounty-hunters who were already buzzing on his trail, commandeered a ship to take him to Mitylene. It was here that he had left Cornelia, in the shadow of its theatre, the model for his own, and a reminder of happier days. Now, wounded by his first taste of defeat, Pompey needed the comfort that only his wife could provide. She did not disappoint. Her father the pornographer may have been a disgrace to his ancestors, but Cornelia, when brought the news of Pharsalus, knew precisely what was expected of her. A swoon, a wiping away of tears, a run through the streets of Mitylene, and Cornelia was in her husband's arms. Pompey, a seasoned hand at playing the antique hero, was jolted by her performance into giving one of his own: a stern lecture on the importance of never abandoning hope. He may even have believed it. Yes, a battle had been lost – but not the East, and therefore not the war. True, many of the kings who owed Pompey their thrones had been at Pharsalus and either perished or surrendered – but not all. One in particular had been absent, and he was the ruler of the kingdom in the Mediterranean that was the richest in money, provisions and ships. Furthermore, he was only a boy, and his sister, who wanted the throne for herself, was in open rebellion against him, leaving his country easy meat for the master of the East. Or so Pompey hoped. The order was given. His small fleet headed south. Barely a month after Pharsalus, Pompey moored off the flat coast of Egypt.

Emissaries were sent to the King. After a few days spent bobbing at anchor off the sand bars, on 28 September 48 BC Pompey saw a small fishing boat rowing towards his ship across the shallows. He was hailed in Latin, then a second time in Greek, and invited to board the boat. Pompey did so, having first embraced Cornelia and kissed her goodbye. As he was rowed towards the shore he attempted to engage his companions in conversation, but no one would answer him. Unsettled, Pompey looked towards the shore. There he could see the King, Ptolemy XIII, a boy dressed in his diadem and purple robes, waiting. Pompey was comforted. When he felt the keel of the boat run against the sand he rose to his feet. As he did so, suddenly, a Roman renegade drew a sword and ran him through the back. More blades were drawn. The blows rained down. 'And Pompey, drawing his toga over his face with both hands, endured them all, nor did he say or do anything unworthy, only gave a faint groan.'[12] And so perished Pompey the Great.

Cornelia, stranded on the deck of the trireme, saw it all. But there was nothing she or any of the crew could do, not even when they saw the Egyptians decapitate the man who had so recently been the greatest in the Roman Republic, and leave his naked body as jetsam on the shore. Instead, his followers had to turn and escape to open sea, leaving only one of Pompey's freedmen, who had accompanied his former master in the fishing boat, to prepare a pyre. In this labour, according to Plutarch's weird and haunting account, he happened to be joined by an old soldier, a veteran of Pompey's first campaigns; and together the two men completed their pious task. Once the body had been burned a stone cairn was raised to mark the site, but the dunes soon engulfed it, and the memory of it was lost. Nothing beside remained. Boundless and bare, the lone and level sand stretched far away.

The Queen of Cosmopolis

The coastline of the Nile Delta had always been treacherous. Low-lying and featureless, it offered nothing to help a sailor find his way. Even so, navigators who approached Egypt were not entirely bereft of guidance. At night, far distant from its shore, a dot of light flickered low in the southern sky. By day it could be seen for what it was: not a star, but a great lantern, set upon a tower, visible from miles out to sea. This was the Pharos, not only the tallest building ever built by the Greeks, but also, thanks to its endless recycling on tourist trinkets, the most instantly recognisable. A triumph of vision and engineering, the great lighthouse served as the perfect symbol for what it advertised: megalopolis – the most stupendous place on earth.

Even Roman visitors had to acknowledge that Alexandria was something special. When Caesar, three days after Pompey's murder, sailed past the island on which the Pharos stood, he was arriving at a city larger,* more cosmopolitan and certainly far more beautiful than his own. If Rome, shabby and labyrinthine, stood as a monument to the rugged virtues of the Republic, then Alexandria bore witness to what a king could achieve. But not just any king. The tomb of Alexander the Great still stood talisman-like in the city he had founded, and the street plan, a gridded lattice lined with gleaming colonnades, was recognisably the same as that mapped out three centuries earlier by the conquering Macedonian, to the roar of the lonely sea. Now, where once there had been nothing except for sand and wheeling marsh birds, there stretched a landscape of exquisite artificiality. Here was the first city ever to have numbered

---

* At least according to the testimony of Diodorus Siculus (17.52), who had visited both Alexandria and Rome: 'The population of Alexandria outstrips that of all other cities.'

addresses. Its banks oiled the commerce of East and West alike, its freight terminals churned with the trade of the world. Its celebrated library boasted seven hundred thousand scrolls and had been built in pursuit of a sublime fantasy: that every book ever written might be gathered in one place. There were even slot machines and automatic doors. Everything in Alexandria was a superlative. No wonder that Cicero, who regarded anywhere that was not Rome as 'squalid obscurity',[13] should have made an exception for the one city that rivalled his own as the centre of the world. 'Yes,' he confessed, 'I dream, and have long dreamed, of seeing Alexandria.'[14]

He was not the only Roman to be haunted by fantasies of the city. Egypt was a land of unrivalled fertility, and the proconsul who conquered Alexandria would have the bread-basket of the Mediterranean in his hands. This was a prospect that had long served to poison the already venomous swirl of Roman politics, breeding endless machinations and bribery scandals – yet no one, not even Crassus, not even Pompey, had succeeded in securing an Egyptian command. By unwritten consent, a prize so dazzling was a prize too far. In the view of most citizens it was safer and just as profitable to leave the ruling dynasty to administer the costs of its own exploitation. A succession of monarchs had played the role of the Republic's poodle to perfection: secure enough to squeeze their subjects dry on behalf of their patrons, weak enough never to present the slightest threat to Rome. On such a humiliating basis was the last independent kingdom of the Greeks, originally founded by a general of Alexander and once the greatest power in the East, permitted to limp along.

But the kings of Egypt were nothing if not survivors. The Ptolemy who had watched Pompey being butchered in the surf was the namesake of a long line of monarchs who had always been prepared to swallow any indignity and perpetrate any outrage to keep a hold on power. To the greed, viciousness and sensuality that had characterised all the Greek dynasties in the East, the Ptolemies had added their own refinement, derived from Egypt's pharaonic past: habitual incest. The effects of their inbreeding could be seen not only in the murderous quality of the Ptolemies' palace intrigues, but also in a decadence exceptional even by the standards of contemporary royalty. The Romans openly regarded the Ptolemies as monstrosities, and saw it as their republican duty to rub this in at every opportunity. If the king were gross and effete, then visiting proconsuls would take delight in forcing him to lumber through the streets of Alexandria, wobbling in his diaphanous robes as he sweated to keep up. Other Romans found more vivid ways of expressing their scorn. Cato, called upon by a Ptolemy while he was administering Cyprus, had greeted the King of Egypt amid the after-effects of a laxative, and spent the entire audience sitting on the lavatory.

So it was that Caesar, arriving in the middle of a dynastic death-struggle with barely four thousand men, more than made up in prejudices what he lacked in troops. The contemptibility of the Ptolemies was confirmed for him from the moment he stepped ashore. There, a welcoming gift on the harbour quay, was Pompey's pickled head. Caesar wept: no matter how relieved he may secretly have felt at the removal of his adversary, he was disgusted by his son-in-law's fate, and even more so when he discovered the full background to the crime.

For Pompey the Great, it emerged, had been the victim of a sinister backstairs cabal, comprising Ptolemy's chief ministers, a eunuch, a mercenary and an academic. Nothing, to Caesar's mind, could have been more offensively un-Roman. Yet the brains behind the crime, Pothinus, the eunuch, was presuming on his gratitude, and confidently expecting him to back the King in the war against his sister. Instead, trapped in Alexandria by adverse winds, Caesar immediately started behaving as though he were a king himself.

Needing somewhere to stay, he naturally chose the royal palace, a vast, fortified complex of buildings that over the centuries had spread and spread, until it now covered almost a third of the city – another of Alexandria's superlatives. From this stronghold Caesar began to issue exorbitant financial demands, and announced, graciously, that he was prepared to settle the civil war between Ptolemy and his sister – not as a partisan, but as a referee. He ordered both siblings to disband their armies and meet him in Alexandria. Ptolemy, without disbanding so much as a soldier, was persuaded by Pothinus to return to the palace. Meanwhile, his sister, Cleopatra, with no free passage to the capital, remained stranded beyond Ptolemy's lines.

But then, one evening, through the deepening shadows of an Alexandrian twilight, a small boat sneaked up to a jetty beside the palace. A single Sicilian merchant clambered out, carrying on his shoulder a carpet in a bag. Once this had been smuggled into Caesar's presence it was unrolled to reveal the unexpected, but bewitching, sight of Cleopatra. Caesar, as the Queen had gambled he would be, was delighted by this *coup de théâtre*. Making an impression had never been a problem for her. While she may not have been the beauty of legend – she appears, from her coins at least, to have been somewhat scrawny and hook-nosed – her resources of seductiveness were infinite. 'Her sex appeal, together with the charm of her conversation, and the charisma evident in everything she said or did, made her, quite simply, irresistible,'[15] wrote Plutarch. Who, looking at Cleopatra's track-record, can doubt it? Not that she was given to sleeping around; far from it. Her favours were the most exclusive in the world. Power, for Cleopatra, was the only aphrodisiac. The female of the Ptolemaic species had always been deadlier than the male: intelligent, ruthless, ambitious, strong-willed. Now, in the person of Cleopatra, all these fierce qualities met and were distilled. As such, she was exactly Caesar's type: after more than a decade of soldiering, intelligent female company must have come as a rare pleasure. Of course, it also helped that Cleopatra was only twenty-one. Caesar bedded her that very night.

When Ptolemy found out about his sister's conquest he was thrown into a violent tantrum. He flounced out into the streets, tossing his diadem down into the dust and screaming for his subjects to rally to his defence. The inhabitants of Alexandria were much given to rioting, and Caesar's high-handed demands for money had already done little for his popularity. Now, when Ptolemy asked the mob to attack the Romans, it obliged enthusiastically. The hated foreigners were besieged in the palace, and so threatened did Caesar's position become that he was obliged not only to recognise Ptolemy as joint monarch with Cleopatra, but also to cede Cyprus back to the pair of them. Even so, such concessions did little to ease him out of his embarrassing scrape. A few weeks into the siege and the rioters were joined by Ptolemy's entire army, some twenty thousand strong. Caesar found his situation going from bad to desperate. Trapped in the hot-house of an Egyptian palace, surrounded by treacherous eunuchs and incestuous royals, he was completely cut off from the outside world. Far beyond the light cast by the flashing Pharos, the Republic was still at war with itself – yet Caesar could not get so much as a letter smuggled through to Rome.

For the next five months the terrible exploits of his previous campaigns were replayed as farce. Burning the Egyptian fleet in the harbour, the bibliophile Caesar accidentally set fire to warehouses crammed with priceless books;* attempting to secure the Pharos, he was forced to jump ship and abandon his general's cloak to the enemy. Despite these embarrassments, however, Caesar succeeded

---

* Or possibly the entire Library of Alexandria, a disaster for which Christians and Muslims have also been blamed.

in retaining control of both the palace and the harbour – and stamped his authority in other ways too. Not only did he have the scheming Pothinus put to death, but he impregnated Cleopatra, an act of king-making to trump anything achieved by Pompey. By March 47 BC, when reinforcements finally arrived in Egypt, the Queen was visibly swelling with the proof of Caesar's favour. Ptolemy, panicking, fled Alexandria. Weighed down by his golden armour, he drowned in the Nile – a convenient accident that left Cleopatra unchallenged on her throne. Caesar had backed a winner once again.

But at what cost? A steep one, it seemed. With his communication lines restored, Caesar was now back in touch with his agents, and the news they sent could hardly have been less promising. The Alexandrian escapade had squandered much of the advantage won at Pharsalus. In Italy Antony's stewardship was provoking widespread resentment; in Asia King Pharnaces, Mithridates' son, had proved himself a chip off the old block by invading Pontus; in Africa Metellus Scipio and Cato were marshalling a vast new army; in Spain Pompeians were fostering renewed unrest. North, east, south, west – war across the world. There were few places where Caesar was not desperately required. But for two more months he lingered in Egypt. With the Republic fatally riven, and the empire of the Roman people collapsing into anarchy, Caesar, the man whose restless ambition had begun the civil war, lolled by his mistress's side.

No wonder that Cleopatra's seductiveness should have struck many Romans as something almost demonic. To tempt a citizen famous for his energies into idleness, to lure him from the path of duty, to keep him from Rome and a destiny that seemed increasingly to have been ordained by the gods – this was a theme worthy of great and terrible poetry. And of obscene chanting too. Caesar's libido had long been a source of hilarity to his men: 'Lock up your wives,' they would sing, 'our commander is bad news/He may be bald, but he fucks anything that moves.'[16] Other jokes, inevitably, harped on the old gossip about Nicomedes. Even to men who had followed their general through unbelievable hardships, his sexual prowess spelled effeminacy. Great though Caesar had proved himself, steel-hard in body and mind, the moral codes of the Republic were unforgiving. A citizen could never afford to slip. Dirt on a toga would always show.

It was the threat of such ridicule, of course, that helped to keep a Roman a man. Custom, wrote the greatest scholar of Caesar's day, was 'a pattern of thought which has evolved to become a regular practice':* shared and accepted by all the citizens of the Republic, it had provided Rome with the surest foundation of her greatness. How different things were in Alexandria! Raised from scratch on sandbanks, the city lacked deep roots. No wonder, to Roman eyes, that it had such a harlot character. Without custom there could be no shame, and without shame anything became possible. A people whose traditions had withered would become prey to the most repellent and degrading habits. Who better illustrated this than the Ptolemies themselves? No sooner had Cleopatra seen off one sibling than she married another. The spectacle of the heavily pregnant Queen taking as her husband her ten-year-old brother was one to put any of Clodia's exploits into the shade. Greek Cleopatra may have been, a daughter of the same culture that had provided the bedrock of a Roman's education, but she was also fabulously, exotically alien. For a man of Caesar's temperament, with his taste for the taboo, it must have been an enchanting combination.

-----

* Varro, yet another of Posidonius' pupils. He was a Pompeian, one of the three generals defeated by Caesar during his first Spanish campaign. He was widely held to be Rome's greatest polymath. The quotation is from his treatise 'On Customs', and is cited by Macrobius, 3.8.9.

Yet if Cleopatra provided him with a delicious erotic interlude, an opportunity, for a couple of months, to drop the guard expected of a Roman magistrate, Caesar was never the man to forget his own future, nor that of Rome. Pondering them, he must have been given much food for thought by what he found in Alexandria. Just like its queen, the city was a disorienting blend of the familiar and the weird. With its library and its temples, it was all very Greek – indeed, the capital of the Greek world. Sometimes, however, when the prevailing winds turned and breezes no longer bore a freshness from the sea, sand would gust through Alexandria, carried from the burning desert to the south. The Egyptian hinterland was too vast and too ancient to be entirely ignored. It made of its capital a dream-like, hybrid place. The spacious streets were decorated not only with the clean-limbed masterpieces of Greek sculptors, but also with statuary looted from the banks of the Nile: sphinxes, gods with animal heads, pharaohs with enigmatic smiles. Just as strikingly – and, to a Roman's eye, bizarrely – however, there were some quarters of the city in which there were no images of gods to be seen at all. As well as to Greeks and Egyptians, Alexandria was home to a vast number of Jews; more, almost certainly, than Jerusalem itself. They completely dominated one of the city's five administrative districts, and despite having to rely on a Greek translation of the Torah, they remained in other ways defiantly unassimilated. Jews entering their synagogue, Syrians camped outside beneath a statue of Zeus, all of them in the shadow of a plundered obelisk – this was the look of cosmopolis.

And was it to be Rome's future too? There were certainly plenty of citizens who feared so. To the Romans, the prospect of being swamped by barbarous cultures had always been a fertile source of paranoia. The ruling classes, in particular, mistrusted foreign influences because they dreaded the enfeebling of the Republic. The world's mistress, yes, but a world city, no: this, essentially, was the

Senate's manifesto for Rome. So it was that Jews and Babylonian astrologers were endlessly being expelled from the city. So too Egyptian gods. Even in the frantic months before Caesar crossed the Rubicon one of the consuls had found time to pick up an axe and personally start on the demolition of a temple of Isis. But the Jews and astrologers always made their ways back, and the great goddess Isis, divine mother and queen of the heavens, had far too strong a hold upon her worshippers easily to be banished from the city. The consul had been forced to lift the axe against her only because no labourers could be found to do the job. Rome was changing, lapped by tides of immigration, and there was little that the Senate could do to hold them back. New languages, new customs, new religions: these were the fruits of the Republic's own greatness. Not for nothing did all roads now lead to Rome.

Caesar, who had always been unafraid of the unthinkable, and had anyway long been a virtual stranger to his own city, could see this with a clarity denied to most of his peers. Perhaps he had always seen it. After all, as a boy, Jews had been his neighbours, and he had offered them his family's protection. Far from alarming him, the presence of immigrants in Rome had served merely to buttress his conceit. Now, as the victor of Pharsalus, he was in a position to patronise entire nations. Throughout the East sculptors were busy chiselling Pompey's name from inscriptions and replacing it with Caesar's — the Republic, naturally, being nowhere mentioned. In city after city the descendant of Venus had been hailed as a living god, and in Ephesus as the saviour of mankind, no less. This was heady stuff, even for a man of Caesar's pitiless intelligence. He did not need to swallow such flattery whole to find it suggestive. Clearly, a role as the saviour of mankind would not easily be accommodated by the constitutional arrangements of the Republic. If Caesar wanted inspiration, then he would have to look elsewhere. No wonder, lingering in Alexandria, that he found Cleopatra so intriguing. Dimly, distortedly, in the figure of the young Egyptian Queen, he surely caught a glimpse of a possible future for himself.

In the late spring of 47 BC the happy couple set out on a cruise down the Nile. To do this was to journey from one world to another. After all, strange as Alexandria struck visiting Romans, it was not altogether alien. Its citizens, like the Romans themselves, were proud of their liberties. Ostensibly, Alexandria was a free city, and the relationship of the monarch to her Greek compatriots was supposed to be that of a first among equals. Civic traditions derived from classical Greece were still cherished, and however hazily they were now understood, Cleopatra could not afford to ignore them altogether. But pass beyond the limits of her capital, glide in her barge past the pyramids or the great pylons of Karnak, and she became something else entirely. The role of pharaoh was one that Cleopatra played with the utmost seriousness. She was the first Greek monarch to speak Egyptian. During the war with her brother she had turned for support not to Alexandria but to her native subjects in the provinces. She was not merely a devotee of the ancient gods, but one of them, divinity made flesh, an incarnation of the queen of the heavens herself.

First citizen of Alexandria and the new Isis: Cleopatra was both. For Caesar, there can have been nothing like taking a goddess to bed to make the scruples of the far-distant Republic appear even more parochial than they had seemed before. It was said that, had his soldiers not started complaining, he would have sailed on with his mistress all the way to Ethiopia. This was scurrilous gossip, but it hinted at a dangerous and plausible truth. Caesar was indeed embarked on a journey into uncharted realms. First, of course, there was a civil war to be won, and it was to achieve this that Caesar, at the end of May, abandoned his Nile cruise and set off with his legions on fresh endeavours and new campaigns. But after victory what then? His time with Cleopatra had given Caesar a good deal to mull over. On the fruits of these reflections much might depend. Not only his own future, perhaps, but that of Rome and the world beyond it too.

Anti Cato

April 46 BC. The sun was setting beyond the walls of Utica. Twenty miles down the shore the ruins of what had once been Carthage were shrouded in the haze of twilight, while off the coast, where ships filled with fugitives dotted the African sea, night had already come. And soon Caesar would be coming too. Despite being vastly outnumbered, he had fought a great battle and been victorious yet again. Metellus Scipio's army, recruited during the long months of Caesar's absence in Egypt and Asia, had been routed with terrible slaughter. Africa was in Caesar's hands. There could be no hope of holding Utica against him. Cato, who was responsible for the city's defence, knew now for sure that the Republic was doomed.

But even though it was he who had provided the shattered remnants of Scipio's army with the ships for their escape, he had no intention of joining them. That was hardly Cato's style. At supper that evening, sitting up, as had been his custom since Pharsalus, he betrayed no sign of alarm. Caesar's name was not even mentioned. Instead, as the wine flowed, the talk turned to philosophy. The theme of freedom came up, and in particular the claim that only the good can truly be free. One guest, adducing subtle and devious arguments, argued the opposite, but Cato, growing agitated, refused to hear him out. This was the only evidence that he was in any way upset. Having reduced the company to silence, however, he was quick to change the topic. He did not want anyone to guess his feelings – or anticipate his plan.

That night, after retiring to his bedroom and reading for a short while, he stabbed himself. He was still alive when his attendants found him on the floor, but while frantic attempts were made to bandage the wound, Cato pushed away the doctors and tore at his own intestines. He quickly bled to death. When Caesar arrived at Utica he found the whole city in mourning. Bitterly, he addressed the man who had for so long been his nemesis, newly laid, like Pompey, in a grave beside the sea: 'Just as you envied me the chance of sparing you, Cato, so I envy you this death.'[17] Caesar was hardly the man to appreciate being cheated of a grand gesture. There had been no one more identified with the flinty spirit of Roman liberty than Cato, and to have pardoned him would have been to destroy his infuriating hold on the Republic's imagination. Instead, thanks to the gory heroism of his death, that hold had now been confirmed. Even as a spectre, Cato remained Caesar's most obdurate foe.

Blood, honour and liberty: the suicide exemplified all the Romans' favourite themes. And Caesar, that master of mass manipulation, knew it. Returning to Rome at the end of July 46 BC, he prepared to put his dead enemies where he felt they now belonged – in the shade. Theatrical as Cato's death had been, Caesar was determined to upstage it. That September, his fellow citizens were invited to share in his victory celebrations. Over the years the Roman people had tended to grow blasé about extravagant spectacle, but the organisation and vision that Caesar brought to his entertainments enabled him to defy the law of diminishing returns. Giraffes and British war chariots, silk canopies and battles on artificial lakes, all were duly gawped at by astonished crowds. Not even Pompey had put on anything to compare; nor had he staged four triumphs in a row as Caesar did now.

Gauls, Egyptians, Asiatics and Africans: these were the foreign foes marched in chains before the cheering crowds. But even

28. Domitius Ahenobarbus. The portrait is either of Caesar's great enemy, or of his son. In 56 BC, the ambitions of the elder Domitius to replace Caesar as governor of Gaul provoked a renewal of the triumvirate, with fateful consequences for the Republic. A denarius struck between 42 and 36 BC. *(Museo Nazionale Romano, Rome/British Museum)*

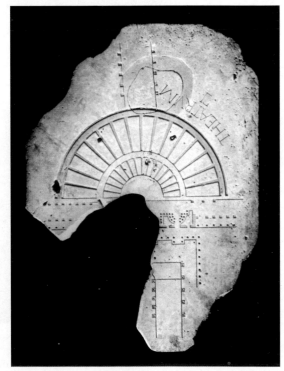

29. A plan of Pompey's great theatre. Begun in 61 BC, and completed in 55, it was the first stone theatre to be built in Rome: an unparalleled – and ominously un-republican – exercise in self-promotion. *(Museo Capitolino, Rome)*

30. The Appian Way, ten miles out of Rome. It was here, in January 52 BC, that Clodius's career came to a fittingly violent end. *(Tom Holland)*

31. 'Vercingetorix throws his arms at the feet of Caesar'. As portrayed by Lionel Royer in 1899. Caesar's victory at Alesia in 52 BC was the most astonishing of his career, and marked the effective end of the Gallic revolt. *(Musée Crozatier, Le Puy en Velay, France/Bridgeman Art Library)*

32. Julius Caesar. 'Your spirit', Cicero told him, 'has never been content within the narrow confines which nature has imposed upon us.' *(Museo Capitolino, Rome/Fratelli Alinari)*

33. 'The Ides of March'. Painted by Edward John Poynter in 1883.
(Manchester City Art Galleries, Manchester/Bridgeman Art Library)

34. A full-length statue of a Roman general, found in the Renaissance on the site of Pompey's theatre. For centuries, it was thought to be the very statue beneath which Caesar fell. Sadly, no one believes that now. *(Palazzo Spada, Rome/Fratelli Alinari)*

ΥΠΕΡΒΑΣΙΛΙΣΣΗΣ
ΚΛΕΟΠΑΤΡΑΣΟΘΕ

35. Cleopatra, Greek queen and Egyptian pharaoh, makes offerings to the goddess Isis.
(*Musée du Louvre, Paris/Art Archive*)

36. Antony and Cleopatra, the reverse sides of a silver tetradrachm, struck in around 34 BC.
No greater affront to the values of the Republic could have been imagined than that a Roman
and a Greek, a triumvir and a queen, should have appeared together on the same coin.

(*Fitzwilliam Museum, Cambridge*)

37. Caesar Divi Filius Augustus. *(Museo Vaticano, Rome/Fratelli Alinari)*

38. A mosaic found in Pompeii. A skull is balanced precariously on a butterfly and a wheel: death haunts life, and fortune is endlessly mutable. *(Museo Nazionale, Naples/Scala, Florence)*

though it would clearly have been obscene for Caesar to have celebrated his victory over fellow citizens in such a manner, he could
not resist the occasional gloat. Having found the time, between his
Egyptian escapade with Cleopatra and his victory in Africa, to
thrash King Pharnaces, Caesar had boasted of the speed of his victory in a celebrated phrase: 'I came, I saw, I conquered.'[18] Now,
written on a billboard and borne in procession through Rome, the
same phrase served to cut Pompey down to size too – for it was
Pompey who had made such a big deal out of conquering
Pharnaces' father, Mithridates. Yet if the spectre of one rival could
be distinguished by knowledgeable citizens trailing Caesar's chariot
in the dust, there was still one shadow who defied the conqueror's
chains. Caesar had defeated Pompey, but he had not beaten Cato –
a failure that led him into a rare propaganda gaffe. In his fourth triumph, ostensibly held to celebrate his victory over Africa, Caesar
ordered a float illustrating Cato's suicide to be wheeled through the
streets. He justified this by claiming that Cato and all the citizens
who had fought with him had been slaves of the Africans, and had
perished as collaborators. The watching crowds did not agree. They
wept at the sight of the float. Cato still eluded the reach of Caesar's
hatred.

But the Republic itself was now securely in his hands. The
Senate, stupefied by the scale of Caesar's achievements, overawed by
the magnitude of his power, had scrabbled to legitimise his victory
and somehow reconcile it with the cherished traditions of the past.
The strain of this attempt had cost constitutionalists a great deal of
pain. Already Caesar had twice accepted the dictatorship: first, in
late 49 BC for eleven days when he had presided over his own hurried election to the consulship, and second, in October 48 when he
had been appointed to the office for a year. Now, in the spring of 46,
he was awarded a dictatorship for the third time – and for the
unprecedented span of ten years. Already consul, Caesar was also

given the right to nominate all the Republic's magistrates, and was created – to sardonic amusement – Rome's 'Prefect of Morals'. Never before, not even under Sulla, had there been such a concentration of authority in the hands of one man. Yet the example of Sulla did offer at least a glimmer of hope. A decade was a long time to endure a dictatorship, but it was not an eternity. Bitter medicine had proved restorative before. And who, after all, could deny that the Republic was very sick indeed?

There was even a measure of sympathy for the man burdened with its cure. 'We are his slaves,' wrote Cicero, 'but he is the slave of the times.'[19] No one could really know what Caesar's plans for the Republic might be, because no one could know how the Republic was to be healed of the wounds of civil war. Yet the vague hope persisted, even among his enemies, that if anyone could find a way out of the crisis, then Caesar was the man. His qualities of brilliance and clemency were clearly incomparable. Nor was there anyone credible left to oppose him: Pompey, Domitius and Cato, all were dead. So too now was Scipio, caught in a storm and lost off the African coast. True, Pompey's two sons, Gnaeus and Sextus, were still at large, but they were young and had vicious reputations. In the winter of 46 BC, when they succeeded in raising a dangerous rebellion in Spain, and Caesar hurriedly left Rome to confront it, even former partisans of Pompey wished their old enemy well. Typical was Cassius Longinus, the officer who had performed so creditably at Carrhae, and who had gone on to become Pompey's most brilliant naval commander, before being pardoned by Caesar after Pharsalus. 'I'd much rather have our old, merciful master', he confessed to Cicero, as the two men discussed the news of Caesar's progress in Spain, 'than have to take our chance with a new and bloodthirsty one.'[20]

Even so, there was a bitterness to Cassius' tone. A master remained a master, no matter how gracious. Most citizens, glad to be alive after the years of civil war, were too exhausted to care. But among Caesar's peers, jealousy and impotence festered, as did humiliation. Better to die than live a slave: this was the lesson that a Roman drew in with his breath. One could submit to the dictator, and be grateful to him, even admire him – but one could never repress the resulting sense of shame. 'To the free men who accepted Caesar's perks, his very power to dole them out was an affront.'[21] And all the more so, of course, because of the memory of what had happened at Utica.

Cato's ghost still haunted the conscience of Rome. Those of his former comrades who had submitted to Caesar and been rewarded for it could not help but see in his death a personal reproach. None more so than Brutus, Cato's nephew, who had initially condemned his uncle's suicide on philosophical grounds, but began to find himself ever more unsettled by the example it had set. Earnest and high minded as he was, Brutus had no wish to be regarded as a collaborator. Still confident that Caesar was, at heart, a constitutionalist, he saw no contradiction between supporting the dictator and remaining loyal to the memory of his uncle. In the cause of making this as clear as he could, Brutus decided that his wife would have to go, and Porcia, Cato's daughter, take her place. Since Porcia's previous husband had been Marcus Bibulus, a bride less popular with Caesar would have been hard to imagine. Brutus had made his point.

But he was not done yet. Wishing his uncle's memory to be immortalised, Brutus turned his hand to an obituary. He also asked Cicero, as Rome's greatest writer, to do the same. The commission was flattering, but Cicero, accepting it after due hesitation, was prompted as much by shame as by vanity. As he was all too painfully aware, he had not had a good war, and his acceptance of a pardon from Caesar had only confirmed his reputation as a trimmer. In the face of widespread contempt Cicero still clung to his self-image as a fearless spokesman for republican virtue, but the reality was that, since making his peace with Caesar, the height of his bravery had been the cracking of an occasional poisonous joke. Now, by lauding the martyr of Utica publicly, he dared to stick his neck out a little further. Cato, Cicero wrote, was one of the few men who had been greater than his reputation. It was a pointed judgement, targeted not only at the dictator, but, by implication, at all those who had bowed to his supremacy – including, not least of course, the author himself.

Far away in Spain, surrounded by dust and blood-fattened flies, Caesar was still keeping abreast of Rome's literary scene. When he read what Cicero and Brutus had written, he was toweringly una-mused. No sooner had the decisive engagement of the campaign been fought and won than he was writing a vituperative riposte. Cato, he argued, far from being a hero, had been a contemptible drunk, obstructive and mad, thoroughly without worth. This com-position, the *Anti Cato*, was then dispatched to Rome, where it was greeted with widespread hilarity, so unrecognisable was the carica-ture of its subject that it gave. Cato's reputation, far from being diminished by Caesar's attack, was raised to new heights.

Caesar himself was left embittered and frustrated. Already, during the Spanish campaign, there had been signs that his con-siderable reserves of patience were nearing exhaustion. The war had been peculiarly brutal. Far from treating the rebels with his cus-tomary clemency, Caesar had refused to recognise them as citizens at all. Their corpses had been used as building material, and their heads stuck on poles. Even though Sextus, Pompey's younger son, had managed to escape Caesar's vengeance, Gnaeus, the elder, had been captured, executed and his head paraded as a trophy of war. These were scenes worthy of Gauls. Yet even though it was Caesar who had turned head-hunter, he accepted no responsibility for the descent of his army into barbarism. Instead, the true fault lay with the treachery and folly of his opponents. It was Fate that had delivered the fortunes of the Roman people into his hands. If they now refused to support him in his efforts to bind their wounds, then not even the blood already spilled would serve to appease the angry gods. Rome, and the world with her, would be lost to a tide of darkness, and the barbarism would prove universal.

Faced with the need to stave off such an apocalypse, what were the sensibilities of a Cicero or a Brutus? What, indeed, was the Republic? Caesar's impatience with traditions still regarded as sacrosanct by his fellow citizens was growing more palpable by the day. Far from hurrying back to the capital to consult the Senate or put his measures to the people, he lingered in the provinces, planting colonies of veterans, extending the franchise to privileged natives. Back in Rome the aristocracy shuddered at the news. Jokes were told of Gauls peeling off their stinking trousers, draping themselves in togas, and asking the way to the Senate House. Such xenophobia, of course, had always been a Roman's right and privilege. Almost by definition, it was those most proud of the liberties of the Republic who proved the worst snobs. But Caesar scorned them. He could no longer be bothered to care what traditionalists thought.

Nor, indeed, was he much interested in the traditions themselves. This was just as well, for his policies raised awkward questions about the future functioning of the Republic. If it had been impractical enough for citizens in Italy to come to Rome to cast their votes, then for those in distant provinces, far away across the sea, it would be impossible. The problem was brushed aside. Caesar was not to be diverted by such quibbles. He had the foundations of a truly universal empire to lay – and with it, not coincidentally, a global supremacy for himself. Every native enfranchised, and every colonist settled, was a brick in his new order. Roman aristocrats had always commanded clients, but Caesar's patronage would extend to the very limits of sand and ice. Syrians

and Spaniards, Africans and Gauls, the far-flung peoples of a shrinking world would henceforward owe their allegiance not to the
lethal amateurism of the Republic but to a single man. As a symbol
of this future, nothing was more potent than Caesar's plan for
Carthage and Corinth. Flattened by the vengeful legions, these two
cities were now to be rebuilt, monuments to a new age of universal
peace and to the glory of their patron. Utica, down the coast from
the new colony of Carthage, would be put forever in the shade. The
future would be raised upon the rubble of the past. For the first
time citizens living in Rome would be made to feel that they were
parts, as well as the masters, of one world.

Which is not to say that Caesar meant to neglect his own city. He
had big plans for Rome: a library was to be founded; a new theatre
to rival Pompey's cut out from the rock of the Capitol; the largest
temple in the world built on the Campus. Even the Tiber, Caesar
had decided, would have to be diverted, because its course
obstructed his building plans. Nothing could better have illustrated
the startling nature of his supremacy than this: that he could not
only build where and what he wanted, but also, as though he were
a god drawing on the landscape with his fingertip, order the city's
topography changed. Clearly, the ten years of Caesar's dictatorship
were going to alter the appearance of Rome for ever. A city that had
always expressed through its ramshackle appearance its ancient liberties would soon look radically different – would soon look almost
Greek.

And specifically, like Alexandria. There had been an early hint
that this might be so in Caesar's choice of house guests. In September
46 BC, just in time to watch her lover's triumphs, Cleopatra had
swept into town. Ensconcing herself in Caesar's mansion on the far
side of the Tiber, she had refused to make any allowances for republican sensibilities, instead playing up the role of an Egyptian queen
to the full. She not only brought her husband–brother and an

entourage of eunuchs with her, but also had an heir to parade, a one-year-old prince. Caesar, already married, had refused to acknowledge his bastard son, but Cleopatra, nothing daunted, had flaunted the obvious by naming the boy Caesarion. Naturally, Rome was scandalised. Equally naturally, everyone who was anyone flocked across the Tiber to gawp. The manner in which Cleopatra greeted visitors reflected her estimation of whether they mattered: Cicero, for instance, who found her hateful, she roundly snubbed. Effectively, of course, the Queen had eyes for only one man. In August 45, when Caesar finally returned to Italy, she hurried off to meet him.* The two of them luxuriated together on holiday in the countryside. Only in October did Caesar finally return to Rome.

He found a city convulsed by wild gossip. It was said – and believed – that he planned to move the seat of empire to Alexandria. Less ludicrously, it was also claimed that he wished to marry Cleopatra, despite the fact that he already had a wife. Caesar himself did nothing to discountenance these rumours by setting up a golden statue of his mistress in the temple of Venus – an unprecedented and shocking honour. And since Venus was the goddess most closely identified with Isis, there was a hint here of an even greater and more ominous scandal. If Cleopatra were to be represented in the heart of the Republic as a goddess, then what plans did her lover have for himself? And exactly why were workmen adding a pediment to his mansion, as though it were a temple? And what was the truth of the rumour that Antony had been appointed his high priest? Caesar was hardly being reticent in scattering out the clues.

Goddess brides and self-deification: he knew that his fellow citizens were bound to be appalled. But there were others, particularly

---

* The sources nowhere state it specifically, but the circumstances make it almost certain.

in the East, who would not be. Rome might have bowed to Caesar, but there were still parts of the globe that had not yet bowed to Rome. Most obdurate of these was Parthia, whose horsemen, taking advantage of the Republic's civil war, had dared to cross the frontier into Syria. There was also Carrhae to avenge, of course, and the lost eagles to regain, responsibilities certainly worthy of the dictator's attention. Yet, coming so soon after his return to Rome, Caesar's plan to set off to war again could not help but leave the city feeling diminished, almost spurned. It was as though the problems of the Republic bored the man appointed to solve them, as though Rome herself were now too small a stage for his ambitions. In the East they would appreciate this. In the East they already worshipped Caesar as a god. In the East there were traditions older by far than the Republic, of the flesh becoming divine, and of the rule of a king of kings.

And there, for anxious Romans, lay the rub. Late in 45 BC the Senate announced that Caesar was henceforward to be honoured as *divus Iulius*: Julius the God. Who now could doubt that he was preparing to break the ultimate taboo and set a crown upon his head? There were certainly grounds for such a horrific suspicion. Early in 44 Caesar began appearing in the high red boots once worn by kings in Italy's legendary past; around the same time he reacted with fury when a diadem that had mysteriously appeared on one of his statues was removed. Public alarm grew. Caesar appears to have realised that he had gone too far. On 15 February, dressed in a purple toga, sporting a golden wreath, he ostentatiously refused Antony's offer of a crown. The occasion was a festival, and Rome was heaving with holiday crowds. As Antony repeated the offer 'a groan echoed all the way round the Forum'.[22] Again Caesar refused the crown, this time with a firmness that brooked no future contradiction. Perhaps, had the crowds cheered, he might have accepted Antony's offer, but it seems unlikely. Caesar knew that the Romans would never tolerate a King Julius. Nor, surely, in the final analysis, did he care. The forms taken by greatness were relative, varying from nation to nation. This was the lesson that his stay in Alexandria had taught him. Just as Cleopatra was both a pharaoh to the Egyptians and a Macedonian queen among the Greeks, so Caesar could be at once a living god in Asia and a dictator to the Romans. Why offend the sensibilities of his fellow citizens by abolishing the Republic when – as Caesar himself was said to have pointed out – the Republic had been reduced to 'nothingness, a name only, without body or substance'?[23] What mattered was not the form but the reality of power. And Caesar, unlike Sulla, had no intention of relinquishing it.

A few days before Antony offered him the crown the Senate had officially appointed him dictator for life.* With this fateful measure the last feeble hope that Caesar might one day return the Republic to its citizens had been snuffed out. But would the Romans care? Caesar's calculation was that they would not. The people he had lulled with games, and welfare, and peace. The Senate he had numbed into quietude, not with open menaces but by the threat of what might result from his removal: 'Better an illegal tyrant than a civil war.'[24] This was the opinion of Favonius, Cato's most loyal admirer. It was a judgement widely shared. Caesar, knowing this, scorned the hatred of his peers. He dismissed his guard of two thousand men. He walked openly in the Forum, attended only by the lictors due to his office. And when informers brought him news of a rumoured assassination plot, and urged him to hunt down the conspirators, he dismissed their anxieties out of hand. 'He would rather die, he said, than be feared.'[25]

Nor was it as though he would be in Rome for much longer. He was due to leave for Parthia on 18 March. True, a soothsayer had

---

* Sometime between 9 and 15 February 44 BC.

advised him to beware the Ides, which fell that month on the fif-
teenth, but Caesar had never shown much regard for superstitions.
Only in his private conversation did he betray any intimations of
mortality. On the evening of the fourteenth, one month after
being appointed dictator for life, Caesar dined with Lepidus, the
patrician who had joined his cause in 49 BC and was now his deputy
in the dictatorship, a position officially entitled the 'Master of
Horse'. Confident that he was among friends, Caesar dropped his
guard. 'What is the sweetest kind of death?' he was asked. Back
shot Caesar's response: 'The kind that comes without warning.'[26]
To be warned was to be fearful; to be fearful was to be emasculated.
That night, when Caesar's wife suffered nightmares and begged
him not to attend the Senate the next day, he laughed. In the
morning, borne in his litter, he caught sight of the soothsayer
who had told him to beware of the Ides of March. 'The day which
you warned me against is here,' Caesar said, smiling, 'and I am still
alive.' 'Yes,' came the answer, swift and inevitable. 'It is here – but
it is not yet past.'[27]

The Senate that morning had arranged to meet in Pompey's
great assembly hall. Games were being held in the adjacent theatre, and as Caesar descended from his litter he would have heard
the roars of the Roman people thrilling to spectacles of blood. But
the noise would soon have been dimmed by the cool marble of
the portico, and even more by that of the assembly hall that
waited beyond. Pompey's statue still dominated the Senate's
meeting-space. After Pharsalus it had been hurriedly pulled
down, but Caesar, with typical generosity, had ordered it restored,
along with all of Pompey's other statues. An investment policy,
Cicero had sneered, against his own being removed – but that
was malicious and unfair. Caesar had no reason to fear for the
future of his statues. Nor, walking into the assembly hall that
morning and seeing the senators rise to greet him, for himself.

Not even when a crowd of them approached him with a petition, mobbing him as he sat down in his gilded chair, pressing him down with their kisses. Then suddenly he felt his toga being pulled down from his shoulders. 'Why,' he cried out, startled, 'this is violence!'[28] At the same moment he felt a slashing pain across his throat. Twisting around he saw a dagger, red with his own blood.

Some sixty men stood in a press around him. All of them had drawn daggers from under their togas. All of them were well known to Caesar. Many were former enemies who had accepted his pardon – but even more were friends.[29] Some were officers who had served with him in Gaul, among them Decimus Brutus, commander of the war fleet that had wiped out the Venetians. The most grievous betrayal, however, the one that finally numbed Caesar and stopped him in his desperate efforts to fight back, came from someone closer still. Caesar glimpsed, flashing through the mêlée, a knife aimed at his groin, held by another Brutus, Marcus, his reputed son. 'You too, my boy?'[30] he whispered, then fell to the ground. Not wishing to be witnessed in his death-agony, he covered his head with the ribbons of his toga. The pool of his blood stained the base of Pompey's statue. Dead, he lay in his great rival's shadow.

But if there appeared to be symbolism in this, then it was illusory. Caesar had not been sacrificed to the cause of any faction. True, one of the two ring-leaders of the conspiracy had been Cassius Longinus, one of Pompey's former officers. But when Cassius had argued for the assassination not only of Caesar but also of Antony and Lepidus, and a wholesale destruction of the dictator's regime, his case had been overruled. Brutus, the other leader, and the conscience of the conspiracy, had refused to hear of it. They were conducting an execution, he had argued, not a squalid manoeuvre in a political fight. And Brutus had prevailed. For Brutus was known to be an honourable man, and worthy to serve as the spokesman and avenger of the Republic.

In the beginning there had been kings, and the last king had been a tyrant. And a man named Brutus had expelled him from the city and set up the consulship, and all the institutions of a free Republic. And now, 465 years later, Brutus, his descendant, had struck down a second tyrant. Leading his fellow conspirators out of Pompey's great complex, he stumbled and ran in his excitement across the Campus. Holding his bloodstained dagger proudly aloft, he headed for the Forum. There, in the people's meeting-place, he proclaimed the glad news: Caesar was dead; liberty was restored; the Republic was saved.

As though in derisory answer, from across the Campus came the sound of screams. The spectators at Pompey's theatre were rioting, crushing one another in their panic. Wisps of smoke were already rising into the sky; shops were being smashed as looters set to work. More distantly, the first wails of grief could be heard as Rome's Jews began the mourning for the man who had always served as their patron. Elsewhere, however, as news of what had happened spread across the city, there was only silence. Far from rushing to the Forum to acclaim the liberators, citizens were rushing to their homes and barring their doors.

The Republic was saved. But what was the Republic now? Stillness hung over the city and no answer could be discerned.

11

THE DEATH OF THE REPUBLIC

The Last Stand

Crisis or no crisis, the Season remained inviolable. Spring, flower-bright and crystalline, was when fashionable society decamped out of town. April 44 BC was no different. In the weeks following Caesar's murder Rome began to empty. Many of those shuttering up their mansions must have felt relieved to be leaving the febrile, panic-racked city behind. Not that the country was without its own headaches. Cicero, for instance, arriving at his favourite villa just south of Rome, found it full of builders. He decided to continue on his way and headed south for the Bay of Naples – where he was promptly ambushed by surveyors. It appeared that a retail complex he had inherited in Puteoli was showing cracks. Two shops had actually collapsed. 'Even the mice have moved out,' Cicero sighed, 'to say nothing of the tenants.' Drawing inspiration from the example of Socrates, however, the landlord professed to be sublimely indifferent to his real-estate problems: 'Immortal gods, what do such trivialities matter to me?'[1]

Yet the consolations of philosophy had their limits. At other times Cicero would confess to being in a permanent mood of irritation.

'Old age', he complained, 'makes me ever more dyspeptic.'[2] Now in his sixties, he felt himself a failure. It was not only his political career that had imploded. So too, over the previous few years, had his family life. First, amid much bitterness and mutual recrimination, he divorced his wife of more than thirty years and hitched himself to one of his wealthy, teenage wards. Twitted for marrying a virgin at his age, Cicero goatishly retorted that she would not be staying a virgin for long – but nor did she stay a bride. Only weeks after the wedding Cicero's daughter, Tullia, died of complications following childbirth. Cicero was devastated. His new wife, transformed from trophy to unwanted distraction, was sent packing back to her mother, while Cicero, obsessively, tended the flame of his grief. Tullia, affectionate and intelligent, had been her father's dearest companion. Now, with her gone, Cicero was desolate. His friends, perturbed by what they saw as unmanly emotionalism, sought to remind him of his duties as a citizen, but the old catchwords, once such an inspiration, served only to deepen his sense of despair. Painfully, to a well-wisher, he sought to explain: 'There was a time when I could find in my home a refuge from the miseries of public life. But now, oppressed by domestic unhappiness as I am, there is no doing the opposite – no taking refuge in the affairs of state, and the comforts they once offered. And so I stay clear of both the Forum and of home.'[3] Glimpsed in the mirror of Cicero's grief, the Republic appeared to have taken on his daughter's semblance: that of a young woman, goddess-like, beloved . . . and dead.

Then the Ides of March. Brutus, raising his dagger wet with Caesar's blood, had called out Cicero's name and congratulated him on the recovery of liberty. Cicero himself, startled and delighted, had reciprocated by hailing the conspirators as heroes, and Caesar's murder as a glorious event. But it was only a start – and maybe, Cicero was soon fretting, not even that. Brutus and Cassius might have succeeded in striking down Caesar, but they had made no attempt to destroy his regime. Instead an awkward truce had been patched up between the dictator's assassins and his henchmen, and as a result the advantage was daily slipping through the conspirators' grasp. Already Brutus and Cassius had been forced by the menaces of pro-Caesarian demagogues to flee Rome. Cicero, who had been urging more ruthlessness and resolution on them, lambasted their strategy as 'absurd'. It was said that the conspirators had decided to exclude him from their plans because they feared that he had grown timid with age. Now the old man paid them back in fitting coin. To the sacred task of redeeming the Republic from tyranny, he complained, the conspirators had brought 'the spirits of men, but the foresight of children'.[4]

Naturally, even in the depths of his despond, the role of knowing elder statesman was one that Cicero could not help but relish. Few would have denied his right to it. The parvenu from Arpinum had become, to younger generations, an almost iconic figure, the very embodiment of tradition, a living relic of a vanished age of giants. Despite his gloating over the murder of their leader, he remained an object of curiosity even to Caesarians. One of these, a particularly startling visitor, was a fair-haired, bright-eyed young man, no more than eighteen, who dropped by to pay his respects while Cicero was still holidaying outside Puteoli. Only a month previously Gaius Octavius, the dictator's great-nephew, had been in the Balkans, stationed with the expeditionary force for Parthia. When the news of Caesar's murder had reached him he had sailed at once for Brundisium. There he had learned of his formal adoption in Caesar's will, becoming, by its terms, Gaius Julius Caesar Octavianus, and being mobbed by crowds of his adoptive father's veterans. With their cheers still ringing in his ears, he had set off for Rome, but, rather than rushing headlong to the capital, had first turned aside to pay a visit to the Bay of Naples. Touring the holiday villas, he had consulted with assorted Caesarian heavyweights and made his pilgrimage to Cicero. The venerable republican, for once proving impervious to flattery, had refused to be charmed. After all, it was Octavian's sacred duty, as Caesar's heir, to hunt down the murderers of his adoptive father. How was such an avenger ever to become a good citizen? 'Impossible,' Cicero sniffed.[5] Pointedly, he referred to the young man by his original name, Octavius, and not – as Octavian himself now preferred to be called – Julius Caesar alone.* For Cicero, one Julius Caesar had been more than enough.

Even so, he can hardly have been seriously alarmed by Octavian's prospects. The young man was heading on from Puteoli armed with little more than the magic of his name and a determination to claim his inheritance in full. In the snake-pit of Rome these were not decisive qualifications. Indeed, for established Caesarians, let alone Caesar's enemies, they verged on the provocative. The dictator might have named Octavian as his legal heir, but there were others, trusted lieutenants in positions of great power, who also had their eyes fixed on their dead master's legacy. Now that Caesar was gone, the ambitions of Rome's leading men once again had free play, but hardly in the manner that Brutus and Cassius had anticipated. 'Freedom has been restored,' Cicero noted in perplexity, 'and yet the Republic has not.'[6]

Which was, as he further noted, 'unprecedented' – and raised a terrifying prospect. Was it possible that the old rules, the old traditions, poisoned by civil war, had been placed forever beyond recovery? If so, then a disorienting and blood-sodden new order threatened, one in which a magistracy would always prove to be of less moment than an army, and legitimacy less than the threat of naked violence. Already, by the summer of 44 BC, the outlines

---

* Since the man born Gaius Octavius changed his name at regular intervals throughout the early years of his career, he is generally called Octavian by historians in order to avoid confusion.

of such a future could be glimpsed. Would-be warlords toured the colonies where Caesar had settled his veterans, currying favour, offering bribes. Even Brutus and Cassius tried to get in on the act. The welcome they received from Caesar's veterans was, unsurprisingly, chilly. By late summer they had come to the reluctant conclusion that Italy was no longer safe for them. Quietly, they slipped away – for the East, it was said, although no one could be sure. For men who had claimed to be liberators, exile anywhere was a bitter defeat.

And for those who had looked to them for leadership it was a disaster. Now, with Brutus and Cassius gone, it would take even more courage to stay behind, to defend the Republic where it still mattered most: in the city that had given birth to its freedoms, before the Senate and the people of Rome. Who was left to make such a stand? Eyes turned to Cicero – but, panicky and a born civilian, he had also vanished from Rome. His intention, painfully arrived at after much vacillation, had been to sail to Athens, where his son, who was supposed to be studying, was instead making a name for himself as the university's foremost drunk. But the anxious father, eager to set his heir back on the straight and narrow, had no sooner set sail than he was swept by bad weather back into port, and it was there, while waiting for the storms to subside, that he learned how his journey was being represented back in Rome. 'Fine! Abandon your country!'[7] even the imperturbable Atticus had written to him. Cicero was mortified. Both shame and vanity served to steel his fluttering nerves. But so too did the knowledge that it was his duty to stand his ground, to beard the warlords in their den. Out came his luggage from the cargo hold. Bracing himself for the fray, Cicero set off back to Rome.

It was the most courageous decision of his life. But it was not entirely reckless. True, Cicero brought no legions to the armed and carnivorous death-struggle – but he did bring his unsurpassed powers of oratory, his well-honed skills in political dog-fighting and his prestige. The news of his arrival in Rome brought out cheering crowds to welcome him, and even among the highest echelons of the Caesarian grandees he did not lack for contacts. If he could only attach some of these to the cause of the constitution, Cicero hoped, then all might yet be well. He had two particular targets: Aulus Hirtius and Vibius Pansa. Both were prominent Caesarian officers, and had been appointed by the dictator as consuls-designate for the succeeding year, 43 BC. Of course, to Cicero, the fact that magistracies had been allocated in advance, without any reference to the electorate, was an outrage, but one which, for the moment, he was prepared to swallow. Hirtius and Pansa were both, by the standards of the troubled times, moderates, even to the extent of having asked Cicero himself for lessons in public speaking. Certainly, there were other Caesarians whom Cicero would far rather have seen excluded from the consulship. And of them all, in his opinion, the most dangerous was Mark Antony, who already held the office, not to mention an army and Caesar's treasure to boot.

As far as Cicero was concerned, even the most attractive aspects of Antony's character – his boldness, charm and generosity – served only to brand the consul all the more a menace. As did his taste in women: after years of pursuing Fulvia, Antony had finally succeeded in hitching himself to Clodius' domineering widow. Pleasure-loving and exhibitionist as he was, Antony appeared to Cicero a worthy heir of Clodius' bed, and as such a self-evident public danger. But there was another spectre, even grimmer, standing at Antony's shoulder. 'Why should it have been my fate', Cicero pondered, 'that for the past two decades the Republic has never had an enemy who did not turn out to be my enemy as well?'[8] No doubt Catiline's spectre would have laughed hollowly at that question. Indeed, Cicero's conceit in 44 BC was, if anything, even greater than

it had been during the year of his consulship. By denouncing
Antony, he was effectively declaring war not on an open rebel, as
Catiline had been, but on a man who was himself the head of state.
But Cicero was unabashed. As with Catiline, so now with Antony,
he believed himself confronted by a monster. Only by cutting off its
head, he trusted, would the Republic be restored at least half-way
to health. So it was that Cicero, the spokesman of legitimacy, prepared to work for the destruction of a consul.

As so many of his campaigns had done, the great orator's assault
on Antony was to prove inspirational and specious in equal measure. With a series of electrifying speeches to the Senate, Cicero
sought to rouse his fellow citizens from the torpor of despair, to
school them in their deepest ideals, to remind them of what they
had been and might be still. 'Life is not merely a matter of breathing. The slave has no true life. All other nations are capable of
enduring servitude – but our city is not.' Here, in Cicero's oratory,
was a worthy threnody for Roman freedom: both a soaring assertion of the Republic's heroic past and a rage against the dying of the
light. 'So glorious is it to recover liberty, that it is better to die than
shrink from regaining it.'[9]

To this claim, ancient generations had borne witness, and Cicero,
by staking his life, was at last proving himself worthy of the ideals he
had for so long aimed to defend. But there were other traditions,
just as ancient, to which his speeches were also bearing witness. In
the public life of the Republic, partisanship had always been savage,
and the tricks of political rhetoric unforgiving. Now, in Cicero's
mauling of Antony, these same tricks received their apotheosis.
Elevated calls to arms alternated with the crudest abuse, as,
throughout Cicero's speeches caricatures of a drunken Antony –
vomiting up gobbets of meat, chasing after boys, pawing at
actresses – were conjured. Malicious, rancorous, unfair – but it was
the mark of a free Republic that its citizens' speech be free too. For

too long Cicero had felt himself gagged. Now, for his swansong, he spoke without inhibition. As only he could, he touched the heights and in his next breath plumbed the depths.

Yet his words, like sparks borne on a gale, needed kindling – and this Cicero could only hope to procure by the dark and time-hallowed arts of political fixing. The Caesarian warlords had to be turned against each other and poisoned against Antony, just as rival noblemen had been persuaded to turn against the over-mighty throughout the Republic's history. Hirtius and Pansa, already suspicious of Antony, needed little encouragement, but Cicero, not content with wooing the consuls-designate, was also luring a far more dramatic recruit to the cause. Only a few months previously he had cold-shouldered Octavian; now, in the dying days of 44 BC, there were few – and certainly not Cicero – who would presume to do that.

Even the gods had blessed the young Caesar with formidable proof of their favour. As Octavian, beneath a cloudless sky, had entered Rome for the first time, a halo in the form of a rainbow had appeared around the sun. Then, three months later, an even more spectacular phenomenon occurred. While Octavian was staging games in honour of his murdered father, a comet had blazed over Rome. It was hailed by the excited spectators as the soul of Caesar ascending to the heavens. Octavian, who privately regarded the comet as a portent of his own greatness, had publicly agreed – as well he might have done, for to become the son of a god was no small promotion, even for Caesar's heir. 'You, boy, owe everything to your name,'[10] Antony had sneered. But if Octavian's good fortune had been prodigious, then so too was the skill that he had brought to exploiting his inheritance. Already, even Antony, the seasoned populist, was finding himself outplayed. Requested to hand over Caesar's treasure so that certain legacies promised to the people could be paid, he had proved obstructive; meanwhile,

Octavian, speculating to accumulate, had coolly auctioned off some of his own estates and paid for the legacies out of the proceeds.

His reward was spectacular popularity – not only with the urban mob, but with Caesar's veterans too. Recruiting head to head with Antony, Octavian soon had a private – and wholly illegal – bodyguard of three thousand men. With this, he briefly occupied the Forum, and although he was soon forced to retreat in the face of Antony's much larger army, he remained a palpable threat to his rival's ambitions.

By now it was late in the year, and Antony's term of office was drawing to its close. Desperate to secure a continued power base, the consul marched north, crossed the Rubicon into Gaul, and proclaimed himself the governor of the province. Blocking his path was Decimus Brutus, the assassin of Caesar, who also claimed the post. Rather than surrender his province to Antony, Decimus chose instead to barricade himself in Modena and sit out the winter. Antony, advancing, settled down to starve him out. The new civil war, long threatening, had finally begun. And all the while, as Caesar's two former lieutenants locked horns, Caesar's heir lurked in their rear, a menacing but imponderable factor, his loyalties uncertain, his ambitions even more so.

Only to Cicero had he claimed to open his soul. Octavian had not ceased to woo the old statesman since their first meeting. Cicero, still suspicious of such flattering attentions, had wrestled painfully with the temptation that Octavian represented to him. On the one hand, as he had wailed plaintively to Atticus, 'Only look at his name, his age!'[11] How could Cicero possibly take Caesar's heir at face value when the young adventurer, sending endless requests for advice, addressed him as 'Father' and insisted that he and his followers were at the service of the Republic? But, on the other hand, bearing in mind the desperate nature of the crisis, what was there to lose? By December, with reports of war arriving

from the north, Cicero had finally made up his mind. On the twentieth he addressed a packed Senate House. Even as he continued to
press for the destruction of Antony, the legitimate consul, he
demanded that Octavian – 'yes, a young man still, almost a boy'[12] –
be rewarded for his recruitment of a private army with fulsome
public honours. To waverers, who were understandably startled
by this proposition, Cicero protested that Octavian was already a
glittering credit to the Republic. 'I guarantee it, Fathers of the
Senate, I promise it and solemnly swear it!' Of course, as Cicero
himself knew full well, he was protesting too much. All the same,
even in private, he was not entirely cynical about Octavian's
prospects. Who was to say how the young man sitting at his knee,
absorbing his wisdom and the ancient ideals of the Republic, might
prosper? And should Octavian, despite Cicero's tutorship, prove an
unworthy pupil, then there would be ways to deal with him, when
the occasion and opportunity arrived. 'The young man should be
lauded, glorified – then raised to the skies.'[13] Just as Caesar had
been, in other words.

This, of course, was precisely the kind of indiscreet witticism
that had landed Cicero in hot water in the past. The joke spread
like wildfire, and, inevitably, Octavian got to hear of it too. Cicero,
however, could afford to shrug off the embarrassment. After
all, Octavian was only one part of the coalition that he had
patched together, nor even the most significant part of it. In April
43 BC the two consuls of the Roman people, Aulus Hirtius and
Vibius Pansa, finally advanced against Antony. Octavian, with two
legions, marched as their lieutenant. In two successive battles
Antony was defeated and forced to withdraw across the Alps. News
of the double victory, when it was brought to a waiting Rome,
appeared the ultimate vindication of Cicero's high-risk, high-stakes
policy. Cicero himself, as he had been in the year of his consulship,
was hailed as the saviour of his country. Antony was officially pro-

nounced a public enemy. The Republic appeared to have been saved.

Then fresh messengers arrived in Rome bringing cruel and bitter news. The two consuls were both dead, one in battle, the other of wounds. Octavian, unsurprisingly, was refusing any form of rapprochement with Decimus Brutus. Antony, in the confusion, had got clean away. He was now marching along the coast beyond the Alps, into the province of another of Caesar's lieutenants, Marcus Lepidus. The army of the 'Master of Horse', seven legions strong, was formidable, and its loyalties, as Antony drew ever nearer to it, had suddenly become an issue of desperate, even decisive, concern. In letters to the Senate, Lepidus reassured its leaders of his continued allegiance – but his men, seasoned Caesarians all, were already making up his mind for him the other way. On 30 May, days of fraternisation between the armies of Antony and Lepidus climaxed in a formal compact between their two generals and the union of their forces. Decimus Brutus, hopelessly outnumbered, attempted to flee but was betrayed by a Gallic chieftain and killed. The armies of the Senate, with baffling speed, had melted away utterly. Antony, on the run only a few weeks previously, had emerged stronger than ever. Now, it was only the young Caesar who stood between him and a march on Rome.

Which way would Octavian turn? The capital swarmed with rumours, and sweated on the answer. It would not be long in coming. In late July a centurion from Octavian's army suddenly appeared in the Senate House. From the assembled gathering he demanded the consulship, still vacant, for his general. The Senate refused. The centurion brushed back his cloak and laid his hand on the hilt of his sword. 'If you do not make him consul,' he warned, 'then this will.'[14] And so it happened. Once again a Caesar crossed the Rubicon. By now Octavian's army numbered eight legions, and there was no one to oppose him. Cicero, sick at the ruinous end of

all his hopes, trudged out with the rest of the Senate to welcome
the conqueror. Desperately, he spun new proposals to Octavian,
new plans. 'Octavian, however, made no answer, save for the mocking reply that Cicero had been the last of his friends to come and
greet him.'[15]

Permitted – or ordered – to leave Rome, the orator retreated to
his favourite country villa. The building work on it had been completed, but there could be no more repairs to its owner's ruined
career. It was over – and with it, much else besides. Cicero followed
his protégé's progress with mute despair. On 19 August Octavian, still
not yet twenty, was formally elected consul. Then, having secured
the condemnation of Caesar's assassins as traitors, he left Rome and
marched northwards, straight towards the advancing army of
Antony and Lepidus. Between the rival Caesarian leaders, unchallenged masters now of the entire Western empire, there was to be no
war. Instead, on an island in a river near Medina, with their armies
lined up on either bank, Antony and Octavian met, embraced and
kissed each other's cheek. Then, along with Lepidus, they settled
down to carve up the world and pronounce the Republic dead.

Naturally, they disguised their purpose with specious and familiar words. They claimed not to be pronouncing the obituary of the
Republic but setting it back in order. In truth, they were executing
it. As a result of the island conference it was agreed that a triumvirate should be established, but not a loose and shifting alliance as
had been established between Pompey, Caesar and Crassus. This
time it would be formally constituted and endowed with ferocious
powers. For five years the triumvirs were to exercise proconsular
authority over the entire empire. They were to have the right to
pass or annul laws as they pleased, without reference to the Senate
or the Roman people. Martial law was extended into the sacred
space of Rome herself. This, after more than four hundred years of
Roman freedom, was effectively the end.

And the Republic's quietus, fittingly, was sealed and signed with blood. The triumvirs, pronouncing their dead leader's policy of clemency a failure, looked back instead to an earlier dictator for inspiration. The return of proscription lists was foreshadowed in Rome by grim and unmistakable portents: dogs howled like wolves, and wolves were seen running through the Forum; in the sky loud shouts were heard, along with the clash of weapons and the pounding of unseen hooves. The lists went up within days of the triumvirs' entry into the city. Ruthless bargaining among the three men had determined whose names would appear on them. One factor more than any other had influenced their decisions: with more than sixty legions needing to be paid, the triumvirate was in desperate need of funds. As a result, the fruit of riches, as it had been under Sulla, became death. Even an exile such as Verres, enjoying his ill-gotten gains in sun-soaked exile, was proscribed – killed, it was said, for his 'Corinthian bronzes'.[16] Some were murdered for factional reasons – to remove potential adversaries of the new regime – and others were victims of personal enmities and feuds. Most chillingly of all, as proof of their commitment to the triumvirate, Antony, Lepidus and Octavian had each sacrificed a man they might otherwise have felt obliged to save. So it was that Antony had agreed to the proscription of his uncle and Lepidus his brother. Octavian, meanwhile, had put down the name of the man he had once called 'Father'.

Even so, Cicero could have escaped. News of his proscription reached him well in advance of the bounty-hunters. Typically, however, he panicked and vacillated over what to do. Rather than setting sail to join Brutus and Cassius, who were even then recruiting a massive army of liberation in the East, he instead flitted despairingly from villa to villa, haunted, as he had been for so long, by the shadow of exile. After all, as Cato had taught him, there were nightmares worse than death. Trapped by his executioners at last, Cicero leaned out from his litter and bared his throat to the sword. This was the gesture of a gladiator, and one he had always admired. Defeated in the greatest and deadliest of all games, he unflinchingly accepted his fate. He died as he would surely have wished: bravely, a martyr to freedom and to freedom of speech.

Even his enemies knew that. When his severed head and hands were delivered by the bounty-hunters, Fulvia, Clodius' widow and now Antony's wife, hurried to gloat. Picking up the grisly souvenirs, she spat on Cicero's head, then yanked out his tongue and stabbed it with a hairpin. Only when she had finished mutilating it was she willing to have the head exposed to the public. The hand that had written the great speeches against Antony was nailed up too. Silenced and pin-pricked as it was, exposed to the gaze of the Roman people, the tongue was eloquent still. Cicero had been the incomparable political orator of the Republic – and now the age of oratory and free politics was dead.

The Winner Takes It All

One year after the establishment of the triumvirate the last hopes for the survival of a free republic perished outside the Macedonian city of Philippi. Trapped and near starving on a Balkan plain, a Caesarian army once again succeeded in tempting its enemies into a fatal engagement. Brutus and Cassius had stripped the East of its legions, possessed command of the sea, and occupied an impregnable position: like Pompey at Pharsalus, they could well have afforded to bide their time. Instead, they chose to fight. In two battles on a scale more massive than any in Roman history first Cassius then Brutus fell on his sword. Other celebrated names also perished in the carnage: a Lucullus, a Hortensius, a Cato. The last of these, removing his helmet and charging into the depths of the

Caesarian ranks, consciously followed his father in preferring death to slavery. So too did his sister. Back in Rome the austere and virtuous Porcia had been waiting for news of Philippi. When it arrived, and she learned that both her brother and her husband Brutus were dead, she slipped free from the grasp of her friends, who had feared what she might do, she ran to a brazier and swallowed burning coals. Women, after all, were Romans too.

But what would that mean in a state no longer free? Not, by definition, the old answer, that it was to value liberty above everything, even life itself. Heroic it may have been, but the grisly example of Porcia was not much emulated. Of those who had lived truest to the ideals of the Republic, most, now that stillness had settled again over Philippi, were dead. The loss of such citizens was impossible to make up, and all the more so because a disproportionate number of the casualties had come from the nobility. The heir to a famous name, in the universal opinion of the Roman people, bore the history of his city in his veins. This was why the extinction of a great house had always been regarded as a matter for public mourning – and why the scything of an entire generation of the nobility, whether at the hands of executioners or amid the dust and flies of Macedon, was a calamity fatal to the Republic. More, much more, than blood had been spilled.

Of the victorious triumvirs, it was Antony who sensed this most clearly. He had come of age at a time when liberty had been something more than just a slogan, and he was not incapable of mourning its death. Searching out the corpse of Brutus on the battlefield of Philippi, he had covered it respectfully with a cloak, then had it cremated, and sent the ashes to Servilia. Nor, now his supremacy was secured, did he abuse it with further bloodbaths. Rather than return to misery-stricken Italy, he elected, as the senior partner in the triumvirate, to stay in the East and play at being Pompey the Great. His pleasures, as he progressed through

Greece and Asia, were those that had long been traditional among
the Republic's proconsuls: posing as a lover of Greek culture while
leeching the Greeks; patronising local princelings; fighting the
Parthians. To die-hard republicans, this was all reassuringly familiar,
and gradually, in the months and years that followed Philippi, the
shattered remnants of Brutus' armed forces would gravitate, *faute de
mieux*, towards Antony. With him, in the East, the cause of legitimacy licked its wounds as its life-blood ebbed away.

For only in Rome could there be any hope of restoring a free
republic – and Rome was in the hands of a man who appeared its
deadliest enemy. Chill and vengeful, Octavian was the man whom
those defeated at Philippi chiefly reviled as the murderer of liberty.
On the battlefield, brought past their conquerors in chains, the
republican prisoners had saluted Antony courteously, but the
youthful Caesar they had cursed and jeered. Nor, in the years following Philippi, had Octavian's reputation grown any the less
sinister. With Lepidus sidelined by his two colleagues to Africa, and
Antony lording it over the East, it was to the youngest member of
the triumvirate that the most invidious task had fallen: finding
land for the returning war veterans. With some three hundred
thousand battle-hardened soldiers waiting to be settled, Octavian
could not afford to delay the programme; nor, for all the efficiency
he brought to executing it, could he avoid inflicting on the countryside the miseries of social revolution. Respect for private
property had always been one of the foundation-stones of the
Republic, but now, with the Republic superseded, private property
could be sequestered on a commissar's whim. Farmers, evicted from
their land without recompense, might find themselves abducted
into slave-pens, or else, lacking any other means of subsistence, end
up as brigands themselves. As in the time of Spartacus, Italy became
bandit land. With armed gangs daring to raid even towns and cities,
rioting flared, impotent explosions of suffering and despair. Amid

all the upheaval crops failed and harvests were lost. As the countryside slipped into anarchy, so Rome began to starve.

The famine was worsened by a familiar plague. More than twenty years after Pompey had swept the pirates from the sea, they were back – and this time their chief was Pompey's own son. Sextus, having escaped Caesar's vengeance in Spain, had profited from the chaos of the times to establish himself as the master of Sicily, and the admiral of two hundred and fifty ships. Preying on the shipping lanes, he was soon throttling Rome. As the citizens grew gaunt with hunger, so the flesh peeled off the city's bones too. Shops were boarded up, temples left to crumble, monuments stripped of their gold. Everywhere, what had once been scenes of luxury were converted to the needs of war. Even Baiae, bright and glittering Baiae, rang to the hammers of Octavian's engineers. On the neighbouring Lucrine Lake, a naval dockyard was built over the fabled oyster beds – a desecration worthy of the times. History itself appeared diminished; and epic, repeating a familiar storyline, was reduced to shrunken parody. Once again a Pompey fought a Caesar, but they both seemed, in comparison to their giant fathers, dwarfish thieves. A pirate and a gangster: fitting generals to scrap over a city no longer free.

Yet, although Sextus was a constant menace and more than capable of bringing misery to his country, he was never a fatal threat to the Caesarians. A much greater danger, and one that cast its shadow over the entire world, was that just as the first triumvirate had finally torn itself to pieces, so too might the second. In 41 BC, only months after Octavian's return from Philippi, this came perilously close to happening. With Antony absent in the East, his wife, the ever pugnacious Fulvia, stirred up a rebellion in Italy. Octavian, responding with swift and calculated atrocities, only just succeeded in repressing it. His revenge on Fulvia herself, however, was limited to the penning of abusive verses on the subject of her nymphomania. His power in Italy was still precarious, and he could not risk provoking Antony. Fulvia was permitted to leave for the East and her husband.

Conveniently, however, she died before she could join him. In September 40 BC Antony's agents and those of Octavian met in uneasy truce at Brundisium. After much haggling the pact between the two men was reconfirmed. To cement it, Octavian gave to the widower the hand of his beloved sister, Octavia. Rome's empire, far more neatly than it had been before, was now sliced in two. Only Sextus and Lepidus still obscured the division – and they were soon swept from the gaming board.

In September 36 BC Octavian finally succeeded in destroying the fleet of Sextus, who fled to the East and ultimate execution at the hands of Antony's agents. At the same time, when Lepidus pushed his resentment at being sidelined too far, he was formally stripped of his triumviral powers, a humiliation staged by Octavian without any reference to the third member of the partnership. The young Caesar, now more firmly established in Rome than his adoptive father had ever been, could afford to shrug aside Antony's inevitable protests. Still only twenty-seven, he had come far. Not only Rome, nor only Italy, but half the world now acknowledged his rule.

Yet his – and Antony's – mastery remained that of a despot. The triumvirate, which had been hurriedly renewed in 37 after its expiry the year before, had no foundations in precedent, only in the exhaustion and misery of the Roman people. The sense of helplessness that the Republic had inspired in other peoples was now its own. As early as 44 BC, following Caesar's assassination, one of his friends had warned that Rome's problems were intractable – 'for if a man of such genius was unable to find a way out, who will find one now?'[17] Since then the Roman people had found themselves ever more storm-racked and adrift. The lodestars of custom were gone, and there seemed nothing to take their place.

No wonder, then, that despair and dislocation should have begun to breed in the Republic's citizens strange fantasies:

> *Now comes the crowning age foretold in the Sibyl's songs,*
> *A great new cycle, bred of time, begins again.*
> *Now virginal Justice and the golden age returns,*
> *Now its first-born is sent down from high heaven.*
> *With the birth of this boy, the generation of iron will pass,*
> *And a generation of gold will inherit all the world.*[18]

These lines were written in 40 BC, in the very teeth of Italy's suffering. Their author, P. Vergilius Maro – Virgil – was from the fertile basin of the River Po, an area where the land commissars had been particularly active. In other poems Virgil had hauntingly depicted the miseries of the dispossessed, nor was his vision of Utopia any the less despairing in its inspiration. Such had been the scale of the catastrophe that had overtaken the Roman people that vague prophetic longings of the kind that Greeks or Jews had long indulged in appeared the only consolations left to them. 'The Sibyl's songs': these were not the Sibyl's songs as they appeared in the books on the Capitol. They contained no prescription for appeasing the gods' anger, no programme for restoring peace to the Republic. They were dreams, nothing more.

And yet dreams, to autocrats, had their uses. Whatever Virgil's talk of messianic babies sent from heaven, there were clearly only two candidates for the role of saviour – and of these two, it was Antony, not Octavian, who had the most suggestive traditions ready to hand. The East, bled white by successive sides in Roman civil wars, yearned for a new beginning even more passionately than did Italy. Visions of apocalypse still swirled through the imaginings of Greeks and Egyptians, Syrians and Jews. Mithridates had demonstrated how an ambitious warlord could turn such hopes to his advantage; but no one had ever done so who was not an enemy of Rome. To present oneself as the saviour god long promised by eastern oracles: no more monstrous crime, for a citizen of the Republic, could possibly have been imagined. For more than a century now proconsuls had been travelling to the East, hearing themselves hailed as divine, mimicking Alexander, handing out crowns – and always dreaded to follow where such indulgences might lead. The Senate would not permit it; the Roman people would not permit it. But now the Republic was dead, and Antony was a triumvir, owing nothing to either the Senate or the Roman people. And temptation came in the form of a great and enchanting queen.

Cleopatra, who had won Caesar's affections by hiding in a carpet, had wooed Antony with overblown spectacle from the start. She knew him of old – his flamboyance, his love of pleasure, his dressing-up as Dionysus – and had calculated accordingly how best to win his heart. In 41 BC, during Antony's progress through the East, she had sailed from Egypt to meet him, her ship's oars made of silver, its poop sheathed with gold, her pages dressed as Cupids, her handmaids as sea nymphs, herself as Aphrodite, goddess of love. Antony had summoned her – an unconscionable humiliation – but Cleopatra, wafting into his headquarters amid the goggling of its stupefied inhabitants, had magnificently turned the tables. Not that she had been foolish enough to hog the limelight for too long. Instead, she had presented Antony with his own part to play in the extravaganza. 'And the word went out everywhere, that Aphrodite had come to feast with Dionysus, for the common good of Asia.'[19] No role could have been better designed to tickle Antony's fancy – no bed-partner either. Just as he had been intended to do, he had speedily made Cleopatra his mistress, and passed a delightful winter with her in Alexandria. Matrons back in Rome would swear by Egyptian methods of birth control, but Cleopatra – at least while taking world leaders to bed – had no time for fiddling around with diaphragms of crocodile dung. As with Caesar, so with Antony, she soon got herself pregnant. Having delivered Caesar a son, Cleopatra now went one better. Aphrodite gave Dionysus twins.

Here, for the father, was the glimmering of a perilous temptation. To found a line of kings: this was the ultimate, the deadliest taboo. No wonder that Antony turned his back on it. For four years – belying the gossip that he was besotted with Cleopatra – he avoided his mistress. Octavia, beautiful, intelligent and loyal, provided him with ample compensations, and for a while – settled in Athens, attending lectures with his intellectual bride – Antony presented a model of uxoriousness. Yet even when with Octavia he could not forget the more glittering possibilities to which Cleopatra had opened his eyes. Outrageous stories began to be told: that Antony was holding orgies in the theatre of Dionysus, dressed like the god in a fetching panther skin; that he was leading torchlit processions up to the Parthenon; that he was pestering the goddess Athena with drunken marriage proposals. All most un-Roman – and the stories were no doubt much improved by the retelling. Not that there was any great scandal in Athens, or among the rest of Antony's subjects. Just the opposite, in fact: in the East it was rather expected that a ruler be a god.

By 36 BC, when Antony and Octavian faced each other as twin masters of the Roman world, undistracted by rivals, the character of their rule was being influenced ever more by the different traditions of their power bases. For both men the challenge was the same: to secure a legitimacy that was not merely of the sword. Here Octavian, as the ruler of the West, had a crucial advantage. Both he and Antony were Roman, but only he had Rome. When Octavian returned to the capital from the defeat of Sextus he was greeted, for the first time, with genuine enthusiasm. The innate conservatism of his fellow citizens had survived the loss of their freedom, and now, grateful for the peace that Octavian had won them, they paid homage in the language of their ancient rights. They offered the conqueror a sacred privilege: the inviolability of a tribune. Only in a restored Republic would this have any meaning – and Octavian, by accepting it, was signalling his anticipation of just such a prospect. Not that this guaranteed anything, of course, for by now the Romans had learned better than to put their trust in rhetorical flourishes. Even so, with Sextus' fleet sunk and Lepidus banished in ignominious retirement, Octavian could at last start to flesh out his claims to be labouring in the cause of peace. Taxes were rescinded, grain supplies re-established, commissioners appointed to bring order to the countryside. Documents relating to the civil wars were ostentatiously burned. The annual magistrates began to have their responsibilities restored. Back to the future indeed.

But not all the way, of course – not yet. Octavian had no intention of surrendering his triumviral powers while Antony held on to his, and for Antony, far distant from his native city, the restoration of the Republic hardly registered as a pressing issue. Instead, his ambitions were tending in a very different direction. For three hundred years, ever since Alexander, dreams of universal empire had haunted the imaginings of the Greeks, dreams that the Republic too, in the end, had come to share. Yet its suspicion of them had lingered, and even the greatest of its citizens – even Pompey, even Caesar himself – had feared to pursue them to the limits. So too had Antony – who had fled the temptings of a Macedonian queen to become the husband of a sober Roman matron. But four years had passed, four years of naked power such as no citizen had ever exercised in the East before – and the temptations, as they were fed, continued to gnaw. In the end Antony proved too self-indulgent, too besotted by his own pretensions, to resist them. Octavia – who was to remain loyal to her husband's memory to the very end – was sent back to Rome. Meanwhile, once again, Aphrodite was summoned to the presence of the new Dionysus.

This time there was to be no backtracking from the affair. In Rome the scandal exploded. Ever since the Republic had begun involving itself in the affairs of the East there had been nothing more calculated to generate moral outrage than the spectacle of a citizen going native — and Antony, if reports were to be believed, was going native with a vengeance. The horrors of his behaviour seemed to have no limits. Why, he used a golden chamberpot, sheltered himself on the parade ground beneath mosquito nets, even massaged his mistress's feet! Extravagance, effeminacy, servility: the charge-sheet was a familiar one to any Roman politician. Antony, playing the bluff man of the world, chose to treat it all with disdain. 'So what if I'm fucking the Queen?' he complained to Octavian. 'What does it matter where you shove your erection?'[20]

But Antony was being disingenuous. His offences were not limited to the field of sex. Nor, even though the slanders that branded Cleopatra a whore were a staple of Roman misogyny, were they necessarily to be discounted for that reason. Her enemies were right to fear her, and to mistrust her seductions. These were not merely, as the cruder propagandists had it, the delights of her body, but charms more insidious and perilous by far. When Cleopatra whispered into Antony's ear, her most honeyed words were not of sensual pleasure, but promises of godhead and universal empire.

And Antony, smitten by such dreams, began to trample where even Caesar had feared to tread. Having previously turned his back on dynastic ambitions, he now began to parade them. First, he acknowledged his children by Cleopatra. Then he gave them provocative, even inflammatory, titles: Alexander Helios, 'the Sun', and Cleopatra Selene, 'the Moon'. Mingling the divine with the dynastic, these names may have been suited to Alexandria, but they could not have been more calculated to raise hackles back in Rome.

Did Antony even care? His fellow citizens, watching him pander to the cheers of servile Greeks and Orientals, frowned in perplexity. And then, just when it seemed as though his offensiveness could go no further, came his – and Cleopatra's – most spectacular stunt of all.

In 34 BC the crowds of Alexandria were invited to witness the inauguration of a dazzling new world order. The ceremony was presided over by Antony, Roman triumvir and new Dionysus. By his side sat Cleopatra, Macedonian queen and Egyptian pharaoh, splendidly robed as the new Isis, mistress of the heavens. Before them, arrayed in equally exotic national dress, stood Cleopatra's children by both Caesar and Antony. To the Alexandrians, these princes and princesses were presented as saviour-gods, the inheritors of a dawning universal harmony, long promised, now drawing near. Young Alexander, garbed as a Persian king of kings, was promised Parthia and all the realms beyond it. Other children, more modestly, were presented with territories that it was actually within the power of Antony to give. The fact that some of these were provinces of the Republic, held in trust for the Roman people, failed to inhibit his generosity. This was partly because, in one sense, he was not being generous at all. Antony had no real intention of handing over the administration of Roman provinces to his children, and to that extent at least the ceremony was show and nothing more. But show mattered – and the message Antony had wished it to proclaim could also be found on his silver coins, jingling in purses throughout the East. His head stamped on one side, Cleopatra's on the other: a Roman and a Greek; a triumvir and a queen. A new age was dawning in which Roman rule would be blended into what the Sibyl had prophesied: the divinely ordained synthesis of East and West, all differences shrunk, presided over by an emperor and an empress of the world.

But Alexandria's meat, of course, was the Republic's poison. Back in Rome, Antony's friends – of whom there were still many – were appalled. Antony himself, alerted to the public-relations disaster, hurriedly wrote to the Senate. He offered, in a grand but vague manner, to lay down his triumviral powers – to restore the Republic. But too late. The gleaming white toga of constitutionalism had already been filched. Distracted as he had been by his grandiose Eastern dreams, Antony turned his gaze back to Rome to discover a most disconcerting sight: the heir of Caesar, adventurer and terrorist, posing resplendent as the defender of the Republic, the champion of tradition and his people's ancient freedoms. And not only posing, but carrying the role off with great style.

True, not everyone was convinced by the young Caesar's impersonation of a constitutionalist – and the mask itself might still occasionally slip. In 32 BC, wishing to browbeat the consuls, both of whom were supporters of Antony, Octavian entered the Senate House with armed guards and stationed them menacingly behind the magistrates' chairs of state. The show of strength had the desired effect: opponents of Octavian's regime were immediately smoked out. The two consuls fled to Antony in the East, and with them went almost a third of the Senate, some three hundred senators in all. Many of these were Antony's placemen, but some, the heirs to a ruined cause, had more principled reasons for refusing to stomach a Caesar as the shield of the Republic. One of the two consuls who fled to Antony, for instance, was Domitius Ahenobarbus, the son of Julius Caesar's old foe. Also in Antony's camp – inevitably – was the grandson of Cato.

Octavian jeered at their choice of loyalties. That such men should end up as courtiers to a queen! Domitius actually made a point of snubbing Cleopatra whenever he could, and was constantly urging Antony to send her packing back to Egypt, but Octavian had always been a master at landing punches below the belt. In the summer of 32 BC, tipped off by a renegade, he even took the supremely sacrilegious step of raiding the temple of Vesta, where Antony had deposited his will, and seizing the document from the hands of the Vestal Virgins. The contents, eagerly pored over, duly proved as explosive as Octavian had anticipated. Stern-faced and censorious, he listed them for the benefit of the Senate. Caesarion to be legitimised; Cleopatra's children awarded vast legacies; Antony himself, on his death, to be buried by Cleopatra's side. It was all very shocking – perhaps suspiciously so.

Yet if there was much that was factitious about Octavian's propaganda, it was not all spin. Antony's partnership with Cleopatra, formalised in 32 when he divorced Octavia, was instinctively recognised by most Romans for what it was – a betrayal of the Republic's deepest principles and values. That the Republic itself was dead did not make these any less mourned, nor its prejudices any less savage. To surrender to what was unworthy of a citizen: this was what the Romans had always most dreaded. It was flattering, therefore, to a people who had become unfree to pillory Antony as unmanly and a slave to a foreign queen. For the last time, the Roman people could gird themselves for war and imagine that both the Republic and their own virtue were not, after all, entirely dead.

Many years later Octavian would boast, 'The whole of Italy, unprompted, swore allegiance to me, and demanded that I lead her into war. The provinces of Gaul, Spain, Africa, Sicily and Sardinia also swore the same oath.'[21] Here, in the form of a plebiscite spanning half the world, was something utterly without precedent, a display of universalism consciously designed to put that of Antony and Cleopatra in the shadow, drawn from the traditions not of the East but of the Roman Republic itself. Undisputed autocrat and champion of his city's most ancient ideals, Octavian sailed to war as both. It was a combination that was to prove irresistible. When, for the third time in less than twenty years, two Roman forces met head to head in the Balkans, it was a Caesar, yet again, who emerged triumphant. Throughout the summer of 31 BC, with his fleet rotting in the shallows and his army rotting with disease, Antony was blockaded on the eastern coast of Greece. His camp began to empty – dispiritingly, even Domitius was among the deserters. Finally, when the stench of defeat had grown too over-powering for Antony to ignore any longer, he decided to make a desperate throw. On 2 September he ordered his fleet to attempt a break-out, past the Cape of Actium, into the open sea. For much of the day the two great fleets faced each other, motionless in the silence of the crystalline bay. Then suddenly, in the afternoon, there was movement: Cleopatra's squadron darting forwards, smashing its way through a gap in Octavian's line, slipping free. Antony, aban-doning his giant flagship for a swifter vessel, followed, but most of his fleet was left behind, his legions too. They quickly surrendered. With this brief, inglorious battle perished all of Antony's dreams, and all the hopes of the new Isis. And for days afterwards the waves washed gold and purple on to the shore.

One year later Octavian closed in for the kill. In July 30 BC his legions appeared before Alexandria. The following evening, as twi-light deepened towards midnight, the noise of invisible musicians was heard floating in a procession through the city, then upwards to the stars. 'And when people reflected on this mystery, they realised that Dionysus, the god whom Antony had always sought to imitate and copy, had abandoned his favourite.'[22] The next day Alexandria fell. Antony, botching his suicide in the manner of Cato, died in his lover's arms. Cleopatra, having discovered that Octavian planned to parade her in chains for his triumph, followed him nine days later. As befitted a pharaoh, she died of a cobra bite, the poison of which, the Egyptians believed, bestowed immortality. It was, for the would-be emperor and empress of the world, a suitably multi-cultural end.

The scare that Cleopatra had given Rome doomed her dynasty. Caesarion, her son by Julius Caesar, was quietly executed, the Ptolemies themselves officially deposed. On temples across Egypt artisans began sculpting the image of their new king: Octavian himself. Henceforward, the country would be ruled not as an independent kingdom, nor even as a Roman province – although the new pharaoh liked to pretend otherwise – but as a private fiefdom. Later, Octavian would boast of his mercy: 'When it was safe to pardon foreign people I preferred to preserve them rather than wipe them out.'[23] Alexandria was the greatest city to have fallen to a Roman general since Carthage, but its fate was far different. Ruthless in the pursuit of power, Octavian was to prove himself cool and cynical in the exercising of it. Alexandria was too rich, too much of a honeypot, to destroy. Even the statues of Cleopatra escaped being smashed.

Such clemency, of course, was the prerogative of a master, a demonstration of his greatness and power. All the world had fallen into Octavian's hands, and now that he had no rivals, bloodshed and savagery had ceased to serve his purpose. 'I am reluctant to call mercy', wrote Seneca almost a century later, 'what was really the exhaustion of cruelty.'[24] But Octavian, if he were exhausted, could not afford to show it. Visiting the tomb of Alexander, he accidentally knocked off the corpse's nose. In a similar manner he chipped at the conqueror's reputation. The greatest challenge, Octavian argued sternly, was not the winning of empire but the ordering of it. He spoke with authority, for this was the challenge he had set himself. No longer to butcher but to spare; no longer to fight but to provide peace; no longer to destroy but to restore.

Such, at any rate as he sailed home, Octavian was pleased to claim.

The Republic Restored

The Ides of January 27 BC. The Senate House seething with anticipation. Senators, crowded on to benches, whispering urgently among themselves. A historic announcement, it appeared, was due. Not only had it been widely trailed, but there were some senators, the leading members of the house, who had been tipped off about the response that was expected. Waiting for the consul to begin his speech, they readied themselves to look surprised, while rehearsing stage-managed answers beneath their breath.

Suddenly, a falling away of voices. The consul, slight still, only thirty-five, rising to his feet. Hushed silence for him, the young Caesar, the saviour of the state. Composed as ever, he began to address the chamber. His words were measured, cool – and freighted with moment. Civil war, he announced, had been extinguished. The extraordinary powers awarded to him – true, by universal consent, but unconstitutional all the same – could no longer be justified. His mission had been accomplished, the Republic had been saved, and so now, at long last, after the worst and most convulsive crisis in its history, the time had come to hand it back to whom it belonged: the Senate and people of Rome.

As he sat down, murmurs of unease, swelling steadily. The leaders of the Senate began to protest. Why, having rescued the Roman people from otherwise certain ruin, was Caesar planning to abandon them now? Yes, he had announced the restoration of constitutional proprieties, and the Senate was duly grateful. But why, just because the traditions of the Republic were set to flourish again, did this mean that Caesar had to resign his guardianship of the state? Did he wish to condemn his people to eternal anarchy and civil war? For this, without him, would surely be their fate!

Perhaps, rather than abandon the Republic to disaster, he would therefore listen to a counter-proposal? Caesar had declared illegal any of his acts or honours that were contrary to the constitution; very well, then let him, just like any consul, be awarded a province. One that would bring with it twenty-odd legions, true, and include Spain, Gaul, Syria, Cyprus and Egypt – but a province, none the less. And let him hold it for ten years, not an unheard-of length of time, after all – for had not Caesar's father, the great Julius, held office for a decade in Gaul? Nothing to offend precedent there. The Republic would flourish and Caesar would fulfil his responsibilities to Rome, and the gods would smile on both. Throughout the Senate there rose a roar of assent.

Who was Octavian to refuse such an appeal? The Republic needed him, so, graciously, as was his duty as a citizen, he announced that, yes, he was prepared to shoulder the burden. The gratitude of the Senate knew no bounds. Magnanimity as great as Caesar's merited spectacular rewards. These were duly voted him. It was agreed that bay leaves should be wreathed over the doorposts of his house, and a civic crown fixed over its door. A golden shield was to be placed in the Senate House, listing his qualities of courage, mercy, justice and sense of duty – time-tested Roman virtues all. And then there was one final honour, novel and supreme, as was only fitting. It was decreed that Caesar should henceforward be known as 'Augustus'.

This, for the man born Gaius Octavius, was the culmination of an entire career spent collecting impressive names. A Caesar at the age of nineteen, he had gone one better two years later when, following his adoptive father's official deification, he had begun calling himself 'Divi Filius' – 'Son of a God.' Extraordinary though such a name was, it had evidently met with divine approval, for the career of Caesar Divi Filius had never ceased to be blessed with success. Now, as 'Augustus', he would be distinguished even further from the common run of mortals. The title would veil him like a nimbus in a glow of unearthly power. 'For it signified that he was something more than human. All the most sacred and honoured things are described as "august"'.[25]

Including Rome herself. A famous phrase, lodged in the mind of every citizen, asserted that the city had been 'founded with august augury'[26] – and now, by becoming Augustus, Octavian had made this phrase his own. To found Rome anew – here was his lifetime's mission, and every time his fellow citizens spoke his name, they would be reminded of it. The artful, almost subliminal, nature of such an association was entirely calculated, for tempted as Octavian had been by the more obvious name of 'Romulus', he had rejected it: the first founder of Rome had been a king and had killed his brother, unfortunate details both. Now that Octavian held supreme power, anything that might jog memories of how he had won it was to be suppressed. Already, eighty silver statues, voted him the previous decade by an obsequious Senate, had been melted down. In official commemorations of his career, the years between Philippi and Actium were left a blank. And most crucially of all, of course, the name 'Octavian' itself was to be buried in oblivion. Augustus Caesar perfectly understood the importance of rebranding.

And he understood it because he understood the Roman people themselves. Augustus had shared in their deepest dreams and desires. That, after all, was what had won him the world. Last and greatest of the Republic's strongmen, he had recognised, with the pitiless eye of a pathologist, the malignancy corrupting his city's noblest ideals – nor had he ever ceased to exploit it. 'Always fight bravely, and be superior to others,' Posidonius had admonished Pompey, citing the impeccable authority of Homer. But the age of heroes was past, and the desire to fight bravely and to be superior to others might now encompass the ruin of Rome. The stakes had grown so high, the resources available to the ambitious so immense, the methods open to them so devastating and lethal, that they had brought the Republic and all its empire to the point of annihilation. No longer a polity of citizens bound by shared assumptions and restraints, Rome had become an anarchy of head-hunters in which only the cruel and fratricidal could hope to advance. This was the hunting-ground into which Octavian, just nineteen, had thrown himself – and there could be no doubt that his aim, from the outset, had been to seize mastery of the state. Having achieved that, however, with his rivals dead or tamed and his people exhausted, he had next faced a momentous decision. Either to continue trampling on the traditions of his city's past, to wield power nakedly with a sword, as a warlord, perhaps, like his father, like Antony, as a god – or to cast himself as the heir of tradition. By becoming 'Augustus' he signalled his choice. He would rule not against the grain of the Republic but with it. He would instruct his countrymen in an ancient lesson: that ambition, if not pursued for the general good, might be a crime. And he himself, the 'best guardian of Romulus' people',[27] would revitalise the ideals of citizenship so that never again would they over-reach themselves and degenerate into savagery and civil war.

Hypocrisy of an Olympian order, of course, but Romulus' people were no longer in a condition much to care. Citizens now imagined their doom inexorable.

> What does the bloodthirsty passage of time not leech away?
> Our parents' generation, worse than their parents',
> Has given birth to us, worse yet – and soon
> We will have children still more depraved.[28]

This was a pessimism bred of more than war-weariness. The old certainties of what it meant to be a Roman had been poisoned, and a confused and frightened people despaired of what had once bound them together: their honour, their love of glory, their military ardour. Freedom had betrayed them. The Republic had lost its liberty, but worse, it had lost its soul. Or so the Romans feared.

The challenge – and the great opportunity – for Augustus was to persuade them of the opposite. Do that and the foundations of his regime would be secure. A citizen who could restore to his fellows not only peace, but also their customs, their past and their pride would rank as august indeed. But he could not do it simply by legislating, 'for what use are empty laws without traditions to animate them?'[29] Decrees on their own would not resurrect the Republic. Only the Roman people, by proving themselves worthy of Augustus' labours, could do that – and therein lay the genius and the greatness of the policy. The new era could be cast as a moral challenge of the kind that the Romans had so often faced – and risen to triumphantly – in the past. Augustus, claiming no more authority than was due to him by virtue of his achievements and prestige, summoned his countrymen to share with him the heroic task of revitalising the Republic. He encouraged them, in short, to feel like citizens again.

And the programme was funded, as was traditional, with the gold of the defeated. The realisation of Augustus' dreams was to be paid for, fittingly, out of the ruin of Cleopatra's. In 29 BC Octavian had returned to Rome from the East with the fabled treasure of the Ptolemies in his cargo-holds – and had immediately begun spending it. Huge tranches of land were bought up, in Italy and throughout the provinces, so that Augustus would never again have to commit the terrible crime of his youth: settling his veterans on confiscated property. Nothing had caused more misery and dislocation, and nothing had struck more brutally at the Romans' sense of themselves. Now, at enormous expense, Augustus worked to expiate his offence. 'The assurance of every citizen's property rights' was to be an enduring slogan of the new regime, and one that did much to underpin its widespread popularity. To the Romans, security of tenure was a moral as much as a social or economic good. Those who benefited from its return saw it as hailing nothing less than a new golden age: 'cultivation restored to the fields, respect to what is sacred, freedom from anxiety to mankind'.[30]

Yet this golden age would impose duties on those who enjoyed it. Unlike the Utopia described by Virgil, it would not be a paradise purged of toil and danger. That would hardly serve to breed hardy citizens. Augustus had not invested the treasure of the Ptolemies merely to encourage his countrymen to lounge around like effeminate Orientals. Instead, his fantasy was the old one of all Roman reformers: to renew the rugged virtues of the ancient peasantry, to bring the Republic back to basics. It struck a deep chord, for this was the raw stuff of Roman myth: nostalgia for a venerated past, yes, but simultaneously a spirit harsh and unsentimental, the same that had forged generations of steel-hard citizens and carried the Republic's standards to the limits of the world. 'Back-breaking labour, and the urgings of tough poverty – these can conquer anything!'[31] So Virgil had written, while Octavian, in the East, was defeating Cleopatra and bringing an end to the civil wars. No vision of an indolent paradise now, but something more ambiguous, challenging – and, by Roman lights, worthwhile. Honour, in the Republic, had never been a goal in itself, only a means to an infinite end. And what was true of her citizens, naturally, was also true of Rome herself. Struggle had been her existence, and the defiance of disaster. For the generation that had lived through the civil wars, this was the consolation that history gave them. Out of calamity could come greatness. Out of dispossession could come the renewal of a civilised order.

For what was Caesar Augustus himself, after all, if not the heir of a refugee? Long before there had been such a city as Rome, Prince Aeneas, the grandson of Venus, the ancestor of the Julian clan, had fled burning Troy and voyaged with his small fleet to Italy, his quest, given him by Jupiter, to make a new beginning. It was from Aeneas and his Trojans that the Roman people had eventually sprung, and in their souls it could be imagined they still retained something of the wanderer. Not to be content with what they had, but always to strive and fight for more, this had been the destiny of the Republic's citizens – and it gave to Augustus and his mission a time-hallowed glow.

In the Romans' beginning was their end. In 29 BC, the same year that Octavian returned from the East to push forward his programme of regeneration, Virgil started a poem on the theme of Aeneas. This was to become the great epic of the Roman people, an exploration both of their primordial roots and of their recent history. Like spectres, famous names out of the future haunt the vision of the Trojan hero: Caesar Augustus, naturally, 'son of a god, who brings back the age of gold',[32] but others too – Catiline, 'trembling at the faces of the Furies', and Cato, 'giving laws to the just'.[33] When Aeneas, shipwrecked off the African coast, neglects his god-given duties to the future of Rome and dallies instead with Dido, the Queen of Carthage, the reader is troubled by knowing what will happen to the Trojan's descendants, Julius Caesar and Antony; Carthage shimmers and elides with Alexandria; Dido with Cleopatra, a second fatal queen. What is gone and what is to come, both cast their shadows, one on the other, meeting, merging, separating again. When Aeneas sails up the Tiber, cattle low in the field that, a thousand years hence, will be the site of the Forum of Augustus' Rome.

To the Romans themselves, who remained a conservative people despite all the upheavals of repeated civil wars, there was

nothing startling about the perception that the past might shadow
the present. The unique achievement of Augustus, however, was
the brilliance with which he colonised both. His claim to be restoring their lost moral greatness to them stirred in the Romans deep
sensibilities and imaginings that at their profoundest could inspire
a Virgil, and make their landscape once again a sacred and myth-
haunted place. But these yearnings also served other, more
programmatic purposes. They encouraged veterans, for instance,
to remain on their farms and not come endlessly flocking to
Rome; to be content with their lot, leaving their swords to rust in
the lofts of their barns. And over the vast tracts of the countryside
that remained the property of agri-business, worked by chain-
gangs of slaves, they cast a veil woven of fantasy.

> *What is happiness? — opting out of the rat race,*
> *Just like the ancient race of men,*
> *Tilling ancestral fields with your own team of oxen,*
> *Spared the horror of overdrafts,*
> *Not a soldier, blood pumping at the fierce trumpet,*
> *Not trembling at the angry sea.*[34]

So wrote Virgil's friend Horace, with delicate irony, for he perfectly appreciated that his vision of the good life bore little relation
to the realities of existence in the countryside. Yet it was no less
precious to him for that. Horace had fought on the losing side in
the civil wars, running away ingloriously from Philippi, and
returning to Italy to find his father's farm confiscated. Like his
political loyalties, his dreams of a modest villa, of a life lived close
to the land, were bred of nostalgia, no matter how self-mockingly
expressed. Augustus, who never held Horace's youthful indiscre-
tions against him, offered the poet friendship and made an
investment in his dreams. Even as the new regime was parcelling

out the huge estates of fallen Antonians to its supporters, it was also subsidising Horace in an idyllic existence outside Rome, complete with garden, spring and little wood. Horace himself was too subtle, too independent, to be bought as a propagandist, but crude propaganda was not what Augustus wanted from him, nor from Virgil. For generations Rome's leading citizens had been tortured by the need to choose between self-interest and traditional ideals. Augustus, with his genius for squaring circles, simply made himself the patron of both.

And he could do this because, like any star performer, he had the pick of roles he wanted. Only the reality could not be acknowledged: Augustus had no wish to end up murdered on the Senate House floor. Instead, with the willing collaboration of his fellow citizens, who flinched from staring the truth in the face, he veiled himself in robes garnered from the antique lumber-box of the Republic, refusing any magistracy not sanctioned by the past, and often not holding any magistracy at all. Authority, not office, was what counted: that mysterious quality that had given to Catulus or to Cato his prestige. 'In all the qualities that make up a man,' Cicero had once acknowledged, 'M. Cato was first citizen.'[35] 'First citizen' – '*princeps*': Augustus let it be known that he could wish for no prouder title. The son of Julius Caesar was to be regarded as the heir of Cato too.

And he pulled it off. No wonder that Augustus boasted of his skills as an actor. Only a man with a supreme talent for dissimulation could have played such various parts so subtly – and with such success. On his signet-ring, the *princeps* carried the image of a sphinx – and throughout his career he posed his countrymen a riddle. The Romans were used to citizens who vaunted their power, who exulted in the brilliance and glamour of their greatness – but Augustus was different. The more his grip tightened on the state, the less he flaunted it. Paradox, of course, had always suffused the

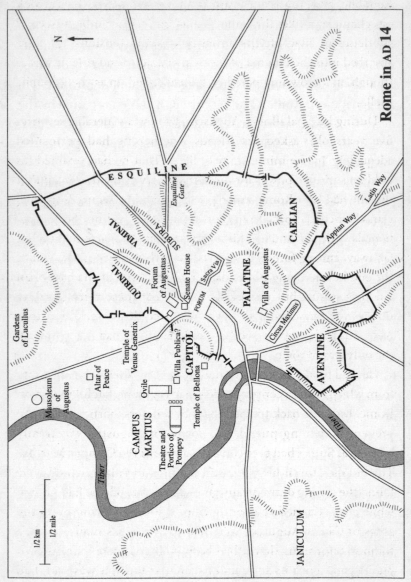

Rome in AD 14

N

ESQUILINE

Esquiline Gate

VIMINAL

SUBURA

QUIRINAL

Forum of Augustus

Senate House

Sacra Via

FORUM

Temple of Venus Genetrix

Villa Publica?

CAPITOL

Gardens of Lucullus

Altar of Peace

Ovile

Mausoleum of Augustus

CAMPUS MARTIUS

Theatre and Portico of Pompey

Temple of Bellona

CAELIAN

Appian Way

Latin Way

PALATINE

Villa of Augustus

Circus Maximus

AVENTINE

Tiber

JANICULUM

1/2 km

1/2 mile

Republic, and Augustus, insinuating himself into its heart, took on, chameleon-like, the same characteristic. The ambiguities and subtleties of civic life, its ambivalences and tensions, all were absorbed into the enigma of his own character and role. It was as though, in a crowning paradox, he had ended up as the Republic itself.

During his final illness, Augustus, by now a venerable seventy-five years old, asked his friends whether he had performed adequately 'in the mime-show of life'.[36] That he had retained his hold on supreme power for more than forty years; that in all that time he had kept Rome, and the world with her, secure from civil war, claimed no special rank for himself that had not been sanctioned by the law, and had his legions stationed not around him but far away, among forests or deserts, on barbarous frontiers; that in the end he was dying not of dagger wounds, not at the base of an enemy's statue, but peacefully in his bed: these were dazzling notices for any citizen to have. Yes, it could be reckoned that Augustus had put on a good show. After all, he had made himself the only star in town.

He died finally in the summer of AD 14 in Nola – the same city from which Sulla, a century earlier, had begun his fateful march on Rome. Escorted back to the capital by senators, borne at night to prevent it turning putrid, the corpse of Augustus was finally burned, as Sulla's had been, on a great pyre in the Campus Martius. The old dictator, if his ghost still haunted the plain, would have found the setting dramatically altered from the one he had known while alive. Carried reverently from the smouldering pyre, the ashes of Caesar Augustus were laid to rest in his mausoleum, a tomb so enormous that it had been built complete with its own public park: both its scale and its circular form, it was said, had been inspired by the tomb of Alexander the Great. The Campus Martius, once the training-ground of Roman youth, was now one

vast demonstration of the virtues of the *Princeps*. Of his magnanimity – for there, to the south, could still be seen Pompey's theatre,
the name and the trophies of Caesar's enemy preserved by the grace
of Caesar's son. Of his benignity – for where once the Republic's citizens had gathered to practise their weapons and be marshalled for
war there now stood an Altar of Peace. And of his beneficence – for
stretching even longer than Pompey's theatre, a whole mile of
gleaming porticoes, rose what had rapidly become, since its completion in 26 BC, Rome's premier entertainment venue, where
Augustus had staged some of the most lavish spectacles ever seen in
the city. Officially, this was the voting hall, the Ovile, an extravagant
upgrading of the old wooden pens into marble. But it was rarely
used for voting. Instead, where the Roman people had once gathered to elect their magistrates, gladiators now fought and bizarre
monsters – giant serpents, for instance, almost ninety feet long –
were displayed. And if there were no shows, then citizens could
always flock there for the luxury shopping.

The Republic had long been dead – now it was passing out of
fashion too. 'Shaggy simplicity is yesterday's news. Rome's made of
gold,/And coins in all the wealth of the conquered globe.'[37]
Greatness might have cost the Romans their freedom, but it had
given them the world. Under Augustus their legions had continued
to display all the martial qualities of old – pushing back the empire's
frontiers, slaughtering barbarians – but to the urbane consumer
back on the Campus Martius, it was only distant noise. War no
longer disturbed his reckoning. Nor, much, did morality, or duty,
or the past. Nor, even, did warnings from the heavens. 'Portents', a
contemporary historian noted with perplexity, 'are never reported
or chronicled nowadays.'[38] But for this there was a self-evident
explanation: the gods, surveying the scene of leisure and peace that
Rome had become, had clearly decided that there was nothing left
for them to say.

'The fruit of too much liberty is slavery'[39] had been the mournful judgement of Cicero — and who was to say that his own generation, the last of a free Republic, had not proved it true? But the fruit of slavery? That was for a new generation, and a new age, to prove.

The Roman World in AD 14

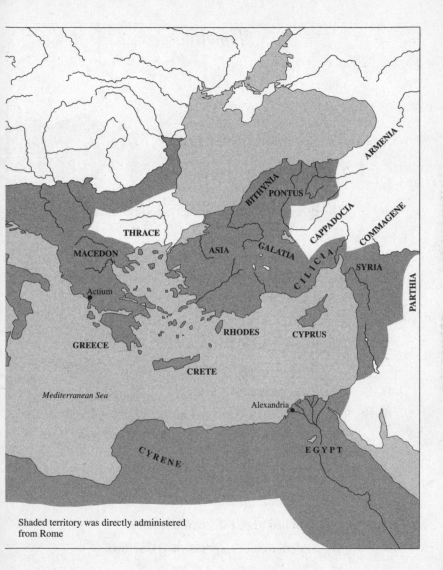

THRACE

MACEDON

ASIA GALATIA BITHYNIA PONTUS ARMENIA

CAPPADOCIA COMMAGENE

CILICIA SYRIA

PARTHIA

Actium

GREECE

RHODES CYPRUS

CRETE

Mediterranean Sea

Alexandria

CYRENE EGYPT

Shaded territory was directly administered
from Rome

Timeline

All dates are BC unless otherwise stated.

753	The foundation of Rome.
509	The downfall of the monarchy, and the establishment of the Republic.
390	The capture of Rome by the Gauls.
367	Legal restrictions on the right of plebeians to hold the consulship are abolished.
343–40	First Samnite war.
321	The Romans are defeated at the Caudine Forks.
290	The Romans complete the conquest of Samnium.
264–41	The first war against Carthage.
219–18	The start of the second war against Carthage. Hannibal marches on Italy, through southern Gaul, and across the Alps.
216	The battle of Cannae.
202	The defeat of Hannibal in Africa.
148	Macedon becomes a Roman province.
146	The destruction of Carthage and Corinth.
133	The tribunate and murder of Tiberius Gracchus. Attalus III of Pergamum leaves his kingdom to Rome in his will.

123	The first tribunate of Gaius Gracchus (starting on 10 December 124). Pergamum subjected to organised taxation.
122	The second tribunate of Gaius Gracchus.
121	The murder of Gaius Gracchus.
118	The establishment of a province in southern Gaul secures the land route to Spain. Probable birthdate of Lucullus.
115	Birth of Crassus.
112	Mithridates VI establishes himself as King of Pontus.
107	Marius' first consulship. He abolishes property qualifications for recruitment to the army.
106	Birth of Pompey and Cicero.
104–100	Marius as Consul. Victorious campaigns against barbarian invaders from the north.
100	Birth of Caesar.
93	Birth of Clodius.
92	The conviction and exile of Rutilius Rufus for extortion.
91	Outbreak of the Italian revolt against Rome.
90	Citizenship offered to Italians loyal to Rome.
89	Sulla, campaigning in Samnium, brings an effective end to the Italian revolt. Mithridates invades the Roman province of Asia.
88	Sulla as consul. Marius, with the assistance of the tribune Sulpicius, has the Mithridatic command transferred to himself. Sulla marches on Rome. The execution of Sulpicius, and escape of Marius into exile. In Asia, Mithridates orders the massacre of 80,000 Romans and Italians.

87   Cinna as consul. Sulla leaves for Greece and the war
         against Mithridates. The death of Pompeius Strabo.
         Marius returns to power in Rome.

86   Cinna as consul. The death of Marius. Athens falls to
         Sulla.

85   Cinna as consul. Sulla signs a peace treaty with
         Mithridates.

84   Cinna as consul. He is murdered by mutineers.

83   Crassus joins Sulla in Greece. Sulla crosses to Italy,
         where he is joined by Pompey. The battle of the Colline
         Gate, and the massacre of the Samnite prisoners in the
         Villa Publica.

82   Proscriptions in Rome. Caesar in hiding.

81   Sulla as Dictator. He launches major constitutional
         reforms, including the hamstringing of the tribunate.
         Cicero's first case.

80   Sulla as consul. Caesar leaves for military service in Asia.

79   Sulla relinquishes his magistracies. Cicero leaves on a
         two-year trip to the East.

78   Catulus as consul. The death of Sulla.

77   Pompey is given a command in Spain.

75   Cicero as quaestor. Mithridates declares war on Rome.

74   Lucullus as consul. Mithridates invades the province of
         Asia a second time. M. Antonius is given a command
         against the pirates.

73   The outbreak of a slave revolt, led by Spartacus.
         Lucullus expels Mithridates from Asia.

72   Crassus is appointed to command of the war against
         Spartacus. The end of Pompey's campaigning in Spain.

Lucullus is victorious against Mithridates in Pontus.
M. Antonius is defeated by the pirates off Crete.

71   The defeat and death of Spartacus. The return of
Pompey to Italy. Lucullus completes the conquest of
Pontus. Mithridates takes refuge with Tigranes of
Armenia.

70   Pompey and Crassus as consuls. Full powers are
restored to the tribunate, after their abolition by Sulla.
The prosecution of Verres.

69   The battle and sack of Tigranocerta.

68   Lucullus' army mutinies. The birth of Cleopatra.

67   Pompey sweeps the seas clear of pirates.

66   Lucullus is replaced by Pompey as proconsul of the East.
Cicero as praetor.

65   Caesar as aedile.

64   Pompey establishes Syria as a new Roman province.
Cato as quaestor.

63   Cicero as consul. Caesar becomes *Pontifex Maximus*.
Lucullus celebrates his triumph. Pompey storms
Jerusalem. The death of Mithridates. The Catilinarian
conspiracy, and execution of the ringleaders. Catiline
raises an army in northern Italy. The birth of Octavian.

62   Caesar as praetor. The defeat and death of Catiline.
Pompey returns to Italy. Clodius profanes the rites of
the Good Goddess.

61   Caesar as governor in Spain. The trial and acquittal of
Clodius. Pompey's third triumph.

60   Caesar returns to Rome. The formation of an informal
alliance between Caesar, Pompey and Crassus.

59   Caesar and Bibulus as consuls. 'The First Triumvirate'. Pompey marries Julia, Caesar's daughter. Clodius becomes a plebeian, and is elected to the tribunate.

58   Caesar campaigns against the Helvetians. Clodius as tribune. Cicero leaves Rome for exile, Cato for Cyprus.

57   Caesar campaigns against the Belgae. Street fighting between the gangs of Clodius and Milo. Cicero returns from exile.

56   The trial and acquittal of Caelius. The conference of Lucca, and the renewal of the Triumvirate. Cato returns to Rome from Cyprus.

55   Pompey and Crassus as consuls. Pompey dedicates his stone theatre. Caesar crosses the Rhine, then leads an expedition to Britain.

54   Domitius and Appius as consuls, Cato as praetor. Crassus leaves for Syria. Caesar leads a second expedition to Britain. The death of Pompey's wife, Julia.

53   The battle of Carrhae, and the death of Crassus.

52   The murder of Clodius, and conviction of Milo. Pompey as sole consul until August. He marries Cornelia, the daughter of Scipio. Caelius as tribune. Vercingetorix leads Gaul in revolt against Caesar, but is defeated at Alesia, and surrenders.

50   Curio as tribune. The death of Hortensius. Pompey is called upon by the consul Marcellus to 'rescue the Republic'.

49   Caesar crosses the Rubicon. The Senate evacuates Rome. Domitius surrenders Corfinium. Pompey leaves Italy for Greece. The defeat and death of Curio in

Africa. Caesar defeats the Pompeian armies in Spain, and is elected dictator.

48   The deaths of Milo and Caelius. The battle of Pharsalus. The murder of Pompey. Caesar trapped in Alexandria.

47   Caesar's cruise with Cleopatra down the Nile. The birth of Caesarion. Caesar defeats Pharnaces, the son of Mithridates, returns to Italy, then crosses to Africa.

46   Caesar defeats Scipio. Cato commits suicide, Scipio drowns. Caesar celebrates four triumphs. Cleopatra arrives in Rome. Caesar leaves for Spain.

45   Caesar defeats the sons of Pompey, and returns to Rome. He publishes his *Anti-Cato*.

44   Caesar is appointed dictator for life. Antony as consul. Caesar is assassinated on the ides of March. Octavian arrives in Rome. Brutus and Cassius leave for the East. Cicero delivers a series of speeches against Antony.

43   Hirtius and Pansa as consuls. They are killed in battle with Antony. The formation of the Second Triumvirate: Antony, Octavian and Lepidus. Octavian's first consulship. The proscriptions. The death of Cicero.

42   The deification of Caesar. The battle of Philippi: the suicides of Brutus and Cassius.

41   Antony meets Cleopatra, then winters with her at Alexandria. Land sequestrations in Italy. War between Octavian and Fulvia.

40   Fulvia flees Italy, and dies. Antony and Octavian make peace, and Antony marries Octavian's sister, Octavia. Cleopatra gives birth to twins.

37   Antony marries Cleopatra.

36	Lepidus is dropped from the Triumvirate. Sextus Pompeius is defeated, and flees to the East.
35	Death of Sextus Pompeius.
34	Antony hands out kingdoms and provinces to his children in Alexandria.
32	Octavia is divorced by Antony. Octavian seizes his will, and presents it to the Senate.
31	The battle of Actium.
30	The suicide of Antony and Cleopatra. Octavian captures Alexandria, and executes Caesarion. Ptolemaic rule in Egypt is brought to an end.
29	Virgil starts work on *The Aeneid*.
27	Octavian is given the title 'Augustus'. The Republic is 'restored'.
19	The death of Virgil.
AD 14	The death of Augustus.

Notes

Unless otherwise stated, author citations refer to the following texts: Appian, *The Civil Wars*; Asconius, *Commentaries of Five Speeches by Cicero*; Aulus Gellius, *The Attic Nights*; Cassius Dio, *The Roman History*; Catullus, *Poems*; Diodorus Siculus, *The Library of History*; Florus, *The Epitome of Roman History*; Livy, *The History of Rome*; Lucan, *The Pharsalia*; Lucretius, *On the Nature of Things*; Macrobius, *The Saturnalia*; Orosius, *The History against the Pagans*; Petronius, *The Satyricon*; Pliny the Elder, *The Natural History*; Polybius, *The Histories*; Publilius Syrus, *Maxims*; Quintilian, *The Education of an Orator*; Strabo, *The Geography*; Valerius Maximus, *Memorable Deeds and Sayings*; Velleius Paterculus, *The Roman Histories*.

Preface

1   Hobbes, *Leviathan*, chapter 29.
2   *Hitler's Table-Talk*, introduced by Hugh Trevor-Roper (1988, Oxford), p. 10.
3   In a review of Hughes-Hallett's book *Cleopatra: Histories, Dreams and Distortions* for the *New York Times* (1990).
4   Niccolò Machiavelli, *Discourses on the First Decade of Livy*, 3.43.
5   Sallust, *Catiline*, 8.
6   Velleius Paterculus, 2.36.

1: The Paradoxical Republic

1   Polybius, 6.56.
2   Cicero, *Concerning the Manilian Law*, 19–21.
3   Polybius, 10.15.
4   Ennius, quoted by Cicero, *The Republic*, 5.1.
5   Livy, 40.5.
6   Cicero, *On the Agrarian Law*, 2.96.

7   Vitruvius, *The Ten Books on Architecture*, 6.1.10.

8   See in particular Cicero, *The Republic*, 2.10–11.

9   See Brunt, *Italian Manpower*, p. 618.

10 Horace, *Odes*, 3.29.12.

11 Dionysius of Halicarnassus, *Roman Antiquities*, 3.43.

12 Horace, *Epistles*, 2.2.72–5.

13 Strabo, 5.3.8.

14 Publilius Syrus, 31.

15 Livy, 4.4.

16 Sallust, *Catiline*, 1.7.

17 Polybius, 6.11.

18 Cicero, *In Defence of Plancius*, 11.

19 Cicero, *In Defence of Murena*, 36.

2: The Sibyl's Curse

1   *The Sibylline Oracles*, 3.464–9.

2   *Ibid.*, 3.175–80.

3   *Ibid.*, 184–8.

4   *Ibid.*, 182–3.

5   Appian, *The Punic Wars*, 132.

6   Badian, in *Publicans and Sinners*, argues that the *publicani* were operating in Pergamum as early as 131 (p. 63). For a convincing refutation, see Gruen's *The Hellenistic World and the Coming of Rome*, pp. 606–8.

7   1 Maccabees, 8.3.

8   See Hughes, *Pan's Travail*, p. 127.

9   For the growth of the Roman money supply during this period, see Crawford, *Coinage and Money under the Roman Republic*, pp. 173–81.

10 According to Valerius Maximus, 9.2. The figures have been treated with some suspicion.

11 Sallust, *Histories*, 4, fragment 67. The words are unlikely to have been Mithridates', but are invaluable all the same, as an indication of the Romans' appreciation of the resentments of their foes.

12 Strabo, 5.4.2.

13 Diodorus Siculus, 37.15.

14 The theory is Luce's (1970). For a counterview, see McGing, *Foreign Policy*, p. 76.

3: Luck Be a Lady

1 Cicero, *On Duties*, 1.123.
2 Plutarch, *Sulla*, 8.
3 Appian, 1.58.
4 Valerius Maximus, 9.7.
5 Appian, 1.60.
6 Cicero, *Laws*, 1.53.
7 Livy, 31.44.
8 Posidonius, fragment 36.
9 Plutarch, *Sulla*, 13.

4: Return of the Native

1 Cicero, *On Duties*, 1.25.
2 Valerius Maximus, 6.2.
3 Velleius Paterculus, 2.26.
4 Plutarch, *Cato the Elder*, 16.
5 Valerius Maximus, 2.9.
6 Plutarch, *Sulla*, 30.
7 Lucan, 2.220.
8 Appian, 2.95.
9 Plutarch, *Sulla*, 31.
10 Sallust, *Catiline*, 51.34.
11 Appian, 1.99.
12 See Cicero, *Laws*, 3.23.
13 Cicero, *On the Ends of Good and Evil*, 5.2.
14 Appian, 1.103–4.
15 Plutarch, *Sulla*, 36.
16 Cicero, *To Atticus*, 9.10.
17 Appian, 1.106.

5: Fame Is the Spur

1 Lucretius, 5.222–5.
2 Cicero, *On the Ends of Good and Evil*, 5.55.

3 Cicero, *Tusculan Disputations*, 1.39.

4 Cicero, *On the Ends of Good and Evil*, 5.55.

5 Tacitus, *The Dialogue on Orators*, 28.

6 Polybius, 6.53.

7 Sallust, *The War against Jugurtha*, 4.5.

8 Cicero, *On Duties*, 1.139.

9 Suetonius, *The Deified Julius*, 56.

10 Plutarch, *Caesar*, 4.

11 Cicero, *Philippics*, 14.17.

12 Lucretius, 2.11–13.

13 Cicero, *Against Verres*, 2.5.180.

14 Cicero, *In Defence of Murena*, 16.

15 For instance, Cicero, *In Defence of Plancius*, 14–15.

16 Cicero, *On the Orator*, 1.197.

17 Cicero, *In Defence of Murena*, 29.

18 By Quintilian, 6.3.28.

19 Aulus Gellius, 1.5.

20 Cicero, *Brutus*, 313.

21 Cicero, *On Duties*, 1.87.

22 Posidonius, fragment 59.

23 Cicero, *Brutus*, 316.

24 Cicero, *In Defence of Plancius*, 66.

25 Cicero, *Against Verres*, 1.36.

26 *Ibid.*, 1.47.

27 *Ibid.*, 2.4.47.

28 *Ibid.*, 2.3.207.

29 Quintus Cicero, *Electioneering Handbook*, 2. The authorship is hotly disputed. Even so, the insights that it provides into electioneering in the late Republic are such that, even if it is a fake, it remains invaluable as a glimpse into the mindset of a new man on the campaign trail.

30 Cicero, *Against Verres*, 2.4.69.

31 Cicero, *On Duties*, 1.109. The description refers to Sulla as well as Crassus.

32 Plutarch, *Crassus*, 7.

33 Seneca, *Letters*, 2.4.

34 Plutarch, *Pompey*, 14.

35 Cicero, *Tusculan Disputations*, 2.41.

36 Sallust, *Histories*, 3, fragment 66 (A).

37 Publilius Syrus, 337.

38 Orosius, 5.24.
39 Sallust, *Histories*, 3, fragment 66 (A).
40 Plutarch, *Crassus*, 12.

6: *A Banquet of Carrion*

1 Plutarch, *Lucullus*, 11.
2 *Ibid.*, 27.
3 Valerius Maximus, 8.14.5.
4 Cato the Elder, *On Agriculture*, preface.
5 Plutarch, *Tiberius Gracchus*, 8.
6 Plutarch, *Lucullus*, 34.
7 *Ibid.*
8 Appian, *The Mithraditic War*, 92.
9 Cicero, *On Duties*, 3.107.
10 Appian, *The Mithraditic War*, 93.
11 Velleius Paterculus, 2.31.
12 Cassius Dio, 36.24.
13 *Ibid.*, 36.34.
14 Strabo, 11.1.6. The line of Homer is from *The Iliad*, 6.208.
15 Pliny the Elder, 7.99.

7: *The Debt to Pleasure*

1 Plutarch, *Lucullus*, 41.
2 Livy, 39.6.
3 Varro, *On Agriculture*, 3.17.
4 Macrobius, 3.15.4.
5 Varro, *On Agriculture*, 3.17.
6 Plutarch, *Lucullus*, 51.
7 Seneca, *Letters*, 95.15.
8 This seems the most probable explanation for the contraction of Clodia's – and Clodius' – family name. See Tatum, *Patrician Tribune*, pp. 247–8.
9 Caelius, speaking in his own defence at his trial in 56 BC. Quoted by Quintilian, *An Orator's Education*, 8.6.52. Literally, '*coam*' (coition) in the dining room, and '*nolam*' (unwillingness) in the bedroom.

10 Lucretius, 4.1268.
11 Cicero, *In Defence of Murena*, 13.
12 Cicero, *Laws*, 2.39.
13 Cicero, *In Defence of Gallio*, fragment 1.
14 Plutarch, *Cato the Younger*, 9.
15 *Ibid.*, 17.
16 Cicero, *To Atticus*, 2.1.
17 Catullus, 58.
18 In Latin '*discinctus*'.
19 Plutarch, *Caesar*, 7.
20 Sallust, *The Catilinarian War*, 14.
21 Cicero, *On Duties*, 3.75.
22 Cicero, *In Defence of Murena*, 50.
23 Plutarch, *Cicero*, 14.
24 Valerius Maximus, 5.9.
25 Cicero, *In Defence of Caelius*, 14.
26 Plutarch, *Cicero*, 15.
27 Cicero, *To Atticus*, 1.19.
28 Suetonius, *The Deified Julius*, 52.
29 Plutarch, *Caesar*, 12.
30 Plutarch, *Pompey*, 43.
31 Cicero, *To Atticus*, 1.14.
32 *Ibid.*
33 *Ibid.*, 1.16.

8: Triumvirate

1 Valerius Maximus, 2.4.2.
2 Plutarch, *Pompey*, 42.
3 Cicero, *In Defence of Murena*, 31.
4 Plutarch, *Cato the Younger*, 30.
5 Cicero, *To Atticus*, 1.18.
6 Cassius Dio, 38.3.
7 Plutarch, *Cato the Younger*, 22.
8 Appian, 2.9.
9 Cicero, *To Atticus*, 2.21.
10 *Ibid.*, 2.3.

11 Plutarch, *Cicero*, 29.

12 Catullus, 58.

13 Cicero, *To Atticus*, 2.15.

14 Cicero, *On the Answer of the Soothsayers*, 46.

15 Caesar, *Commentaries on the Gallic War*, 2.1.

16 Quoted by Strabo, 17.3.4.

17 Diodorus Siculus, 5.26.

18 Cicero, *The Republic*, 3.16.

19 Caesar, *Commentaries on the Gallic War*, 4.2.

20 *Ibid.*, 1.1.

21 *Ibid.*, 2.35.

22 Cicero, *On the Consular Provinces*, 33.

23 Plutarch, *Pompey*, 48.

24 Cicero, *On his House*, 75.

25 Cicero, *To Quintus*, 2.3.

26 *Ibid.*

9: The Wings of Icarus

1 Cicero, *In Defence of Caelius*, 49–50.

2 Cicero, *To Friends*, 1.7.

3 *Ibid.*, 1.9.

4 Cicero, *To Atticus*, 4.8a.

5 Cicero, *On Duties*, 1.26.

6 Cicero, *To Atticus*, 4.13.

7 Lucretius, 2.538.

8 Plutarch, *Crassus*, 17.

9 *Ibid.*, 23.

10 Caesar, *Commentaries on the Gallic War*, 3.16.

11 *Ibid.*, 4.17.

12 Cicero, *To Atticus*, 4.16.

13 Goudineau, *César*, p. 335.

14 Caesar, *Commentaries on the Gallic War*, 7.4.

15 *Ibid.*, 7.56.

16 Plutarch, to be specific: *Caesar*, 15.

17 See, for instance, Goudineau, *César*, pp. 317–28.

18 Caesar, *Commentaries on the Gallic War*, 8.44.

19 Plutarch, *Pompey*, 12.

20 Petronius, 119.17–18.

21 Cicero, *Against Piso*, 65.

22 Cicero, *To Friends*, 7.1.

23 Pliny the Elder, 36.41. It is possible that the fourteen captive nations were gathered round Pompey's statue, rather than his theatre. The Latin is ambiguous.

24 Pliny the Elder, 8.21.

25 Cicero, *To Atticus*, 4.17.

26 Asconius, 42C.

27 Plutarch, *Pompey*, 54.

28 Cicero, *In Defence of Milo*, 79.

29 Pliny the Elder, 36.117–18.

30 Cicero, *To Friends*, 8.7.

31 *Ibid.*, 8.1.

32 *Ibid.*, 8.8.

33 *Ibid.*, 8.6.

34 Petronius, 119.

35 Plutarch, *Pompey*, 57.

36 Cicero, *To Friends*, 8.14.

37 *Ibid.*, 2.15.

38 Appian, 2.31.

10: World War

1 Cicero, *To Atticus*, 7.1.

2 Lucan, 1.581. A poetic touch, no doubt, but a haunting and apt one.

3 Cicero, *To Atticus*, 8.2.

4 Cicero, *To Atticus*, 8.11.

5 Plutarch, *Cicero*, 38.

6 Cicero, *In Defence of Marcellus*, 27.

7 Anon., *The Spanish War*, 42.

8 Caesar, *The Civil War*, 3.8.

9 Plutarch, *Caesar*, 39.

10 Caesar, *The Civil War*, 3.82.

11 Suetonius, *The Deified Julius*, 30.

12 Plutarch, *Pompey*, 79.

13 Cicero, *To Friends*, 2.12.
14 Cicero, *To Atticus*, 2.5.
15 Plutarch, *Antony*, 27.
16 Suetonius, *The Deified Julius*, 51.
17 Plutarch, *Cato the Younger*, 72.
18 Suetonius, *The Deified Julius*, 37.
19 Cicero, *To Friends*, 9.15.
20 *Ibid.*, 15.19.
21 Florus, 2.13.92.
22 Cicero, *Philippics*, 2.85.
23 Suetonius, *The Deified Julius*, 77.
24 Plutarch, *Brutus*, 12.
25 Velleius Paterculus, 2.57.
26 Plutarch, *Caesar*, 63.
27 Cassius Dio, 44.18.
28 Suetonius, *The Deified Julius*, 82.
29 Or so it was claimed by Seneca. See *On Anger*, 3.30.4.
30 Suetonius, *The Deified Julius*, 82.

11: The Death of the Republic

1 Cicero, *To Atticus*, 14.9.
2 *Ibid.*, 14.21.
3 Cicero, *To Friends*, 4.6.
4 Cicero, *To Atticus*, 14.21.
5 *Ibid.*, 14.12.
6 *Ibid.*, 14.4.
7 *Ibid.*, 16.7.3.
8 Cicero, *Philippics*, 2.1.
9 *Ibid.*, 10.20.
10 *Ibid.*, 13.24–5.
11 Cicero, *To Atticus*, 16.8.1.
12 Cicero, *Philippics*, 3.3.
13 Cicero, *To Friends*, 11.20.
14 Suetonius, *The Deified Augustus*, 26.
15 Appian, 3.92.
16 Pliny the Elder, 34.6.

17 Cicero, *Letters to Atticus*, 14.1.

18 Virgil, *Eclogues*, 4.4–9.

19 Plutarch, *Antony*, 26.

20 Suetonius, *The Deified Augustus*, 69.

21 *The Achievements of the Divine Augustus*, 25.2.

22 Plutarch, *Antony*, 75.

23 *The Achievements of the Divine Augustus*, 3.2.

24 Seneca, *On Mercy*, 1.2.2.

25 Cassius Dio, 53.16.

26 Ennius, *Annals*, fragment 155.

27 Horace, *Odes*, 4.5.1–2.

28 *Ibid.*, 3.6.45–8.

29 *Ibid.*, 3.24.36–7.

30 Velleius Paterculus, 2.89.

31 Virgil, *Georgics*, 1.145–6.

32 Virgil, *Aeneid*, 6.792–3.

33 *Ibid.*, 8.669–70.

34 Horace, *Epodes*, 2.1–6.

35 Cicero, *Philippics*, 13.30.

36 Suetonius, *The Deified Augustus*, 99.

37 Ovid, *The Art of Loving*, 3.112–13.

38 Livy, 43.13.

39 Cicero, *The Republic*, 1.68.

Bibliography

Ancient . . .

Classical sources are often given the blanket label 'primary', when in reality they may be no such thing. Call Plutarch, who was born in the reign of the Emperor Claudius, a primary source for the fall of the Republic and one might as well call Carlyle a primary source for the life of Frederick the Great. Even so, documents from the period covered by this book *have* been preserved – and, by the standards of ancient history, a voluminous quantity of them. Most were written by Cicero: speeches, philosophical works and letters. A few works by his contemporaries have also survived: most notably the commentaries of Caesar, two monographs by Sallust, fragments of works by the great polymath Terrentius Varro, maxims culled from the dramas of a mime-writer, Publilius Syrus, and the work of two poets, Lucretius and Catullus. Lucretius' poem *On the Nature of Things* provides a fascinating counterpoint to the letters of Cicero: the work of a man who consciously withdrew from the clamour and frenzy of public life. Catullus, who was almost certainly a lover of Clodia Metelli, and a friend of Caelius – though see Wiseman's *Catullus and His World* – paints vivid sketches of the capital's party set, sometimes full of pathos, more often scabrous, witty and abusive.

Greeks also wrote about Roman affairs. One of the first to do so was Polybius, brought to Rome as a hostage in 168 BC, befriended by Scipio Aemilianus, and a witness to the destruction of Carthage. His *History* provided a penetrating analysis of the Roman constitution and the rise of the Republic to mastery over the entire Mediterranean. Of Posidonius' writings, little has survived – only a few scraps here and there. Bulkier fragments have been preserved of the *Library of History*, an immense, forty-volume universal history written by Diodorus Siculus, a Sicilian writing even as the Republic collapsed. A generation later, the geographer Strabo, who came from Mithridates' old kingdom of Pontus, wrote an exhaustive gazetteer of the Roman world – including Italy and Rome herself. This was supplemented by the labours of Dionysius of Halicarnassus, whose *Roman Antiquities* was written as an introduction to Polybius, and contains invaluable information derived from the earliest Roman annalists.

In a sense, the entire literature of the Augustan period can be seen as a commentary on the fall of the Republic: in profoundly different ways it is a theme that runs throughout the poetry of Virgil, Horace and Ovid; and through Livy's great history of Rome. Even though the books of that history which covered the late Republic have been lost, an abridgement of Livy's work by the late-first-century AD poet Florus has survived. Then there is the testimony of Octavian himself, in the form of *The Achievements of the Divine Augustus* – a lengthy self-justification set up in public places throughout the empire and a superlative exercise in spin.

Even after Augustus' death, Roman writers kept returning to the heroic years of the Republic's end. Details from the period filled Valerius Maximus' compendium of *Memorable Deeds and Sayings*, and Velleius Paterculus' *Roman Histories*, both composed during the reign of Augustus' successor, Tiberius. The philosopher Seneca, tutor and adviser to Nero, mulled over the lessons of liberty betrayed. So too did his nephew, Lucan, in his epic poem on the civil wars, *The Pharsalia*, and Petronius, in his considerably less elevated prose work, *The Satyricon*. All three ultimately committed suicide, the only gesture of republican defiance still permitted Roman noblemen under the rule of the Caesars. 'A monotonous glut of downfalls' – so Tacitus, writing at the beginning of the second century AD, described the judicial murders that had blotted the recent history of his country. Rome's ancient inheritance of freedom seemed to have vanished, drowned in blood. In Tacitus, bleakest of historians, the ghost of the Republic haunts what the city has become.

None of his near contemporaries could rival Tacitus for the clarity and mercilessness of his perspective. Instead, for most, the history of the Republic had become a quarry to be mined for entertainment or elevated anecdotes. The elder Pliny's *Natural History* provided character sketches of Caesar, Pompey and Cicero, along with an inexhaustible supply of more eclectic information. Quintilian, in his treatise on rhetoric, *The Education of an Orator*, often referred back to Cicero and the other orators of the last years of the Republic, and is an invaluable source of quotations for writers who have otherwise been lost. So too is Aulus Gellius, in his chatty collection of essays, *The Attic Nights*. Suetonius, author of a racy *Lives of the Caesars*, wrote muck-raking portraits of the two deified warlords, Julius and Augustus. King of the biographers, however, was Plutarch, whose portraits of the great men of the late Republic have been the most influential, because they are the most readable, of any historian's. Vivid with moralising and gossip, they portray the Republic's collapse not as a revolution or a social disintegration, but as the ancients tended to see it: a drama of ambitious and exceptional men.

Plutarch, a patriotic Greek, demonstrates the fascination that Roman history continued to exert over the Empire's subject peoples. Increasingly, from the second century AD onwards, historians who wrote about the Republic's collapse tended to do so in Greek. The most significant of these was Appian, a lawyer from Alexandria, who wrote a detailed history of Rome and her empire. For the events from the tribunate of Tiberius Gracchus to 70 BC, his book, *The Civil Wars*, is our only surviving narrative source. For events from 69 BC onwards, however, he is supplemented by another historian, Cassius Dio, who wrote at a time when the Roman world, at the beginning of the third century AD, was once again tearing itself to pieces. Even as Rome slipped into terminal decline, citizens of the dying Empire continued to look back at a period that was by now becoming very ancient history indeed. Among the last to do so, around AD 400, was Macrobius, whose *Saturnalia* is full of anecdotes and jokes lovingly culled from the records of the late Republic. A few years later, a friend of Saint Augustine, Orosius, wrote a history of the world that also covered the period, but by then the Empire – and with it the classical tradition itself – had only a few decades left to live. With the fall of Rome, the history of the city passed into myth.

. . . and Modern

APA = *The American Philological Association*
JRS = *Journal of Roman Studies*

Adcock, F. E.: *Marcus Crassus: Millionaire* (1966, Cambridge)
Badian, E.: *Foreign Clientelae, 264–70 BC* (1958, Oxford)
———: 'Waiting for Sulla' (1962, *JRS* 52)
———: *Roman Imperialism in the Late Republic* (1967, Oxford)
———: *Lucius Sulla, the Deadly Reformer* (1970, Sydney)
———: *Publicans and Sinners: Private Enterprise in the Service of the Roman Republic* (1972, Oxford)
Balsdon, J. V. P. D.: 'Sulla Felix' (1951, *JRS* 41)
———: *Julius Caesar: A Political Biography* (1967, New York)

Barton, Carlin A.: *The Sorrows of the Ancient Romans: The Gladiator and the Monster* (1993, Princeton)

———: *Roman Honor: The Fire in the Bones* (2001, Berkeley and Los Angeles)

Beard, Mary and Crawford, Michael: *Rome in the Late Republic: Problems and Interpretations* (1985, London)

Beard, Mary, North, John and Price, Simon: *Religions of Rome, Volume 1: A History* (1998, Cambridge)

Bell, Andrew J. E.: 'Cicero and the Spectacle of Power' (1997, *JRS* 87)

Broughton, T. R. S.: *The Magistrates of the Roman Republic*, 2 vols (1951/2, New York)

Brunt, P. A.: 'Italian Aims at the Time of the Social War' (1962, *JRS* 52)

———: *Italian Manpower, 225 BC–AD 14* (1971, Oxford)

———: *Social Conflicts in the Roman Republic* (1971, London)

———: *The Fall of the Roman Republic, and Related Essays* (1988, Oxford)

Cambridge Ancient History: The Last Age of the Roman Republic, 146–43 BC, ed. J. A. Crook, Andrew Lintott and Elizabeth Rawson (1994, Cambridge)

Cambridge Ancient History: The Augustan Empire, 43 BC–AD 69, ed. Alan K. Bowman, Edward Champlin and Andrew Lintott (1996, Cambridge)

Carney, Thomas F.: *A Biography of C. Marius* (1961, Assen)

Casson, Lionel: *Travel in the Ancient World* (1994, Baltimore)

Chauveau, Michel: *Egypt in the Age of Cleopatra*, trans. David Lorton (2000, Ithaca)

Claridge, Amanda: *Rome: An Archaeological Guide* (1998, Oxford)

Clarke, M. L.: *The Noblest Roman: Marcus Brutus and His Reputation* (1981, London)

Collins, J. H.: 'Caesar and the Corruption of Power' (1955, *Historia* 4)

Crawford, M. H.: *The Roman Republic* (1978, Glasgow)

———: *Coinage and Money under the Roman Republic* (1985, London)

Dalby, Andrew: *Empire of Pleasures: Luxury and Indulgence in the Roman World* (2000, London)

D'Arms, John H.: *Romans on the Bay of Naples: A Social and Cultural Study of the Villas and Their Owners from 150 BC to AD 400* (1970, Cambridge, Mass.)

———: *Commerce and Social Standing in Ancient Rome* (1981, Cambridge, Mass.)

Dixon, Suzanne: *The Roman Family* (1992, Baltimore)

Dupont, Florence: *Daily Life in Ancient Rome*, trans. Christopher Woodall (1992, Oxford)

Edwards, Catharine: *The Politics of Immorality in Ancient Rome* (1993, Cambridge)

Earl, D. C.: *The Moral and Political Tradition of Rome* (1967, London)

Epstein, David F.: 'Cicero's Testimony at the *Bona Dea* Trial' (1986, *Classical Philology* 81)

Evans, John K.: *War, Women and Children in Ancient Rome* (1991, London)

Evans, Richard J.: *Gaius Marius: A Political Biography* (1994, Pretoria)

Everitt, Anthony: *Cicero: A Turbulent Life* (2001, London)

Fagan, Garrett G.: 'Sergius Orata: Inventor of the Hypocaust?' (1996, *Phoenix* 50)

Favro, Diane: *The Urban Image of Augustan Rome* (1996, Cambridge)

Frederiksen, Martin: *Campania* (1984, British School at Rome)

Gabba, Emilio: *Republican Rome, the Army and the Allies*, trans. P. J. Cuff (1976, Oxford)

Galinsky, Karl: *Augustan Culture* (1996, Princeton)

Garnsey, Peter, Hopkins, Keith and Whittaker, C. R. (eds): *Trade in the Ancient Economy* (1983, London)

Gelzer, Matthias: *Julius Caesar: Politician and Statesman*, trans. Peter Needham (1968, Cambridge)

———: *The Roman Nobility*, trans. Robin Seager (1975, Oxford)

Goudineau, Christian: *César et la Gaule* (2000, Paris)

Grant, Michael: *Cleopatra* (1972, London)

Green, Peter: *Classical Bearings: Interpreting Ancient History and Culture* (1989, Berkeley and Los Angeles)

———: *Alexander to Actium: The Historical Evolution of the Hellenistic Age* (1990, Berkeley and Los Angeles)

Greenhalgh, Peter: *Pompey: The Roman Alexander* (1980, London)

———: *Pompey: The Republican Prince* (1981, London)

Griffith, R. Drew: 'The Eyes of Clodia Metelli' (1996, *Latomus* 55)

Gruen, Erich S.: *The Last Generation of the Roman Republic* (1974, Berkeley and Los Angeles)

———: *The Hellenistic World and the Coming of Rome* (1984, Berkeley and Los Angeles)

———: *Culture and National Identity in Republican Rome* (1992, New York)

Gurval, Robert Alan: *Actium and Augustus: The Politics and Emotions of Civil War* (1998, Ann Arbor)

Hallett, Judith P. and Skinner, Marilyn B. (eds): *Roman Sexualities* (1997, Princeton)

Hanson, J. A.: *Roman Theater-Temples* (1959, Princeton)

Harris, William V.: *War and Imperialism in Republican Rome, 327–70 BC* (1979, Oxford)

Higginbotham, James: *Piscinae: Artificial Fishponds in Roman Italy* (1997, Chapel Hill)

Hoff, Michael C. and Rotroff, Susan I.: *The Romanization of Athens* (1992, *Oxbow Monograph* 94)

Hopkins, Keith: *Sociological Studies in Roman History, Volume I: Conquerors and Slaves* (Cambridge, 1978)

———: *Sociological Studies in Roman History, Volume II: Death and Renewal* (Cambridge, 1983)

Horden, Peregrine and Purcell, Nicholas: *The Corrupting Sea: A Study of Mediterranean History* (2000, Oxford)

Horsfall, Nicholas: 'The Ides of March: Some New Problems' (1974, *Greece & Rome*, 21)

Hughes, J. Donald: *Pan's Travail: Environmental Problems of the Ancient Greeks and Romans* (1994, Baltimore)

Hughes-Hallett, Lucy: *Cleopatra: Histories, Dreams and Distortions* (1990, London)

Jashemski, W. F.: *The Origins and History of the Proconsular and Propraetorian Imperium* (1950, Chicago)

Jenkyns, Richard: *Virgil's Experience: Nature and History, Times, Names and Places* (1998, Oxford)

Kahn, Arthur D.: *The Education of Julius Caesar* (1986, New York)

Keaveney, Arthur: *Sulla: The Last Republican* (1982, London)

———: *Lucullus: A Life* (1992, London)

Keppie, L.: *The Making of the Roman Army: From Republic to Empire* (1984, London)

Lacey, W. K.: 'The Tribunate of Curio' (1961, *Historia* 10)

———: *Cicero and the End of the Roman Republic* (1978, London)

Lintott, Andrew: *Violence in Republican Rome* (1968/99, Oxford)

———: 'Cicero and Milo' (1974, *JRS* 64)

———: *The Constitution of the Roman Republic* (1999, Oxford)

Lo Cascio, E: 'State and Coinage in the Late Republic and Early Empire' (1981, *JRS* 71)

Luce, T. J.: 'Marius and the Mithridatic Command' (1970, *Historia* 19)

Machiavelli, Niccolò: *The Discourses*, ed. Bernard Crick (1970, London)

Marshall, B. A.: *Crassus: A Political Biography* (1976, Amsterdam)

Mattern, Susan: *Rome and the Enemy* (1999, Berkeley and Los Angeles)

McGing, B. C.: *The Foreign Policy of Mithridates VI Eupator, King of Pontus* (1986, Leiden)

Meier, Christian: *Caesar*, trans. David McLintock (1995, London)

Millar, Fergus: 'The Political Character of the Classical Roman Republic, 200–151 BC' (1984, *JRS* 74)

———: *The Crowd in Rome in the Late Republic* (1998, Ann Arbor)

———: *The Roman Republic in Political Thought* (2002, Hanover)

Mitchell, Thomas N.: *Cicero: The Ascending Years* (1979, New Haven)

———: *Cicero: The Senior Statesman* (1991, New Haven)

Mouritsen, Henrik: *Plebs and Politics in the Late Roman Republic* (2001, Cambridge)

Néraudau, Jean-Pierre: *Être Enfant à Rome* (1984, Paris)

Nicolet, Claude: *L'Ordre Équestre à l'Époque Républicain*, 2 vols (1966/74, Paris)

——: *The World of the Citizen in Republican Rome*, trans. P. S. Falla (1980, London)

—— (ed.): *Des Ordres à Rome* (1984, Paris)

North, J. A.: 'The Development of Roman Imperialism' (1981, *JRS* 71)

Ormerod, Henry A.: *Piracy in the Ancient World* (1924, Liverpool)

Parke, H. W.: *Sibyls and Sibylline Prophecy in Classical Antiquity* (1988, London)

Patterson, John R.: 'The City of Rome: From Republic to Empire' (1992, *JRS* 82)

Plass, Paul: *The Game of Death in Ancient Rome: Arena Sport and Political Suicide* (1995, Madison)

Pomeroy, Sarah B.: *Goddesses, Whores, Wives and Slaves: Women in Classical Antiquity* (1994, London)

Porter, James I.: *Constructions of the Classical Body* (1999, Ann Arbor)

Raaflaub, Kurt A. and Toher, Mark (eds): *Between Republic and Empire* (1990, Berkeley and Los Angeles)

Rathbone, D. W.: 'The Slave Mode of Production in Italy' (1983, *JRS* 71)

Rawson, Elizabeth: 'The Eastern Clientelae of Clodius and the Claudii' (1973, *Historia* 22)

——: *Cicero: A Portrait* (1975, London)

——: *Intellectual Life in the Late Roman Republic* (1985, London)

Richardson, J. S.: 'The Spanish Mines and the Development of Provincial Taxation in the Second Century BC' (1976, *JRS* 66)

Richardson, Keith: *Daggers in the Forum: The Revolutionary Lives and Violent Deaths of the Gracchus Brothers* (1976, London)

Robinson, O. F.: *Ancient Rome: City Planning and Administration* (1992, London)

Rosenstein, Nathan: *Imperatores Victi: Military Defeat and Aristocratic Competition in the Middle and Late Republic* (1990, Berkeley and Los Angeles)

Rousselle, Aline: 'The Family under the Roman Empire: Signs and Gestures', in *A History of the Family*, Vol. 1 (1996, Cambridge)

Sacks, Kenneth S.: *Diodorus Siculus and the First Century* (1990, Princeton)

Salmon, E. T.: *Samnium and the Samnites* (1967, Cambridge)

——: *The Making of Roman Italy* (1982, London)

Santosuosso, Antonio: *Storming the Heavens* (2001, Boulder)

Schiavone, Aldo: *The End of the Past: Ancient Rome and the Modern West*, trans. Margery J. Schneider (2000, Cambridge, Mass.)

Scullard, H. H.: *From the Gracchi to Nero* (1959, London)

Seager, Robin J.: *Pompey: A Political Biography* (1979, Oxford)

—— (ed.): *The Crisis of the Roman Republic* (1969, Cambridge and New York)

Sedley, David: 'The Ethics of Brutus and Cassius' (1997, *JRS* 87)

Shackleton-Bailey, D. R.: *Cicero* (1971, London)

Shatzman, Israël: *Senatorial Wealth and Roman Politics* (1975, Brussels)

Shaw, Brent D.: *Spartacus and the Slave Wars* (2001, Boston)

Sherwin-White, A. N.: 'Violence in Roman Politics' (1956, *JRS* 46)

——: *The Roman Citizenship* (1973, Oxford)

Skinner, Marilyn B.: 'Pretty Lesbius' (1982, *APA* 112)

——: 'Clodia Metelli' (1983, *APA* 113)

Staveley, E. S.: *Greek and Roman Voting and Elections* (1972, London)

Stockton, David: *Cicero: A Political Biography* (1971, Oxford)

——: *The Gracchi* (1979, Oxford)

Syme, Ronald: *The Roman Revolution* (1939, Oxford)

Tarn, W. W.: 'Alexander Helios and the Golden Age' (1932, *JRS* 22)

Tatum, W. Jeffrey: *The Patrician Tribune: Publius Clodius Pulcher* (1999, Chapel Hill)

Taylor, Lily Ross: *The Divinity of the Roman Emperor* (1931, Middletown)

——: *Party Politics in the Age of Caesar* (1948, Berkeley and Los Angeles)

Tchernia, André: *Le Vin de l'Italie Romaine* (1986, École Française de Rome)

Ulansey, David: *The Origins of the Mithraic Mysteries: Cosmology and Salvation in the Ancient World* (1989, Oxford)

Walker, Susan and Higgs, Peter: *Cleopatra of Egypt: From History to Myth* (2001, London)

Wiseman, T. P.: 'The Census in the First Century BC' (1969/70, *JRS* 61)

——: *Catullus and His World: A Reappraisal* (1985, Cambridge)

Woolf, Greg: *Becoming Roman: The Origins of Provincial Civilization in Gaul* (1998, Cambridge)

Yakobson, A.: *Elections and Electioneering in Rome: A Study in the Political System of the Late Republic* (1999, Stuttgart)

Yavetz, Zwi: 'The Living Conditions of the Urban Plebs in Republican Rome' (1958, *Latomus* 17)

——: *Plebs and Princeps* (1969, Oxford)

——: *Julius Caesar and His Public Image* (1983, London)

Index